THE JEWS
IN THE WORLD OF THE
RENAISSANCE

THE JEWS
IN THE WORLD OF THE
RENAISSANCE

BY

MOSES A. SHULVASS

TRANSLATED BY ELVIN I. KOSE

LEIDEN — E. J. BRILL
and
SPERTUS COLLEGE OF JUDAICA PRESS
1973

ISBN 90 04 03646 6

Library of Congress
catalog card number: 72-97357

PRINTED IN THE NETHERLANDS

To Celia

for her love and companionship

BOOKS BY MOSES A. SHULVASS

CONTENTS

PREFACE

The Renaissance is justifiably regarded as one of the most significant eras in human history. When people tired of the burdensome limitations imposed upon them during the Middle Ages, they discarded them and broke through to a broad avenue of new social and cultural creativity. The cultural treasures of the Antiquity were rediscovered. Men began to consciously perceive the world with all its vastness and beauty, and to extol the worth of the individual, his powers, his talents, and his aspirations for creativity and fulfillment.

The new approach that opened society to the individual, offered hitherto unimaginable opportunities to the Jew. Renewed interest in the ancient world and its culture effected a changed relationship between enlightened Christian and Jew. Affection for the Jew displaced hatred, for he was the keeper of an important part of ancient culture—Hebrew language and literature. Simultaneously, new economic conditions gave rise to a new, more liberal attitude to "Jewish" professions. The social significance of the Jewish humanist and moneylender became enhanced and many sought their services. Some came to the Jewish humanist to study Hebrew language and Scripture; others visited synagogues to listen to his interesting sermons. On the basis of a special contract (*condotta*), that offered many privileges to the Jew, Jewish moneylenders were invited to many cities and states throughout the peninsula.

This astonishing change awakened a powerful response in Jewish hearts. The new attitudes and patterns of life penetrated the Jewish quarter. Almost feverish activity seized the Jews. They began to express interest in areas of knowledge which the Renaissance created. Political problems and events began to concern them, and even the visual arts engaged their interest.

In the area of visual arts, however, it becomes apparent that the Jews did not immerse themselves in the culture of the Renaissance unconditionally. The meagerness of Jewish creativity in the visual arts reveals that where new views clashed with a fundamental of the Jewish faith, Judaism emerged the winner. After perusing the description of the various areas of life, the reader will conclude that in virtually every respect the Jews accepted the Renaissance "cautiously". They honestly strove to create a harmonious blend of Judaism and Renaissance culture in life and thought patterns, and to a large degree they succeeded.

As a result of specific historical conditions another social development of considerable importance became crystallized during the first half of the Renaissance period. Persecutions of Jews in Germany and their expulsion from France and Spain, while favorable conditions prevailed in Italy, stimulated a Jewish mass migration into the Italian peninsula. This migration transformed the Italian Jewish community from a unicultural group (Italiani) into a composite of Italiani, Ashkenazim, Sephardim, and Levantines. The immigrants also repopulated many areas on the peninsula which had become devoid of Jews at the close of the Middle Ages.

It is thus readily understood that the path of the Renaissance Jew is due to attract the attention of the historian. The Jewish scholar is further drawn to this period because of the "modern" problems that the Renaissance Jewish community faced: How to live in a friendly, highly cultured non-Jewish environment without losing its own specific Jewish character. Equally challenging to the scholar is Renaissance Jewry's composite structure, within which different groups lived in close proximity to one another, and where tension and cooperation were perpetually interchanging. The complex historical experience of the Renaissance Jewish community may be of special interest to the modern Jew in his quest to understand his position in the contemporary world.

The present work originally was published in Hebrew (New York, 1955). The English translation was prepared by Elvin I. Kose, except for Chapter 1 of Section I, which was translated by Joshua Starr, and appeared in *Jewish Social Studies*, vol. XIII (1951), pp. 3-24. Thanks are due the editors of *Jewish Social Studies* for permission to reprint that chapter.

Hebrew words were generally transliterated in accordance with the system used in the *Jewish Encyclopedia*. Italian surnames were mostly given as they are listed in Marco Mortara's *Indice alfabetico dei rabbini e scrittori Israeliti di cose Giudaiche in Italia* (Padua, 1886). Hebrew books were generally listed in the *Notes* by their original titles. Whenever the frontispiece also listed the title in Latin characters, or in the vernacular, they were used.

A number of my friends, and expecially: Dr. Martin J. Goldman, Dr. Robert S. Mendelsohn, Dr. Ludwig Rosenberger, Dr. Ralph Simon, Dr. Maurice Spertus and Dr. David Weinstein, gave me much encouragement during the process of publication.

My colleague and friend Byron Sherwin and my former student Benita Masters made many constructive and felicitous stylistic suggestions. Mrs Mildred Crane of the secretarial staff of Spertus College of Judaica prepared the typescript, and my student Mary Pattison prepared the index.

I am deeply grateful to all of them. But it was, above all, the untiring patience of my wife Celia and her steadfast devotion to my research work, which made it possible for me to overcome the many difficulties and obstacles encountered in the process of publishing this book.

Spertus College of Judaica   Moses A. SHULVASS
Chicago, Illinois, December 1972.

ABBREVIATIONS

Balletti	Gli Ebrei e gli Estensi, by A. Balletti, Modena 1913.
Berliner, Rome	Geschichte der Juden in Rom, by A. Berliner, Frankfort/Main 1893.
Burckhardt	Die Kultur der Renaissance in Italien, by Jacob Burckhardt, Hebrew edition, Jerusalem 1949.
Cassuto, Florence	Gli ebrei a Firenze nell'eta del Rinascimento, by Umberto Cassuto, Florence 1918.
Cenni storici	Cenni storici ed amministrativi delle Comunità israelitiche Italiane, Rome 1914.
Ciscato	Gli ebrei in Padova, by A. Ciscato, Padua 1901.
Colorni, Magistrature maggiori	Le Magistrature Maggiori della Comunità Ebraica di Mantova (Sec. XV-XIX), by Vittore Colorni, Bologna 1938.
Divan Modena	The Divan of Leo de Modena, edited by Simon Bernstein, Philadelphia 1932.
Emeḳ habaka	Emek Habaca, by Joseph Hacohen, second edition, Cracow 1895.
Erik, History	The History of the Yiddish Literature, by Max Erik, Warsaw 1928.
Ferorelli	Gli ebrei nell'Italia meridionale, by Nicola Ferorelli, Turin 1915.
Finkelstein	Jewish Self-Government in the Middle Ages, by Louis L. Finkelstein, New York 1924.
Foa, Monferrato	Gli ebrei nel Monferrato, by S. Foa, Alessandria 1914.
Ge ḥizzayon	Ge ḥizzayon, by Abraham Jaghel Gallichi, Alexandria (Egypt), 1880.
Giovanni de Giovanni	L'ebraismo della Sicilia, by G. de Giovanni, Palermo 1848.
Guedemann	Geschichte des Erziehungswesens und der Kultur der abendlaendischen Juden waehrend des Mittelalters und der neueren Zeit, by M. Guedemann, Hebrew edition, vol. 2, Warsaw 1899.
Graetz-Rabinowitz	Geschichte der Juden, by H. Graetz, Hebrew edition by S. P. Rabinowitz, Warsaw 1908.
Hamagiha	Chronicle of the "Annotator", published in Emek Habaca by Joseph Hacohen, second edition, Cracow 1895.
HB	Hebraeische Bibliographie.
Historia de gli Riti Hebraici	Historia de gli Riti Hebraici, by Leon da Modena, Paris 1637.
HUCA	Hebrew Union College Annual.

Iggeret oreḥot olam	Iggeret oreḥot olam, by Abraham Farissol, Cracow 1822.
Iggerot Ereẓ Yisrael	Iggerot Ereẓ Yisrael, edited by Abraham Yaari, Tel Aviv 1943.
JQR	Jewish Quarterly Review.
Kaufmann, Gesam- melte Schriften	Gesammelte Schriften, by David Kaufmann, Frankfort/Main 1908.
Lagumina	Codice diplomatico dei Giudei di Sicilia, edited by B. and G. Lagumina, Palermo 1884-1909.
Landsberger	A History of Jewish Art, by F. Landsberger, Cincinnati 1946.
Leo Modenas Briefe	Leo Modenas Briefe und Schriftstuecke, edited by Ludwig Blau, Budapest 1905.
Luzzatto, Urbino	I banchieri ebrei in Urbino, by Gino Luzzatto, Padua 1902.
Maḥberot Immanuel	Maḥberot Immanuel, by Immanuel of Rome, edited by A. M. Habermann, Tel Aviv 1950.
Marx, Studies	Studies in Jewish History and Booklore, by Alexander Marx, New York 1944.
Meor enayim	Meor enayim, by Azariah dei Rossi, edited by I. A. Benjacob, Vilna 1865.
Meshullam da Vol- terra's Travelogue	Meshullam da Volterra's Travelogue, edited by Abraham Yaari, Jerusalem 1949.
MGWJ	Monatsschrift fuer Geschichte und Wissen- schaft des Judentums.
Milano, Rome	Ricerche sulle condizioni economiche degli ebrei di Roma, by A. Milano, Città di Castello 1931.
Morpurgo, Padua	L'universita degli ebrei in Padova, by E. Morpurgo, Padua 1909.
M. Stern, Stellung der Paepste	Urkundliche Beitraege ueber die Stellung der Paepste zu den Juden, by Moritz Stern, Kiel 1893.
Natali	Il ghetto di Roma, by E. Natali, Rome 1887.
Neppi-Ghirondi	Zeker ẓaddiḳim liberakah, by Hananel Neppi and Toledot gedole Yisrael, by Mordecai Samuel Ghirondi, Trieste 1853.
REJ	Revue des études juives.
RI	Rivista Israelitica.
RMI	La Rassegna mensile di Israel.
Roth, History	The History of the Jews of Italy, by Cecil Roth, Philadelphia 1946.
Roth, Venice	Venice, by Cecil Roth, Philadelphia 1930.
Sepher Chaje Jehuda	Sepher Chaje Jehuda, by Leon da Modena, edited by Abraham Kahana, Kiev 1911.
Shalshelet haḳabbalah	Shalshelet haḳabbalah, by Gedaliah Ibn Jachia, Lemberg 1864.
Shilte hagibborim	Shilte hagibborim, by Abraham Portaleone, Mantua 1612.
Sippur David Hareubeni	Sippur David Hareubeni, edited by A. Z. Aescoly, Jerusalem 1940.

Sonne, Hateḳufah	Isaiah Sonne, The Waad Kelali in Italy as the Prototype of the Council of the Four Provinces in Poland, Hateḳufah, vol. 32-33, New York 1948, pp. 617-689.
Vogelstein-Rieger	Geschichte der Juden in Rome, by Hermann Vogelstein and Paul Rieger, Berlin 1896.
Ẓaḥut bediḥuta deḳiddushin	Ẓaḥut bediḥuta deḳiddushin, edited by Jefim Schirmann, Jerusalem 1946.
ZfhB	Zeitschrift fuer hebraeische Bibliographie.
Zinberg	The History of the Jewish Literature, by I. Zinberg, vol. 4, Vilna 1933.

THE JEWISH POPULATION

CHAPTER ONE

GEOGRAPHIC DISPERSION, COMMUNAL COMPOSITION, AND SIZE

Statistics on the Jewish population in any period usually present a difficult problem for historians. The data available for calculating the size of a population in a distant period are particularly complicated when they refer to a persecuted minority, which is not the master of its own fate. For the most part, the particular figure in a contemporary source is incorrect, and occurs not incidentally but in relation to a specific need. This renders the source suspect and the historian does not always have the means to check that source or to distinguish between its tendentious aspect and the grain of truth imbedded in it.

As far as the investigation of statistics on the Jews of Italy is concerned, there are in fact further difficulties to be overcome. Until the last quarter of the nineteenth century Italy comprised a multiplicity of states, large and small. The treatment of the Jews varied widely; while those in one area enjoyed a measure of freedom, their contemporaries in another suffered oppression. It is, therefore, necessary to examine the data bearing on the individual republics, duchies and towns. In the end one may hope to ascertain the approximate extent of the Jewish population in the peninsula as a whole, during the period in question.

a.

This study will deal with the number, distribution and communal divisions of the Jewish inhabitants of Renaissance Italy (1300-1600). It was during these centuries that separate groupings developed within the Jewish population. On the threshold of this age began the mass immigration from

1

Germany,[1] and two hundred years later came the refugees from Spain and Portugal. Groups from the same countries continued to arrive during the sixteenth century, the end of which saw the immigration of the Levantine Jews, particularly to the important center at Leghorn. The age of the Renaissance consequently transformed the composition of the Jewish population; the original homogeneous *italiani* now lived together with Askenazim, Sephardim, and Levantines.

A study of the distribution of this population must reckon with the fundamental fact that it consisted of migratory groups. It is a general rule that after their arrival immigrants tend to change their residence within the new country. In the case of the Jews who migrated to Renaissance Italy, this tendency was intensified by two circumstances: the widespread expansion of loan banks,[2] and the political disunity of the peninsula. The settlements of the Ashkenazim arose in towns to which a Jew was invited for the purpose of establishing a pawnbroking establishment. He received the privilege of residence for himself, his family and others attached to the household. The agreement was limited to a specified number of years and upon its expiration either party frequently declined to renew it. This marked the end of the residence of the Jewish group in the given town and its transfer to another.

A rather instructive example is offered by the duchy of Parma-Piacenza. Between 1562 and 1578 the 16 localities, which harbored Jewish moneylenders, declined to eight. Characteristically, thereafter the Jews remained in these eight towns until the nineteenth century, the only places with any recorded Jewish population in the duchy.[3]

It was the Jews of Rome and vicinity who started the trend of new loan establishments, which sprang up to the north,

[1] The author has dealt at length with this immigration in his study "Ashkenazic Jewry in Italy." See Moses A. Shulvass, *Between the Rhine and the Bosporus*, Chicago 1964, pp. 158-183.

[2] Cf. Vittore Colorni, *Il prestito ebraico e communitá ebraiche nell' Italia centrale e settentrionale*, Bologna 1935, and Moses A. Shulvass, *In the Grip of Centuries*, Tel-Aviv and Jerusalem 1960, pp. 23-32 (Hebrew).

[3] Cf. Roberto Bachi, *Dante Lattes Jubilee Volume*, p. 272, Note 2. See also Cassuto, *Florence*, p. 230.

south and east of that city. Thus, these established Jewish residents of Italy, no less than the newcomers, contributed to the spread of the Jewish population.

The second circumstance reflected in the population shifts which was mentioned above was the division of Italy into numerous political units. When one state expelled the Jews they simply moved to a town in an adjacent state under another ruler. Small-scale expulsions of this type were particularly frequent throughout the fifteenth and sixteenth centuries. There were, indeed, towns which invited the Jews to return after their expulsion and repeated the procedure again and again.[1]

In brief, the characteristic feature of the Jewish scene in Renaissance Italy was migration within the country's borders. This makes it all but impossible to depict the distribution of the Jewish population without it, however, having much bearing on the question of the total number of Jews in Italy. This feature of Italian-Jewish history evidently had little relation to the numerical growth or decline.

b.

How many Jews were living in Italy at the beginning of our period, at the end of the thirteenth century? There is as yet no way of answering this question, but the geographic distribution of the population can be established. There were few, if any, Jews north of the Rome district, in which their number was fairly large. The movement of moneylenders from Rome to numerous small towns [2] marks the beginning of the spread of the Jewish population and implies a rather large group in their original place of residence. This trend apparently did not cause any sharp decline in the size of the Jewry of Rome, whose natural increase was presumably sufficient to make good the loss.

To the south, in the Kingdom of Naples,[3] there was an equally dense Jewish population until the beginning of our

[1] For a list of these expulsions see Bachi, *op. cit.*, p. 269.
[2] Cf. Colorni, *op. cit.*
[3] Cf. *Ferorelli*, p. 42 ff.

period. It was just at this point that the first Angevin kings carried out their systematic policy of forced conversion.[1] The story of the Jews' resettlement in southern Italy during the age of the Renaissance will be presented in a later portion of this study. At this point we need only mention that, apart from the groups who adhered to Judaism in secret, there were very few Jews in the Kingdom of Naples in 1300.

There was, on the other hand, a large Jewish population in Sicily. As early as the twelfth century Benjamin of Tudela provides figures greater than those referring to the Italian mainland.[2] Whatever our judgment of this traveller's reliability in regard to statistics there is no doubt that in visiting this area he received the impression that the Jews of Sicily outnumbered those of the peninsula. To this must be added the fact of the considerable number of communities in the Sicilian towns.[3] There is no reason to suppose that these consisted for the most part of tiny groups, such as spread later in other parts of Italy, on the basis of contracts for moneylending activities.

In what way did this scene change during the ensuing three centuries? The question of whether an upward or downward trend occurred is a complicated one. The period was, on the one hand, one of relative tranquility and freedom for the Jews. Despite the recurrent anti-Jewish actions, it was essentially a favorable era, one in which we would find a substantial increase, particularly in view of the influx from the north and from the Iberian peninsula. The increase was stemmed, however, by trends toward conversion produced by passing phases of political pressure, as will be shown below, and secondly, by the fact that Sicily was included in the decree of Ferdinand and Isabella. It may be doubted whether the

---

[1] See Cassuto, *Hermann Cohen Jubilee Volume*, p. 389 ff. and *Asher Gulak and Samuel Klein Memorial Volume*, p. 139 ff. See also Joshua Starr, "The Mass Conversion of Jews in Southern Italy (1290-1293)," *Speculum* 21:203-211.

[2] Benjamin of Tudela, *Masaot*, ed. Gruenhut, Frankfort 1904, p. 12 ff. and p. 100 ff.

[3] According to *Giovanni de Giovanni*, p. 19 ff. there were 55 Jewish communities in Sicily.

refugees from Sicily, who crossed the Strait of Messina *en masse*, settled there.[1] Throughout the sixteenth century we find Sicilian Jews only in a few southern towns and in Rome, but none farther north.[2] This contrasts with the fact that Sicilian congregations spread throughout the Near East.[3] We can only conclude that the Italian mainland was merely the first stop in the migration of the Jews from Sicily in 1492 to the Levant (the Balkans in particular.)[4]

The main factor in the growth of the Jewish population was the waves of immigration, the first of which brought Jews from Germany.[5] Even before 1300 we find Ashkenazic communities in the region under the Republic of Venice, and as the fourteenth century advances the references become increasingly frequent. These immigrants attained a numerical strength reflected in their flourishing communities in northern Italy, which had no Jewish population at the time the Ashkenazic influx began. According to the account of Elijah Capsali, the principal source for this area, the Ashkenazic population was extremely large, but one must discount the exaggeration in view of this scholar's penchant for painting the local scene in the brightest of colors. At all events, the Ashkenazim clearly formed the largest group among the Jewish immigrants who came to Italy during the Renaissance.

The second wave brought Jews expelled from France in 1394, who crossed the border into Savoy, a mixed French and Italian region. As the chronicler Joseph Hakohen relates: [6] "After their departure from France, Jews lived happily in Savoy, *where they waxed greatly in strength*. And it came to

[1] Cf. *Ferorelli*, p. 79. A small number of Jews from Sardinia also came there. *Ibid.*, p. 81.

[2] In M. Stern, *Stellung der Paepste*, Part 1, p. 91, there are references to refugees from "Sicily" in several cities of Le Marche. Careful reading of the Latin text reveals, however, that these references are to the Kingdom of Sicily and not to the island of Sicily.

[3] Cf. S. A. Rosanes, *Dibre yeme Yisrael betogarmah*, vol. 1, p. 150 ff. and *Sefer masaot* of Moses Bassola, ed. by Itzhak Ben-Zvi, Jerusalem 1938, pp. 36, 39, 67.

[4] See A. Milano, *Ricerche sulle condizioni economiche degli Ebrei di Roma durante la clausura nel ghetto*, Rome 1931, p. 7.

[5] See page 2, Note 1.

[6] *Emek habaka* of Joseph Hacohen, 2d ed., Cracow 1895, pp. 88, 94.

pass thereafter that they were expelled in the year 5221, which is 1461, and they went to live in the land of Lombardy and Romagna, and remained there unto this day". Thus, the number who settled in the Lombardy-Romagna was greater than the number who immigrated from France sixty-six years earlier. The Piedmont area, on the northwestern frontier of Italy, likewise received an influx of refugees from France (1410),[1] an event which accounts in part for the numerical rise of the Jews in Lombardy during the latter part of the century.[2]

The third move, which brought the Spanish Jews, was apparently smaller in extent than the influx from Germany, yet much greater than the number who came from France. Jews from Spain were a familiar sight in Italy, beginning with the persecution of 1391,[3] and the connection between the two countries became very close with the conquest of the Kingdom of Naples by Aragon. After the expulsion of 1492 the tide of immigration swelled,[4] and of the estimated 9,000 persons who came to Italy in that year,[5] many remained after the others departed eastward.

Although each of the three waves is associated with a particular period they respectively occupied a span of years. The influx from Germany reached its peak toward 1400,[6] but immigrants continued to arrive in larger or lesser numbers throughout the ensuing two centuries. A similar curve may be perceived in the case of the Spanish Jews who in 1492 went to Portugal, which presently decreed their forcible conversion.[7] Throughout the entire sixteenth century there was a steady stream of marrano families, arriving singly or in groups from the Iberian peninsula, who threw off the cloak of Christianity

---

[1] *Ibid.*

[2] C. Invernizzi, *Gli Ebrei a Pavia*, Pavia 1905, p. 4.

[3] Cf. Stern, *op. cit.*, pp. 21, 36; V. Colorni, *Legge ebraica e leggi locali*, Rome 1945, p. 367; *Ciscato*, p. 12 f.

[4] Cf. Alexander Marx, *Studies in Jewish History and Booklore*, New York 1944, p. 85 ff. and Moses A. Shulvass, *The Jews in Spain from 1391 to the Expulsion*, Jerusalem 1947, p. 41 ff. (Hebrew).

[5] Cassuto, *EJ*, vol. 8, p. 694.

[6] Cf. Elijah Capsali, *REJ* 79:28.

[7] *Emek habaka*, p. 108.

in Italy. In 1513 there came from Sicily alone 400 marranos, part of the population which had not left in 1492.[1] Similarly, Jews from France continued to migrate to Italy for years after the main group of immigrants appeared. The partial expulsion from Provence in 1491 brought immigrants as far south as Palermo (Sicily).[2] A case of a Provencal Jew, settled in Mantua, occurs as late as 1566.[3] In the sources four our period, individuals hailing from all parts of the Mediterranean world (Corfu, Tunis, Ragusa, Tripoli, Balearic Isles) are mentioned, indicating a small but steady immigration in addition to the important waves discussed above.

In the middle of the sixteenth century, the Levantine sector of the Jewish population, consisting of immigrants from Palestine and other parts of the Near East, began to achieve prominence, and in the following century this new element assumed considerable importance. In Venice, the Levantines attained their prominence as early as the first half of the sixteenth century.[4] In later years their progress kept pace with the strengthening of the connection between Italy and Palestine,[5] culminating in the leading role of the Levantines in the development of Leghorn, the youngest of the leading Jewish centers.[6]

Some increase in population also resulted from the ransoming of Jewish captives brought to Italy. This activity forms one of the brightest chapters in the social life of Italian Jewry, and it would require an extensive collection of material to show its full scope. Here we can only take into account the fact that over the centuries the liberated captives totalled more than a negligible addition to the population. A few examples may the cited. In 1509 all of the Jews captured by the Spaniards in Tripoli were transported to Naples.[7] No doubt

[1] Cf. Roth, *History*, p. 284.
[2] *Giovanni de Giovanni*, p. 96.
[3] Cf. *Haẓaah al odot haget*, Venice 1566, 30b.
[4] Roth, Venice, p. 61.
[5] See Moses A. Shulvass, *Rome and Jerusalem, the History of the Relations between the Jews of Italy and the Holy Land*, Jerusalem 1944, p. 72 (Hebrew).
[6] Roth, *History*, p. 347.
[7] *Emek habaka*, p. 110.

many of them succumbed to harsh treatment, but the survivors remained in Italy. When Charles V attacked Tunis in 1535, Jewish captives were brought to Genoa and Naples, where 150 were ransomed.[1] When Andrea Doria took the Greek towns of Modon, Coron and Patras in 1533, part of his many captives were also ransomed in Italy.[2]

The factors which favored the upward population trend were counterbalanced by various contrary factors. To begin with, the exodus from the Kingdom of Naples, which continued for some decades,[3] must have reduced the number of Jews,[4] even though some of the refugees gradually found a haven elsewhere in Italy. Apart from such cases, Jews often emigrated from specific localities, when the situation made it necessary. Thus, in 1509, when the war of the League of Cambrai struck the large Ashkenazic center, many of the Jews went to Mantua and Ferrara, "but many went to Germany to look for a peaceful place." [5] Again, under the impact of the hostile policy of Pope Paul IV, another reduction occurred and "the poor folk sailed away in ships for Turkey." [6] Added to this was the migration to Palestine, which rose to a high level under the stress of the persecution in the Papal States.[7]

In considering the effect of conversions to Christianity, we must naturally distinguish individual cases and large groups. The low rate of individuals forsaking Judaism is attested by the large community of Ferrara, where conversion claimed no more than 94 persons in a seventy year period (1531-1600).[8] Much more significant for their effects on the numerical strength of Italian Jewry were the recurrent cases of mass conversion, usually a result of official persecution. First in this

---

[1] *Ibid.*, p. 118.

[2] *Shalshelet hakabbalah*, Lemberg 1862, p. 173.

[3] *Ferorelli*, p. 218 ff.

[4] *Emek habaka*, p. 118; *Dibre hayamim lemalke Zarephath umalke bet Ottoman*, Amsterdam 1733, vol. 2, p. 28a.

[5] *REJ* 79:56.

[6] Cf. "The History of Pope Paul IV," Tarbiẓ 2:347.

[7] Shulvass, *Rome and Jerusalem*, p. 69 f. and p. 74 f.

[8] L. Livi, *Gli Ebrei alla luce della statistica*, Florence n. d., p. 290.

series was the Kingdom of Naples, where the Jews had re-established themselves following the mass conversion effected under the first Angevin kings. After almost two centuries, however, they fell prey to the fanaticism of a conqueror, King Charles VIII, and only secret Jews remained in southern Italy. In a letter of 1504, written by Fernando Gonzales de Cordoba, the Spanish viceroy, extant in the library of the Jewish Theological Seminary in New York, we read that the number of converts far exceeded the loyal Jews.[1] Despite the fact that the former continued to practice Judaism in secret, the conversion unquestionably diminished the size of the Jewish population. In the end the marranos either left the Kingdom of Naples and migrated to other lands or became indistinguishable from their neighbors.

The second instance of this type occurred as a result of the policy of Pope Paul IV. Benjamin Nehemiah, the most important chronicler for this period, reports that in a certain small town "seventeen persons were converted together, while elsewhere in the Papal States a few here and there were converted, so that there was no city without an apostate." [2] A document of 1582 attests the conversion of many of the wealthier Jews of Rome.[3] We have also a letter from Cori, which states that "every day there come families of the great and the small, the wise and the intelligent, the poor and the rich, who change their religion...." [4] The disillusionment, which followed the exposure of Asher Laemlein, likewise took the form of numerous conversions.[5]

The rate of natural increase among the Jews of Renaissance Italy, it should be noted, was quite low. As Rabbi Judah Minz explicitly indicated, "it is not customary for the *Romaneschi* [Jews of Rome or families which came from Rome] to marry girls of minor age."[6] Where data are available, we find families

[1] An English translation of this letter was published in the *Register* of the Jewish Theological Seminary for 1940, p. 65 ff.
[2] *Tarbiz, Ibid.*, p. 346.
[3] Milano, *op. cit.*, p. 47.
[4] Published in *Graetz-Rabinowitz*, vol. 7, p. 420.
[5] *Shalshelet hakabbalah*, p. 64.
[6] *Responsa of Rabbi Judah Minz*, par. 2.

averaging no more than two or three children each.[1] The
theory of a student of Sicilian Jewish history that polygamy
prevailed in that group [2] cannot be proven. The refugee
families from Spain, moreover, were fairly small.[3]

These various population trends extended down to the very
end of the Renaissance. About a century later, Rabbi Simone
Luzzatto estimated the number of Jews as 25,000.[4] This important figure refers to the year 1638, by which time the
migrations into and out of Italy were a thing of the past, so
that the numerical strength of the country's Jewry was
governed until the mid-nineteenth century almost entirely by
the rate of natural increase. In view of Luzzatto's profound
grasp of economic and political affairs we may assume that
his estimate was well-founded.

The figure of 25,000 must be considered in the light of the
losses suffered during the severe epidemic of 1630-1631, and
as a consequence of the entry of the Imperial army into
Mantua.[5] It would, accordingly, follow that in 1630 the
Jewish population numbered about 30,000. This estimate,
however, appears somewhat conservative; our estimated
figures, covering most of the political divisions of Italy, yield
a total of about 35,000.

If either of these estimates be accepted, we must conclude
that the number of Jews on the mainland *and* Sicily in 1300
dropped considerably during the Renaissance period. On

---

[1] Of the eight Jewish families living in Asolo in 1547, five had 2
children each, one had 5 children, one had 3 children, and one had 1
child. Cf. M. Osimo, *Narrazione della strage compita nel 1547 contro gli
Ebrei di Asolo*, Casale Monferrato 1875, p. 27. Rome had 1,772 Jews
and 373 families in 1520. Cf. Bachi, *op. cit.*, p. 271, Note 1, making an
average of 3 children to each family. Only one instance is found of a
family of 9 children, cf. *Meor enayim*, Part 1, Section *Ḳol Elohim*,
p. 11.

[2] *Giovanni de Giovanni*, p. 21.

[3] In a group of 11 families that came from Spain to southern Italy
in 1492, there was a total of 28 children, averaging less than 3 children
per family. Cf. *Ferorelli*, p. 84, Note 1.

[4] *Discorso circa il stato degli Ebrei*, Venice 1638, p. 91.

[5] Cf. the chronicles *Olam hafuk* of Abraham Catalano, *Kobez al jad*,
N.S., vol 4; *Hagalut wehapedut* of Abraham Massaran, *Hayekeb*, St.
Petersburg 1894.

the other hand, on the Italian mainland there was a greater number at the end of the Period than at its beginning. This increase means that the losses resulting from the persecution in the Papal States were outweighed by immigration. This numerical rise is one of the factors in the unique development of social and cultural activities which marks the life of the Jews of Renaissance Italy.

c.

The influx of Jews from other countries changed the composition of the population, which had been culturally homogeneous in the preceding period. Small as the population was, various groups now lived side by side, Italian, German, Spanish, French and Levantine, together with a sprinkling from the Greek islands and north Africa. The three groups which set the tone of communal life were the Italian, the German and Spanish Jews. The Levantines began to play a prominent role only at the close of the Renaissance, while the French group lost its identity and left only some families with a vague memory of their origin.[1] The French prayer ritual persisted only in the three northwestern communities, Asti, Fossano, Moncalvo (the *Afam* mahzor).

While the three principal groups (*tre nazioni*) represented distinctive cultural-religious currents, each had its regional focus in a particular Italian region. This geographic distribution was a result both of the diverse directions from which the immigrant groups arrived and of the internal migrations; that is to say, the result of the resettlement of Italy as a whole by Jews during the Renaissance period. The earliest movement was that of the Jews of Rome and vicinity who sent forth settlers to new localities.[2] While starting their loan-banks they founded communities in Le Marche and later in Romagna and Umbria. There they spread northward as far as Padua, while others at the same time moved in the opposite direction and began to penetrate into the Kingdom of Naples.[3] The

[1] An example of this was the family of Leon Modena. See *Sepher Chaje Jehuda*, ed. by A. Kahana, Kiev 1912, p. 10.

[2] Cf. Colorni's study mentioned in Note 2 (p. 2).

[3] *Ferorelli*, p. 72 f.

influx from Germany brought immigrants to Friuli and later
to Istria; expanding eastward, this group re-established a
Jewish population in Dalmatia, then a Venetian colony.

Concurrently there arose communities on Venetian territory,
closer to the capital, and as far west as Brescia and Cremona.
The German Jews came into contact with the established
Jewish groups to the southwest of Venice, in the Po Valley.
It was not long before the newcomers increased to the point
of putting an Ashkenazic stamp on the Jewish scene at
Padua, a change facilitated by the temporary suspension of
the loan-banks and the departure of the Italian-Jewish
residents.[1] The growth of the German element in the cities of
the Republic prior to 1509 is clearly portrayed in the chronicle
of Elijah Capsali. In the Duchy of Milan (Lombardy), which
saw a considerable increase in the Jewish population between
1400 and the time of Francis Sforza, the Ashkenazim likewise
predominated.[2] The names of the first Jews to reappear in
Pavia are Ashkenazic, and a document of 1459 designates one
as *hebreus de Alemania*, an immigrant from Germany.[3] In the
principalities of Monferrato and Piedmont, where French
and Spanish refugees were the first Jewish settlers, the residue
of the Jewish population was again Ashkenazic. This is shown
by the retention of their prayer ritual to our own day. The
once flourishing Ashkenazic congregations of Venice and
Padua, on the other hand, ultimately adopted the Spanish and
Italian ritual, respectively.[4]

The Spanish Jews were concentrated in the Kingdom of
Naples, which received the main body of the refugees in 1492,[5]
and even after the great majority became nominal Christians
the remainder consisted primarily of Sephardim. The well-
known document in which David Ibn Jachia lodged his
complaint against the Naples community [6] makes it clear

---

[1] E. Morpurgo, *L'Università degli Ebrei in Padova nel XVI secolo*,
1909, p. 19.
[2] Invernizzi, *Ibid.*, p. 4, and *Emek habaka*, p. 92.
[3] *Ibid.*, p. 13, Note 2.
[4] *Lunario israelitico*, 1928, ed. by F. Serve.
[5] *Ferorelli*, p. 78 f.
[6] Published by Alexander Marx, HUCA 1:616 ff.

that the leaders and most of the population were Sephardim.

In sum, the Jews in the north were chiefly of German origin, in central Italy Italian, and in the south Spanish. Within the three geographic divisions there were other groups as well, largely as a result of the expulsions. As noted above, in 1461 French Jews had to move from Savoy to Romagna, where the Italian element predominated. Following the final expulsion from Naples, many Spanish Jews found a haven in Le Marche: Ancona, Fano, Ascoli and Camerino.[1] The war of the League of Cambrai drove many Ashkenazic Jews from Venetian territory southward, particularly to Mantua and Ferrara.[2]

The mixed character of the Jewish population in the big cities was primarily a result of the fact that these centers attracted Jews of diverse background. This was especially true of Rome, Venice and Ferrara. At the beginning of the sixteenth century the non-Italian elements in the Rome community became strong enough to vie for communal power. When the struggle ended, as a result of the mediation of Daniel da Pisa, the power was shared between the Italian and the more recent elements, although the former retained some minor privileges.[3] At this junction non-Italians evidently formed about half of the Jewish population of Rome, but during the course of the century the Italianic Jews regained their pre-dominance. Following the closing of the Ashkenazic synagogue, as a result of the machinations of the Inquisition, it was not reopened,[4] and the local Ashkenazim scarcely figure in the community life during the rest of our period. By an order of the state, in 1571, the council of the community (*congrega*) was to consist of 60 members, of whom 35 should be Italiani, thus reflecting the relative decline of the non-Italian groups within the Jewry of Rome.

The community of Venice was divided into three major "nations", of which the German was the dominant sector.

[1] M. Stern, *Stellung der Paepste*, p. 91.
[2] Elijah Capsali, *REJ* 79:56.
[3] A. Milano, *RMI* 10:324, 330.
[4] A. Berliner, *Censur und Konfiscation hebraeischer Buecher im Kirchenstaate*, Berlin 1891, p. 5.

Yet the Spanish and Levantine groups, reinforced to a degree by the Italian, rose in importance and ultimately the Spanish Jews wrested the control of the community from the Ashkenazim. The influx of non-Ashkenazic Jews into Venice, attracted by the city's economic opportunities and the liberal regime, coincides with the flight of such Jews from nearby Padua, which was mentioned above. The majority status of the German Jews declined until the Spanish and Levantine Jews together gained a majority in the communal executive committee, a trend which continued in the same direction thereafter.[1]

The development of the Spanish Jews' preponderance in Ferrara is especially noteworthy. Around 1500 this was one of the most important cities in Italy, with a total population of close to 100,000 (as compared with 30,000 at present), and the capital of a duchy, which played a prominent role in the politics of that day. So great was the influx of Jews from Spain that the city's limits had to be enlarged in order to accomodate them.[2] The number grew following the flight of marranos from Portugal, where the Inquisition was established in 1531. Joseph Hakohen relates that "most of them returned to the Lord, God of our fathers, who had mercy on them, and they worshipped the Lord, God of Israel, and Ercole, Duke of Ferrara, permitted them to dwell in his land....."[3] Again, a decade later, many Spanish Jews, including the Abrabanel family, when compelled to leave the Kingdom of Naples, came to Ferrara. This important city likewise attracted Ashkenazim, who founded a synagogue in 1532.[4]

There were other places as well in which the Jewish population included "cultural islands" in addition to the predominant group. But the tripartite concentration of the major categories, which was indicated above, remained until the last decades of the Renaissance period, when the Spanish Jews lost their stronghold in the south. Thereafter this group

[1] Roth, *Venice*, p. 129.
[2] A. Pesaro, *Memorie storiche sulla comunita israelitica ferrarese*, Ferrara 1878, p. 16.
[3] *Emek habaka*, p. 108.
[4] Pesaro, *op. cit.*, p. 19.

formed compact units elsewhere in Italy; in time, as the
Leghorn community became a flourishing center, the Jewry of
Tuscany as a whole took on a Sephardic complexion.

d.

We have thus far described the Jewish population in general
terms, for one cannot reconstruct the demographic picture
in every one of the divisions of the Italian peninsula. The
effort must, nevertheless, be made to obtain at least a partial
picture. The available materials provide a basis for certain
conclusions, which, despite their incompleteness, may contribute toward the understanding of the historical course of the
Jews in Italy.

The Republic of Venice

On Venetian territory, where the settlement of Jews proceeded in accordance with agreements between the moneylenders and the town councils, the Jews appear in the smaller
towns first and in the larger places afterward. Until 1516 the
Jewry of Venice proper—from which Jews were excluded—
resided not in the capital but at Mestre, a small town on the
adjacent mainland. In the case of Verona, an important
document indicates that while the Jews settled in the nearby
villages, they did not take up residence in the city until it was
annexed by the Republic of Venice (1408).[1] The Jewish
population in the small towns persisted long after the Renaissance, as late as the second half of the eighteenth century.
The list of places inhabited by Jews is sufficiently broad to
warrant the generalization that they were scattered throughout
Venetian territory.

The size of this Jewish population cannot be estimated with
any certainty. At all events, in the writer's opinion, the
number in the three principal centers (Venice, Padua and
Verona) exceeded the combined number in all other parts of
the Venetian state. Typical of the tiny communities was

[1] The document was published by Salo W. Baron in *Samuel Krausz
Jubilee Volume*. See offprint, p. 6.

Asolo, with seven Jewish families (37 persons) about 1550.[1] One must bear in mind that in the small towns, in which the basis of the residence of Jews was a *condotta*, we must assume that they numbered only one or two families. The account of the attempt of Jews to settle in the fortress-town of Palmanova, which was built at the end of the sixteenth century, indeed refers to a single family from an adjacent small town.[2] It would accordingly not be far from the truth to estimate the combined Jewish population of the 25 small local groups under the Republic of Venice as about 1,000 persons.

Our information regarding the three principal cities is clearer. The Jewish population of Venice rose from less than a thousand in the middle of the sixteenth century to 1,694 in 1586.[3] The reason for this rapid increase is obscure, but the fact that the number grew from 923 to 1,424 between 1556 and 1563, suggests a connection with the flight of Jews from Rome (under Paul IV and thereafter). This persecution, which culminated in the expulsion of 1569, probably accounts for the continued upward trend in Venice during the years 1563-1586. The influx of Jews into Venice was in fact greater than that reflected by the net population figures, for one must take into account those who left in 1571, fearing that the order of expulsion issued that year would be enforced.[4] The figure for 1586 also reflects the mortality due to the plague of 1575.[5] The sudden decline of the population from 1,694 to 1,043 in a seven-year period (1586-1593) has yet to be explained. At the close of the Renaissance there were about a thousand Jews in Venice.

In Padua the Jews numbered about 600-700. This estimate is based on the fact that the plague of 1576 killed 220 Jews, while the population numbered 439 in 1603 and 721 in 1631.[6] In Verona there were more than 400 Jews at the end of the

[1] Osimo, *Op. cit., Ibid.*
[2] Published in *Italyah* 1:26 ff.
[3] Roth, *Venice*, p. 106, Note 12.
[4] *Emek habaka*, p. 153, and the *Chronicle of Hamagiha*, printed with the *Emek habaka*, p. 167.
[5] *Hamagiha*, p. 171.
[6] Rabbi Isaac Cantarini, *Paḥad Yiẓḥaḳ*, Amsterdam 1685, p. 10b.

sixteenth century.[1] Their number probably rose in 1597, when refugees from Lombardy arrived.[2]

Lombardy

The Jews were expelled from the duchy of Milan in 1225.[3] Then in the latter part of the following century (1387), Jews received authorization to establish loan-banks in the duchy.[4] In Pavia, one of the chief cities, there were at this date more than 50 Jews.[5] The population increased in the fifteenth century with the arrival of the French Jews, who were driven out of their temporary haven in Savoy [6] and were welcomed by the famous Duke Francis Sforza.[7] In 1489, however, a century after the restoration of the Jews to this state, Lodovico Moro, the son of Sforza, decreed the expulsion of the Jews.[8] A second restoration ensued on the basis of the *condotta* of 1522, which authorized 80 families to settle, indicating a total population of at least 400, all dependent on moneylending. In addition, we may assume that Jews engaged in other pursuits joined the bankers. A number of those expelled from Bologna and its district by Pope Pius V settled in the Milan region.[9] Cremona with a Jewish population of more than 450 had an important community at this time.[10] There were small groups inhabiting other places as well; the historians of the Jews of Pavia and Brescia mention a considerable number of localities in which individual Jews or small groups are recorded.[11] According to an estimate the Jewish population as a whole was in 1550 about 900.[12] At the time of the expulsion of 1597,

---

[1] Baron, *Ibid.*
[2] *Hamagiha*, p. 184.
[3] *Invernizzi*, p. 4.
[4] *Ibid.*, and Colorni, *op. cit.*, p. 41.
[5] *Invernizzi*, p. 10.
[6] *Emek habaka*, p. 94.
[7] *Ibid.*, p. 92.
[8] *Ibid.*, p. 98.
[9] *Hamagiha*, p. 159; *Invernizzi*, p. 62, Notes 1, 63.
[10] *Cenni storici*, p. 25 gives a figure of 456 Jews in Cremona in 1588. This is probably based on an article on the Jews of Cremona that escaped my investigations.
[11] *Invernizzi*, p. 25; F. Glissenti, *Gli Ebrei nel Bresciano*, Brescia 1890.
[12] Roth, *History*, p. 322.

the Jewish bankers were concentrated in Cremona, Pavia, Allesandria, and Lodi. The capital, Milan, was closed to Jews as a place of residence.[1]

Piedmont and Monferrato

The medieval Jewry of Piedmont and Monferrato appeared much later than that in the eastern portion of north Italy. The first to appear in Piedmont were the French Jews in the fifteenth century,[2] and the refugees from Savoy (1461)[3] were evidently the first to settle in Monferrato. There are signs that some Spanish Jews came to Monferrato in 1492 and by 1509 the population was sufficiently large to warrant the appointment of a state official (conservatore) to deal with the community. Some years later (1522), when the sum of 25,000 scudi was appropriated for the army, the Jewry was taxed 500 scudi. In view of the disproportionate share of the taxes regularly levied on this group, I am inclined to consider that it constituted one percent of the total population, and paid double that ratio of the military levy. Later in the same century the importance of the bankers in the Jewish population became pronounced, a change attributable not only to the arrival of French Jews from the Savoy and of Jews from Spain but to the migration of German Jews. This hypothesis is supported by the remarkable persistence of the Ashkenazic prayer ritual, which was pointed out above. The documents name numerous towns, to which the condotta applied, but the list was repeatedly revised and it is doubtful whether Jewish bankers settled in all of these places. The existence of local Jewish groups is, however, certain in those places where we know both of a condotta with the rulers of Monferrato and papal authorization. The papal authorization was undoubtedly obtained for the specific purpose of taking advantage of the condotta by Jews about to settle in the localities in question. We have a list of 13 towns, for which

[1] *Invernizzi*, p. 76, 85.
[2] *Emek habaka*, p. 88.
[3] Cf. Salvatore Foà, *Ebrei nel Monferrato*, Alessandria 1914, pp. 7, 9, 66, 73, 74, 75, 124, Note 58.

papal approval of Jewish residence was obtained in 1589-1594, which attests the distribution of the Jewish population in the smaller centers. These were tiny groups, and only in those in which a synagogue is known to have existed (such as Capriata or Monastero) may we assume that the issued comprised ten male adult Jews. The bulk of the Jewish population was naturally concentrated in Casale, the capital, an important community in post-Renaissance times, and four other towns (Acqui, Asti, Moncalvo, Nizza Monferrato). In the second half of the sixteenth century the Jewry of Piedmont likewise increased. Duke Emanuel Philibert published in 1572 a sort of official invitation to the Jews [1] of all varieties—Italian, German, Spanish, Portugese, Levantine, North African, and Syrian—which undoubtedly brought a number of newcomers.

In regard to Monferrato, we have an important item in a memorial addressed by the Jews to the state (1601), to the effect that the Jewry comprised 100 families, many of which were large. This justifies an estimate of 600-700 persons.

Mantua

The capital of a small but strong duchy, Mantua was from the fifteenth century one of the most celebrated Jewish communities in Italy. This Jewry was noted for its unusually rich communal activity, which implies a degree of numerical strength. Like Venice, this Jewry was composed of groups of diverse origin. Founded in the familiar manner by money-lenders, the original Italian-Jewish settlers from the Rome area were joined by immigrants from Germany (Speier, Erfurt, Nuremberg, Heidelberg) and the region around Venice. In the second half of the sixteenth century came the French Jews from Piedmont. Within this mixed population the Italiani formed about two-thirds of the total.[2] As the influx into Mantua continued, this group grew with the arrival of exiles from Romagna under Pius V,[3] who had been preceded

---

[1] The text is published in *REJ* 5:231.

[2] Cf. Colorni, *RMI* 9:219.

[3] *Hamagiha*, p. 159.

fifty years earlier by Ashkenazim fleeing from Padua.[1] At the
close of our period came a number of exiles from Lombardy,
likewise chiefly Ashkenazim. The names figuring in the
sources for this century also attest the presence of Jews of
other origins (Tunis, Provence, Corfu). Although as early as
1431 there appeared a Spanish Jew at Mantua,[2] surprisingly
few came from that country toward the end of the century;
considering the large influx of exiles into Ferrara, this situation is enigmatic and calls for investigation.

At the end of the Renaissance period there were close to
2,000 Jews in Mantua,[3] (twice as many as in Venice) constituting, according to some authorities, 20 percent of the
city's total population.[4] The relative position of the Jewish
group in Mantua in respect to its sister communities in Italy
was paramount, and the local Jewry's social and cultural
activities were correspondingly noteworthy.

Ferrara, Modena, Reggio, Parma

Ferrara was a typical Renaissance development. The dukes
of Este succeeded in building a small but strong state, the
principal cities of which, besides the capital, were Modena and
Reggio, and which comprised a great number of small towns
and villages. The house of Este had a very liberal Jewish
policy and the duchy had a relatively dense Jewish population.
During the fifteenth century a number of Ashkenazim settled
in Ferrara beside the established Italian community but were
too few as yet to have need of a separate synagogue.[5] The
population rose quickly in 1492, as was seen above. The
number in Modena and Reggio likewise increased, but these
were apparently Ashkenazi centers.[6] In the early part of the

---

[1] Capsali, op. cit., p. 56.
[2] Colorni, Legge ebraica, p. 367.
[3] Ibid., p. 338; also in RMI 9:230.
[4] Cf. Abraham Kahana, in Hagoren, 5682, p. 178. I was not able to
consult the works of Carnevali and Rezasco.
[5] Pesaro, op. cit., p. 16 f.
[6] Cf. Balletti, passim.

succeeding century we also find Jews scattered in the villages around Reggio.[1]

Throughout this century Ferrara received Jewish exiles from other parts of Italy, belonging to the several groups. In 1510 came those who fled Padua (chiefly Germans) during the war of the League of Cambrai.[2] In 1531 there arrived many marranos from Portugal,[3] and a decade later the exiles from the Kingdom of Naples, including the Abravanel family. The two latest additions to the population came from the Papal States: a large part of the wealthy class from Rome in 1556 [4] and the exiles from Bologna and Romagna in 1569.[5] The constant stream of immigration during this period in which Ferrara reached the zenith of its power resulted in a Jewish population estimated as about 2,000 by a reliable local historian.[6]

In 1597 Duke Alphonso II died without issue, whereupon the pope annexed Ferrara, leaving the new duke to rule Modena and Reggio. As a contemporary chronicler succinctly describes the exodus from Ferrara: "There went out Don Cesare (the duke) and the Jews." [7] According to the modern historian cited previously, however, the number leaving was one-fourth of the Jews, so that 1,500 remained.[8]

No doubt a large part of those who left Ferrara came to nearby Modena and Reggio, as did some of the exiles from Lombardy,[9] who preferred not to settle in Ferrara under papal rule. Thereafter the importance of that city's Jewry declined considerably, while Modena and Reggio assumed greater importance during the seventeenth and eighteenth centuries.

In the duchy of Parma, the western neighbor of Ferrara, the residence of Jews was likewise based originally on the

[1] This is evident from a responsum by Rabbi Azriel Diena published in *Kirjath sepher*, vol. 14.
[2] *Sefer hapesakim*, Venice 1519, p. 34a.
[3] *Emek habaka*, p. 108.
[4] *Tarbiz*, 2:346.
[5] *Hamagiha*, p. 159.
[6] Pesaro, *op. cit.*, p. 33.
[7] *Hamagiha*, p. 187.
[8] Pesaro, p. 34.
[9] *Hamagiha*, p. 184.

condotta.[1] In 1562 we learn of 16 towns to which Jewish moneylenders were admitted, but in 1578 there were only 8. The Jewish population persisted in these eight localities down to the nineteenth century.

Tuscany

The Jewry of Florence, the principal city of Tuscany, had its beginnings at the opening of the Ranaissance, and the names of the earliest residents point to Rome.[2] The community remained predominantly Italianic almost throughout this period. Rabbi Joseph Colon mentions the arrival of newcomers[3] but without indicating where they hailed from. Few of the Spanish exiles came here or elsewhere in Tuscany and this region is not mentioned in our principal sources regarding the distribution of that population in Italy.[4] Here and there, nevertheless, we meet with individual families, such as the Jachia in Pisa (1495).[5] The number of Jews in Tuscany increased as a result of the persecution in the Papal States and the expulsion from Romagna,[6] which brought chiefly Italianic Jews.

The distribution of the population outside of Florence in 21 towns of the district is attested by the fact that in 1571 the Jews thereof were concentrated in the newly established ghetto at Florence. Somewhat later a similar concentration took place in the ghetto of Sienna, and the circumstances imply that the population outside of the two cities was quite limited. In Florence, according to one scholar, the ghetto period opened with some 500 residents.[7] The researches of Professor Umberto Cassuto tend, however, to make this appear somewhat too high.

Papal States

During the Renaissance the Papal States rose in extent to second rank among the states of the peninsula. This domain

---

[1] E. Loevinson, "Gli Ebrei di Parma, Piacenza e Guastalla," *RMI* 1932.

[2] Cf. Cassuto, *Florence*, Chapter 1.

[3] No. 172.

[4] Marx, *op. cit.*, p. 86.

[5] *Shalshelet hakabbalah*, p. 91.

[6] *Hamagiha*, p. 159.

[7] Livi, *op. cit.*, p. 24.

comprised nearly all of central Italy from coast to coast and in the north took in Romagna with its capital Bologna. As the period ended the pope also added Ferrara.

As far as the pattern of the Jewish population was concerned, the essential feature of this state was the concentration of the Italian-Jewish element within its borders. While it is impossible to make any reliable estimate, the number must have formed a high ratio of the total Jewish population of Italy. The list of Jews taxed for the *Casa dei Catecumeni* in 1569 covers 42 towns in the Rome district, in which synagogues existed; there were in addition 34 such towns in Le Marche and 13 in Romagna. This is in accord with the fourteenth-century report, which mentions moneylending establishments in 30 towns in the latter province[1]. We may accordingly figure that the total number of local communities was about 80. This agrees with the impression given by the chronicler Benjamin Nehemiah,[2] who as a captive traversed the route from Civitanova on the Adriatic to Rome and found Jews living in virtually every one of the places he passed through.

In 1527 there were close to 1,800 Jews in Rome,[3] and in 1556 about 1,500.[4] The downward trend undoubtedly continued beginning with the reign of Paul IV. According to a report of unknown reliability, however, more than 200 families returned under Sixtus V (1585-1590).[5] The number in Bologna is estimated as 800-900 persons,[6] and there were a few hundred or more at Ancona.

Among the smaller towns, in 1566 there were 200 Jews in Cori, after the conversion of a substantial number.[7] In view of the numerous communities scattered throughout the Papal States, and especially in the Rome area, and of the fact that they did not originate on the basis of the *condotta*, we may

[1] Colorni, *Il Prestito*, p. 32; M. Stern, *Stellung der Paepste*, p. 144 f.
[2] *Tarbiz*, vol. 2, p. 480 ff.
[3] Livi, *op. cit.*, p. 23.
[4] Milano, *op. cit.*, p. 71.
[5] Cf. *Natali*, p. 217.
[6] Cassuto, *EJ*, vol. 4, p. 926.
[7] *Graetz-Rabinowitz*, vol. 7, p. 421.

assume that their combined Jewish population was relatively great. I would conjecture that the smallest numbered no less than 100 and some had 200 or more.

Throughout the first half of the sixteenth century the Papal States received Jews from other areas. There were during 1492-1511 five waves of immigration to Rome from Spain, Sicily, Portugal, Navarre, Provence, Naples, Calabria and Tripoli, as a result of which the newcomers formed a slight majority of the Jewish population.[1] The province of Le Marche, for its part, received an influx from the Kingdom of Naples; the exiles came to Ancona, Fano, Ascoli and Camerino.[2]

On the basis of the foregoing figures and the estimates for the smaller communities, the Papal States comprised half of the total Jewish population of Italy, as estimated by Luzzatto (25,000), or one third according to the writer's conclusion (see below). These figures refer to the middle of the sixteenth century, after which a decline occurred under the pressure of the policy initiated by Paul IV. The numerical loss was the result both of mass conversions and departures, as pointed out above. Regardless of the occasional return of some Jews to Rome and Bologna conditions were unfavorable for checking the numerical decline and the population was clearly smaller in 1600 than in 1500.

Duchy of Urbino

Jews appeared in Urbino, the duchy in which the Adriatic port of Pesaro is situated, at the beginning of the fourteenth century.[3] Under the Montefeltre and the first of the Rovere dukes, the political situation was favorable for the Jews, and we may assume that their number rose during the fifteenth and sixteenth centuries. It is known that many of the wealthier Jews in the papal provinces of Le Marche and Umbria moved to Urbino immediately after the famous bull of Paul IV against the Jews.[4] A number of the exiles from Romagna came

[1] Cf. A. Milano, *RMI* 10:325 f.
[2] M. Stern, *Stellung der Paepste*, pp. 87, 91.
[3] G. Luzzatto, *I banchieri ebrei in Urbino*, Padua 1902, p. 21.
[4] *Tarbiz* 2:346.

to Urbino and Pesaro.[1] The expulsion of the marranos from
Pesaro in 1558 [2] presumably did not affect the size of the
Jewry, since the former were recent refugees from the Papal
States and their sojourn was temporary, while awaiting an
opportunity to proceed to Turkey. At the end of our period
the number of Jews in the duchy was about 1,500,[3] divided
into Italian, Spanish and Levantine groups; [4] German Jews
do not figure in the sources.

Kingdom of Naples

The Jewish situation in the Kingdom of Naples, which was
the largest of the Italian states, was subject to recurrent
changes. The history of this Jewry, which goes back to
antiquity, was terminated at the end of the thirteenth century,
as has already been mentioned. Shortly afterward the Jews
reappear and in 1311 they received the privilege of re-estab-
lishing synagogues in various towns, a sure sign of the rise of
new communities. In 1393 the Jews of the Balearic isles
received a special invitation to immigrate. The distribution
of this population extended to the provinces on the northern
frontier and Jewish communities were found in various towns
in the Abruzzi hills.[5] We have already had occasion to see how
the influx of Italian and German Jews increased the population.

The immigration of Spanish exiles was quite considerable,
and was supplemented by others from Portugal, Sicily and
Sardinia. Although the absolute total is not known, these
immigrants outnumbered the resident Jews (*regnicoli*) two
to one.[6] But no sooner did the new arrivals settle that a new

---

[1] *Hamagiha*, p. 159.

[2] *Emek habaka*, p. 136; *REJ* 20:70; *JQR* 4:510.

[3] Luzzatto, *op. cit.*, p. 43.

[4] An ordinance of one of the rabbis of Pesaro of the year 1584,
published in *Finkelstein*, p. 315 contains a passage implying that
there were at least three groups in the community.

[5] *Ferorelli*, p. 63 f.

[6] Of a tax of 6,000 ducats imposed on all the Jews of the kingdom,
2,000 ducats were paid by the *regnicoli* and 4,000 by the immigrants.
Cf. N. Ferorelli, *Immigrazione degli Ebrei spagnoli nel Napoletano*,
1906, p. 7. We may assume that the immigrants were not burdened
with a disproportionate share of the taxes, thus indicating that they
made up two-thirds of the Jewish community.

conqueror, Charles VIII of France, decreed a persecution. The Spanish conquest was followed by the restoration of the Jews, including small groups of immigrants or captives of war who had been ransomed. At this stage, however, the plans for the final expulsion (1540) were ripening. The population during these closing decades was prosperous but small in number.

The greatest expansion was undoubtedly that which occurred in the latter part of the fifteenth century. The Jewish population at this time was distributed in at least 153 localities.[1] There is, however, no means of estimating the extent of this population and Ferorelli's calculation of 150,000, based on certain taxation data,[2] is plainly a gross exaggeration. That figure is entirely out of keeping with the restricted scope of the cultural and social activities of the Jewry of southern Italy and is not reflected in any way in the Jewish sources. It is, nevertheless, amazing that there were small towns in which according to Ferorelli, hundreds of Jews are known to have lived.

As for the composition of the Jewish population, the first to return to this kingdom were moneylenders from the Rome area. Later came the German and Provencal Jews.[3] After 1492, however, the population was predominantly Spanish.

Sicily, Malta, Sardinia

It will be recalled that Sicilian Jewry was relatively populous on the threshold of the Renaissance era, and it retained its density until the expulsion of 1492. There were some 50 communities, the largest of which greatly outnumbered the population of the principal mainland communities. Visiting the island in 1488, Obadiah of Bertinoro reported 850 Jewish families in Palermo,[4] or about 5,000 persons, a figure corroborated by non-Jewish sources.[5] Elsewhere this traveler found 400 families in Messina, 5,000 persons in Syracuse, and lesser groups in Trapani, Catania and Agrigento. While Giovani de

---

[1] A list of these is given in *Ferorelli*, p. 98, Note 1.
[2] *Ibid.*, p. 97 f.
[3] *Ibid.*, p. 71 f.
[4] *Iggerot Erez Yisrael*, p. 104.
[5] *Guedemann*, vol. 2, passim.

Giovanni's claim that the Jews formed 10 percent gof the island's total may be fairly correct his estimate of 100,000 Jews is definitely too high. This is made clear by statements of the Jews submitted to the authorities on various occasions in reference to taxation.[1]

The rulers of Sicily usually held Malta and Gozzo, where the Jewish situation was similar. About 1250 there were 25 Jewish families on Malta and 8 on Gozzo. By the time of the expulsion a century and a half later, the number had risen to 500 and 350 persons, respectively, judging from the tax records.[2] Of the Jews of Sardinia we know only that in 1492 the exiles landed at Gaeta and Naples.[3] This was apparently a very small population, which has left no traces in Jewish literature.

e.

Summarizing the population figures and estimates presented above, we arrive at the following:

Region	Jewish Population
Venice (city)	1,000
Padua	700
Verona	400
Other localities (ca. 50) under Venice	2,000
Lombardy	900
Monferrato	700
Mantua (city)	2,000
Ferrara (city)	2,000
Florence	400
Papal States	12,500
Urbino (duchy)	1,500
Total	24,100

The foregoing list does not include several places, for which no estimates are available, namely, Piedmont, Mantua (outside of the capital), Reggio and vicinity, Modena and vicinity

[1] *Giovanni de Giovanni*, p. 21 and passim.
[2] C. Roth, *The Jews of Malta*, London 1931, pp. 191, 195.
[3] *Ferorelli*, pp. 83, 95, Note 1.

(both in the duchy of Ferrara), the duchy of Parma, and Tuscany. With the exception of Parma, all of these had a fairly important population in the seventeenth and eighteenth centuries. The Piedmontese communities, those in the vicinity of Mantua and the two large centers of Modena and Reggio [1] with the smaller groups in the vicinity, all played an important role in Italian-Jewish communal and cultural life down to the last years of the eighteenth century. We may accordingly estimate that there were some 10,000 Jews in the places named. If so, the total Jewish population of Italy at the close of the Renaissance was about 35,000.

CHAPTER TWO

THE JEWISH PHYSICAL TYPE

The paucity of portraits depicting Jews of the Period, limits the possibility of identifying their physical appearance. However, a few extant portraits plus various literary sources do permit several conclusions regarding Jewish physical characteristics.

During the period of the Renaissance the Jewish community changed from a unitypical group to a composite. This leads us to raise the question of the extent of intermarriage among the various Jewish groups and of how this phenomenon affected the emergence of a "new" Jewish type by the end of the Renaissance, after migratory movements had ceased. This question cannot be answered clearly, since there is no way of assessing the number of "mixed" marriages between the Italiani, Ashkenazim and Sephardim. No figure can be entirely authoritative. We are, therefore, compelled to conclude merely that mixed marriages among the different groups did take place. This can be ascertained with regard to all three groups. When the Spanish Jews arrived in the Kingdom of Naples they found a settlement of Italiani bankers, many of whom were their social peers. Thus no barrier prevented members of thes groups from intermarrying. After the ex-

[1] In the second half of the 17th century, for example, there were about 900 Jews in Reggio.

pulsion from Naples, Spanish Jews spread throughout Tuscany which was inhabited by Italianic Jews. Spanish Jews also established important communities in the Republic of Venice in close proximity to the Ashkenazic settlements there.

The historic conditions that brought Ashkenazim close to the Italiani were different. To be sure, the Ashkenazim lived their own settlement area in which there were very few Italiani. However, in the latter years of the Renaissance their Ashkenazic character began to wane and their life patterns began to approximate those of the Italiani. This change established a basis for intermarriage between the two groups even though absence of geographical contact in fact resulted in fewer intermarriages between Ashkenazim and the Italiani than between the Spanish Jews and the Italiani or between the Spanish Jews and the Ashkenazim. In the light of the foregoing, we may assume that mixed marriages and the existence of similar life conditions over a period of two to three hundred years served to create a single Jewish type which was a composite of all three groups.

We have no drawings of the fourteenth century by which to ascertain the Jewish physical appearance of that period. The only fact definitely known is that Immanuel of Rome was blond.[1]

On the other hand, several portraits of the fifteenth century show a more or less common type. In the Daniel Norsa [2] family both men and women have oval faces. Similar faces are shown in a drawing from the end of that century.[3] Both

[1] The portrait of Jews greeting King Henry VII on his arrival in Rome in 1312 which appeared in H. Vogelstein, *Rome*, Philadelphia, 1940, p. 202, apparently comes from a German source and depicts German Jews wearing the well known pointed Jewish hat. See *Mahberot Immanuel*, p. 131. "For my hair has whitened, and my beard has turned from gold to silver". On p. 122, however, he states that his locks were black.

[2] See Roth, *The History of the Jews of Italy*, Philadelphia, 1946, p. 174.

[3] See Elkan N. Adler, *Jewish Travellers*, 1930, Frontispiece. The drawing shows two scenes: The upper drawing shows two mature men standing alongside the holy ark; in the lower scene a group of seated pupils are studying. The sketch of a Jewish pharmacy in fifteenth century Italy from a manuscript in the University of Bologna

portraits depict men with thick eyebrows. The noses, however are different. The Norsa family is characterized by long, slightly hooked noses, while both the adults and children in the sketch show short ones. The shape of the beard is alike in both pictures: short, as it remained during the entire Renaissance period.[1] The figures in the sketch are short in stature.[2]

Much more information is available from the sixteenth and early seventeenth centuries.[3] Here too the faces are mostly oval, with the exception of Rabbi Menahem Azariah da Fano who has a long, narrow face. The noses, like those in the fifteenth century Norsa family, tend to be long and hawk-shaped in virtually all the portraits. This nose shape is also seen some years later in the portrait of Rabbi Samson Morpurgo (1681-1740).[4] The beards are all short and the eyebrows are thick.

This physical type, evident in portraits, accords with detailed information available in literary sources. Leon da Modena described both his father and his oldest son Mordecai as being thin and of average height. Their beards were short

that is reproduced in Suessman Muntner, *R. Shabtai Donnolo*, Jerusalem, 1949, p. 16 is so small that nothing can be learned about the facial appearance of the people. The same is true of the beautiful drawing of a Jewish wedding from the first half of the fifteenth century that was uncovered in a manuscript at the Vatican library, a copy of which was published in Franz Landsberger, *History of Jewish Art*, Cincinatti, 1946, p. 213. The only thing to be derived from the sketch is that their heads tend to be oval.

[1] Roth, *History*, p. 360 recounts that most Italian Jews shaved their beards. In a sketch of six Jews of Trento in 1475, found in *Geschichte des zu Trient ermordeten Christenkindes*, Trento, 1475 (Reproduced in Joshua Trachtenberg, *The Devil and the Jew*, New Haven, 1943, p. 136) only one of them has a beard.

[2] It is possible that the artist had to shorten the height of his subjects for technical reasons.

[3] The portrait of Rabbi Leon da Modena can be found in Nehemia S. Libowitz, *Leon Modena*, New York, 1901, after the English title page. It was reprinted enlarged in Roth, *History*, p. 400. The portrait of Rabbi Menahem Azariah of Fano is available in all encyclopedias. For a portrait of a Venetian Jewish peddler see Roth, *Venice*, p. 174. Cf. ibid., p. 123 for a picture of Venetian ghetto leaders.

[4] See Roth, History, p. 401. We find a different, small nose on Elijah Lattes (see *Universal Jewish Encyclopedia*, vol. 6, p. 548 for a picture of his medallion). He was, however, probably a native of Provence who settled in Italy.

and their complexion dark. Thomas Coryat, the English traveler wo visited Venice in 1612 was impressed by the appearance of the ghetto Jews, especially the women, whose beauty, he believed, was unequalled elsewhere.[1]

The ideal of the people of the Renaissance was the man perfect both physically and intellectually. Thus an extensive discussion on ideal physical beauty appeared in the literature of most European peoples beginning with the close of the Middle Ages. Efforts to establish virtually dogmatic standards of womanly beauty [2] proliferated, efforts in which writers of the Italian Renaissance participated prominently in a lively fashion. The most important contribution was Angelo Firenzuola's detailed description of ideal womanly beauty, based upon the opinions of earlier writers and artists as well as on his own observations.[3]

A similar interest in feminine beauty is found in contemporary Hebrew literature. Various writers occasionally presented their criteria of beauty. Messer Leon in *Nofet zufim* [4] comments on women's physical beauty and quotes Aristotle's views on the subject. Abraham Jaghel Gallichi maintains [5] that "red headed young men and women with ruddy faces" have "ideal complexions." The subject is also treated extensively in the poetic debate on the status of women, in which many sixteenth century Hebrew writers participated.[6] The most specific details on the subject are found in a poem entitled "Prerequisites of womanly beauty are three and thirty", [7] by the physician and chronicler Joseph Hakohen. The author enumerates the parts of a woman's body and

---

[1] *Sepher Chaje Jehuda*, pp. 26, 36; cf. T. Coryat, *Coryat's Crudities*, vol. I, p. 372.

[2] See Burkhardt, vol. 2, p. 67

[3] Ibid., vol. 2, p. 64 ff.

[4] p. 101.

[5] *Moshia Ḥosim*, p. 6a. "Red" (hair) in his terminology probably means a soft yellow blending toward brown that Firenzuola places in the highest category. See *Burckhardt*, op. cit. vol. 2, p. 65.

[6] Published by Neubauer in *Rendiconti* of the *Academia dei Lincei*, 1891, vol. 7, 2nd Semester, Number 6. Cf. also article by Isidore Loeb in *REJ* 16:29.

[7] Published by Israel Davidson in his edition of *Sepher Shaashuim* by Joseph ben Meir Ibn Zabara, New York 1914, p. 88 ff.

establishes criteria for their form as prerequisites of beauty. He generally agrees with Firenzuola, whose treatise he may have known,[1] although at times he offers independent views. Like other Renaissance writers who dreamed of *occhi neri* he also felt that black eyes were the most beautiful. His prerequisites and groupings reflect a certain dogmatism in the presentation of ideal beauty. A comparison of the Hebrew writers' description of ideal beauty with that of gentile authors indicates that there were no striking physical differences between Italian Jews and their Christian neighbors.

CHAPTER THREE
NAMES AND SURNAMES

The source material available to us yields a general idea of the names and family names that were customary among Italian Jews during the Renaissance.[2] In this area of life, more than in any other, each group followed its own path and observed its own tradition. Among the Ashkenazim in the North we encounter well known Ashkenazic names whose sound or meaning is Germanic. On the other hand, Sicilian Jewish names are clearly Arabic, a remnant of Arab dominion over the island. In the central part of the peninsula, between these two groupings we find a definite Italianic tradition with names that are unknown in other lands.[3] Among the Italiani we also encounter an elaborate pattern of parallel Hebrew and Italian male names and surnames.[4] This is readily understood against the backdrop of social proximity between Jews and

[1] Firenzuola's *Dialoghi sulle bellezze delle donne* was published in 1541.

[2] Cassuto, *Florence*, p. 231 ff. devotes a chapter to the subject of names. Florence was at that time a pure Italiani community and we get an insight into the naming customs of the Italiani. Cf. Isaiah Sonne's many studies on the history of the Italian Jews for additional information.

[3] The material in this chapter is drawn from virtually all sources on the history of the Jews of Italy and various monographs on individual communities. I cannot, therefore, cite here the references with the exception of special points from which a generalized conclusion on some custom may be derived.

[4] Burckhardt's (10th German edition, vol. I, p. 388) statement that Roman Jews customarily named their sons after Semitic enemies of the Romans, such as Hannibal, has no basis in fact.

Christians in addition to economic relationships that necessitated writing many documents in the vernacular. On the other
hand, Jews show no special inclination to rare biblical names in
contrast to the gentile pattern of latinizing or hellenizing
names in an attempt to lend an antique flavor to daily living.
Aside from the name Joab, which was rather common among
the Italiani before 1500, we find no biblical name that was
not used by Jews in all places and times.

The practice of using non-Hebrew names antedated the
Renaissance period. Women's names that appear in *Maḥberot
Immanuel*, composed at the beginning of the Period, with very
few exceptions,[1] are non-Hebraic. The names of the men
however, are virtually all Hebrew. Evidently non-Hebraic
names were the rule among women and were used even in the
privacy of the home. At least in the area of religious usage the
men, on the other hand, retained Hebrew names.[2]

A great number of Italianic men's names and their vernacular parallels are listed in a special chapter of Umberto
Cassuto's work on the Florence Jewish community. The
connection between the two names is generally clear; they
are linked by direct translation or phonetic similarity.
Additional names that have been uncovered after Cassuto
justify this premise. Elhanan is Angelo, Abtalyon is Ottavio,
and Simone is used by men named Shimeon, Simḥah, She-
maryah, and Shemuel.[3] In one source [4] we find the combination

[1] See index of names in the Habermann edition, p. 981 ff.

[2] However, Immanuel's heroes undoubtedly bore gentile names as
well. It is worth noting that Italian names (Teofilo, Silano) are mentioned in the *Megilat Ahimaaz* which was written about two hundred
and fifty years before the Renaissance.

[3] See *Annuario di studi ebraici*, vol. 1, p. 178. Cf: *Graetz Jubilee
Volume*, p. 53; F. Luzzato, *La Comunita ebraica di Rovigo*, Citta di
Castello, 1932, p. 7; *Luḥot Abanim*, part 2, Simon Bernstein ed.,
Cincinnati 1938, p. 15; I. Sonne, Zion, N.S. 3:155, note 66. The names
compiled by Zunz in his biography of Azariah dei Rossi in I. A.
Benjacob's edition of *Maẓref Lakesef*, p. 14 bolster this principle.
Regarding the name *Jekuthiel*, in Italian Consiglio (Cassuto, *Florence*,
p. 237) it should be noted that German Jews regularly transcribed
it as Kosel, from which the Italian Consiglio may have resulted.

[4] *Elleh hadebarim*, Mantua 1566, in the membership list of the
Italianic community. For Mordecai's identity with Malachi cf. tractate
Megillah 15.

Malachi Mordecai, no doubt because customarily the name
Angelo was used as the Italian parallel to Mordecai. Menaẓeaḥ,
unquestionably a parallel to Vittorio, is found in several
places.[1] Similarly, Maẓliaḥ is named Prospero (perhaps
Pompeo,[2] as well), Yom Tob — Bondie, Tobijah — Bonsignor.[3]
Names with special meaning were given rarely. Leon da
Modena, a patriotic citizen of the port city Venice named one
of his sons Zebulun in Hebrew and Marino in Italian,[4] following
the verse "Zebulun shall dwell at the shore of the sea." [5]

It is more difficult to clearly describe the evolution of
women's names among the Italiani. The majority of such
names appear even in Hebrew sources in a non-Hebraic form
and it is difficult to perceive the Hebrew parallel. A woman's
Hebrew name will appear sporadically,[6] so rarely, however,
that it offers no clue.

The custom among Ashkenazim and Sephardim was completely different. Most of the male names appear, with a slight
accomodation to the Italian transcript, in their Hebrew forms
even in non-Hebrew sources. Much information can be
derived from a list of Ashkenazim and Sephardim in Verona.[7]
While the date of the list is 1660, it is undoubtedly no different
than if it were composed fifty years earlier. Moreover, it is a
list of middle aged men, some of whom certainly were born
before the year 1600, while others were born close to it. Whenever the list shows a set of parallel names, it follows the
Italianic pattern by employing either a phonetic similarity, as
for instance Elisha-Allesandro, Abigedor—Vidal, Meir-Maggio,
or a translation, like in the case of Kaufmann-Mercante,
Joshua-Salvador, and Neeman-Fedel. However, in Ashkenazic
Verona Mordecai becomes Marco, not Angelo. Many German
names prevail among the Ashkenazim such as Isserlein,

[1] *Kirjath sepher* 14:540; *Responsa of Maharam of Padua* No. 3.
[2] Berliner, *Rom*, vol. 2, part 1, p. 123.
[3] *Keneset hagedolah*, Eben haezer Section, No. 129, par. 119.
[4] *Sepher chaje Jehuda*, p. 28.
[5] Genesis 49:13.
[6] Such as *Bath-sheba*=Fioretta. See *Maabar Jabbok*, Lemberg,
1867, pp. 6b and 92b.
[7] See Sonne, *op. cit.* p. 154 ff. Mordecai=Marco is found on p. 157
(No. 78 on the list).

Gumprecht, and Kaufmann, even though we find also the
purely Christian Giovan Battista.[1] Eliezer often appears in
its German form Leiser and Mordecai is translated as Gumprecht. The sources verify that the German names brought by
the Ashkenazim to Italy endured for centuries. One case is
especially interesting: In 1459 we find a Jew in Pavia [2]
called Mercadante Di Bassano (Kaufmann of Bassan) and in
1660 we find someone in Verona called Mercante Bassan.[3] It
is fairly certain that Kaufmann Bassan of Verona in 1660
was a descendant of Kaufmann of Bassan who lived in that
area two hundred years earlier and kept the family name. It
should be noted that we also find a grandson named after a
living grandfather.[4]

Ashkenazic women in North Italy retained their German
names, such as Edelein, Zierlein, and Braeundlein, throughout
the Period and beyond. When necessary, German names were
translated into Italian.[5]

Important, though fragmentary information is available in
the sources regarding surnames of Italian Jews, and here too
there are striking differences in the three communities. To
begin with,[6] the Italiani rarely used family names. In a list
of seventy-five Roman Jews [7] twenty-five have no last names
and are identified by their fathers' names, twenty-six are
identified by a city or place of origin, and only five have
genuine family names. Names of Jews who entered Bologna

---

[1] See Osimo, *op. cit.* p. 10.

[2] Invernizzi, *op. cit.* p. 13.

[3] In Sonne's list, *ibid.*, No. 4.

[4] J. Shatzky, *Elye Boḥer*, Buenos Aires 1950, p. 26; Elijah Baḥur's
grandson was called Elijah while the grandfather was still alive.

[5] See the Yiddish poem of Gumprecht of Szczebrzeszyn, edited
by Moritz Stern in *Deutsche Sprachdenkmaeler in hebraeischen Schriftcharakteren*, vol. 1, Berlin 1922, pp. 16 and 54; Max Weinreich,
Studies in History Of the Yiddish Literature (Yiddish), Vilna 1928,
p. 142; "Italian Marriage-Contracts", edited by I. Joel, *Kirjath Sepher*
22:27 (Edelein = Gentile).

[6] I have limited myself to an examination of 3 lists: The list in
Berliner, *Rome*; the list of Jews who entered Bologna in the fifteenth
century published by E. Levinson in *Annuario di studi ebraici* 2:125 ff.;
Sonne's list cited above.

[7] Berliner's list.

between 1412 and 1419 [1] corroborate this usage. To judge from the Verona list mentioned above, the situation among Ashkenazim and Sephardim was entirely different. There are virtually no people identified only by their father's names; they all bear familiar types of family names. This distinction between the Italiani and Ashkenazim-Sephardim is because the former were long time citizens who, principally remained rooted in Rome and central Italy, even when banking and the *condotta* led to a broadening of the area of Jewish settlement. These people and their places of origin were well known and needed no special designation. Ashkenazic and Sephardic immigrants, on the other hand, needed family names to distinguish them. There were, however, differences between the Ashkenazim and Sephardim as well. While three quarters of the Ashkenazim are designated by places of origin, German or North Italian cities, the vast majority of the Sephardim carry family names that are unrelated to cities or countries, a practice that these two communities imported from their lands of origin.

The limited number of Italiani with family names took pride in them and several claimed that according to a preserved tradition they belonged to the families that were brought to Rome by Titus after the Temple's destruction. A legend circulated in Italy that "four family heads left Jerusalem for Rome with Titus: Anavim, Nearim, Adumim, and Latifim founded the synagogue in Rome called Synagogue of the Four Heads (*Dei Quattro Capi*)".[2] This tradition was apparently created prior to the Renaissance,[3] but received special significance during this period when everyone strove to prove ancient family lineage. Thus we find more than ten families who claimed descent from the four families who allegedly came from Jerusalem.[4] A similar tendency is also apparent in the remarks of Rabbi Yehiel Manoscrivi who claimed that

---

[1] Levinson's list.

[2] See *REJ* 85:64; *Meor Enayim*, section Yeme olam, p. 112; David de Pomis, *Ẓemaḥ David*, Venice 1587, Introduction.

[3] Roth, *History*, p. 13.

[4] *Vogelstein-Rieger*, vol. 1, p. 24 ff.

he was a "descendant of Ezra the Scribe",[1] as the name
"Manoscrivi", meaning scribe, attests. The old families, in
imitation of Italian aristocracy, generally added the word *min*
to their Hebrew names, "dei" in the Italian translation. The
best known of such names are: *Adumim* (dei Rossi), *Tapuhim*
(de Pomis), *Anavim* (degli Umani, Mansi, Piatelli), *Nearim*
(degli Adolescenteli), and *Zekenim* (del Vecchio). Other
families also adopted the custom of prefacing *min* before the
family name and thus we find a name *min Hazebuim*,[2] and
even the great sage who lived at the end of the Period, Rabbi
Samuel Archivolti signed his name *min Haarchivolti*.[3]

Ashkenazic family names, as we have seen, were linked
mostly to towns and cities in North Italy. This resulted from
the fact that German immigrants in Italy did not remain in
their first places of residence but, like all immigrants of all
times kept moving. This was especially true of Italy where
migration was linked to the opening or liquidation of banking
businesses. Thus when these German immigrants or their sons
left their first area of settlement in Italy to settle elsewhere,
they named themselves after the Italian town they came from
rather than the German place of origin of their parents or
grandparents. There was also a case of a man who came to
Italy from Cracow, Poland, and named himself after a North
Italian town.[4]

In addition to family names that appear regularly in the
sources, a goodly number of names appear periodically that
reflect certain occupations such as Orefice, (goldsmith), or
names that have no rationale such as *Bath-sheba*—Bassevi
and *Anshe kodesh*—Gentilli. One man,[5] undoubtedly German,
named Neeman Treutlin, in Italian becomes Fedel Fedeli.
However, these are exceptions which, despite numerical
frequency do not affect the general pattern.

[1] *MGWJ* 47:180
[2] A. Freimann, *Thesaurus Typographiae Saeculi XV*, Berlin 1924,
p. 63.
[3] *Catalogue Kaufmann*, p. 84, No. 187.
[4] Rabbi Jacob Soresina. See the Introduction to his *Seder nikur*,
Venice 1595.
[5] Sonne's list, *Ibid.*, No. 96.

CHAPTER FOUR

LANGUAGES SPOKEN BY THE JEWISH POPULATION

Communal heterogeneity was also evident in the variety of languages used by Jews. Gedaliah Ibn Jachia, discussing Italian scholars says: [1] "They spoke many tongues...these rabbis scattered throughout Italy used all languages." At the end of the Period editions of Passover Hagadot appeared frequently with three translations: Italian, Spanish, and Yiddish,[2] and a guide to ritual dietary regulations concerning the removal of fat and veins transmits the information in these three languages, that it be understood "in every city and to all people in their language". [3]

Ashkenazim, Italiani, and Sephardim each used its own cursive Hebrew and one group could not always understand the script of another. A Sephardic writer of the second half of the sixteenth century found it necessary to transcribe his work into "another script" in order "to benefit them (the Italiani) as well, if they chance upon the book". [4] This at a time when Ashkenazic and Sephardic immigration had ceased; Ashkenazim resided in the country close to three hundred years and the Sephardim close to one hundred years, and yet among the Italiani there still were people who did not know how to read Sephardic or Ashkenazic cursive script. Italianic cursive was the most widespread and it may be assumed that most Italian Jews used it.[5]

---

[1] *Shalshelet hakabbalah*, pp. 92, 96.

[2] Appeared in Venice in 1599, 1601, 1603, and 1604. For a description of these Haggadot see Isaac Rivkind, *Pinkos* 1:37-38. This trilingual Haggadah was published in 1609 in a fifth edition, in three separate booklets: Hebrew-Yiddish, Hebrew-Italian, and Hebrew-Spanish. In 1568 a bi-lingual Haggadah (Italian-Yiddish) was published in Mantua (*Ibid.*), undoubtedly due to the fact that Mantua's Jewish population consisted of Ashkenazim and Italiani with a negligible Sephardic minority.

[3] Jacob Soresina, *Seder Hanikur*, Venice, 1595.

[4] *Kirjath Sepher* 3:237.

[5] A study of the list of manuscripts in the *David Kaufmann Collec-*

Understandably, multiplicity of languages gave Hebrew a unique position as a common means of communication among the various groups. When a French scholar visited the Ashkenazic academy in Padua at the beginning of the sixteenth century "...they conducted their dialectics in the academy in the holy tongue that he too might understand".[1] Undoubtedly this was one of the factors that helped to create a common Hebrew pronunciation among all the Italian Jews with a decisive influence of the Italian language.[2] On the other hand, the languages that Jews spoke influenced Hebrew vocabulary and grammar.[3] The extent of the knowledge of the Hebrew language and the degree of its use among Jews as a living language cannot be ascertained.[4] Moreover, even in inner communal life the Hebrew language did not enjoy a monopoly. Communal ordinances in the sixteenth century were often issued in Italian.[5]

tion, of which the large majority are from Italy, reveals that in the forty-two manuscripts that could definitely be placed in the Renaissance, thirty-six were in Italianic cursive, three in the Sephardic, and three in the Ashkenazic. See *Ibid.*, p. 115, no. 366 for a prayerbook in the Sephardic ritual that was copied by an Ashkenazi in Italianic cursive. This manuscript, written in 1706, shows the extent of the dominance of the Italianic cursive among all Italian Jews in post-Renaissance times.

[1] Related by Rabbi Elijah Capsali, *REJ* 79:35

[2] For example, Italian Jews pronounced the name Matityah "Matassia" and Nathan as "Nasas" or "Nasan" (See Cassuto, *Florence*, p. 237, note 6 and p. 238), the ת was thus pronounced ss or s. For the pronunciation of various letters see A. S. Artom, *Leshonenu* 15:52 ff.

[3] Italian Jews often used in Hebrew masculine adjectives with feminine nouns when the parallel Italian noun was masculine, and vice versa. See *Italia* 1:26, note 1. Rabbi Elijah Capsali used the word מבחוץ (instead of בעל פה) to signify "oral". He doubtlessly was influenced by the Yiddish word אויסנווייניק ("by heart"). See *REJ* 79:34. In the minutes of the Verona community of 1539 (I. Sonne, *Kobez al jad*, N.S. 3:152) we find a resolution that the rabbi must teach the congregation Torah כל מחרת בהשכמה ("early every morrow"), a translation of the Yiddish word פרימאַרגן (early morning).

[4] Leon da Modena complains (Preface to Galut Yehudah) that "the exile has made us forget the sacred tongue and writing as well." Two learned rabbis like Leon da Modena and Manoah Corcos of Rome corresponded in Italian. See Cecil Roth in *Jewish Studies in Memory of Israel Abrahams*, New York 1927, p. 392.

[5] Such as the statutes of the Florence community mentioned above.

Italian and the Judeo-Italian dialect were the most widely used languages. While the Jewish-Italian dialects are not as different from Italian in the degree that Yiddish differs from German,[1] they do, nevertheless, have a unique dialectic character because of the many Hebrew words which they absorbed.[2] These dialects, preserved in literary form in old manuscripts, all belong to a group of Central-Southern dialects prevalent in the Marche region, Umbria, and the environs of Rome.[3] This accords with the fact that when these dialects were created Italian Jews were concentrated in the central and southern areas, while Northern Italy was virtually Jewless. When Jews of the Roman region began to expand Northward, they brought their Southern dialects with them. In time, however, these were eventually forgotten under local influence.[4]

The Judeo-Italian dialect never occupied among Italian Jews the place that Yiddish occupied among Polish or North Italian Ashkenazim, since Italian Jews understood Italian well and knew how to use it. Thus the Judeo-Italian dialect appears as a literary language confined to religious subjects (prayerbooks, translations of the Scriptures, Biblical dictionaries, etc.). A secular literature in this dialect is virtually non existent. The need to read belles-lettres was easily filled by Italian literature. At the end of the Period we find Biblical translations moving away from the dialects and approaching literary Italian.[5] To be sure, in certain areas, particularly Rome and Tuscany, the lower classes continued until the present to use the Judeo-Italian dialect.

The use of Italian in daily life was, understandably, more

[1] Steinschneider stresses the fact that the Italian language was born when Jews had already settled in Italy and thus participated in its creation (*MGWJ* 42:116). Cf. *JQR*, N.S. 42:75, 77.

[2] See prayer texts published by Cassuto *REJ* 5:146 ff. A small sized prayerbook according to the Roman usage, which appeared in 1486, was called *sidurello*. See A. Freimann, *Thesaurus Typographiae Hebraicae*, Berlin-Wilmersdorf 1924, p. 355.

[3] See U. Cassuto in *Miscellanea di studi ebraici in memoria di H. P. Chajes*, Florence 1930, p. 25.

[4] *Ibid.*

[5] *Ibid.*

widespread among the Italiani than among the Ashkenazim
and Sephardim. Fourteen of the sixteen known Italian
translations of the prayerbook follow Roman usage.[1] Italian
was doubtless the language used in preaching sermons in
Italianic synagogues, which is indicated by the presence of
Christian listeners.[2] By the second half of the sixteenth
century most of the Ashkenazim too spoke Italian.[3] The
Sephardim clung to their language with greater tenacity, and
there were places in Italy where Sephardim spoke Ladino
literally until the twentieth century.

The large Ashkenazic group that settled in North Italy used
the Yiddish language during most of the Renaissance period.
The rich Yiddish literature that was created in North Italy
during the Renaissance implies the existence of a large Yiddish
speaking population. Yiddish terminology that appeared in
many areas of life as well as rabbinic responsa in Yiddish
attest further to this.[4] Moreover, North Italian Ashkenazim
played a creative role in the formation of the Yiddish language
by assimilating Italian words that became so much a part of
Yiddish that only linguists can detect their Italian origin.[5]
It is also certain that the Bible was taught in Yiddish trans-

[1] See U. Cassuto, "Bibliografia delle traduzioni giudeo-italiane
della Bibbia" in *Kaminka-Festschrift*, Vienna 1937, p. 140.

[2] See Alexander Marx, *HUCA* 1:617 and *Sepher Chaje Jehuda*, p.
25, 39. Sermons in the second half of the sixteenth century like those
of Rabbi Mordecai Dato were originally composed in Italian (Steinschneider, *MGWJ* 42:521).

[3] See Moses A. Shulvass, "Ashkenazic Jewry in Italy", Yivo Annual
of Jewish Social Science 7:110-131. Available also in Moses A. Shulvass,
Between the Rhine and the Bosporus, Chicago 1964, pp. 158-183.

[4] See: *Nahalat Yaakob* by Jacob Heilpron, Venice 1623, par. 1, 42;
de *Pragmatica* of the Venice community of 1543 (I. Sonne, *Kobez al jad*,
Ibid., p. 159). The word *Jahrzeit* is used in Italy until today. A "German" responsum is mentioned in a document of about 1460, published
by I. Sonne in Hatekufah 32-33:643.

[5] See Max Weinreich, *Ibid.*, p. 143 ("A Story from Danzig") and
Shtaplen, Berlin 1923, p. 80. Cf. also Juda A. Joffe's Introduction
to his edition of *Bovobuch*, New York 1949, (p. 14). The *Bovobuch*
contains sixty-seventy Italian words from all areas of life. The vocabulary added by Elijah Baḥur at the end of the book was surely
meant for readers outside of Italy since the book was published in
Isny.

lation in Ashkenazic schools.[1] What is more difficult to trace is
the process whereby Yiddish was forgotten by North Italian
Jews. At the end of the Renaissance Yiddish books were still
published in Italy and Leon da Modena mentions specifically
in his book *Historia de gli Riti Hebraici* that the Ashkenazim
in Italy speak "German".[2] However, as we progress further
into the seventeenth century the Yiddish language keeps
disappearing. This process had already started in the middle
of the sixteenth century. A letter of that period [3] dealing with
the engagement of a teacher suggests that "the Scriptures be
taught in the German tongue and Talmud in Italian". This
indicates that the children spoke Yiddish at home and that
the Pentateuch therefore was taught in this language. However, when the youngsters grew up and started to study
Gemara, the language of instruction was Italian. An allusion
to the diminishing knowledge of Yiddish is also found in
Abraham Basevi's postscript to Elijah Baḥur's *Paris un
Wyena*.[4] He remarks that various people will find the book
difficult to understand, but if they persist in reading, they
will comprehend it. The disappearance of the Yiddish language reflected one aspect of the evaporation process of
Ashkenazic content from the lives of Ashkenazim in Italy.
By the middle of the seventeenth century Yiddish speech had
become so rare, that even a wave of Yiddish speaking refugees
from Poland who came to Italy in 1648-1650 failed to revive
it. At the end of the seventeenth century there are no indications of Yiddish language usage in Italy.

In contrast to the comparatively clear picture the sources
yield regarding the Yiddish and Italian languages, it is
extremely difficult to receive such a view of the use of Spanish
and Portuguese spoken by Sephardic Jews who immigrated en
masse in 1492, and in small groups throughout the sixteenth
century. On one hand the sources prior to 1600 yield virtually

---

[1] This is clear from Elijah Baḥur's preface to his Yiddish translation
of the Psalms, Venice 1545.
[2] *Historia de gli Riti Hebraici*, part 2, Chapter 1, par. 1.
[3] *REJ* 105:56.
[4] Published in Erik, *History*, p. 437 ff.

no trace of Spanish as a language spoken by Jews in Italy, which is rather surprising since we know that spoken Spanish thrived vigorously in various parts of Italy even to the present. Moreover, a number of Jewish books in Spanish and Portuguese were published in the course of the sixteenth century.[1] Most of these books were liturgical works while editions of the Bible occupied the second place. Curiously and surprisingly, all these books appeared after 1550.

Nonetheless, we can safely assume that the Sephardic community continued to use Spanish in its new home in Italy. For this group settled mainly in the Kingdom of Naples where the Spanish influence was strong during most of the fifteenth century since its kings were of Aragonian lineage. This influence was further strengthened at the turn of the century when the territory was conquered by Ferdinand the Catholic and transformed into a Spanish colony. Jewish community leaders in Naples were always close to the Spanish viceroy and surely would have used the Spanish language in significant areas of contact with the gentile world. Even when a letter from a Neapolitan Jewish family was sent to the government of Ferrara, where there was no particular Spanish influence, it was written in Spanish.[2] Nor is it surprising that the Sephardim in small Tuscany towns still spoke Spanish until close to our time. Tuscany, more than any other Italian province, was close to Spain in the second half of the sixteenth century and willingly accepted its cultural influence and life pattern.[3] Neither should one overlook the fact that the large community that formed in Leghorn at the close of the Period was overwhelmingly Spanish-Portuguese and Spanish served as its official language until the beginning of the nineteenth century.[4]

[1] The information given below on the Spanish literature of Italian Jews is based on M. Kayserling, *Biblioteca Espagnola-Portugueza-Judaica*, Strassburg 1890. Additional Spanish books appeared in the first half of the seventeenth century, which include compilations of religious law. See Cecil Roth, "The Marrano Press at Ferrara, 1552-1555", *Language Review* 38:307 ff.

[2] See *Balletti*, p. 78, note 1.

[3] See C. Chledowski, *Rom. Die Menschen des Barock*, Munich 1921, p. 8.

[4] C. Roth, *A History of the Marranos*, Philadelphia 1941, p. 217.

SECTION II
THE COMMUNITY

CHAPTER ONE
JEWISH SETTLEMENTS

In the areas where Jewish settlement existed during all or part of the Renaissance era it was generally scattered over the entire province, in both large and small cities. As a rule both large and small communities were established simultaneously. Only in rare instances did larger communities emerge following the dissolution of smaller ones and vice versa.

The numerical growth of communities in Venice, Florence, and Siena offers interesting examples. The Venetian community was founded when Jews who resided in small towns on the Italian mainland fled during the invasion of the Emperor's armies in 1509. Not only did the Jews of Mestre, who formerly also conducted their affairs in the capital city, settle in Venice at that time, but Jews from other places came there as well.[1] The large communities in Florence and Siena arose in similar manner, although the motivation was different. In 1570 Duke Cosimo I ordered the four hundred Jews of the Florence principality into the Florence ghetto, and the Jews of the Siena principality into its ghetto.[2] Not much different was the situation in the Kingdom of Naples. At the end of the fifteenth century antisemitism among the Christians became so intensified that small town Jews began to stream to the large cities.[3] Curiously, at the time the small com-

[1] *REJ* 79:45. ". . .not only did they come from Padua, but they came from all over Italy as numerous as locusts".

[2] See U. Cassuto, *Florence*, p. 111. The order to create a ghetto in Siena was issued in December, 1571.

[3] N. Ferorelli, p. 197. We also know that the Jews who lived in the villages about Verona came to settle there in 1408 when the city was conquered by the Venetians. See S. Baron, *Samuel Krausz Jubilee Volume*, p. 222. However, this does not imply that Jewish settlement in villages ceased.

munities in the Tuscany Duchy were dissolved and their populations resettled in Florence and Siena on Ducal order, the Jewish community in Parma was liquidated, also by government fiat, and its people scattered in six small neighboring towns.[1]

Small towns with Jewish communities were numerous. One hundred fity-three towns with a Jewish population are known in the Kingdom of Naples, about fifty in Sicily, more than seventy in the Papal States, and twenty-five in Monferrato.[2] Many sources offer information of Jewish residence in villages.[3] Accurate statistics about the Jews who lived in large communities and those who lived in small communities are not available. However, it can be surmised that approximately sixty percent of the Jews lived in small communities.[4]

The Italiani and Ashkenazim settled almost exclusively in small towns, since the overwhelming majority of pawnbrokers about whom small town settlements clustered, came from these groups. Sephardim, on the other hand, settled mainly in large cities, since most of them were engaged in commerce. Only in Tuscany, as we have seen, Sephardic communities developed in small towns as well.

Virtually every city and town had its Jewish neighborhood in which most or all the Jews lived. This separatism was partially voluntary. A seventeenth century account [5] describing an attempt to establish a Jewish community in one

[1] Cf. *Cenni storici*, p. 54.

[2] See above Section I, Chapter 1.

[3] For example: Baron, *Ibid*; *Kirjath Sepher* 14:545.

[4] See Section I, Chapter 1. Of the twenty-four thousand Jews who lived in areas where a realistic figure can be made, about thirteen thousand five hundred lived in small cities: State of Venice two thousand, Lombardy nine hundred, Monferrato seven hundred, Papal State nine thousand (after deduction of three thousand five hundred from the Jewish population of Rome, Ancona, and Bologna), Urbino one thousand (after a deduction of five hundred Jews who may have lived in the city of Urbino). Of the approximately ten thousand who lived in Piedmont, Mantua (exclusive of the city of Mantua), Parma and the environs of Modena and Reggio, at least two thirds lived in small communities. Thus about twenty thousand Jews lived in small towns and only fifteen thousand in large cities.

[5] "Account of the Tribulations that Took Place in Italy", in Moses A. Shulvass, *In the Grip of Centuries*, pp. 76-102 (Hebrew).

of the towns of the Venetian Republic tells that the Jews prepared for themselves "houses and a yard, that is a *separate street* on which to live". This is a characteristic description of the general process of Jewish settlement, especially in small towns where all Jewish residents sometimes lived in one, two, or three buildings.[1] Larger communities too were concentrated in one spot, at times for the purpose of living close to the synagogue.[2] The Jews of Palermo, the capital of Sicily, lived "assembled in one street *in the best part of the city*",[3] an indication that they settled there of their own free will.

In other places, mainly in large cities, the separate Jewish neighborhood was created under pressure of the government or the populace. In the early fourteenth century the Jews of Padua, fearing the wrath of the masses, settled in a section removed from the center of the city.[4] In Mantua, Jews in 1484 settled in one place "of their own free will".[5] Rome offers the classic example of the Jewish neighborhood. There Jews had lived on the left bank of the Tiber since ancient times, and this area remained their principal neigborhood virtually to the present. However, prior to the establishment of the ghetto, Jews lived in other areas of the city as well.[6] In Venice and Verona too, early Jewish settlement prior to the creation of their ghettos, was unrestricted.[7]

Voluntary Jewish removal into separate neighborhoods did not always satisfy those circles that tried to completely sever contacts between Jew and Christian. They therefore attempted to legalize the de facto segregation of the Jew. An example is the decision of the Padua city council in the first half of the sixteenth century compelling Jews to live in a restricted area that they themselves had selected one hundred and fifty

[1] Such as Asolo or Trent. See J. E. Scherer, *Die Rechtsverhaeltnisse der Juden in den Deutsch-Oesterreichischen Laendern*, Leipzig 1901, p. 596.

[2] As in Civitanova. See *Tarbiẓ* 2:477.

[3] See letter of R. Obadiah of Bertinoro in *Iggerot Eretz Yisrael*, ed. by A. Yaari, Tel-Aviv 1943, p. 104.

[4] *Ciscato*, p. 13.

[5] See L. Carnevali, *Il ghetto di Mantova*, Mantua 1884, p. 7.

[6] *Vogelstein-Rieger*, vol. 1, pp. 261, 301.

[7] Roth, *Venice*, p. 47, and Baron *Ibid.*, p. 225: "And the Jews lived in houses scattered throughout the city".

years earlier.[1] In 1427, under the influence of one of the great
Christian preachers, it was decided in Ancona that Jews should
live on "Jews's Street". A similar order was issued in Urbino
about a century later.[2] Similar attempts are found in the
South as well. In 1312 King Frederick II of Sicily ordered that
in all towns of the island the Jews should live *outside the walls*.[3]
A demand to establish a ghetto in Naples was presented to
King Charles VIII of France when he conquered that province.[4]

The last step in separating Jewish neighborhoods was the
creation of the ghetto. Venice was the first to establish the
closed off ghetto surrounded by walls in 1516. This event
created much bitterness among the Jews and they vigorously
attempted to protect their right of unrestricted residence
in the city. The wealthy financier Anselmo del Banco conducted his battle like a true Renaissance man. He argued
against the ghetto on moral grounds and hinted at the same
time that the Jews might leave the city. Even after the
ghetto had become a fait accompli, he still tried to secure the
right of unrestricted residence at least for himself in exchange
for substantial sums of money.[5]

Jewish reaction was different when the closed off ghetto
became a major objective in the policy of the Church towards
the Jews. They accepted the ghetto with virtually no opposition, and at the end of the Period they even cooperated in
establishing ghettos.[6] Despite many delays in the implemen-
tation of the policy introduced by the papal bull *Cum nimis
absurdum*, the movement to create ghettos spread throughout
Italy by the end of the Period. By that time Jewish neighborhoods in Italian cities had a fixed, homogeneous character:
A separate open or closed quarter in which the community
lived in extremely crowded conditions.[7]

[1] *Ciscato*, p. 47.
[2] Luzzatto, *Urbino*, pp. 18, 43.
[3] *Giovanni de Giovanni*, pp. 23, 25.
[4] In 1495. Cf. *Ferorelli*, p. 198 ff.
[5] L. A. Schiavi, *Gli ebrei in Venezia*, 1893, p. 325.
[6] See Sonne, *Zion*, N.S., 3:127 ff.
[7] The crowded conditions in the Venetian ghetto, for example, are
mentioned in a fragment of a letter published by Alexander Marx,
Louis Ginzberg Jubilee Volume, Hebrew Section, p. 299.

CHAPTER TWO

EVOLUTION OF THE COMMUNITY, ITS CHARACTER, AND AUTHORITY

In evaluating the Italian Jewish community of the Renaissance period, consideration must be given to the fact that in Central Italy and Sicily Jews lived uninterruptedly for more than one thousand years. There can, therefore, be no doubt that the communal organization of these areas was based upon old principles and foundations.[1]

The situation in the north of the Peninsula and in the Kingdom of Naples in the south was completely different. The South entered the Renaissance era at a time, when in the Kingdom of Naples, following grave persecutions, only a handful of Jews could practice their religion openly. In the North there was virtually no Jewish population during most of the thirteenth century. Both in the North and the South therefore, a new network of communities was established shaped by the altered historical conditions created by the Renaissance. The historical conditions were generally not favorable to the establishment of a strong communal organization that encompassed and regulated all areas of Jewish concern. The individualistic tendency of Renaissance men resisted communal restrictions that might limit personal freedom. This trend dominated Jewish life as much as it prevailed among the Christians, and did not contribute to the strengthening of the community structure. Numerous attemps to cast off communal control were typified by evading payment of taxes,[2] exaggerated patronage of non-Jewish

---

[1] In Sicily, for example, community leaders were called by the Greek term *proti* and one of the taxes goes by the Arabic term *gisia*. This proves that the communal organization retained elements that reached back to Moslem domination of the island, and the Byzantine period.

[2] Cf. *Sefer pesaķim*, Venice 1519, p. 30b. Immanuel Norsa of Ferrara is accused that even though he is the second richest Jew in the city, he pays the community no higher a tax than any average member.

courts, and widespread anarchy in the rabbinate.[1] The rap-prochement between Jews and gentiles and the partial integration of Jews in Christian society also deprived the Jewish communal institutions of much of their significance. Further limitation of community scope was caused by the widespread practice of establishing private schools and welfare institutions. Every city had a multitude of societies that assumed obligations for services ordinarily supplied by Jewish communal institutions.

The most important factors, however, in limiting the power and scope of the community derived from the con-glomerate character of the Jewish population (see below) and the establishment of Jewish settlements in many places by individuals or small groups.

Many communities were founded or re-established during the Renaissance on the basis of a permit to open a money-lending business. This license, *condotta*, also granted the recipient the right to settle in a city with his family and entourage (employees, teachers, ritual slaughterers, etc.), and to establish a synagogue and cemetery. The moneylenders were not always interested in developing community in-stitutions on the basis of the *condotta*. At times they were only temporarily bound to a location by business prospects and very often discovered that it was not financially profitable to renew the *condotta* after its expiration. They would then leave that place and seek a *condotta* in another locale. However, even if communal agencies were established on the basis of a *con-dotta*, the early membership of the community was composed of the moneylender, and a small number of associates and dependents. As a result, when a Jewish settlement arose that was independent of the banking business, the bankers still tried to rule the community, since they controlled the legal residence sanction and economic power. This condition en-gendered numerous conflicts that lasted until the end of the Renaissance and resulted in ultimate victory for a democratic community.[2] As early as 1416 at a congress of communities in

[1] See below, Section V (Religious and Moral Life).
[2] See Moses A. Shulvass, *In the Grip of Centuries*, p. 23 ff.

4

Bologna with representatives of several regions, it was decided
that every community must establish "an organized administration", that is, a communal authority. About two
years later, in 1418, the leadership of the community league
met in Forli to review the effectiveness of the decisions of the
Bologna congress. They found that the resolution about "the
organized administration...has not yet been completely
carried out" and have, therefore, again decided that
every community must permanently have "an organized
administration that shall care for the existence of the community, and the aforementioned administration shall be
empowered to issue ordinances and establish rules in their
community... and let no man disobey their command"...[1]

In addition to this general effort to enforce the organization
of well governed communities "where no one will disobey their
command," we have data from other places regarding the
struggle of the non-banking Jewish population to gain an
influence in the administration of community affairs.[2] Prospects of victory in this struggle were very good, for not only
was it supported by a majority of the community, but it also
was aided by the bankers' desire to involve the rest of the
people in sharing expenses, especially the taxes that were paid
to the state. The bankers could not, therefore, entirely exclude
the majority from exerting an influence on community administration.

However, the most significant stimulus toward strenght-
ening the communal organization came at the end of the
Period when most of the peninsula's states adopted the
policy of Pope Paul IV that aimed at severing social bonds
between Jews and Christians. The need for a strong community
to serve as a frame for organized Jewish life then became
apparent to all Jews. The confinement of many communities
in ghettos that was effected in the last decades of the sixteenth
century was not only an external symbol of a changed attitude,

---

[1] See the document summarizing the decisions of the Congress in
Finkelstein, p. 284.

[2] This struggle as it was waged in Mantua, one of the most important
communities, is described in detail by Vittore Colorni in *Le magistrature maggiori della comunita ebraica di Mantova*, Bologna 1938.

but it exerted a powerful influence in strenghening the communal organization, which became a religio-secular institution
concerned with all aspects of Jewish life.[1]

With the development of communities and the increase
of their membership, there apparently developed a need to
adopt community constitutions. Regrettably, it is difficult
to obtain clear data on the subject since very few community
constitutions have as yet been found. However, the legislation of two communities—Rome and Florence—that codified
their laws as a result of a rapid population expansion, is available. The legislation of the Roman community of 1524 [2]
clearly reflects heightened immigration. Similarly, the community constitution of Florence was adopted in 1571 after
Duke Cosimo transferred all the small surrounding Jewish
communities to that city.[3] It would be fairly safe to assume
that other cities also formulated fundamental laws. The constitution adopted in Rome aimed at neutralizing community
strife and establishing peace between the social classes and
among various communal groups. The Jews of Rome considered such legislation as extremely important and elected a
special committee (*Defensori dei capitoli*), whose purpose was
"to protect the constitution" that is, to oversee its execution
and the interpretation of its various clauses. We know that
similar conditions prevailed in other places too and undoubtedly necessitated enactment of community laws.

The character of the community organization and its scope

[1] See the interesting material on the Verona community published
by Isaiah Sonne, *Zion, Ibid.*, and Moses A. Shulvass, *Ibid.* One of the
signs of the times is the decision of the Ferrara Congress in 1554 that
in every city that had a community appointed rabbi, no other rabbi
had the right to issue any ordinances (the document is available in
Finkelstein, p. 302), or the decision of the Padua community that
forbade under a threat of severe punishment, telling any non-Jew of
decisions made by community authorities (see Morpurgo, *Padua*, p.
15). These were steps in the direction of strengthening the communal
organization.

[2] The text of the Roman constitution was published by A. Milano,
RMI 10:409 ff. The introduction to the constitution was published
in German translation by Berliner, *Rom*, vol. 2, section 1, p. 89 ff.

[3] The Florence constitution was published by U. Cassuto in *Rivista
Israelitica*, vols. 9-10. The article also appeared as an offprint.

of authority developed in a uniform manner. The Italianic and Ashkenazic communities established their control over their constituents and extended their services in various areas of life according to objective needs and in response to the attitudes of the various states on the peninsula. Two major types of community organization stood out and both were represented to an equal degree in the Italianic regions and the Ashkenazic North. One type was chiefly concerned with the religio-moral life of its constituents and represented them before the governments only to a limited extent. Such communities, for example, existed in Italianic Rome and Ashkenazic Verona prior to the concentration of their Jews in ghettos. Conversely, where a ghetto was established, the community took on the character of a municipal administration. This was the case in Rome, Florence, Venice, and Verona after the establishment of their ghettos.[1]

The communal organization in Sicily also had a definite municipal character "with secular and administrative functions that were far more important than its religious functions". [2] Similar was the situation in several places in the Kingdom of Naples in the fifteenth century. The Jewish community of Lecce had such a marked municipal character that the city council thought it necessary to appeal to the king to ban the existence of two city administrations, Christian and Jewish.[3]

The base of community strength lay in its authority to govern, in specific areas, all Jews within its province. Thus, for example, the Verona community had the power to decide in 1589 that all Jews of the city must pray in the communal synagogue and to forbid the establishment of private houses of worship.[4] Likewise, any Venetian Jew who wanted to settle

---

[1] Note the differences in community character as they appeared in the constitution of Rome in 1524 and in the minutes of the Verona community before 1598 (Sonne, *Kobez al jad, Ibid.*) and the municipal character expressed in the Florence constitution and the minutes of the Verona community in the seventeenth century (Sonne, *Zion, Ibid.*).

[2] See R. Strauss, *Die Juden im Koenigreich Sizilien*, Heidelberg 1910, p. 79.

[3] Ferorelli, p. 104, note 2.

[4] Sonne, *Kobez al jad, Ibid.*, p. 172 ff.

in Verona could do so only with the permission of the community.[1] In Reggio, when land was purchased for a new cemetery, the community levied a special tax not only on the Jews who dwelt in the city, but upon "all family heads who lived in villages under jurisdiction of the city of Reggio". [2] Thus, also Jewish residents in the surrounding area were occasionally subject to the rule of the city's community.

A clear manifestation of the community's claim for exclusive control over the local Jewry was its unyielding stand against the intrusion of non-resident rabbis or unauthorized local rabbis in civil law cases affecting its members. The community persisted in its stand all through the sixteenth century, successfully overcoming the opposing forces. As a result, the seventeenth century community no longer faced the difficulties of its Renaissance predecessor in this respect.[3]

The Italian community had recourse to an array of sanctions in exercising its authority, which included excommunication [4] and financial and corporal penalties, depending upon the extent of government support. Such information is available from all regions of the peninsula. Rabbi Obadiah da Bertinoro who visited Sicily in 1488, four years prior to the final expulsion of Jews from the island, attests succinctly to the

[1] *Ibid.*, p. 174 ff.

[2] *Kirjath sepher* 14:545.

[3] No issue in the history of this period is so thoroughly documented as this one. The Responsa of the Period are filled with information from various locales. The Congress of Ferrara in 1554 decided that "in a place where one rabbi resides no other non-resident rabbi can write decrees there... and where a rabbi is appointed by the community or community heads, no other rabbi, even if he is a resident of that city, can order any decree either in writing or orally... and if he should make a decree, it shall be null and void" (the document is available in *Finkelstein*, p. 302). A dramatic description of a dispute concerning jurisdictional authority over residents of two different communities is found in A. Marx, *Studies in Jewish History and Booklore*, p. 107 ff. For a comprehensive study of the subject see Isaiah Sonne, "On the History of the Bologna Community in the Beginning of the Sixteenth Century," *HUCA* 16:35 ff.

[4] It was customary in Italy to insert in a certificate of ordination a clause stating that the ordained is authorized to "excommunicate anyone so meriting". Cf. Isaiah Sonne, *Kobez al jad*, N.S. 5:207, note 1 for a fragment of such a certificate of ordination.

community's vast power: "They (the elected officers) are authorized by the king to levy taxes, to fine property, and to imprison". [1] In Mantua the communal court had the right to imprison lawbreakers. South-Italian communities would punish violators by flogging, and the Roman community had the authority to punish not only those who acted against the general community welfare, but even those who inflicted damage upon a fellow Jew.[2] Information from Alessandria, in the Ashkenazic region, tells of a Jewish transgressor in 1587 who was turned over to the local rabbi by the government to investigate him even with "pangs and throes" (cf. Isaiah 8:13),[3] that is, the rabbi was permitted to resort to torture during the questioning. From Ashkenazic Verona comes information of a community practice to levy monetary fines and to take collateral that would be sold in the event of non payment.[4] Apparently in the Ashkenazic communities in the North, communal civil courts operated regularly. In Verona in 1545 the rabbi was obligated to sit as a judge together with the community leaders in the synagogue every Sunday. In 1577 we find a similar court in session every Sunday in Padua.[5] Significantly, in Florence in 1571 the government endorsed the validity of documents signed by the community secretary.[6] Here and there the governments even agreed to enforce decisions of the community or its agencies.[7]

Although the community encountered perpetual difficulties

[1] *Iggerot Erez Israel*, p. 105.
[2] *Ferorelli*, p. 105, note 9; *RMI* 9:229; *Vogelstein-Rieger*, vol. 2, p. 128.
[3] The document was published in Isaiah Sonne, *Expurgation of Hebrew Books*, New York 1943, p. 40.
[4] Isaiah Sonne, *Kobez al jad*, N.S., 3:58.
[5] Sonne, *Ibid.*; Morpurgo, *op. cit.*, p. 14. The fact that the courts in both Verona and Padua met every Sunday, may, perhaps, suggest a move toward a unified legal procedure among the Ashkenazic communities.
[6] U. Cassuto, *I più antichi capitoli del Ghetto di Firenze*, p. 10.
[7] Responsa of Rabbi Isaac ben Immanuel de Lattes, Vienna 1860, p. 55; Responsa of Rabbi Joseph Colon, par. 9. For the factors that encouraged government support of Jewish community authority cf. S. W. Baron, *The Jewish Community*, Philadelphia 1942, vol. 1, p. 235 ff.

in asserting its authority, it was extremely cautious in using excommunication, which was its strongest weapon of compulsion. Generally, a rabbi could issue a ban only if authorized by the lay leadership of the community.[1] In some communities even more rigid controls were applied. For example, in Venice the Church authorities could prevent the issuance of bans even when these were to be imposed by the rabbis with the approval of the executive council.[2]

In addition to the positive efforts by the community to strengthen its position and extend its authority, a struggle arose to prevent Jews from patronizing non-Jewish courts, to which many resorted in order to cast off dominion of the Jewish community. This struggle is echoed in the entire Responsa literature where numerous plaints are registered over this practise. True, there was no real religious transgression in patronizing non-Jewish courts in a land and period where the social barriers between Jew and Christian were few and Jews trusted non-Jewish judges. It was, nevertheless, corrosive from the community viewpoint and more than anything else reflected the weakness of the Jewish communal organization. The battle against patronizing non-Jewish courts was never fully won.[3] Only at the end of the Period, a heightened moral and pietistic trend in Jewish life, characteristic of the time, evoked public reaction to this flaw,[4] and avoidance of non-Jewish courts was part of the great revival in Italian Jewish communal life of that time.

Two periods can be discerned regarding the scope of the activities of the Italian Jewish community. In the early

[1] *RMI* 10:332 (Rome); *Responsa of Rabbi Isaac de Lattes*, p. 143 (Padua); Isaiah Sonne, *op. cit.*, p. 165, document 13 (Verona); Morpurgo, *op. cit.*, p. 14 (Padua); Cf. also the interesting information offered by Isaiah Sonne, *Kobez al jad*, N.S. 5:207.

[2] Roth, Venice, p. 131 ff. Cf. the document at the beginning of *Seder hanikur* by Rabbi Jacob Soresina, Venice 1595.

[3] See A. Marx, *op. cit.*, p. 122, where even Rabbi Judah Minz failed to wean Jews from non-Jewish courts. Cf. below Section V (Religious and Moral Life).

[4] Cf. the by-laws of the society *Yeshibat shalom* in Ancona for the ordinance prohibiting this practice to the members (*Heasif* 3:214 ff.).

Renaissance period, prior to the ghetto confinement of the Jews, the community limited itself to general matters such as, relations with the government, supervision of synagogues, dietary laws and ritual slaughter, the appointment of officials and tax collection. Even the concern for Torah study was shared only partially by the community,[1] since specially organized voluntary societies assumed part of this responsibility. Many voluntary organizations operated in other areas of life as well.

However, when the community was transformed into a ghetto, the scope of its activities broadened to hitherto unprecedented proportions. The community undertook sanitation of the ghetto, protection of the peace, maintenance of a Jewish hostel in the city, and even provided a physician who was under contract to minister to Jewish patients.[2] The community continued to function in this manner until the beginning of the Emancipation period.

CHAPTER THREE

GROUPS WITHIN THE COMMUNITY

In the framework of the composite Jewish community a definite affinity prevailed between the Italiani and Ashkenazim. Very rarely did serious tension arise between them, and this only if there were no other groups in the community. For where the Sephardim appeared as a third party, a kind of "united front" formed between the Italiani and the Ashkenazim against the Sephardim. In Venice where the Italiani were always a small minority compared to the Ashkenazim and Sephardim, they were, from a "political" viewpoint, counted as Ashkenazim, even though they had their own synagogue.[3] In a situation where the Ashkenazic minority was unable to establish a synagogue with its own ritual, the common base

[1] See Section VIII, chapter 3, Torah Learning.
[2] *The Florence Capitoli*, pp. 10, 12; *Vogelstein-Rieger*, Part 2, p. 129 ff.; Isaiah Sonne, *Kobez al jad*, N.S. 3:166; *JQR* 2:306.
[3] See Roth, *Venice*, p. 60 ff. The Italianic synagogue in Venice already existed in the middle of the sixteenth century.

they shared with the Italiani in prayer order and customs [1] led them to attend Italianic synagogues rather than those of the Sephardim. An example of this pattern can be found in Ancona where the Ashkenazim were a minority vis-a-vis large groups of Italiani and Sephardim.[2] The most illuminating example, however, comes from Ferrara. Until 1492 the community was composed of an Italianic majority and Ashkenazic minority. However, in that year such a mass of Spanish refugees arrived that the Duke had to expand appreciably the city's boundaries. The Sephardim naturally built their own synagogue, while the Ashkenazim prayed in the Italianic synagogue. This situation lasted until 1532 when the Ashkenazim, too, built their own synagogue. The independent Ashkenazic synagogue existed about forty years until the terrible calamity of 1571 when most of the city was destroyed by an earthquake.[3] Despite the community's shrinkage, the Shephardim continued to pray by themselves, but the Ashkenazim reverted to praying with the Italiani in one synagogue.[4] Moreover, there then arose an Italiani-Ashkenazic partnership in other communal areas such as the administration of charitable funds and of the financial aid for the poor in the Holy Land.[5] It is interesting to note, parenthetically, that at the same time that the Ashkenazim in Ferrara founded their synagogue, the Ashkenazim in neighboring Mantua also built a synagogue for themselves (1530). Apparently the Ashkenazic element in the Po valley had become so numerous in those years that they could strive for independence.

To be sure, there were also incidents of tension and strife between Ashkenazim and Italiani. In a small town where both elements were numerically equal it was natural that conflict

[1] See below, Section V and Section VIII, Chapter 3.

[2] *RMI* 10:312, continuation of note 1.

[3] This earthquake was beautifully described by Rabbi Azariah dei Rossi in the first chapter of *Meor enayim*.

[4] See A. Pesaro, *Memorie storiche sulla communita israelitica Ferrarese*, Ferrara 1878, pp. 16, 17, 19, 31.

[5] See the Introduction to the Minute Book of the united community published by Isaiah Sonne, *Kobez al jad*, N. S. 5:204, note 28. Cf. *Ibid.*, p. 203.

over synagogue ritual should erupt.[1] Occasionally, too, an Italiani would make unfriendly remarks about the Ashkenazim. Such was the case with an Italiani who about 1550 attempted to dissuade his friend from going to Ashkenazic Venice to study. He wrote: "I have heard it said that the Venice ghetto is corrupt, with many people of impure lips, arrogant haters of the Italiani..." [2] This, however, is mild compared to the open hostility of the Sephardic chronicler Joseph Hakohen, author of *Emek habaka* toward the Ashkenazim in Italy. In his opinion they lacked good manners and were responsible for a series of disasters and expulsions that befell the Italian Jews of his time. He never failed to add to the name of a culprit that he was an Ashkenazi.[3]

A situation of tension often emerged in cases of business or marital conflict where one party was Italiani and the other Ashkenazi. In such instances the Ashkenazic party sought the aid of Ashkenazic rabbis while the other party looked to Italianic rabbis, as mutual recriminations of partiality were made. Rabbi Isaac ben Immanuel de Lattes, an Italianic rabbi of Provençal origin, twice accused the Ashkenazic rabbis of bias, "for such is their manner... to side with the Ashkenazim... whether they are wrongers or wronged and to find the Italiani guilty without examining the legal positions of the litigants". [4] But all these incidents do not obscure the fact that in the Italian composite community of the Renaissance period the Ashkenazim and the Italiani were very close to each other and both were discriminating against the third group, the Sephardim.[5]

In contrast to the Ashkenazim who established a network of communities in cities that had no Jews, the Sephardim generally avoided this. They preferred to concentrate in places that

---

[1] See *Kirjath sepher*, 15:125.
[2] See A. Marx in *Louis Ginzberg Jubilee Volume*, Hebrew section, p. 299.
[3] *REJ* 16:35; *Emek habaka*, pp. 122, 141, 143, 148.
[4] *Responsa of Rabbi Isaac de Lattes*, p. 141 ff.
[5] In 1611 a Jew of Ferrara left a large sum in his will for the poor of the Holy Land limiting his aid to the Ashkenazic and Italianic poor (*Balletti*, p. 85).

already had Jewish settlement. They settled chiefly in regions where the main Jewish element was Italianic (Kingdom of Naples, Tuscany, the Adriatic ports, and Ferrara), and the communal struggle against the Sephardim was, therefore, waged primarily by the Italiani. The Sephardim emerged victorious from this battle, since they were economically more powerful and wielded strong influence in government circles. No Jewish family in the middle of the sixteenth century could approximate the influence of the Abravanel family in the courts of the Kingdom of Naples, Ferrara, and Tuscany.[1] The dukes of Tuscany invited Sephardic and Levantine Jews, who were active in international trade, to settle in their land as early as 1551. By the end of the sixteenth century the magnificent community in Leghorn emerged, which was exclusively Sephardic and Levantine.[2] The Sephardim did not act like shy refugees. Since they constituted a majority of taxpayers in many places, their influence on the administration of the community was great.[3] They often knew how to utilize government support to achieve this end.[4] Fear of the Sephardic aggressiveness was possibly the reason why the Roman community besought Pope Alexander VI to forbid the settlement of Spanish refugees in the city.[5] And indeed, after the arrival of the Sephardim the harsh struggle erupted that led to the adoption of the community constitution prepared by Daniel da Pisa.[6] David ben Messer Leon's angry indictment of the Sephardim for their ambition to dominate the communities,[7]

[1] See S. H. Margulies, *Rivista Israelitica* 3:147 ff.; Cassuto, *Florence*, p. 384 ff; M. A. Shulvass, "The House of Abravanel in Italy", *Ḥayim Ḥezekiah Medini Memorial Volume Ḥemdat Yisrael*, p. 114 ff. (Hebrew).

[2] Cassuto, *Florence*, p. 409; G. Sonnino, *Storia della tipografia ebraica in Livorno*, Turin 1912, p. 3.

[3] In seventeenth century Venice there were sixty Sephardic and twelve Levantine taxpayers. In contrast, there were only forty Ashkenazic taxpayers. See Roth, *Venice*, p. 128. The majority of the population who could not pay any taxes were Ashkenazim.

[4] As in Verona in the mid seventeenth century. Cf. Isaiah Sonne, *Zion*, N. S. 3:149.

[5] *Shalshelet haḳabbalah*, p. 172.

[6] *RMI* 10:327.

[7] *Kebod haḳamim*, edited by Simon Bernfeld and published by M'kize Nirdamim, Berlin 1899.

no doubt expressed the feelings of most Italiani. The Sephardim cared little about the bitterness that they aroused and
continued to establish their separate or autonomous communities. As a result, Sephardic communities preserved their
identity far more successfully than did the Ashkenazic communities. The affinity between the Ashkenazim and Italiani
led inexorably to the partial assimilation of the former, even
though the Ashkenazim were probably numerically equal to
the Italiani. The Italiani proved to be "stronger" because they
spoke Italian or the Judeo-Italian dialect. Although the
Ashkenazim spoke Yiddish for a long time; their use of
Italian was steadily progressing.

We have seen how the partisan tendencies of the various
groups led to a weakening of the communal organization.
Moreover, in some places the various groups established their
own communities with separate administrations. Such was
the case, for example, in Venice in 1516 when the Ashkenazim
and the Italiani were placed in the ghetto while the Sephardim
and Levantines continued to live all over the city until 1541
and maintained a separate community. When the Sephardim
entered the ghetto, even then a special section was assigned
to them where they continued to have a separate communal
organization.[1] Sephardic Jews who came to the Kingdom of
Naples after the Spanish expulsion had their own community
leaders, *Proti*, in many cities. Also the Sicilian refugees of
1492 who settled there had their own leader in the person of
the *Consul Siculorum Ebreorum*.[2] It is furthermore certain
that the Sephardim who came to the Marche region after the
Naples expulsion in 1541 established their own separate communities. To be sure, upon their arrival, the Pope ordered that
they pay their taxes as part of the Marche Jewry and join
its communal organization. However, this applied only to the
regional communal organization, *Universitas Hebreorum
Marchiae*,[3] and not to local communities. In 1553 Pope Julius

[1] Roth, *Venice*, p. 61 ff.
[2] Ferorelli, *Immigrazione degli ebrei spagnuoli nel Napoletano*, 1906,
p. 9.
[3] This is clearly seen in the document published by Stern, *Stellung
der Paepste*, Part 1, p. 91.

III granted special rights to the Portuguese Jews in Ancona and referred to them specifically as a separate community, *Universitas Hebreorum Portugalensium in Civitate Nostra Anconitana.*[1]

There were also communities where the divisiveness was less articulate. Here united communities did function but left to the synagogues of the various groups the freedom to conduct their internal affairs autonomously. The constitution prepared by Daniel da Pisa in Rome clearly stated that while all synagogues must submit to the community's legislative body (*Congrega*) in general matters, they may remain autonomous in internal affairs.[2] In 1584 in Pesaro there were at least three communities that cooperated in matters of common interest.[3] The Levantines in Venice referred to themselves as "The Easterners' Sacred Community" during the period that a united community undoubtedly existed.[4] This type of communal separatism is further expressed in the prohibition that the various groups placed upon their membership not to worship in the synagogues of the other groups, in encouragement to preserve their own customs, and to support the charities of their own group exclusively. Prohibitions of praying in a synagogue with a different rite are known from the seventeenth century, after the close of the Period.[5] We may safely assume that earlier, before the composite community had fully crystallized, these trends were even stronger. Rabbi Judah Minz, the great Ashkenazic leader during the flowering period of this community in North Italy, reminded

---

[1] *Ibid.,* p. 95. Cf. *RMI* 10:312.

[2] *RMI* 10:331.

[3] A text incorporating an ordinance by the rabbis in Pesaro, published in *Finkelstein,* p. 314 ff. states that it should apply "to *all* the sacred communities here in Pesaro". This indicates that there were at least three communal organizations.

[4] At the beginning of the seventeenth century. See *Ḳuntres elleh hadebarim,* Mantua 1564. Cf. Judah da Saltara of Fano, *Miḳweh Yisrael,* Venice 1607, p. 9a.

[5] In Venice, where the Italiani, Sephardim, and Levantines issued such a prohibition in 1636. In Ancona too, the Italianic *ḳehillah* in 1668 forbade its members to pray in the Levantine synagogue. See *Oẓar tob,* 1885-6, p. 13.

the Jews of Treviso of their Ashkenazic origin and urged them to conduct themselves according to "their old customs". [1] Preference for their own group also motivated the leaders of a Levantine society for dowering brides when they resolved that funds should be màde available first and foremost to girls of Levantine origin.[2]

These examples clearly indicate the complexity of intracommunal relationships within the Italian Jewish community. People of varied background, orientation, and customs, with conflicting economic interests, resided in close proximity to one another. The only possibility of an organized Jewish life lay in the mutual consent of all parties to communal cooperation. In most cases, indeed, an agreement generally emerged from the tangled conflicts that granted representation to each group in the administration of the community. Rome was the first of such communities. By 1524 there were in Rome, in addition to the old Italianic synagogues, Castilian ,Catalan, Sicilian, and Ashkenazic synagogues.[3] The difficulties that arose from this situation were removed by the enactment of the already mentioned constitution, prepared by Daniel da Pisa which gave satisfactory representation to all interested parties. Significantly, representation was arranged along group as well as social [4] principles, indicating the existence of additional areas of conflict within the community. The introduction to the constitution [5] makes it clear that after extended conflict, the community recognized that the only solution was intracommunal cooperation.

With all the rights that the constitution granted to the *ultramontani*, the immigrants from the "other side of the mountains", it nevertheless accorded more privileges to the Italiani who were the majority, or at least fifty percent of the community. This pattern was adopted in other places as well. In Mantua it was resolved in 1589 that two of the three com-

[1] *Responsa of Rabbi Judah Minz and Maharam of Padua*, Venice 1553, par. 7.

[2] A. Marx, *ZfhB*, 1907, p. 120. The decision was taken in 1653.

[3] Berliner, *Rom*, vol. 2, Part 1, p. 96.

[4] *RMI* 10:324 ff.

[5] Berliner, *op. cit.*, p. 89 ff.

munal officers, *massari*, should be Italiani and one Ashkenazi.[1]
Even prior to this time, when the Italianic synagogue was
built, it was decided that meetings of the community's
general council must take place in this synagogue.[2] Here, the
Italiani clearly dominated. Definite Ashkenazic dominance
prevailed in sixteenth century Padua. The Ashkenazic
synagogue was recognized as the community's official house
of worship and the community leadership controlled its budget
and appointed its officers. To be sure, in matters affecting this
synagogue, Italiani members of the community administration
abstained from voting. As could be expected, the Italianic
synagogue enjoyed internal autonomy.[3]

Another large community that attained intra-group administrative accord was Venice. A unified community was
organized close to the end of the Renaissance period with the
creation of an executive council, *waad ḳatan*. The council was
composed of seven members, three Ashkenazim, three
Sephardim, and one Levantine.[4] The Ashkenazim, although
constituting a majority of the population were a minority in
the community administration because the franchise was
linked to tax payments.[5] Intra-group cooperation in Venice
extended to the rabbinate as well. Assuming that the first
signature on rabbinic documents was that of the "chief"
rabbi or head of the board of rabbis, we find that this title
was apparently bestowed on the basis of personal merit rather
than group affiliation. In 1605 we find Rabbi Benzion Zarfadi signing first and in 1623 it is Rabbi Isaac Gherescion,
a Levantine rabbi.[6] After them, with the advance of the seventeenth century, came the Italianic Rabbi Leon da Modena, and
the Ashkenazic Rabbi Simone Luzzatto.

[1] Colorni, *Magistrature maggiori*, p. 45.
[2] *Ibid.*, p. 38.
[3] Morpurgo, *Padua*, p. 3, note 1 on the basis of the community's
minutes.
[4] Roth, *Venice*, pp. 70, 129.
[5] See the following chapter.
[6] Solomon de Rossi, *Hashirim asher lishelomoh*, Francfort/M 1925,
p. 6.

CHAPTER FOUR

ADMINISTRATION AND FINANCIAL STRUCTURE OF THE COMMUNITY

a.

The problem of community organization preoccupied Italian Jewry during the entire Renaissance period. The many communal and social conflicts prevented the stabilization of administrative systems, and the frequent changes that occured in every locale are indicative of the efforts to devise effective administrative practices.

In Rome where the community was old and populous, the situation was less complicated and became stabilized by the constitution adopted in 1524. An executive board composed of only three directors,[1] *fattori*, proved to be an efficiently functioning administrative body. Supervision of the directors and decisions on major matters, or projects that necessitated the expenditure of large sums, were in the hands of a sixty man council called the Assembly, *Congrega*. The Assembly was elected annually at a general convocation by members of the community. Apparently this function was the only prerogative of the general convocation, and the Assembly was the decisive community authority. From its midst the Assembly elected the three directors, and, to effectively supervise their activities, it also elected a twenty man council *Consiglio ristretto* that assisted the directors in their work. This form of community organization continued even after Roman Jews were placed within the walled ghetto in 1555.

This administrative structure, fully crystallized in Rome as early as 1524, was not common in most communities of the North until the last decades of the Period. Such developmental disparity resulted from the fact that all the communities of the North were founded in the Renaissance period with very limited populations. Many of these communities were controlled by the family with *condotta* privilege and did not attain any form of public administration until the end of the Period.

[1] See the Roman constitution in *RMI* 10:409 ff.

When such a community freed itself from the control of the
condotta bearer, its membership was so limited that the most
logical form of dealing with community matters was through a
general assembly of all members. This assembly was called
waad kelali—(General council), with various Italian titles
such as, *Vicinia, Assemblea,* or *Convocazione,* with the adjective
Generale.[1]

The first step in the establishment of representative institutions probably came shortly after a community was founded,
through the election of directors (*memunim, parnasim*). The
election of directors was discussed as early as 1416 at the
congress of communities held in Bologna.[2] Clearly, when the
congress sought to organize communities in the various cities,
it weighed the need of an administrative body to assist the
assembly of family heads. Indeed, *parnasim* are mentioned in
North Italy even prior to 1500. In Treviso there were *parnasim*
close to 1500.[3] In Padua we encounter one *parnas* before 1533.
Later, two *parnasim* were in charge of community affairs.
We also find two *parnasim* in Verona in 1539. At the same
time Mantua had three *memunim*, as did Venice, and this
became the usual number of the members of the directorate.[4]
The Italian titles of the directors were *fattori, capi, gastaldi,
deputati,* and, mainly, *massari.*

About the middle of the sixteenth century an increase in
population and a broader scope of religious and communal
activities by the community created the need in North Italy
also to elect a council of limited size to represent the General
Council, see that its decisions in important matters were
carried out, and supervise the work of the directors. At first
such a council was, undoubtedly, temporary and was only
convened periodically for some specific purpose. Presumably
its size and composition were as yet undetermined. This is

[1] See Colorni, *op. cit.,* p. 27.
[2] See *Finkelstein,* p. 284.
[3] *Responsa of Rabbi Judah Minz and Maharam of Padua.*
[4] See Morpurgo, *op. cit.,* p. 13; Isaiah Sonne, *Kobez al jad,* N. S.
3:152, 159; Colorni, *op. cit.,* p. 27. Since the officers of the community
administration were called in Hebrew *memunim*, the community
board was called *minuy.*

clear from the decisions of the Mantuan General Council stating that in the event that the General Council cannot be convened, the directors were authorized to consult with ten worthy family heads and their decision would be as binding as that of the General Council.[1] Soon everybody became aware of the effectiveness of a council of limited size and such councils sprang up in the communities of North Italy. However, the communities were still groping, and the number and authority of the members on the council of limited size, generally called Great Council, *waad gadol*, kept changing perpetually. Ultimately, the *waad gadol* became the major legislative body in the community, and by the end of the Period was solidly entrenched. On the other hand, the General Council gradually lost its influence on all important matters, including taxation and budget.[2]

During the period of the development of the Great Council, the executive body also experienced broader development. A directorate of three no longer sufficed. Seven, nine or ten members replaced it, and, known in many places as the Small (Executive) Council, *waad katan*, it quickly occupied a powerful place in community life. The original three directors were generally incorporated within the frame of the Small Council and functioned like a modern day secretariat of an executive committee. Venice was an exception: it never elected a Great Council. The community was administered by a *waad katan*, and theoretically upheld the prerogatives of the General Council, called in Venice *ḳahal gadol*, Great Congregation.[3]

The method of electing community officers varied from place to place. Generally, the right to vote hinged upon a specific tax payment. In Venice the franchise was extended to those who paid the community a minimum of twelve ducats a year. In Padua only those who paid a higher rate of taxes could be elected to the position of *parnas*. Other community posts were open also to those who paid taxes at a lower rate.[4]

[1] Colorni, *op. cit.*, p. 28.
[2] *Ibid.*, p. 29.
[3] Roth, *Venice*, p. 127 ff.
[4] *Ibid.*, p. 128. Cf. Morpurgo, *op. cit.*, p. 15.

Elections were either by lot or by casting balls into voting boxes, which was also the most popular form of voting within the various communal administrative bodies. Some communities also elected alternates for the directors or the members of the Executive Council, who were called *niknasim*, "entrants", that is those who enter to conduct community affairs in place of absent colleagues. The tenure of office of directors and of members of the various councils also varied greatly among the communities—from three months to two and a half years. In Venice, toward the end of the Period, when the Executive Council consisted of twenty members, the president would rotate every week.[1]

Various communities attempted to establish rules regarding the validity of the decisions of their councils. Generally, the majority of those present ruled. There were, however, communities which required a larger majority. For example, at the end of the Period the decisions of the Mantuan General Council were not valid unless passed at a meeting with a minimum of thirty two members in attendance. The constitution of the Roman community called for a two thirds majority of those present. In Verona in 1589 the decisions of the executive council were mandatory only if two thirds of its membership participated in the meeting and were passed by two thirds of those present.[2] These rules undoubtedly resulted from the fact that community leaders were generally wealthy merchants and moneylenders who often were away on business trips. The strict rules thus aimed at giving decisions a basis of true majority within the framework of the aristocratic democracy that prevailed in the community.

Alongside the central administrative agencies, the Italian community had a number of committees with specialized tasks, such as a tax committee, an education committee, and a committee for charities, where the membership was most frequently limited to three. To these committees were appointed either members of the executive body or other members of the community. Members of such committees

[1] Jacob Soresina, *Seder haniḳur*, Venice 1595, Introduction.
[2] Colorni, *op. cit.*, p. 37; *RMI*, *Ibid.*; Sonne, *Ibid.*, p. 173.

were also designated as *parnasim* or *memunim* with an
appropriate addendum: *parnas* of the education fund, *parnas*
of food (for the poor), etc. To distinguish between these and the
memunim of the community, the words *ḳahal* or *ḳehillah
ḳedoshah* were added to the latter's title—*memunim* of the
community, *parnasim* of the sacred community. In the
decisions of the Forli congress the community directors were
also called *memunim peratiyim*, local directors as opposed to
the *memunim kelaliyim*, general directors, a title used by
leaders of the all-Italian or regional organization of Jewish
communities.[1]

An entirely different type of community administration was
instituted in Florence in 1571.[2] In that year Jews were
expelled from all the small towns in the Duchy of Florence
and herded into the ghetto that was established in the capital
city. The rules by which the ghetto was to be administered
were imposed by the duke and had a definite autocratic
character. The entire government of the ghetto community
was placed in the hands of two people called *soprastanti*,
overseers. They alone decided upon everything, except in
dealing with tax levies, when they had to consult with three
others, elders or men of community status. Apparently the
Jewish community was not satisfied with this form of administration and, as early as 1572 the government decided that ten
men should be chosen by the community, from whose midst
they should elect the two overseers and other officers. They
were also instructed to select an officer called *sindaco* whose
duty was to inform the government of transgressions of the
ghetto inhabitants. Obviously, this office offended the Jewish
population. Small wonder then that a harsh ordinance was
issued against ridiculing the overseers and the informer. At
the end of the Period the election of the ten men was abolished
and the community was administered by a few government
appointees. Thus, a handful of men controlled the community

---

[1] Sonne, *Ibid.*, pp. 153-156; Roth, *Venice*, p. 129; *Ḳuntres elleh
hadebarim*, list of eminent community figures; *Finkelstein*, p. 282 ff.

[2] *Capitoli . . . Firenze*, published in *Rivista Israelitica*, 9-10, also
available in an offprint.

administration, and the once proud community of Florence lost its autonomy despite its official title of *Republica delli Hebrei*.

Not fully known is the story of the Jewish Renaissance community in the cities of the Kingdom of Naples.[1] It seems that during the reign of the Aragon dynasty community institutions arose that were generally similar to those in the North, since a large part of these communities came into being in similar fashion, through the spread of the loan business. Among the community leaders we find officers bearing the title *proti*. These were wealthy and prominent men who paralleled the directors of the northern communities in number and function. In Hebrew documents they too are called *memune hakahal*.[2] With them appear *consiglieri*, members of an advisory council, and *thesaurieri*—treasurers. Officers elected for limited functions were called *eletti per...*, i.e. elected for specific tasks.

A different organizational pattern prevailed in Sicily.[3] A general assembly of all Jews would annually elect a forty man board of electors, that in turn elected twelve *proti*. These twelve were divided into four groups of three with each group administering community affairs on a three month rotation. There was no legislative or advisory council. The elections of the board of electors took place annually in all the island communities in the month of May and its orderliness impressed Rabbi Obadiah da Bertinoro who stayed in Sicily for a while on his way to the Holy Land.[4]

While community authority was concentrated in the hands of a few people, it did, nevertheless, have a definite democratic base through the annual elections of boards of electors. To be sure, the *proti* sometimes tried to eliminate the board of electors. Such was the case in Palermo where an attempt was

---

[1] Most of this material is based on *Ferorelli*, p. 105 ff.

[2] Marx, *HUCA* 1:617.

[3] In this connection see *Giovanni de Giovanni*, p. 116 ff. Cf. S. F. Lionti, *Documenti relativi agli ebrei di Sicilia*, 1885, pp. 328-371. Cf. also his *Protesto di un ebreo della Giudecca di Palermo*, Palermo 1889.

[4] *Iggerot Erez Yisrael*, p. 105.

made by the *proti* to bypass the electors and appoint their own candidates for the successive year. The members of the community took legal action against this attempt and succeeded in forcing the *proti* to revert to the legal method of election.[1]

However, what the Palermo *proti* failed to achieve, was attained on a regional scale when the government started to appoint the *dienchelele* (*dayyan kelali*, general judge) for the Jews of Sicily (see below). The elections of *proti* by a special board of electors were eliminated and *proti* were henceforth appointed by the general judge. Even when the office of general judge was abolished, the communities were not able to return to the constitutional method. Instead, the outgoing *proti* appointed the new ones. Thus, government intervention destroyed the semi-democratic foundations upon which the Sicilian community was built.

b.

The financial means at the disposal of the community and its budget were quite modest. Most of the funds that passed through the community treasury came from government imposed taxes, for which the communities were merely agents. The character and sums of these taxes varied according to place and time. They are virtually impossible to enumerate and, moreover, belong more properly to the area of external political relationships of the community.

Very little money remained under community control to finance its work. General community weakness was apparent in the budget. To be sure, the Italian communities never felt a need for a ramified community budget. Prior to the establishment of ghettos, a large part of the life of the Jews was spent within the framework of the gentile community. Moreover, many of the inner Jewish needs were filled on a voluntary basis.

It seems that the direct tax upon community members amounted approximately to the sum that the communities paid to the various governments. A large and important community like Verona did not pay the rabbi's modest salary

[1] S. F. Lionti, *op. cit.*

(in 1539) from its regular budget and raised the required amount through private generosity. When support was needed for the *yeshibah*, the rabbi and a few interested individuals solicited the needed funds. Even when the Reggio community had to purchase a new cemetery in the first half of the sixteenth century after it had already become a prominent community, it could not manage the purchase from regular community funds, but had to levy a special tax on community members and Jews living in outlying villages.[1]

The chief source of community revenue apparently came from all kinds of fines imposed for breach of community discipline. At the congress of communities which met in Forli in 1418, fines were set for transgression of its anti-luxury ordinances, payable to the "treasury of each community".[2] In virtually every locale fines were levied on those who refused to accept a community appointment or failed to participate in meetings of the community or its institutions. The energetic collection of fines by taking collateral which was sold in the event of non payment, attest to their importance as both a means of preserving community discipline and a source of income.[3]

The importance attached to the income from fines was negligible however, compared with the serious concern for collecting the heavy sums of the direct tax levied upon communities by the governments. Here we find all kinds of attempts by powerful individuals to rid themselves of this burden at the expense of others in the community. We know of one Sicilian family that was exempted by the king from its community tax obligations in 1237, and in 1325 this privilege was again renewed. In the early sixteenth century a powerful figure in Ferrara, regarded as the second richest Jew in Italy, eluded tax payments.[4] The fact that Italy was divided into a host of small states made it easy to evade paying taxes since

---

[1] Sonne, *op. cit.*, pp. 153, 157; *Kirjath sepher* 14:545; Cf. Baron, *op. cit.*, p. 246 ff. for general information on tax matters with some references to Italian communities.

[2] See *Finkelstein*, p. 285 for the text of the decision.

[3] Sonne, *Ibid.*, p. 167; *Vogelstein-Rieger*, vol. I, p. 343.

[4] *Sefer hapesakim*, Venice 1519, p. 30 b; *Lagumina*, vol. I, p. 26, 40.

many people who moved from one place to another came under the dominion of another gouvernment and were no more under the control of their former community. Public reaction against tax evaders was bitter, and Rabbi Joseph Colon even tried to prove that it was permissible to resort to governmental power against recalcitrants.[1] Another great rabbi, Azriel Diena recommended the use of the practice common in the Jewish communities in Germany of first collecting the tax and afterwards considering the pleas of those who claimed not to owe it.[2] Only towards rabbis did the public assent to tax exemption, even if they were wealthy or active in business. When a contract was drawn with a rabbi in Verona in 1592 it was regarded proper to emphasize that he would not be exempt from taxes.[3] Obviously, it was customary for rabbis not to pay taxes.

The community tax was collected exclusively from property owners. Being simple and direct, this tax system spread quickly among the communities.[4] This was the pattern, for example, in such major communities as Rome and Mantua. Information coming from the early seventeenth century may well be indicative of what was Renaissance period practice. For example, in Mantua in 1624 every man who possessed at least two hundred scudi (its purchasing power was the equivalent of approximately two thousand dollars) had to declare his worth to a board of assessment. The board had the right to exempt from taxes anyone who possessed less than four hundred scudi. In some communities, the board had the right to have the declarer verify his declaration by an oath. If he refused, the board had the right to make its own tax evaluation. In some places those who declared falsely were excommunicated. In Mantua, dealers in precious stones were

[1] Ibid.; Responsa of Rabbi Joseph Colon, par. 17, 127.
[2] See the document published by Sonne, Hatekufah, p. 661. Cf. Introduction to Responsa of Maharam, Berlin, 1891, p. 207.
[3] Sonne, Ibid., p. 178.
[4] What follows on property tax and its collection is based on various sources relating to community affairs in Rome, Florence, Verona, and Mantua referred to in the preceding Notes of this chapter. For important additional information relating to Mantua see Marx, ZfhB, 1911, p. 139 ff.

especially warned to make honest declarations, probably because it was easy to hide their wares or because of the difficulty in assessment. At a later time, and perhaps already during the Renaissance period, the tax rate was one and one half percent of one's capital.

Boards of assessment were organized along different lines in the various cities. However, there was a common denominator: In no community was the matter placed entirely in the hands of the directors, and often the directors had no influence whatsoever on tax assessments. In Rome, following the adoption of the 1524 constitution, the Assembly selected once every three years from its midst a four man assessment board whose members were called *tasatori*. Such was the procedure in Naples as well. On the other hand, beginning with 1571 in Florence the two directors joined by three "elders" served as a board of assessment. When it was decided to elect the ten member community executive board, it also acted as a board of assessment.

The collection of taxes was handled either by a special committee (Naples) or a specially elected official (Mantua) who was called *esattore* or *colettore*. The tax collector generally turned over community funds to a treasurer, known in Italian as *camerlengo* (Rome, Florence). The entire matter of tax collection and account keeping was, apparently, well organized. In Mantua assessments periodically appeared in writing, and in a later period, an assessment roll was prepared regularly every three years. Many such rolls were printed.

Little is known of the expenditure budgets of the communities. The only thing that may be said with certainty is that as we approach the end of the Period when the community assumed greater importance, the expense budget expanded and incorporated broader areas of the religious, social, and cultural life.[1] Understandably, the primary expense went for

---

[1] The two complete community budgets known to the author were published by Sonne, *Ibid.*, p. 165 (of the year 1550) and p. 181 (of the year 1603). The 1550 budget is less than 50 Ducats, aside from the minor expense of a *lulab* and *etrog*. The 1603 budget, on the other hand, amounts to 274 Ducats, aside from the salaries of the preachers Rabbi Gershon, Rabbi Joḥanan, and Rabbi Abraham Porto. Both

salaries of various functionaries, who will be discussed in the next chapter. A large share was allocated for the maintenance of a security force and for political action. Even with these expenses, however, the budget for expenditures was not very large. The many voluntary societies, active in most communities, in keeping with Renaissance custom (see below) usurped various important areas of communal responsibility and thus relieved the *kehillah* of a large portion of its financial burden.

CHAPTER FIVE

INSTITUTIONS AND COMMUNITY OFFICIALS

In the period prior to the enclosure of the Jews of various cities in ghettos, before the community assumed municipal duties, the *ḳehillah* limited its activities to the care for Jewish religious needs and compensation of community officials.

The primary community institution was the synagogue. The number of synagogues was very large. In major communities like Rome, Mantua or Ferrara there were about ten; in other places there were, generally, two or three.[1] The multiplicity of groups with different ritual patterns was the primary reason for this condition. Individualistic tendencies and the Renaissance effort to excel in good works also resulted in the foundation of many synagogues by individuals.[2] It was the multiplicity of synagogues that provoked the popes to limit their number and to allow no more than one synagogue in each

budgets contain a paragraph with a hidden expense "money paid to the priests" (in the 1603 budget it reads to "preachers", that is, the *predicatori* friars). The fact that no sum is recorded in either budget leaves the impression that this refers to a bribe to the priests to silence their anti-Semitic propaganda. This sum should therefore be considered an expense to secure peace for the community.

  [1] See *Meor Enayim*, p. 20; *Hayeḳeb*, St. Petersburg, 1894, p. 12; *RMI* 10:326; Berliner, *Rom*, vol. 2, Part 1, p. 96. In circa 1569 there were at least 115 synagogues in the Papal States (the document is available in Stern, Part 1, p. 144 ff), which certainly refers to non-urban communities.

  [2] See Moses A. Shulvass, *In the Grip of Centuries* (Heb.), New York, Tel Aviv, and Jerusalem, 1960, p. 326; *REJ* 79:43; Vogelstein-Rieger, vol. 1, p. 341.

city.[1] There were fewer synagogues, it seems, in Southern Italy and Sicily because of the poverty of these communities in comparison to the northern communities, and as a result of the ban on building new synagogues in effect in the Kingdom of Naples until the Aragon dynasty ascended the throne (1435).[2]

Various names were applied to the Italian house of worship. In northern communities it was identified by the customary name *bet keneset, sinagoga* in Italian. In Rome, the house of worship was known as *keneset*. In the Kingdom of Naples too, it was referred to as *sinagoga* in Italian. Often, however, it was called *moschetta*, mosque, a remnant of the period of Arab domination in parts of the South.

The interior of the synagogue was as far as we know, attractive, with ornaments enhancing its appearance. A Jew of Capri solicited the government to permit murals in the synagogue, justifying his request by indicating that all synagogues had many fine murals.[3] A wealthy Paduan attempted to build a synagogue for himself with gold leaf covered walls, and when the government refused to permit it, he made an ark cover that was valued at five hundred ducats,[4] an enormous sum in those days. In the Ascoli synagogue two life size statues of lions stood beside the stairs that led to the holy ark, and when the Jews were expelled in 1569, they brought the statues to Pesaro,[5] surely because of their artistic quality. An exquisite holy ark of Modena, made in 1472, is now kept in the Musée Cluny in Paris.[6] Its form is reminiscent of the door that Donatello made for the San Lorenzo church in

[1] The anti-Jewish law of Pope Paul IV contains this ban in the first paragraph (see *Tarbiz* 2:345. A similar ban of 1415, enacted by the anti-pope Benedict III is cited by Baron, *Ibid.*, vol. 1. p. 200.

[2] Ferorelli, p. 100.

[3] Balletti, p. 86. While this petition was submitted in 1620, there is no question that in the preceding period decorations in the synagogue were even more numerous.

[4] *REJ* 79:43.

[5] *JQR* 9:254 ff. Cf. David Kaufmann, *Gesammelte Schriften*, vol. 1, Francfort/Main, 1908, p. 89.

[6] A picture of this holy ark is reproduced in E. R. Bevan and Ch. Singer, *The Legacy of Israel*, Oxford, 1927, facing p. 377.

Florence. The sacred objects were often works of art and sometimes made by gentile craftsmen. One of the Roman synagogues still has a pitcher and a chain, which, according to tradition, were made by Benvenuto Cellini.[1]

The cemetery was another community institution found in virtually every city. Oddly enough, there were places where the cemetery belonged to individual families. Even in so large and important a community as Modena "the administration of the cemetery" still belonged to an individual family in the first half of the seventeenth century.[2] This is understandable when we consider that many communities were founded by families of pawnbrokers. However, private control of cemeteries steadily diminished,[3] while private ownership of synagogues continued.

It is difficult to describe the appearance of Italian Jewish Renaissance cemeteries, since very little written material or pictures of monuments are available. However, the extant material shows a decisive decorative trend. A historian of the Jews of Venice noted that the lanscaped Jewish graveyard in that city looked much like the Christian cemetery[4]. There was, evidently, a strong trend to set up monuments upon graves. Leon da Modena, whose words and acts are representative of Jewish Renaissance attitudes, expressed a desire that there be set for him "a monument that will last as long as possible".[5] It was also customary to engrave the coats of arms of prominent families upon monuments.[6]

There were virtually no community institutions other than the synagogues and cemeteries, except for scattered mention of such institutions as, *mahaneh*,[7] that is, a lodging house for transients. Most of the charitable institutions generally found in Jewish communities were maintained by voluntary societies,

---

[1] *RMI* 2:111. Cf. *Menorah Journal*, 1946, spring issue, p. 76.

[2] *Sepher Chaje Jehuda*, p. 10.

[3] Moses A. Shulvass, *Ibid.*, pp. 23 ff.

[4] L. A. Schiavi, *Gli ebrei in Venezia*, 1893, p. 497 ff.

[5] *Sepher Chaje Jehuda*, p. 70.

[6] F. Luzzatto, *La comunita ebraica di Rovigo*, Citta di Castello, 1932, p. 7, end of Note 3.

[7] As in Verona. Cf. Sonne, *Ibid.*, p. 166.

which will be discussed in the following chapter. The concern for general education, which was under community auspices, will be discussed in the chapter dealing with education (Section IV, Chapter 2).

The circle of communal functionaries, including rabbis, sextons, ritual slaughterers, cantors, and a community scribe, was more diverse than community institutions. The community sometimes retained a physician to administer to its constituency, and sometimes one person would perform a number of functions. The usual combination was the office of rabbi and scribe; sometimes the office of rabbi and physician was held by one man.[1] The rabbi as a spiritual leader will be discussed in the chapter dealing with the religious life. Here, the position of the rabbi as a community official will be discussed insofar as he actually served the entire community. The "private rabbi" was a frequent phenomenon in the rabbinate. He was a learned man who was supported by a patron, in the manner Christian humanists were supported by the nobility. The main duties of the private rabbi were to study Jewish lore with the patron and his sons and to copy for him manuscripts. Often he also served his patron as a legal adviser, especially when the latter wished to dispute rulings of official rabbis.[2] While there were men of stature among these private rabbis and they did constitute an integral part of the rabbinate, the official rabbinate far surpassed them in both communal prestige and authority. The famous Roman rabbi Bonet de Lattes designated himself as "an ordained rabbi accepted by the community" and added that "he is authorized by the papal court...to decree and order".[3] Conversely, when Messer Leon tried to extend his rabbinic authority over all of Italian Jewry and many important rabbis opposed him, they argued that "neither the rulers of the nations nor Jewish communities...appointed him as prince and judge..."[4] Ultimately, full recognition was accorded to the official rabbis

[1] Marx, *HUCA* 1:617; Sonne, *Ibid.*, p. 145 ff.; *Graetz-Rabinowitz*, vol. 7, p. 420.

[2] See below Section III, Chapter 4 and Section VIII, Chapter 3.

[3] Berliner, *Rome, Ibid.*, p. 122.

[4] Moses A. Shulvass, *Ibid.*, p. 59.

on a national scale through the decision of the congress of communities held in Ferrara in 1554, that where there was "an official rabbi appointed by the community" his authority extended also over the "private" rabbis who resided in his city.[1]

It seems, however, that the position of the rabbi was relatively unimportant at first. Documents of the Verona community clearly indicate that at the beginning of the sixteenth century the rabbi served only as head of the *yeshibah* or as a teacher, and only later in the Period did he gradually assume the additional duties of preacher and judge. The rabbi's position as an inconsequential community official was also reflected in the budget. As mentioned above, Verona paid its rabbi's salary from contributions, not from community funds. Only later, when the rabbi achieved importance, did they pay his salary from the regular community budget. And if such was his status in Ashkenazic Verona, his position in the Sephardic communities with their tradition of domination by the lay leadership, was certainly no stronger.[2]

Whenever rabbis served as official community functionaries they were engaged by contract for a limited time. If a rabbi was to serve through his lifetime, this too was sealed by contract. The rabbi was generally designated by the usual titles: rabbi, head of the court, our teacher, but sometimes also as chief or servant of the community.[3] Rabbis' salaries varied and were generally not less than fifty ducats per annum and no more than one hundred ducats, which was considerably

---

[1] *Finkelstein*, p. 302.

[2] Compare the recurrent efforts in Venice at the end of the Period to strip the rabbis' power, *Tarbiz* 13:145 ff. and Sonne, *Ibid.* 5:207 ff. An interesting allusion to rabbinic dependence upon community lay leaders is found in the ordinances of the Ferrara Congress of communities that no book can be published unless it contains an endorsement by three rabbis *and* the heads of the community next to the place of publication (*Finkelstein*, p. 301). Even the endorsement of books, a matter of rabbinic scholarship, was not left entirely to them.

[3] These terms are so frequent in the literature that references are unnecessary. The rabbis in Rome (Berliner, *Rom*, p. 122), Pesaro (*Finkelstein*, p. 314), and the Levantine congregation in Venice (Kaufmann, *Gesammelte Schriften*, vol. 3, p. 91), were called "servants".

lower than the salaries paid to Christian humanists by their employers.[1] The disparity is understandable considering the fact that Christian humanists were mostly engaged by kings and dukes.[2]

A second senior official who sometimes even surpassed the rabbi in importance was the community scribe. His regular duties included recording the minutes of the meetings of the community executive bodies in the minute book, to conduct the official correspondence, and carry out various occasional functions. This is why communities made certain that they had their own scribe, and from the beginning of the sixteenth century there is authoritative testimony that "each community engages a regularly employed scribe to write its letters, notes, and documents"...[3] Considering the importance of the position, communities strove to find a scribe with literary talents, capable of composing elegant letters in rhetorical style, in accord with the tastes of the Period. The Roman community, for example, engaged the famous poet Immanuel to compose its important letters.[4] Understandably, a community-scribe of this caliber received adequate compensation, and the early sixteenth century source mentioned above tells that "the scribe's salary corresponded to his rhetorical proficiency".

The official language of community records and of many of the official documents was mostly Hebrew. However, in the second half of the sixteenth century the Italian language began to appear alongside the Hebrew and, sometimes, to replace it. This process of displacing Hebrew lasted several centuries, achieving its climax in the nineteenth century. The Hebrew style of the community records varied with the authors, but employed a common terminology.[5] In the Ashkenazic North, community records contained many

---

[1] See Burckhardt, vol. I, p. 377 ff.

[2] Rabbi Jacob Provenzal who lived in Naples at the end of the fifteenth century treated the causes and results of this fact with great clarity. Cf. *Dibre Ḥakamim*, edited by Eliezer Ashkenazi, Metz, 1849, p. 73.

[3] *HUCA, Ibid.*, p. 620.

[4] *Maḥberot Immanuel*, p. 658 ff.

[5] e.g. *nishear*, it so remained = it was resolved; *niknas*, entrant = substitute.

Yiddish words, while Italian words proliferated in the documents of the Italiani. The Sephardim mostly used Spanish as the official language of the community. It should be noted that rabbinic bodies and charitable societies also used expert scribes. Leon da Modena was such a scribe.[1]

Other community officials that appear regularly in the sources are the cantor, ritual slaughterer, and sexton. The cantor, sometimes called *deputato* in Italian (a translation of *sheliah zibbur*), received a fixed but rather modest salary from community funds.[2] The sexton's salary was even less, about half of what the cantor received. In Rome the sexton was referred to as *sheliah hakahal* in Hebrew, in Monferrato as *sagrestano* in Italian, and in Sicily as *manigliore* in Italian. The ritual slaughterer had several Italian designations such as *sciattatore*, *scammatore*, and *sagatino*.

CHAPTER SIX

VOLUNTARY SOCIETIES

Earlier chapters referred to the fact that a significant share of communal activity was conducted by private societies motivated by a desire to do good works. Most communities were sparsely populated and voluntary efforts sufficed in lieu of imposed community management. These groups were primarily interested in helping the needy. The relatively large number of welfare societies compared to educational groups attest to this fact. Some places did not have any community group to support Torah study (such as Verona),[3] but in virtually no place did burial of the dead or visitation of the sick become a direct community concern.

The desire of the people to organize societies for the purpose of doing charitable work led to decentralization and duplication

[1] *Sepher Chaje Jehuda*, p. 64 and *Leo Modenas Briefe*, passim.

[2] Sonne, *Ibid.*, vol. 3, p. 165; Berliner *Rom*, p. 100. It is noteworthy that in both Rom and Verona the cantors received identical salaries: nine ducats annually.

[3] Sonne, *Ibid.*, pp. 157, 182. Here the community appointed special officials responsible for the collection of funds for Torah study.

of activities in virtually every community. In Rome, for example, a special society for laving the dead existed side by side with the regular burial society, *Gemilut ḥasadim*.[1] In a later period we know of at least five burial societies.[2] The proliferation of burial societies derived partially from the desire to lend order and dignity to the hour of death and burial. Aaron Berechiah da Modena's book *Maabar Yabok*, a widely accepted guide for last rites, was composed in response to this demand.

Another factor in organizational multiplicity, as in many areas of life, was group variety. In Venice, for example, each group had a separate burial society,[3] and also *Shomerim laboḳer* societies were periodically organized along the same lines. The societal multiplicity and the extreme fragmentization of charitable activities were liable to damage the general framework of community needs. It, therefore, comes as no surpise to see an effort in Padua in 1580 to consolidate charitable activities by uniting the society for the education of the poor with the burial society into one organization under the name of *Talmud Torah ugemilut ḥasadim*. Its scope included aid to education, visiting the sick, and burying the dead. Moreover, a ban was issued against the formation of new societies, explicitly to protect the interests of the centralized organization. Apparently the experiment succeeded, and in 1597 the community decided to transmit to the united society all contributions that were pledged in the synagogue in behalf of the indigent sick.[4]

In addition to the two primary societies of *Gemilut ḥasadim* [5] and *Talmud Torah*, other organizations of more limited scope functioned, such as that for aiding indigent brides, clothing orphans and needy students, providing the poor with prayerbooks, prayer shawls and phylacteries. While most sources

[1] This was the name of the burial societies in Italy.
[2] See A. Milano-R. Bachi, *Storia e riordinamento del archivio*, Rome 1929, p. 21 ff.
[3] Roth, *Venice*, p. 52.
[4] Morpurgo, *Ibid.*, p. 16 and p. 18, especially p. 18 Note 2.
[5] See Sonne, *Zion, Ibid.*, p. 140, that the *Gemilut ḥasadim* society was the oldest philanthropic organization in Italian communities.

dealing with this subject are from a later time, some data indicate that a sizable share of these societies were organized before the close of the Period.

The societies' income apparently came mainly from contributions and, perhaps, from membership dues as well. Sometimes a considerable sum was accumulated, which enabled them to broaden their charitable deeds even beyond their main concern. In Rome, for example, the *Gemilut ḥasadim* society supplied free medical care for the poor. We know of one society, in a later period to be sure, whose expenses for collateral charitable purposes far surpassed the expenses of its primary function.[1] It is noteworthy that there were also communities (e.g. Rome) in which contributions in behalf of the Holy Land were collected by societies specifically organized for this purpose. However, this was exceptional, and most communities merely placed charity boxes in the synagogues for the poor in Palestine.[2]

In addition to these philanthropic societies whose chief concern was fund raising for the needy, there were other organizations of an entirely different category. There were groups organized for the study of Torah, more rigorous fulfillment of the ritual, or similar religio-pietistic purposes. These societies will be discussed in forthcoming chapters dealing with Torah study and religious life. However, these groups were so widespread throughout Italy that they must be included in a general review of societal activity paralleling the functions of the communal authorities.

[1] This information is scattered throughout the sources making it difficult to specify references. See the author's Introduction to the minute book of the society *Ḥesed weemet* in Reggio, *In the Grip of Centuries*, pp. 107-110. Even though this society was founded in the eighteenth century, it obviously was modeled after earlier societies of this type. Cf.: *Vogelstein-Rieger*, vol. 2, p. 316.

[2] For fuller treatment of this subject see the author's *Rome and Jerusalem* (Hebrew), a history of the relationship of Italian Jews to the Holy Land, Jerusalem 1944, passim.

CHAPTER SEVEN

GENERAL AND REGIONAL COMMUNITY ORGANIZATION

a.

Despite the fact that during virtually the entire Renaissance period the Italian community never attained the stability of the Central and Eastern European *ḳehillah*, and despite the fragmentization of the Italian peninsula into a large number of states, serious efforts to create unified general and regional communal organizations were undertaken during the entire epoch. The establishment of regional community organizations was due to the influence of two unconnected factors: the governments' desire to centralize the collection of taxes from its Jewish subjects, and inner pressure by responsible community circles that tried to counteract the weakness of the local community administration. These factors undoubtedly operated even prior to our period and continued through and beyond the entire Renaissance. As a result, a series of firm regional community organizations developed, with a more or less well defined scope of activity.

Conversely, the basis of the general community organization was rooted essentially in several phenomena that were specifically related to the Renaissance period, and, therefore disintegrated toward the end of the Period. The most important element in the establishment of the *waad kelali*, as the general community organization was called, was the fact that the Pope resided in Rome. During the entire period of almost two hundred years, from the Popes' return to Rome from Avignon until the Counter-Reformation and the Council of Trent, there was no consistent papal policy toward the Jews, but the general attidute was not hostile. It was usually possible through certain actions to obtain privileges from the Popes that would appreciably ameliorate the Jewish position in the entire Peninsula, prevent the spread of anti-Jewish legislation or annul unfriendly laws even after their promulga-

tion. The *waad kelali*[1] was thus created to choose the proper
men and to provide the sizable sums of money that were
needed for this purpose. On the other hand, a less friendly
papal attitude toward the Jews crystallized during the
Counter-Reformation, which could not be changed after the
principles on which it was based became solidified. This policy
was sometimes administered harshly and sometimes leniently,
depending upon the personal inclinations of the various Popes.
Since, however, the basic principles of this policy remained
firm as an inseparable part of a system to strengthen the
Church, there was no more a raison d'etre for the *Waad Kelali*.
No effort was able to alter the basis for the new anti-Jewish
policy of the Church. The only area left where a policy change
could be effected was acquiring permission to publish the
Talmud under censorship. Thus we find in the second half of
the sixteenth century a *waad kelali* whose sole concern focused
upon this question. This *waad kelali* existed until the end of the
Period.

Other matters too that periodically concerned the *waad
kelali* such as marriages of girls without parental consent and
similar problems that resulted from the excessive adherence
to the life patterns of the Renaissance, also disappeared in
the last decades of the Period when a religious revival swept
over Italian Jewry. Even the loan business, the main area of
economic endeavor of Italian Jews (excluding Sicilian Jews)
during a great part of the Renaissance, which was often on the
agenda of the *waad kelali*, lost much of its significance at the
end of the Period. A considerable portion of Jews now earned
a livelihood in other areas of endeavor and, moreover, within
the community, arguments emerged that the loan business was
immoral and anto-social. The political, economic, and spiritual
life of the Jews was gradually adjusted to the local patterns of
the small Italian principalities, especially with the onset of the
movement toward ghettoization and the concurrent growth of
the circles who favored a stronger *kehillah*. Under these

[1] This fact proves that the "general *waad*" in Italy was a unique
creation, produced by conditions of place and time and cannot be
compared to central community organizations in other countries.

circumstances there was only room for regional organizations and the *waad kelali* disappeared as soon as the factors that originally promoted its existence vanished.

This distinction in the factors that led to the creation of two types of central community organization is validated by the fact that heretofore no non-Jewish sources were uncovered that mention the *waad kelali*. It was an internal Jewish institution and had no "official" status. Conversely, regional organizations are quite frequently mentioned in official documents of various states. These were, indeed, community organizations, vital to both the Jews and the governments in whose lands they lived.

b.

It is impossible to determine the exact time of emergence of both the regional organizations and the *waad kelali*. However, it is certain that at the start of the Renaissance period the concept of the *waad*, a regional or general community organization, as a unifying communal institution was already accepted by Italian Jewry. We have concrete proof of the existence of such a regional organization in the Marche province,[1] which later became the most stable of all such bodies throughout the peninsula.

It seems that the origin of the *waad kelali* was rooted in the attempt by the Roman community to have other Italian communities share the expenses of obtaining papal privileges. The Roman Jews argued that such privileges benefited or lessened the burdens of all Italian Jews, and not Roman Jews exclusively. The Italian Jews seem to have accepted this argument and from circa 1300, the communities participated

[1] See Sonne, *Hatekufah*, p. 632 ff. In this important study Sonne has collected a large majority of the documentary material pertaining to the general and regional community organizations in Italy. These documents will be quoted here frequently. Where other sources not published by Sonne will be mentioned, references will be brought. The great importance of Sonne's study lies in the large amount of material that he brings from hitherto unpublished documents. The texts that deal with the all-Italian communal organization I will cite from *Finkelstein*.

in paying the "Roman tax".[1] The general participation in payment of this tax probably followed a decision taken by a congress of communities, or of rabbis and lay leaders. A circular of the Roman community of the middle of the fifteenth century, sent in connection with collection of the tax, claimed that great was "the wisdom of the sages (or: leaders) of old who introduced this tax".[2] Such a statement in the Hebrew style in use in fifteenth century Italy may imply a decision by an authoritative communal assembly. Although generally the communities felt a fundamental obligation to pay the tax, some defaulted and some tried to have the Roman community reduce the amount it demanded by threats of non-payment. The Roman community, on the other hand, also occasionally threatened "to exclude" recalcitrant communities who did not pay their share.[3] To be sure, it is difficult to determine what was meant by the exclusion of unwilling communities, whether it referred to expulsion from a general community organization that may have existed, or merely deprivation of the rights granted by the papal privileges. The system of collecting the tax was well organized and provided that the tax must be paid by the communities "through some of their brethren who dwelt among them", that is, assigned collectors in every locale. The fact that Immanuel of Rome wrote a letter dealing with this tax in behalf of the Ancona community ("and we the people of

[1] There is no doubt that the letter written by Immanuel of Rome (end of *Maḥberet* 24, p. 690) in behalf of the Ancona community to the Roman community deals with the levy that was later called Roman tax. It is doubtful that the letter in *Maḥberot Immanuel* is identical with the letter actually sent. Possibly the Roman community first sought this tax only from *Romaneschi* communities that were established by emigrants from Rome (Italiani) who opened pawnshops in various cities, since Immanuel says that the Roman community ordered the collection of taxes from "all their brethren scattered from their flock".

[2] The document is from 1450 approximately and was published from a manuscript by Sonne, *Hatekufah*, p. 640 ff.

[3] Immanuel, *Ibid.*, specifically attests to such a threat by the Roman community, and in the letter of response he hints that it would also be advantageous to the Roman community if "the entire land spoke one language and one speech" (comp. Genesis 11:1).

Ancona") clearly indicates that the Roman tax was collectable from communities, and not individuals. In the course of time the collection of this tax became so well organized that its collection procedure in the fifteenth century became a model for other tax collections by the general organization of communities.[1] It can thus clearly be ascertained that the Roman tax payment at the outset of the Renaissance period was associated with some sort of a general organization of communities in Italy, even though there is no proof that the organization of communities at that time undertook other projects than the assessment and collection of this tax. The "Roman tax" concept survived to the very end of the Period. When, in 1586, the last meeting of communities took place in connection with efforts to obtain permission for the printing of the Talmud, the question of expenses was discussed in terms of "what the general organization (of communities) needs (to spend) in Rome".[2]

The earliest information we have of a meeting of community representatives from all, or a great portion of Italy, is from the beginning of the fifteenth century. In 1416 a congress of community delegates met in Bologna, adopted a series of resolutions and elected a number of people, called *memunim kelaliyim*, general directors,[3] whose function was to supervise matters of the Italian Jewish community in the ensuing ten years. They also received permission to impose a tax on the communities when they considered it necessary.[4] Since the general directors were elected for a ten year term, participants in the Bologna meeting evidently planned to convene a congress of communities once every decade. Indeed, a certain

[1] See the decisions of the Bologna Congress in *Finkelstein*, p. 282.
[2] See the important document of 1587 published by Sonne, *Zion*, N. S. 17:152.
[3] To distinguish between them and directors of individual communities.
[4] Only one decision dealing with the election of the general directors is left of the decisions of this Congress, and is recorded among the decisions of the Congress that met two years later in Forli. See *Finkelstein* for the text. The Bologna Congress also adopted other resolutions, which is apparent from the minutes of the Forli Congress that state: "And this is the text of that resolution as far as is relevant now".

document attests that twelve years later, in 1428, another
meeting of communities was held in Florence.[1] The heading
of the document records that the Florence meeting was "the
third congress for community needs", which was surely due
to the fact that the meeting of general directors in Forli in
1418 was actually transformed into a plenary session of
communities and came to be regarded as the second congress
of communities. It can, therefore, be safely stated that the
Bologna gathering represented the first attempt at the
creation of an inter-communal congress of Italian Jews which
would convene regularly once every decade and discuss all
their political and communal problems.

After the Bologna congress the institution seemed to take
root. Two years later a meeting of the general directors took
place in Forli with the participation of additional community
representatives and dealt with a number of important matters
relating to the Jewish political position in Italy and the relations with the Christian population. They also discussed
internal religious issues and various social problems. The
document incorporating their decisions is the most complete
of all documents relating to the all-Italian organization of
communities and it indicates that at the time it seemed that
this congress would become an effective force. However, from
the minutes of the ensuing congress of communities which
took place in Florence in 1428, it appears that great difficulties
prevented the execution of the organization's decisions.
Apparently, the difficulties increased and, henceforth, we

---

[1] Published in *Finkelstein*, p. 296. The convocation of the Florence
Congress twelve years after the Bologna meeting, rather than ten
years, can be explained by the fact that in 1418 the general directors
met in a large assemblage at Forli, in which various additional community representatives participated. This is evident from the fact
that signatories to the decisions of the Forli Congress included representatives other than the general directors. As a result, the Forli
conference regarded itself as authorized "to validate and execute all
the decisions taken at Bologna". The document is available in *Finkelstein*, p. 282 ff. The second document relating to this Congress published by *Finkelstein*, p. 298 ff, indicates that the Florence gathering
adopted a number of decisions. See Cassuto, *Florence*, p. 29, note 4
and Sonne, *Hatekufah*, p. 637 that both documents belong to one conference despite the difference of one year in their dates.

have no further information of a congress of communities that dealt comprehensively with communal problems. Moreover, it is quite certain that by about 1450 the general organization of communities founded in Bologna about thirty years earlier no longer existed. The Roman community's effort to pressure Italian communities to pay their assessments for the "Roman tax" was directed to the leadership of the regional organizations.[1] Had there been a general organization of communities in accord with projected plans of the Bologna and Forli congresses, the collection of the "Roman tax" would have been its concern. In the middle of the sixteenth century the idea of a congress of communities was revived and such congresses met twice in Ferrara [2] and perhaps once also in Padua.[3]

In addition we do have information of conferences of communities that met under circumstances of extreme peril and, judging from the sources, dealt only with the emergency situation. Such meetings took place close to the middle of the fifteenth century in Tivoli and Ravenna when Pope Eugene IV (1431-1447) [4] issued a number of anti-Jewish decrees, and close to 1500 when Jews were threatened with expulsion from Florence.[5] We also know of a plan to call a special conference

[1] See the document quoted from a manuscript by Sonne, *Ibid.*, p. 640 ff.

[2] The sources on the two Ferrara Congresses are published in *Finkelstein*, p. 301 ff, and p. 307. It is clear that there were two meetings in Ferrara since the decision of 1555 found on p. 307 is missing in the council decisions of 1554. Nor is it identical with decision 7 of the 1554 Congress.

[3] See the document from a manuscript published by Sonne, *Ibid.*, p. 669 ff.

[4] See *Shalshelet Haḳabalah*, p. 170. A description of the events is found in *Vogelstein-Rieger*, vol. 2, p. 11 ff. It is difficult to understand why they write that these were rabbinical meetings, since the minutes do not mention any rabbis and state specifically that they called "a general congress of all Italian Jews".

[5] See *Catalogue Kaufmann*, p. 165, No. 494. Written on the back of this manuscript is: "Letters concerning the great convocation called from all districts of Italy to send delegates to Rome regarding the expulsion that they intended viciously for us, from which God in His manifold mercy saved us, see letters Nos. 886 to 906." The writer of the letters was Solomon of Poggibonsi (see *Ibid.*) and the expression "they intended viciously for us" refers to the Jews of Florence, who, during Solomon's time were in constant danger of

to deal with the problem of redeeming Jewish captives taken by Emperor Charles V when he attacked Tunis [1] in 1535, but we do not know if the meeting actually took place.

The last congresses of Italian communities met in 1564-1586, and they too dealt only with one specific goal, to get the consent of the Catholic Church for printing of the Talmud. The effort to save the Talmud is one of the most glorious chapters in the history of Italian Jewry, and the numerous congresses during the aforementioned period indicate how important this issue was.[2] After 1586 we have no further information of congresses of Italian communities, which surely suggests that such meetings no longer took place. The general organization of Italian Jews is virtually always referred to as the *waad kelali*, General Council, and once as *waad gadol*, Great Council.[3] It is worth noting that when the Napoleonic Sanhedrin was convoked in Paris, its leadership studied the decisions of the Ferrara congress of 1554 from a manuscript, in the belief that they might guide them in solving the problems they faced.[4]

The composition [5] of the congress of communities was

expulsion and, actually were driven from the city. For this, see Cassuto, *Florence*, p. 61 ff.

[1] See *Kirjath sepher* 4:548.

[2] See *Hamagiha*, pp. 157, 175; Colorni, *Magistrature maggiori*, p. 16; *Sepher Chaje Jehuda*, p. 12; M. Stern, *Stellung der Paepste*, Part 1, p. 153; *Alim* 2:49. Significantly, both *Hamagiha* and Leon da Modena described the congress of communities or organization of communities who delt with this matter as *haḳehillot meitalyah*, which leaves no doubt regarding the all-Italian character of this action. The documents in *Alim, Ibid.*, specifically mention the existence of a body of elected officers who received information from Rome on the state of the matter. It is difficult, however, to define the duties of these officials. There is no way of telling whether they were elected to deal specifically with the issue of printing the Talmud or whether their functioning indicates the recurrent convocation of congresses of communities that dealt with other matters as well. The former possibility is more probable, since we have no information of general directors after 1429.

[3] See the interesting material regarding the concept of the *waad* presented by Sonne, *Ibid.*, p. 628 ff. Regarding a "great *waad*" cf. *Catalogue Kaufmann*, p. 165, manuscript No. 494.

[4] See J. I. Carmi, *All' assemblea ed al sinedrio di Parigi*, Reggio 1905, p. 119.

[5] The following is based on the documentary material in *Finkel-*

never clearly crystallized, due no doubt to the fact that the all-Italian organization of communities did not become firmly established and could not develop a tradition of fixed representation. Judging from the extant documentray material, representatives of states, districts, and individual towns participated. Such a system of representation was inevitable since some Italian states had strong, well organized country-wide organizations of communities, while others had none. One thing seems certain—all delegates to the congresses represented communal bodies. They were generally called *murshim*, delegates. The delegates' authorization was, apparently, closely scrutinized, for we know that Rabbi Baruch Uzziel Forti, the scribe at the Ferrara congress of communities kept in his possession all the authorization letters of the delegates together with the official text of the decisions.[1] True, one source mentions that "all the great leaders" participated in one of the congresses, but it can be safely assumed that they attended as representatives of communal bodies and not as individuals. Even Meir of Padua, the greatest rabbi of the Period, who was the head and moving spirit of the Ferrara congress clearly signed the decisions as an "authorized delegate from the Republic of Venice". Only in the 1418 Forli congress do we find that the *memunim kelaliyim* who were elected at the Bologna congress enjoyed full delegates rights equal to community representatives. They were given this status because they convoked the assembly and transformed it from a meeting of the *memunim kelaliyim* to a congress of far broader scope. Moreover, those *memunim kelaliyim* who were unable to come to Forli had the right to delegate their authority to anyone they chose, and certain people who were in Forli at the time (by chance?) participated in the congress as personal representatives of *memunim kelaliyim*.

The number of delegates attending the congresses was not large. It was probably due to the delicate political character of the central problem constantly on the agenda, namely,

stein, pp. 282-308 and on the aforementioned study by Sonne. Wherever I based a conclusion upon another source I indicated it specifically.

[1] See *Kirjath sepher* 14:540.

the pope's relationship to Italian Jews, which necessitated a great deal of secrecy.[1] The Forli congress was the largest one with twenty two signatories on the decisions. Participants in the Bologna congress surely equaled this figure, since twelve *memunim kelaliyim* were elected. On the other hand, only fourteen people participated in the Ferrara congress in 1554. This meager representation at the congresses followed a pre-conceived plan. That such was the case can be clearly seen from the plan of a meeting of communities to redeem Tunisian captives that was prepared by the famed Rabbi Azriel Diena. He suggested that only five or six people attend the meeting as representatives of Jewish communities of various Italian states. He even suggested that Mantua and Ferrara, which were two separate principalities with large Jewish populations, send a common delegate in order to keep representation to a minimum.[2] And when we consider that some communities sent two, or even more, delegates to the Bologna and Ferrara congresses, it is apparent that these meetings were, indeed, limited exclusively to the leadership of the most important communities, or officers of regional organizations. Thus, the non-democratic, "private" character of all Jewish communal life was also reflected in these congresses.

In this aspect the congresses of communities in the first half of the fifteenth century and those of the second half of the sixteenth century were similar in character. However, from the aspect of composition there was a great difference. While the Ferrara congress of 1554, for example, had representation from all three Italian Jewish groups, Italianic, Ashkenazic and Sephardic, the Bologna and Forli congresses were, apparently, attended only by the Italiani. To be sure, the Sephardim were not as yet in Italy at the time. However, the North Italian Ashkenazic community, especially in the State of Venice, was strong and populous. Despite this, we find no Ashkenazic

---

[1] Slander was one of the sorest social plagues (see below, Section V). Even the effort to attain permission to reprint the Talmud was damaged by informers. See *Alim, Ibid.*, p. 52. The obscure and allusive style of the document relating to the Florence Congress of 1428 (in *Finkelstein*, p. 296) is noteworthy.

[2] See *Kirjath sepher*, 14:548.

representation at these congresses. The only participating community of the Republic of Venice was Padua, which, at the time, was still an Italianic community.[1] Moreover, several decisions of the Forli congress applied specifically to "the communities of the Romaneschi Jews", namely, the Italiani [2] as if to exclude the Ashkenazim. This further limited the narrow communal perimeter of the general organization of Italian Jewry. Not until the second half of the sixteenth century after both new subcommunities had become firmly established and jointly outnumbered the Italiani by far, could genuine all-Italian congresses of communities be called. However, by then the external conditions had changed and no objective possibility remained for such an institution to function and develop.

We do not know how deliberations were conducted at the congresses of communities. However, it is certain that meticulous care was taken to record the decisions. The Forli congress that met one and a half years after the Bologna congress quotes the exact language of one of its decisions. The congress scribe was in charge of recording the decisions. A good example is Rabbi Baruch Uzziel Forti, who served as scribe of the Ferrara congress and was the keeper of its minutes and other documents. Some of the Ferrara decisions were published in several editions in a later period. Resolutions were passed by majority vote, unanimous decisions were periodically emphasized and all participants of the congress signed them in order to add to their strength.

It is not possible to fully describe the officialdom that was elected by the congresses for the purpose of enforcing their decisions. Regarding the first congress in Bologna there is definite information of the election of twelve directors, known collectively as the General Directorate. The authority granted

---

[1] See Morpurgo, *Padua*, p. 4.

[2] Italianic Jews who spread throughout all of southern and central Italy during the first half of the Renaissance Period were sometimes called Romaneschi because they spoke the Roman Italian dialect (see Cassuto, *Miscellanea di studi ebraici in memoria di H. P. Chajes*, Florence 1930, p. 25). In the *Responsa of Rabbi Judah Minz*, Munkacs 1898, p. 7b, he too speaks of the Romaneschi usage, in reference to what we generally call the Roman *minhag*.

these directors was quite broad, especially in regard to levying taxes for community needs. They were elected explicitly to watch "new situations that might arise". They were to meet whenever they felt such a need, and, in the event of a director's inability to attend, a substitute could be sent, provided that the full Directorate approved. It is possible that the Ferrara congress (1554), too, elected a number of officials to supervise community affairs after its adjournment.[1] Baruch Uzziel Forti, the scribe, surely felt that his duties were not terminated when the congress adjourned. As guardian of the official document containing the congress' decisions, he had to determine whether the communities abided by these decisions. Another official elected to serve after the congress' adjournment was a treasurer who was responsible for funds that were made available to the general organization.

Virtually all money that was disbursed collectively by all Italian Jewry flowed into the Pope's treasury. While it is difficult to estimate these sums precisely, they were, undoubtedly, substantial. Many contemporary documents clearly allude to very large sums. A document of 1586 concerned with the effort to attain permission to print the Talmud [2] specifically mentions the sum of ten thousand scudi that must be raised, which, in our terms would be the equivalent of over one hundred thousand dollars. In addition to these unanticipated expenses, there was the regular tax paid by the Roman Community to the papal treasury, which was regarded even at the beginning of our Period as payment in behalf of all Italian Jewry. Despite this, there were times when it was

---

[1] A letter dealing with the issue of the printing of the Talmud, published in *Alim, Ibid.*, contains the clear statement that it was being sent to "the leaders of the hosts of Israel who serve as officers of the general *waad*". If, indeed, this letter is from 1554, as its editor believes, it would constitute strong evidence of the election of officials by the Congress. It is also possible that the reference here is not to the directors but to the Congress itself and that the letter was sent to the Congress during its deliberations. However, if this were the case, it would be difficult to understand why the Congress' decisions contain nothing about the necessary funds to achieve its goals, since the letter writer speaks specifically of the need of large sums.

[2] M. Stern, *Stellung der Paepste*, Part I, p. 154.

difficult to collect the tax, and the Roman community had to resort to all sorts of measures to secure participation in the payment of this tax.[1] It also enlisted the aid of various district leaders where regional community organizations existed. In the early fifteenth century there were permanent collectors of the Roman tax in many places. However, this did not suffice and the congresses of Bologna and Forli were compelled to exert maximal public pressure to force communities to pay their taxes.

The minutes of the Forli congress in 1418 contain quite clear details of the types of special taxation periodically levied by the communal congresses and the method of collection. The directors were authorized "to collect money in accordance with immediate need", which implies that they could collect even very large sums. Collecting the taxes was the duty of the directors, but keeping the money was the function of a treasurer. Apparently, the tax assessment was quite substantial at that time and was collectable in part from the communities and partly from individuals. It was a progressive tax assessed according to the wealth of community members or the capital they employed in their loan operations. Only charity receiving poor were exempted from taxation. Even rabbis who ordinarily enjoyed large tax reductions had to pay for this tax in full. The collection apparatus through which the directors collected the tax was composed of the permanent collectors of the Roman tax in every locale plus a few additional special collectors. The main burden, to be sure, was carried by the collectors of the Roman tax who had considerable experience in the collection of Jewish communal taxes.

We cannot, because of the very meager documentary material, fully comprehend the authority and function of the communal congresses. However, it seems certain that the organizers of the communal congresses both in their early

---

[1] See Berliner, *Rome*, vol. 2, Section 1, p. 70 ff. The famous poet Moses Rieti was the emissary. Cf. *Vogelstein-Rieger*, vol. 2, p. 11 ff. that the Tivoli congress negotiated with Francesco, duke of Mantua, about allowing Jews to settle in his territory. However, this is uncertain, since the source only states that "a few Jews tried (to negotiate with Francesco), but does not mention a *waad*.

period, in the beginning of the fifteenth century, and in their later period, the middle of the sixteenth century, envisaged a fully representative organization that would act on all public matters of Jewish interest and would try to regulate the inner life of Italian Jewry and its relationships with external forces that affected its destiny. The Forli congress, for example, regarded itself as the authority to select an official delegation representing all of Italian Jewry to obtain from the pope the rights that were vital to its existence.[1] Although the need to win privileges from the pope was probably the principal factor in convoking this assembly, many important decisions emerged from its deliberations, which would have certainly resulted in a complete regulation of Jewish life on the Peninsula if the congresses would have continued to meet. Moreover, the Forli congress was also concerned with a budget to carry out some of its plans that were unrelated to immediate needs. When the Forli congress levied a general tax upon Italian Jewry it explicitly announced that in addition to the necessary expenses for the papal court, the tax was also "for other expenses vital to improve the general position of the communities". It was also concerned with publicizing its decisions and demanded that communities do so. And indeed, only one week after the adjournment of the Forli congress, its decisions were publicly disseminated in Bologna at the behest of the local rabbis. We have a number of sources which indicate that the Forli congress was not the only one to adopt many resolutions. The main body of resolutions by this congress refers to all kinds of decisions adopted two years earlier by the Bologna congress. The Ferrara congress of 1554 also passed a series of decisions that dealt with various areas of Jewish life. Even in the case of the Florence congress of 1429, of which we know only one decision pertaining to money lending, we are told that this decision is only one "among other decrees they promulgated".

[1] *Shalshelet hakabbalah*, p. 170. It is interesting that the official document containing the decisions of the Forli congress does not mention the selection of this delegation or the names of the delegates. This indicates that the document does not reflect all of the activities of the congress.

The matters that most required strong communal intervention included the strengthening of local *kehillot* that were too weak to counteract the individualistic tendencies of the Renaissance Jew,[1] and the excessive absorption in Renaissance life patterns. The organization of local communities was the most important of all the problems, and the congresses devoted a large portion of concern to its solution. Both the Bologna and Forli congresses tried to solve it on a national scale and ordered that every city should have "an organized communal authority" empowered to decide on all local Jewish matters. We know that this effort failed and local community affairs remained completely disorganized until the end of the Period. It is, therefore, understandable why the Ferrara congress more than a century later tried to correct the situation in at least one area of communal life, the rabbinate. It called attention to the widespread practice of patronizing non-Jewish courts, tried to introduce consistency in rabbinic court procedure, and, above all, tried to strengthen the position of the official rabbis vis a vis unofficial and private rabbis of various magnates who disputed the authority of the official rabbinate.

The congresses were equally concerned about the excessive indulgence in feasts, lavish parties, and expensive clothing, and they tried to curb these extravagances. They also attempted, unsuccessfully to be sure, to limit card playing and dice gambling, which was one of the worst vices of Renaissance society. A serious, energetic effort was made to curb sexual licentiousness that was widespread during most of the Period.

On the other hand, it is rather surprising how limited was the concern with the loan business, which was one of the main areas of economic endeavor. The few decisions of the congresses on this subject appear inadequate in view of the abundance of cases recorded in the responsa literature. It is possible that the basically local character of the *condotta* and of the loan business in general made all-Italian regulation unnecessary. Conversely, a problem of special concern which became central

[1] See Moses A. Shulvass, *In the Grip of Centuries*, p. 23 ff. There the subject is treated at length.

at the last congresses was, as we have seen, the question of publication of Hebrew books. The decision of the Ferrara congress of 1554 that required rabbinic and communal endorsement of every new book prior to publication, belongs to this category. The struggle of Italian Jewry in behalf of the sacred books will be discussed in a later chapter.

So far public efforts to create a general organization of communities have been discussed. This description cannot be complete without mention of an attempt by Messer Leon, one of the greatest rabbis of the fifteenth century, to impose his spiritual authority over all Italian Jews. If this effort had succeeded, it would have created a different form of general Jewish organization, a chief rabbinate. Messer Leon made his attempt about 1455,[1] by promulgating a number of ordinances with a demand that every Italian community obey them under threat of excommunication. This attempt was apparently made at a time when no general organization of communities existed. About twelve years had passed since the earlier congresses met in Tivoli and Ravenna in 1443,[2] and the ensuing congress, regarding which we only know the date, did not meet until 1469.[3] The absence of a general organization, coupled with a pressing need for organized religious guidance, especially in view of the heightened Jewish immigration from Germany and France, may have induced Messer Leon to make his single handed attempt at achieving unity. There are also allusions in the sources indicating that Messer Leon assembled a congress of rabbis or community representatives in Ancona, where he resided, and based his attempt upon its decisions.[4]

It appears from the fragmentary, vague sources that Messer Leon's attempt was only partially successful and that in any event, there was no continuity to the chief rabbinate as an institution, even if we assume that Messer Leon attained limited recognition as a chief rabbi. He failed because of the

---

[1] For a description of these events see *Ibid.*, p. 56 ff.

[2] See *Shalshelet hakabbalah, Ibid.*, and *Vogelstein-Rieger*, vol. 2, p. 11.

[3] See the catalogue of the antiquarian bookseller Raphael Nathan Rabinowitz for 1885, manuscript No. 62, and Sonne, *Hatekufah*, p. 643, that this congress apparently met in Pisa.

[4] See *In the Grip of Centuries, Ibid.*

bitter opposition by a number of prominent Italian rabbis who recoiled from the very idea of rabbinic domination that would limit the authority of local rabbis. It is noteworthy that exactly a century later an effort to organize the rabbinate was again strongly opposed by the rabbis themselves. When the Ferrara congress adopted resolutions opposing unofficial rabbis, one of these rabbis, Moses Basola, a brilliant author and scholar, sharply attacked them. He bitterly assailed all the decrees of the congress [1] and termed them, in typical Renaissance style as "pitfalls created by the accursed congress", substituting takalot (pitfalls) for takanot (ordinances), and ḳelali (accursed) for ḳelali (general). His arguments against the main body of resolutions were pale, to be sure, compared to the raging plaints directed at the aforementioned decision regarding an organized rabbinate. In addition to the resistance of many rabbis, writers, and persons of influence, negligence and opposition by local community leaders undermined all efforts at unity. At the Florence congress of 1428, where the tradition of the important conferences that were held in Bologna and Forli twelve and ten years earlier was still alive, the complaint was heard of the difficulty in assembling community representatives: "what ordeals in trying to get together. . . and still no fruit from barren thoughts". Even the painful effort of acquiring permission to publish the Talmud encountered the opposition of an important community like Venice. A contemporary chronicler specifically recorded that all efforts were unsuccessful because "the residents of the sacred community of Venice refused to join them and the group came apart. . ." [2] All of these factors, opposition in certain circles, inertia in others, and the objective conditions of a country divided into a large number of states combined to prevent the establishment of a permanent organization of all Italian Jewry. Under these circumstances, the recurrent efforts by responsible elements within the Jewish community to establish a framework of a general organization succeeded only sporadically, and in a limited form.

[1] S. Z. Ch. Halberstamm, Taḳḳanot Haḳamim, Brody 1879, p. 11.
[2] Hamagiha, p. 175.

C.

Earlier in this chapter it was indicated that for objective reasons far better possibilities existed for the establishment of regional community organizations than for a general organization of Italian Jewry. Indeed, we find this institution widespread throughout most of Italy. During the three hundred years of the Renaissance Period regional community organizations appeared in thirteen principalities and regions, that is, in virtually every place of Jewish residence. At the beginning of the Period there existed only one such organization in the Marche region. In the following century we encounter similar organizations in the islands of Sicily and Sardinia, and the Rimini region in central Italy. In the fifteenth century five new regional organizations appear, and the final four appear in the sixteenth century.

An examination of the emergence patterns of regional organizations reveals that no specific local factor contributed to their establishment. For example, two new regional organizations, one in the extreme north (Monferrato, 1522) and another in the extreme south (Naples, early sixteenth century), emerged virtually simultaneously. Likewise, there was no special similarity in the factors that encouraged the establishment of the regional organizations or in the scope of their activities. Only occasionally was there a common phenomenon, such as the position of a regional rabbi: Naples and the Marche region had official district rabbis at the same time whose duties were very similar.[1] The chief rabbi of Sicilian Jewry had an entirely different role, since he was an official appointed by the government for its own purposes. The function of an unofficial regional rabbi was different from either, in that his authority was recognized in his district by virtue of his personal qualities and his fulfillment of local religious needs.[2] The multifaceted character of the regional organizations and their scope of activities can only be understood by examining the history of each regional organization.

[1] See Marx, *HUCA* 1:616 ff. and Sonne, *Ibid.*, pp. 655-657.
[2] See below, Section V.

The Marche region [1]

As mentioned above, the first of the regional community organizations was in the Marche region. The earliest information is from circa 1290 and it tells of a *waad*, assembly, that met in Foligno. Since the source does not indicate that this was the first *waad*, it may be safely assumed that it was organized quite some time earlier. About one hundred and thirty years later we again encounter the regional organization of the Marche region. This time it appears as a powerful community institution, whose leaders, the directors, were energetically engaged in thwarting attempts at community tax evasion. About this time the *waad* also collected the "Roman tax". In the beginning of the sixteenth century we encounter a *bet waad*, that is, a regional upper court that claimed judicial authority over all Jews who resided in the district.

The organization of communities in the Marche region was officially recognized by the government, at least from 1532 when the region was annexed to the Papal States. In 1542 it appeared in an official document as *Universitas Judeorum Marchiae*, and from other sources we know that it was a well organized body. The organization was headed by representatives of the various communities whose number it is difficult to ascertain. The *neeman*, trustee, who apparently presided over the organization had an important role. The organization's decisions and activities were recorded in a book of minutes, (*sefer hazikronot, pinkas*), and all secretarial work was done by a scribe who was a paid employee. Among the scribes of the Marche region were great scholars like Rabbi Obadiah da Bertinoro, the famous Mishnah commentator, and Rabbi Joseph Arli, one of the great humanists. It appears that the regional rabbi often served as the scribe. His main task,

[1] For all that follows in connection with the Marche region see the sources in: Sonne, *Ibid.*, pp. 632 ff., 636, 639, 644 ff., 649, 651 ff., 654 ff., 677 ff.; *HB* 17:18; M. Stern, *Stellung der Paepste*, Part 1, p. 91 ff.; Sonne, *Tarbiz* 2:483; *Alim* 2:49; *Sefer hapesakim*, Venice 1519, p. 32b; *REJ* 23:254 ff.

however, was to adjudicate conflicts that arose between individuals. He was appointed for a specific number of years and received his salary from the regional treasury. It is possible that the rabbi's residence was in Macerata, since two rabbis of the region (Jehiel Trabot and Joseph Arli) resided in that city. The (annual?) salary of Rabbi Jehiel Trabot was forty eight florins. It thus seems that the rabbi of the Marche region earned as much as Jewish humanists who served as teachers or private rabbis.

It appears that the Marche region organization of communities enjoyed the support of the pope because of its role as a centralized agency for tax collection. Thus, when Sephardic Jews, who formerly resided in Naples came to the Marche region in 1542, the pope ordered that they submit to the regional *waad* and pay their taxes together with the other Jewish residents. This was a clear endorsement of the authority of the *waad* in view of the separatist tendencies generally manifested by the Spanish exiles. The regional community used to send one of the directors to Rome to act as its agent. In the course of time this representation apparently became a permanent institution. An uninterupted contact between the Marche region *waad* and the Roman Jewish community was established regarding the Roman tax. It also seems that the Roman rabbinic court claimed the status of a superior court with jurisdiction over the Jewry of the Papal States, and consequently took the prerogative of reviewing judicial decisions of the court of the Marche region.

The latest information regarding the Marche region's organization of communities is from the second half of the sixteenth century. We cannot determine how long it continued to exist. It is possible that the radical shift in papal policy toward the Jews beginning in 1555, the expulsion from various cities, and the increased Jewish emigration from the pope's territories caused the disbandment of this regional *waad*, which was an exemplary model of permanent community organization within Italian Jewry.

Sardinia [1]

With reference to the general organization of Sardinian Jews, we know only that close to 1390 the king appointed a man named Judah ben David of the city of Alghero to serve as the chief rabbi for all the Jews who resided on the island.

Sicily [2]

The old Jewish community of Sicily that had a very highly developed system of communal management (see above, chapter two of this section), did not establish a general organization until the fourteenth century. Even then this was due not to inner Jewish initiative but to governmental planning that sought to extend its grip over the Jewish community. The government's effort was in line with the character of the Sicilian state and was further prompted by the fact that the Jewish community grew to ten percent of the island's total population.

The centralized organization of communities imposed upon the Jews was concretized through the appointment of a *Dienchelele (dayyan kelali)*, chief justice. It is difficult to ascertain the precise authority of this official. His title "chief justice" clearly implies that he had jurisdiction over all of the island's Jews. He undoubtedly also supervised the administration of the communities. We find that he appointed his own representatives (*Vicari*) in various communities. Once when he was absent from the island, his authority was transferred to two other people, one of whom was a Christian. This clearly suggests that his duties were essentially administrative. In 1430 the king explicitly ordered that the laws that would henceforth be enacted in the various communities must be confirmed by the chief justice. During the fifty years that the position of chief justice lasted, five men served in that capacity, most of whom were physicians of the king's entourage. The

[1] Roth, *History*, p. 265.
[2] What follows is based upon *Giovanni de Giovanni*, p. 115 ff. and *Lagumina*, vol. 1, p. 166 ff., as well as other sources.

Jews of the island did not generally favor the office and their opposition finally forced its abolition in 1448.

In addition to the chief justice, we also find traces of the existence of general community representation in the capital, and of community congresses. It is certain that the congresses were convoked by government order and not by community initiative. The general representation (*Deputati di tutto il Corpo dell'ebraismo della Sicilia*) was probably selected by the communities. It also happened that one of the chief justices, Moses Bonavoglia, appeared before the king in 1431 as a *deputato* in connection with an intercession in behalf of the communities. Such emissaries are also mentioned at a much later period after the abolition of the office of chief justice.[1]

Community congresses were convoked in 1469 and 1489 at the invitation of the Viceroy. They met in Palermo, and representatives of various communities and districts in the kingdom participated. The government ordered each community to send one or two delegates and, apparently, each community had only one vote. The Palermo community, too, had only one vote despite the fact that it sent six delegates to the 1489 congress. The congresses dealt with tax matters and "gifts" for the king, above the tax figure that was regularly paid each year. Evidently, at the 1489 congress the Jews demanded an endorsement of their privileges, (*capitoli*), in exchange for "the gift". And, indeed, King Fernando did validate their rights about a half year later.[2]

Rimini [3]

During most of the Renaissance Period Rimini was an independent principality governed by the Malatesta family, and this evidently prompted the Jews to organize as an independent region. Information regarding this region is available from the year 1399. At that time community leaders and representatives met in Rimini (in assembly ?), and in connection

---

[1] *Giovanni de Giovanni*, p. 63.

[2] *Lagumina*, vol. 2, pp. 87, 94, 430 ff., 432, 433, 437, 461.

[3] See *Responsa of Rabbi Isaac ben Sheshet Perfet*, par. 127; a portion of the document was published by Sonne, *Hatekufah*, p. 634 ff.

with a conflict between a husband and his wife, they decided to seat a special court in Fano on a date they were to designate, and they compelled the unwilling husband to appear before that court. There is also mention of the district's "distinguished men", and while it is difficult to ascertain the meaning of this title, it is possible that it alludes to the fact that the communities of the Rimini region were organized as an independent district.

Lombardy [1]

The regional organization of the Jews of Lombardy was created in connection with the government's policy of centralizing the collection of taxes from its Jewish subjects. The exact date of its formation is unknown. However, the earliest information on centralized tax collection comes from the middle of the fifteenth century. The first attempts to establish a central community organization were made somewhat later when the Lombardian dukes adopted the custom of levying the payment of large sums of money beyond the regular tax figures. The leaders [2] of the communities would then negotiate with the government for as large a reduction as possible and would simultaneously strive to involve all Jewish residents in the payment of these sums. This action was carried out very energetically and received rabbinic support. Rabbi Joseph Colon, the greatest of the Lombardian rabbis of the Period, declared emphatically that whenever the communities entered an agreement with the duke they acted as representatives of every Jewish household in Lombardy. Conversely, Rabbi Joseph Colon regarded decisions on internal Jewish affairs binding only when all Lombardy Jews assented. Deliberations

[1] See *Responsa of Rabbi Joseph Colon*, pars. 2, 181; *Hamagiha*, pp. 180, 186; *Leo Modenas Briefe*, No. 146; M. Stern, *Stellung der Paepste*, Part 1, p. 126; *Invernizzi*, pp. 17, 73; Sonne, *Hatekufah*, p. 660 ff.

[2] It is difficult to determine whether this refers to a united action by the heads of individual communities, which was merely an important step toward the organization of a district *waad*, or whether it refers to the heads of an actual organization of communities. The fact that when the general organization was founded it was called *hakehillot*, the communities, suggest the latter possibility.

on these matters clearly indicate that in certain Jewish circles
there was an effort to establish a broader general community
organization. However, the opposition was apparently also
strong. The most prominent rabbi evidently felt that a communal organization of all Jews of the duchy could be established only as a result of the voluntary assent of all Jewish
residents.

Midway in the first half of the sixteenth century we encounter in Lombardy the existence of a *waad* that appointed
one of the well known rabbis as the sole tax assessor. Again in
1559 we find this *waad* protesting before the government the
attempts of the Inquisition to confiscate the books of the
Jews of Cremona. The leaders of the organization of communities were called *Li Eletti della Università deli Hebrei del Stato
de Milano*, attesting that the government regarded all Jews
of the duchy as organized into one community.

The general organization of Lombardian Jews lasted until
the end of the Renaissance Period, which also marked the end
of Jewish settlement in this province. When exile was decreed
upon the Jews of Lombardy, the activities to nullify the decree
or delay its execution, as well as the orderly liquidation of
Jewish property were carried out by the general organization.
The decisions in these matters were accepted in specially
convoked *waadim*, and the three directors of the organization
of Lombardian Jews still functioned in 1604, several years
after the expulsion. In that year they called a meeting in
Viadana, near Mantua, of all the Jews who formerly resided in
Lombardy to terminate the liquidation of Jewish property
from that state.

Piedmont [1]

We have no information regarding the date of establishment
of the organization of communities in Piedmont. However, it
is certain that in the latter half of the fifteenth century it
already existed as a permanent organization. Rabbi Joseph
Colon described it as "government of the communities" and he

[1] See *Responsa of Rabbi Joseph Colon*, pars. 14, 95, 124; M. Stern,
Stellung der Paepste, Part 1, p. 153 ff; Joseph Conzio, *Ot letobah*,

felt, contrary to his opinion regarding Lombardy, that its leadership had authority "to do as they saw fit regarding communities and their needs". This altered position undoubtedly resulted from the fact that the Piedmont organization of communities was older and had a tradition of authority over the Jewish population, while the *waad* of Lombardy was then in its early organization stage. The decisions referred to by Rabbi Joseph Colon were accepted at regularly convened congresses. It should be noted that Jews of the Savoy region, which was a part of Piedmont since the mid-eleventh century, apparently had an independent organization of communities (Rabbi Joseph Colon spoke specifically of "leaders of the Savoy communities"), and we do not know why they separated and what kind of relationship existed between the two organizations of communities in one state.

While the Piedmont organization of communities was a firmly established institution as early as the second half of the fifteenth century, we have no information regarding its activities until virtually the end of the Period. In 1583 Joseph Conzio dedicated his book *Ot letobah* to Judah Segrè of Chieri, "the faithful leader of the general community organization, who is the most famous among its three directors". We thus see that the leadership of the organization was conducted by three *parnasim*. About three years later a representative of Piedmont Jews journeyed to Rome with delegates from Milan, Ferrara, and Mantua to negotiate permission to publish

Chieri 1583, Dedication; *Miḳweh Yisrael*, Venice 1607, p. 78a; *Responsa of Rabbi Joseph Colon*, par. 14 unquestionably refers to Piedmont and not Lombardy, since a strong organization of communities is mentioned, and Rabbi Joseph Colon was somewhat vague about Lombardy regarding that organization's authority over the Jews of the state. See *Ibid.*, par. 181. This is also why responsum 95 certainly refers to Piedmont. The text clearly indicates that the meetings of the organization were already a permanent feature of Jewish communal life. On the other hand, I doubt whether the responsum of Rabbi Jehiel Trabot the Elder, published in Sonne from a manuscript, *Ibid.*, p. 643 ff. deals with a district organization. It seems to me that the author was reminiscing about his stay in Piedmont, and by stating "and all the great (scholars) of the land were there" he only intended to say that at that time a number of sages, including himself, lived in Piedmont.

the Talmud. It is possible that at the time Piedmont Jews also had a chief rabbi.

Venice [1]

The earliest information regarding a general organization of the communities of the Republic of Venice or, at least common action among them, is from 1483. In that year the representatives of the *Università degli Ebrei del Dominio Veneto* petitioned the doge on the subject of the Jewish badge. The very settlement of the Jews in the Republic on the basis of their obligation to maintain several pawnshops in the capital city also necessitated common action among the communities to raise the required funds for such a project. We know, in fact, that the Jews in most of the mainland communities of the Venetian Republic contributed to the support of these shops.

In the course of time the executive council of the Venetian community apparently attained control over the mainland communities. However, there is no detailed information on the extent of this domination. We know that the executive council convoked meetings of representatives of various communities when necessary. We know of an invitation to such a meeting sent shortly after the end of the Renaissance Period with an appended threat of ex-communication of the communities that refused to participate. The executive council used to issue ordinances and obligated all Jews in the Republic to abide by them; it regarded itself as authorized to threaten non-conformists with excommunication and to appoint overseers to enforce its orders upon communities of the mainland. To be sure, the executive council's authority was considerably limited by the practice of the important mainland communities to send permanent delegates to Venice to protect their interests. These community delegates presumably constituted an advisory group to the executive council on matters affecting Jews of the entire state.

---

[1] See Sonne, *Kobez al jad*, N. S. 3:157, 158, 159, 163; F. Glissenti, *Gli ebrei nel Bresciano*, Brescia 1890, p. 16; A. Milano, *RMI*, vol. 17; Sonne, *Hatekufah*, p. 675; *Leo Modenas Briefe*, p. 121.

The executive council's powerful dominance could not prevent the organization of independent regions by Padua and Cremona.[1] The autonomy of the Padua region was strengthened by an organizational pact between the Paduan *ḳelillah* and the neighboring small communities, and by the fact that its rabbis, by virtue of their scholarly stature and activities, achieved a kind of regional rabbinic status for the entire area. The first of the Paduan rabbis with regional authority was Judah Minz, perhaps the most famous Italian rabbi at the end of the fifteenth and early sixteenth centuries. In 1509 he assembled in Padua "a gathering of sages and men of affairs" and with their consent promulgated several ordinances on the subject of matrimony. These ordinances remained in force in Padua for at least one hundred and twenty years, and certain circles even tried to impose them upon other North Italian areas of Ashkenazic settlement. Furthermore, a ban was pronounced upon a man who refused to be bound by the rabbinic court during the presidency of Rabbi Judah Minz "with the assent of all the district heads (i.e. rabbis)". The general recognition of Rabbi Judah Minz's rabbinic leadership was also expressed through an annual subvention of one hundred ducats by the regional community organization to his rabbinical school. This may also be regarded as a common community effort to support Torah study.

Rabbi Meir Katzenellenbogen (Maharam) of Padua also enjoyed the status of a regional rabbi. Not only did the people of Verona submit their internal conflicts which the local rabbi could not manage to his adjudication, but we are specifically told that all the rabbis of the region functioned as one body under his leadership, exactly as under Rabbi Judah Minz. Moreover, Maharam also represented the Padua region in Venice "on vital matters of the district", undoubtedly in communal matters of secular nature.

Our information regarding the organization (or, perhaps,

---

[1] Sonne, *Ibid.*, p. 646 ff.; Sonne, *Kobez al jad, Ibid.*, p. 156 ff. *Responsa of Maharam*, pars. 45, 68; *Sefer Hapesaḳim*, Venice 1519, p. 28a and 29b. The documents regarding Cremona were published in David Kaufmann, *Gesammelte Schriften*, vol. 3, pp. 92-94.

reorganization) of the Padua district is accurate only for the
end of the Period. In 1581 a formal agreement was made
between the *ḳehillah* of Padua and the surrounding communities to take common action on matters of mutual concern.
A "central board" (*waad kelalut*) composed of representatives
of both Padua and its environs was created to lead the new
organization. The agreement guaranteed representation of the
surrounding communities, consisting of at least one central
board member with voting rights, one tax assessor, and one
accountant. Proportionate payments to cover the district's
expenses were also clearly delineated and a scribe (the famous
scholar Rabbi Samuel Archivolti) was appointed, whose
salary was paid from the district's "public fund". Thus we
have here a formal organization of communities in all its
details. We find that this organization functioned several
years after 1581, and was known officially in Italian as
Capitolo Generale degli Ebrei della Provincia; the word "*provincia*" is undoubtedly a translation of the Hebrew term *galil*,
which is constantly repeated in the sources in connection with
Padua and its environs.

In the second half of the sixteenth century Cremona also
emerged as a separate district. Several documents that describe
the polemic of the rabbi of Cremona against Azariah dei
Rossi's book *Meor enayim* clearly indicate that the Jews of
that city and its environs were regarded as "members of the
district" who obeyed the rulings of the Cremona rabbi. A
"district director" is also specifically mentioned whose
authorization was prerequisite to any announcements by the
rabbi in the synagogue.

The Kingdom of Naples [1]

The lack of stable Jewish settlement and the recurrent
cessation of its existence in the Kingdom prevented the
development of communal life. However, when the Spanish
exiles brought a tradition of a strong communal organization
and imposed a virtually pure Sephardic character upon the

---

[1] Marx, *Ibid.*, pp. 6-621; *Shalshelet hakabbalah*, p. 97; *Ferorelli*,
p. 106 ff.; Ferorelli, *Immigrazioni*, p. 9.

Jewish community, a union of communities was apparently created, led by members of the Abravanel family.

It is difficult to ascertain whether the family's leadership resulted from elections or from its prominent position in the Jewish community and in the Spanish viceroy's court. A chief rabbi who also served as scribe kept a minute book in which he regularly entered the ordinances and decisions of the Union.[1] The only chief rabbi we know was David Ibn Jachia. He apparently served simultaneously as the rabbi of the Kingdom and the local rabbi in the city of Naples. There were other local rabbis in other cities. The chief rabbi had many varied administrative duties and also visited other cities to adjudicate civil cases. His salary was one hundred scudi per annum and was paid from the treasury of the Union.

In addition to the statewide Union there were regional organizations, similar to those in the Venetian Republic, that were led by an officer known as *sindaco* or *procuratore*. The scope of activity of these officials was quite broad, especially in the area of tax distribution and collection. They also traveled frequently to the capital city to lobby for their districts.

Urbino [2]

There was no permanent organization of communities in the Duchy of Urbino. Only once, possibly in 1510, did a congress of community delegates meet to allocate the amount of a tax imposed upon them by the pope. The council met in Pesaro.

Mantua [3]

No stable organization of communities existed in Mantua either, probably because of the conflict over community dominance in the capital city between the pawnbrokers and the rest of the Jewish population (see above). We do know

---

[1] *HUCA, Ibid.* The term *hakehillot*, the communities, can refer to either an organization of communities or to a number of individual communities. In either event, it is apparent that Rabbi David ibn Jachia worked for all of the communities in the kingdom.

[2] Sonne, *Hatekufah*, p. 650 ff.

[3] Colorni, *Magistrature maggiori*, p. 12.

that in 1511 the marquis decided that every tax that he levied
upon the Jews of his state be assessed by a three man committee, two to represent the pawnbrokers and one *tutti gli
Ebrei del Dominio*. Thus, all Jews of the state, exclusive of the
pawnbrokers, were regarded in tax matters as one group and
one person represented their interests.

Monferrato [1]

The Jews of Monferrato who were not numerous, established
an orderly inter-communal organization as early as the beginning of the sixteenth century. Since there were few family
heads (see above, Chapter 1 of Section I), they all met together
in a general assembly. This gathering elected general directors
who managed all community matters. The first general
assembly we know of met in 1552, to deal with an irregular
tax that was levied upon the Jews. Such meetings were
convoked until well after the close of the Renaissance Period.
The number of general directors varied at different times:
They numbered two, three, and even four. In Italian they
were called *eletti*, *deputati*, or *massari*. The government
regarded the Jews of all the duchy as one communal body and
referred to them in official documents as the *Università del
Monferrato*, the (Jewish) community of Monferrato. The
general organization of Monferrato Jewry lasted until the
second half of the eighteenth century.

Romagna [2]

The all-Italian congress that met in Bologna in 1416
appointed one man as general director in Romagna. However,
we do not know if a regional community organization existed
at that time, or whether the man who was appointed represented the congress in the Romagna district. On the other hand,
we do know that such an organization did exist in the middle
of the sixteenth century. In the month of Adar, 1554, a
meeting was held of all the Romagna communities that dealt
with tax matters, among others. In the following month of

---

[1] *Foa*, p. 9, Note 4; p. 12, Note 18, and p. 129; Sonne, *Ibid.*, p. 658.
[2] *Finkelstein*, p. 303; Sonne, *Ibid.*, p. 668; *Alim*, *Ibid.*, p. 49.

Tammuz "a representative of the Romagna communities" participated in the Ferrara congress. There are also indications that the Romagna communities participated as a corporate body in the efforts to obtain permission to publish the Talmud.

Reggio Emilia [1]

All we know of the Reggio district is that its rabbi, Isaac ben Vardama Foà who served there in the second half of the sixteenth century, was "the recognized rabbi of the entire district".

[1] *Responsa of Rabbi Menachem Azariah da Fano*, Dyhernfurt edition, par. 32.

SECTION III

ECONOMIC LIFE

CHAPTER ONE

THE LOAN BUSINESS

a.

While Italian Jews of the Renaissance were active in various areas of business and industry, banking, and especially pawnbroking, became the major field of their economic endeavor. In the early Renaissance the merchant and craft guilds in many cities managed to oust a large portion of Jews from these economic fields, thereby forcing them to engage in usury. Simultaneously, Italian economic life began to expand, creating a demand for credit. However, precisely because of the enhanced significance of the loan business in the contemporary economic system, the Church increased its opposition to usury and campaigned to remove Christians from this business area. These positive and negative factors combined at the beginning of the Period to impel the development of the loan business among Jews.[1]

To be sure, not every sector of Jewry participated in the development of the loan business. It was the Jews of Central Italy who were mainly involved in this business. During the Middle Ages they engaged in trade and accumulated sizable wealth, which in turn enabled them to develop pawnbroking businesses.[2] Conversely, virtually no Sicilian Jews entered this business, since they were mostly poor artisans who lacked the necessary funds for pawnbroking.[3] In addition to many Jews

---

[1] See *RMI* 11:257 ff. Cf. A. Milano, *I primordi del prestito ebraico in Italia*, Città di Castello 1953.

[2] Colorni, *Il prestito*, p. 28.

[3] See the letter of Rabbi Obadiah of Bertinoro in *Iggerot Erez Israel*, p. 104. It also offers partial explanation of the perplexing fact that even though the Sicilian exiles of 1492 were geographically and linguistically close to Italy, they did not settle there (see above,

in Rome and in its environs who were in the loan business, a large number of German Jews who migrated to Italy during the entire Renaissance also participated. Many of them engaged in pawnbroking while still in Germany [1] and brought with them enough capital to develop the trade in their new environment. In terms of required capital for pawnbroking, the Spanish exiles who came to Italy were also equipped for it and, doubtless, many of them entered this business.[2] However, many others entered the business of trade with the Near East.[3] It was easy for them to establish trade bonds with the Levantine countries because of their relations with the many Sephardic Jews who lived in all parts of the Turkish Empire. One important factor which prevented their wholesale entry into the pawnbroking business was the strong attack by the Church and the *Monti di Pieta* (see below) upon the Jewish loan business precisely at the time of their arrival in Italy.[4]

Even though the Sicilian Jews and most of the Sephardim did not participate in the loan business, the Italian Jewish community still derived its livelihood mainly from usury. In

Section I, Chapter 1), while thousands of those who came from Spain did remain. Sicilian Jews did not fit into the economic framework of Italian Jewry, which was based mainly on the loan business and required substantial capital. Most of the Spanish Jews who came to Italy were either wealthy merchants (see A. Milano, *Roma*, p. 7) or scholars. They thus became integral to the Jewish economic system either as bankers or humanists.

[1] See James Parkes, *The Jew in the Medieval Community*, London 1938, p. 344, that as early as the eleventh century the Jews of Germany were involved in pawnbroking. A source from the year 1244 indicates that this constituted the major occupation of the Jews. We thus see that about fifty years prior to the first appearance of German Jews in Italy, the loan business was their major economic mainstay.

[2] For a list of pawnbrokers see *Ferorelli*, p. 148 ff. While the vast majority were Italianic Jews, some obviously were Spanish Jews. See *RMI* 10:306 ff. Further proof of Sephardic participation in the loan business comes from the charter granted to the Jews of the Naples Kingdom in 1520 (*Ferorelli*, p. 224) which stated specifically the Jews' right "to open pawnshops and to lend money" at a time when most of them were Sephardim.

[3] The close trade relations between Sephardic Jews and the Levant are evident in most of the sources. For example, see the document mentioned in *Balletti*, p. 65, Note 3 and Cassuto, *Florence*, p. 89 ff.

[4] *RMI, Ibid.*, p. 226 ff.

the beginning of the Period, Kalonymos ben Kalonymos wrote in his *Maseket Purim*: "no usurious loans are to take place on Purim...that is, in the land of Israel, but it is permitted in Babylonia and in Greek Italy (that is, Southern Italy)... Inhabitants of Babylonia and Italy have nothing else but usury upon which to rely (for their support)..."[1] Near the close of the Period Jehiel Nisim da Pisa also attested "that in these lands more than anywhere else in the entire Diaspora has the custom of lending to the non-Jew become widespread".[2] These testimonies are buttressed by a mass of information from both Jewish and non Jewish official documents indicating that the business of usury was practiced by Jews throughout the entire Period in all sections of the peninsula.

Local Jewish historiography in Italy has devoted much attention to the history of usury in various places, and several decades ago much of the scattered information was collated and the line of the general development was charted.[3] The trend of establishing Jewish pawnshops started in the last decades of the thirteenth century, that is, precisely at the beginning of the Period. A Jewish pawnshop was established in 1287 in Matelica, in the Marche region, in Central Italy, and in a neighboring city in 1309. Between these two dates the first Jewish pawnbrokers from Germany appeared in North Italy, in the territory of the Republic of Venice (Cividale, 1294 and Treviso, 1296). After 1300 the banks began to multiply and reached Venice, which opened its gates to the Jews in 1366. During the last decades of the fourteenth century which were generally an expansion period for the pawnbroking business,[4] the banks spread over the southern portion of the

---

[1] Cited by Israel Davidson, *Parody in Jewish Literature*, New York 1907, p. 23, Note 40.

[2] Cited in Cassuto, *Florence*, p. 429.

[3] Colorni, *Ibid.*, p. 28 ff.

[4] For information regarding the establishment of various pawnshops see, for example: *RMI* 9:219; *RMI* 11:224; A. Ciscato, *Gli ebrei in Montagnana*, Este 1899, p. 75. A number of documents contain information of the Jewish loan business in Trieste in 1263 (*Corriere Israelitico*, 1913, p. 175) and in Cremona in 1278 (Cassuto, *Encyclopaedia Judaica*, vol. 5, p. 693).

Republic, especially around Padua, as well as to the western-most sections of North Italy. The movement also spread from the center of the peninsula, especially toward the Adriatic Sea, and in the beginning of the fifteenth century we find pawn-shops in approximately thirty cities in the Marche region. Some decades earlier the first signs of the Jewish loan business appeared in various cities of Tuscany including Florence, even though we have no information of an official agreement between the city government of Florence and Jewish money-lenders until the end of the fourteenth century.[1]

At that time the movement to open pawnshops also started in the Kingdom of Naples where a Jewish community began to re-establish itself in the fourteenth century. In 1409 [2] the people of Brindisi petitioned King Ladislao to permit Jews to engage in the loan business in their city in view of the great need for credit. The need for credit prevailed in the entire kingdom since it underwent a severe economic crisis during the entire first half of the fifteenth century. It therefore is not surprising that Queen Giovanna II in 1427 permitted the Jews to engage in the loan business throughout the entire kingdom and issued regulations regarding the interest rate. The Jewish loan business had reached such proportions that national regulations became necessary.

Thus, by the start of the fifteenth century the geographic expansion of the loan business by Jews was complete and became a general economic phenomenon in all parts of Italy. A process of inner expansion also began and Jewish money-lenders penetrated into many small towns of various regions. It became customary among city leaders to invite a Jewish moneylender to settle in their midst much in the way they would invite a physician or a teacher.[3] Several large cities like Bologna, Mantua, and Padua were known as centers of the loan business. In 1432 there were no less than seven Jewishly owned pawnshops in Padua. When the city council of Conegliano was seeking a Jewish moneylender to open a loan-bank for

[1] See Luzzatto, *Urbino*, p. 14 ff. and Cassuto, *Florence*, pp. 10, 14.
[2] *Ferorelli*, p. 66 ff.
[3] Luzzatto, *Ibid.*, p. 14 ff.

its residents, it sent emissaries to the Jewish moneylenders in
Padua, Mantua, and Treviso.[1] The business began to burst
from its local frame and started to become a large banking
venture. Several wealthy moneylenders began to open
branches of their loan business in various places. Similarly,
partnerships began to appear which pooled the capital
necessary to open banks in the larger cities.[2]

At this point opposition to Jewish loan-banking began to
emerge among the Christian population. The economic
depression of the masses caused by endless wars waged
throughout all of Italy, contrasted with a rise in the living
standard of Jewish pawnbrokers, aroused strong anti-Jewish
feelings. The movement was led by the Franciscans who
during this period had a number of outstanding itinerant
preachers with tremendous influence upon the masses.[3] The
preachers agitated for the annulment of the *condotte* and a ban
upon the granting of new *condotte*. They believed that the
abolition of the Jewish loan business would heal all social ills.
The masses also believed that the loan business was ruining
the country. An early sixteenth century Christian author
arguedt, hat the Jews "have consumed the land" through
usury. Likewise, a seventeenth century Italian Jewish
chronicler, evaluating the expulsions from various Italian
cities at the end of the fifteenth century, considered usury their
main cause, since the moneylenders "consumed the people's
bones". [4]

Both Franciscans and the Christian masses were well aware
of the need for loan institutions to extend small amounts of
credit. But they felt that with the elimination of Jewish
businesses this function could be filled by the *Monti di Pieta*,
lending institutions sponsored by wealthy Christians that
would extend credit on a non-profit basis. And, indeed,
monastic circles succeeded in stimulating the foundation of
such institutions, the impact of which was felt during the

[1] *Ciscato*, p. 242; Morpurgo, *Padua*, p. 4.
[2] Cassuto, *Florence*, p. 123 ff.
[3] See *Burckhardt*, p. 350 ff.
[4] See *RMI, Ibid.*, p. 266 ff. and Moses A. Shulvass, *In the Grip of
Centuries*, p. 93.

entire second half of the fifteenth century. It is difficult to
give a complete list of cities with a *Monte di Pieta*. From a
partial list compiled by a scholar [1] it is evident that the
movement evoked a strong response in North and Central
Italy. The list contains more than twenty institutions that
were founded between 1462 and 1496 in most of the important
cities and, undoubtedly, in smaller towns as well.

The immediate effect of this movement was the closing of
established Jewish pawnshops in many places. A classic
example of the movement's activities was in Florence where
both the elimination of pawnshops and the expulsion of the
Jews from the city were effected by the preachers under their
leader Girolamo Savonarola. While Savonarola did not as a
rule attack the Jews in his sermons, he did devote a great deal
of attention to the *Monti*. He directed his sermons at the
wealthy and urged them to contribute substantially to the
fund. He also demanded that the women donate their jewelry
to the institution. [2] And, indeed, the city council in 1495
authorized a law regarding the establishment of a *Monte di
Pieta*. The text of the law contains the argument that the
high interest paid to Jewish moneylenders increased the
payment of a loan of one hundred florins to millions over a
fifty year period. The law permitted a limited interest rate on
loans to cover administrative expenses which was fixed at
a seven and a half percent maximum. [3]

As mentioned above, the movement to establish charitable
loan funds was widespread through North and Central Italy.
Conversely, the movement barely touched Southern Italy,
that is, the Kingdom of Naples, undoubtedly because of a
greater credit need that could not be satisfied by charitable
loan funds. The drastic need for credit is illustrated by the
fact that precisely during the retrenchment period through

[1] *Ciscato*, p. 56, Note 2.
[2] Such a request was also voiced by a great preacher in Modena in
1505 (see *Balletti*, p. 49). Apparently, those who conceived of the
Fund expected many contributions from women.
[3] This matter is treated at length in P. Villari, *Life and Times
of Savonarola*, London and New York 1888, p. 294 ff. Cf. Cassuto,
Florence, p. 66 ff. and p. 73 ff.

which other parts of the peninsula were passing, the Jewish loan business in Naples attained climactic development. Here the legal interest rate was also higher than what was ever permitted in other Italian areas. Jewish loan banks were located in more than fifty cities and their growth and organization displayed all the characteristic signs of Jewish pawnbroking in North Italy at its most prosperous period fifty years earlier.[1] The famous humanist Antonio Ferrari, known as Galateo (1444-1517) pointed out that Neapolitan Jews engaged in trade and free professions but enjoyed an actual monopoly in the lending business.[2]

Not until the second half of the sixteenth century did the Jewish loan business in North and Central Italy recover fully from the propaganda blow of the monks and the movement to establish *Monti di Pieta*. To be sure, the charity institutions apparently fulfilled only part of what was anticipated. They depended upon the largess of the wealthy and people of good will who, periodically, rose to the task moved by great religious experiences or the poverty of the masses. But the lack of a firm business base undermined the stability of the *Monti*. Even at the height of the movement a Fund that was established in as large a city as Padua in 1469 could not begin its operation until 1491. In Forli even though a charity foundation was established in 1545 through the efforts of a "pious man", Jewish loan banks continued to function and their proprietors enjoyed many privileges.[3] The end result was a mutual accommodation of charity funds and Jewish pawn banks, and after some time both institutions continued to function side by side without hostility. Certain contracts between city councils and Jewish pawnbrokers that obligated Jews to lend at a low interest rate [4] indicate that the charity funds achieved part of their main goal—the lowering of the interest rate. There were also cases where Jewish lenders lent their own money to

---

[1] See *Ferorelli*, p. 148 ff. (a list of pawnbrokers) and p. 136 (the rate of interest).

[2] *RMI* 15:378.

[3] See Ciscato, *Ibid.*; *La Romagna*, 1908, p. 268.

[4] *RMI* 10:306; *RMI* 11:452.

charity funds at a very low interest rate.[1] No doubt, the Jewish loan business now operated within far more limited confines. Large Jewish capital was now engaged in big business and loan ventures. Those with limited capital were no longer able to expand as formerly. As a result, the problem of internal Jewish competition which heretofore was nonexistent now emerged. This is why in 1554 the Ferrara congress promulgated a stern decree "that no one dare to intrude upon the domain of his neighbor...for interest lending..." [2] There was evidently much Jewish capital in search of investment. Further limitation of the loan business resulted from the expulsion of the Jews from the Kingdom of Naples in several stages during the first half of the sixteenth century. This expulsion closed that sector of the peninsula to the Jewish loan business.

It appears that the mid-sixteenth century marked the end of the war between Jewish pawnshops and Christian charity foundations and the start of a shared parallel existence. This peace was most vividly attested to in the second half of the century by the large number of Jewish pawnshops, mainly in smaller communities. Most of these loan-banks undoubtedly existed earlier and survived the struggle with the charity foundations. It seems that during this struggle the large pawnbanks with branches in many locales ceased to exist. Possibly, these large banks were the principal factor in the mass revolt against Jewish pawnbrokerage. Most of the pawnshops that operated during the last fifty years of the Period were small shops in small towns: eighteen in the Province of Modena, eight in the Principality of Parma, twenty-five in the Monferrato Duchy, and thirty-two in the Principality of Urbino.[3] As for the large cities, there were so many Jewish pawnshops that we must assume that they were mainly small establishments with a limited clientele and capital. Thus we find fifteen moneylenders in Casale Monferrato, twenty-five

---

[1] *Balletti*, p. 60.

[2] The text is in *Finkelstein*, p. 303.

[3] *Balletti*, p. 55 ff.; *RMI* 12:272; *Foà*, p. 72 ff.; Luzzatto, *Urbino*, p. 43.

in Verona, and in Rome in the middle of the seventeenth century were one hundred Jewish moneylenders whose individual capital did not exceed 1500 scudi.[1] A further reflection of the new friendly relationship between the gentile society and the Jewish loan business was the renewal of issuing permits to open pawnshops (e.g. in the province of Piedmont). In addition, the various states made general provisions regarding the maximum number of pawnshops to be owned by Jews within their territories. That these general provisions were not intended as a stringent limitation is apparent from the permit given by the small principality of Monferrato to open forty pawnshops, fifteen of which were to operate in the capital. Further indication of a nonrestrictive attitude comes from the Parma Principality where the Jews did not use their quota of sixteen pawnshops and only established eight.[2] At the conclusion of the Period Jewish pawnshops numbering in the hundreds existed all over Italy both in large and small cities.[3]

b.

The legal base of Jewish interest lending was the *condotta*, an agreement between governing agencies and Jewish loan brokers that incorporated all contractual terms. Since the *condotta*'s primary condition was the right of Jewish settlement in a municipal area or specific district in exchange for an obligation to open a pawnbank, the *condotta* became an important legal factor in the history of Italian Jewry during the Renaissance Period. It served, in effect, as the legal base for the establishment of many Jewish communities. Essentially, however, the *condotta* regulated the business and, as such, concerns us here.[4]

[1] See S. W. Baron, *Krausz Jubilee Volume*, p. 223; Foà, *Ibid.*; A. Milano, *Roma*, p. 16.

[2] See *Cenni storici*, p. 75; *RMI* 12:273; Foà, p. 44.

[3] From a document published in *Talpioth* 6:344 is evident that there was a great demand for money, to the extent that one banker feared lest he will have insufficient funds to fill his borrowers' demands. It appears that at the end of the Period when peace was restored between the charity foundations and Jewish loan banking, most of the Jewish capitalists re-entered the field.

[4] Many *condotta* texts have been published and we also know the

Most *condotte* applied to a specific municipal area and were granted to the Jewish loan banker by the municipal administration or the ruler in whose territory the city lay. There were, however, cases of statewide *condotta* grants such as in Parma and Monferrato.[1] The *condotta* obligated an individual Jew (or a group) to open one or more pawnshops for money lending. The document specified the number of years the contract was to be in effect. Some agreements called for a short term such as three years, while others were for longer periods, up to twenty years. Sometimes the terms of the *condotta* were changed upon renewal even in the same locality. In one instance a contract was good for three years, then for five years, and finally for seven years.[2]

One of the characteristic features of the *condotta* was that it was not a government issued statement of rights to Jews, but clearly a bilateral agreement. This is evident from the fact that conditions were changed regularly upon renewal and that many contracts contained a clause permitting their transfer to someone else. Because of this the Jewish moneylender attached great importance to the matter of assuring exclusive rights for himself that could not be abrogated unilaterally by the other side. One method was to guarantee exclusiveness with an explicit clause in the *condotta*. This, however, apparently did not suffice, especially in the sixteenth century when there was more Jewish capital than could possibly be invested. Internal Jewish effort then came to aid the Jewish *condotta* holder in the form of the above mentioned resolution by the Ferrara congress of 1554 stating that wherever a Jewish pawnbroker had an exclusive right, it was forbidden for

details of many unpublished ones. Typical are a routine *condotta* published in *JQR* 4:225, and on that was transferred to another man, published in *Romagna*, 1908, p. 266 ff. Cf. also A. Milano, *RMI* 9: 263.

[1] See *RMI* 12:272, Note 2 and *Foà*, p. 72 ff. The statewide *condotta* also reveals that any Jew who wanted to leave the territory of Piedmont had to pay his tax share to the *ḳehillah* up to the termination date of the *condotta* (see M. D. Anfossi, *Gli ebrei in Piemonte*, Turin 1914, p. 79 ff.).

[2] A. Ciscato, *Gli ebrei in Montagnana*, p. 76.

anyone else to engage in lending in that place without his permission.[1]

Rabbi Meir Katzenellenbogen (Maharam) of Padua, who participated in the congress, lent the full support of his great prestige to the resolution in behalf of the principle of *condotta* exclusivity. Since the *condotta* affected the Jewish right of settlement, he equated it with the concept of *herem hayishub*, the prohibition against strangers taking up residence in an established community without formal permission of that community. The resolution was periodically reindorsed during the last fifty years of the Period by both communal ordinances and rabbinic court decisions.[2]

The clause enabling the *condotta* holder to transfer it to someone else apparently was very important to the Jewish party, and we find that the new contract holder usually also secured this right for himself. On the basis of this clause, it seems, the *condotta* rights would be "subleased" for several years and, upon termination, would then revert to the original owner. The Jewish moneylender sometimes also secured for his heirs the right to inherit the *condotta*.[3]

The main regulations of the *condotta* can be divided into two categories. The first dealt with matters of the projected loan bank, such as the amount of money that must be invested, the interest rate, a definition of items to be considered as pawns, and conditions under which they may be sold. The second pertained to the personal rights of the Jewish pawnbroker and was intended to enable him to live peacefully in accordance with his religious convictions. The various municipal *condotte* reveal a great deal of similarity with regard to the first section of conditions. There were, however, significant variations regarding the personal and religious rights of the Jewish pawnbroker. Some *condotte* granted the Jews quite extensive rights, including the right to bear arms and exemp-

---

[1] *Finkelstein*, p. 303.

[2] See *Responsa of Maharam*, pars. 39 and 41; Sonne, *Hatekufah*, p. 668; *Finkelstein*, p. 310 ff. For the concept of *herem hayishub* comp. L. Rabinowitz, *The Herem Hayyishub*, London 1945, p. 13.

[3] See *Responsa of Maharam*, par. 39 and *Capitoli sopra gli Hebrei*, Ferrara 1601, paragraph 1.

tion from wearing the Jewish badge. Conversely, some *condotte* limited Jewish rights and firmly insisted upon the obligation to wear the badge. The city of Florence offers a classic example. Between the years 1437 and 1481 the clause regarding the badge was periodically changed upon the reissuance of the *condotta*. When the city needed the Jews it was forced to be lenient on the badge. However, in 1463 when the Jews were threatened by a great loss if the *condotta* were not renewed, they were compelled to agree to wear the badge.[1] In conclusion, despite changing circumstances, the *condotta* generally enabled Jews to live fairly comfortably in a significant number of Italian cities.

c.

One of the important clauses which appeared in virtually every *condotta* was the amount of capital that the Jew must retain in his pawnshop for moneylending. Surprisingly, in a large number of cases this sum was relatively modest even by the standards of that era. In some small localities the required amount to open a pawnshop was less than a thousand ducats. In medium sized cities the figure was from three to five thousand, and only in the large cities did the basic sum for each pawnshop rise to ten thousand or slightly more.[2] Even in Florence, where in 1437 four *condotta* partners were obligated to maintain a total of forty thousand florins, that is, ten thousand in each shop, they were permitted to open the first pawnshop with 4,000 florins on condition that they invest the total sum within two to three years.[3] The situation was completely different in Venice. There in the sixteenth century the loan business ceased to be the principal occupation of most Jews and the capital city pawnshops were no longer business

[1] Regarding Jewish living conditions under the *condotta*, see the sources listed in Note 4 on p. 122. Cf. Luzzatto, *Urbino*, p. 66 ff. The data regarding Florence are available in Cassuto, *Florence*, pp. 123, 141, 142, 148.
[2] It is superfluous to cite the sources here. The sums invested in the various shops appear in most of the sources mentioned in this chapter. The ducato, fiorino, and zecchino had equal value.
[3] See Cassuto, *Florence*, p. 120 ff.

institutions. In exchange for residence rights within the Republic, the Jewish pawnbrokers had to lend money to indigent Christians at such a low interest rate that it was necessary to involve Jews of the entire country in the maintenance of the pawnshops. The capital that was invested in the shops diminished so that by the end of the Period it amounted to fifty thousand ducats,[1] a rather modest figure in proportion to a city like Venice, especially when we consider the fact that money was raised from Jews of the entire state.

The preceding facts reveal that where Jewishly owned pawnshops were opened for actual business, and this was the case in the vast majority of cities, the moneylenders had rather small revolving assets and were compelled to demand a high interest rate in order to derive a livelihood. The other party to the *condotta*, the city council or the duke, usually took this under consideration and the *condotta* generally permitted an interest rate of 20-25 per cent per annum. In unusual cases, especially in the Kingdom of Naples, the interest rate reached 40-45 percent. There were some cases, however, where the *condotta* specified a rate of only 15 per cent per annum.[2] The rate of interest was also determined by the size of the loan. Usually, the interest rate rose with the increased size of the loan in conformity with the basic concept that the Jewish loan business was created in response to the needs of the indigent Christian. But there were also occasions when the interest rate decreased as the size of the loan increased. In evaluating the profit of Jewish moneylenders it should also be noted that many *condotte* included a provision which obligated the Jewish moneylender to advance each year a specific amount of cash, often quite substantial, to the city council without any interest charge. This practice, obviously, reduced the lender's actual income from his invested capital. During the entire sixteenth century the interest rate was also lowered by competition from the charity foundations. The government sometimes ordered an examination of the pawnbroker's

[1] For details see Roth, *Venice*, p. 133 ff.
[2] See *Ferorelli*, pp. 68, 136; Cassuto, *Florence*, p. 68 ff.; *RMI*, 10:306 ff.; *Romagna*, 1908, p. 269.

financial records "to take an interest tally" and, on such occasions, confiscated part of the lender's capital under a variety of pretexts.[1] In sum, the moneylending business offered Jewish moneylenders the opportunity of a decent livelihood but did not permit the amassing of large personal fortunes.

There were, to be sure, several magnates among Italian Jews during the Renaissance such as the Da Pisa and Meshullam families, Elhanan of Fano, and the Abravanels. The latter undoubtedly brought a large portion of their wealth from Spain, since the Spanish exiles generally brought a great deal of money into Italy with them in 1492. The others, however, did amass a large share of their wealth through the money-lending business. The Italian name of the Meshullam family, Del Banco, indicates that the essential business of the famous brothers Asher, Hayim, and Mendlin was banking. The expert knowledge of exchange notes that Jehiel Nisim da Pisa demonstrated in his book *Eternal Life* [2] illustrates that the large scale business of banking was widespread in his family. However, the sources leave no doubt that large scale banking was rare among Italian Jews. It is worth noting that Jehiel Nisim da Pisa discussed exchange notes purely on a theoretical basis, since, according to him, this form of lending business was not widespread among Italian Jews. Great fortunes were only amassed in the field of trade, which will be discussed in the following chapter.

d.

The majority of Jewishly owned pawnshops were established in small cities where the *condotta* holder was generally the owner of the pawnshop. The amount of capital needed to open a business was modest, as we have seen. One family could usually fulfill the terms of the contract by itself. Such was not the case in the large cities. There, large investment funds were

[1] See *Tarbiz* 2:354.
[2] See Marx, *Studies in Jewish History and Booklore*, p. 167 and *REJ* 6:19. See also Gilbert S. Rosenthal's edition of *Eternal Life*, New York 1962.

needed and, in order to fulfill the terms of the *condotta*, groups of pawnbrokers were organized who would collectively raise the full investment. Such businesses [1] were limited partnerships. They were managed solely by one of the partners and became his responsibility. He did not rely upon the opinion of the partners in the actual conduct of the business and he received a certain amount of the profits for his managerial work. A balance sheet was taken at the end of the business year and each partner received his share of the profits proportionate to the amount of his investment. A special share of the profits was paid to the partner who owned the *condotta*.

This organizational structure of the pawnshop business began to develop in the second half of the fourteenth century, the period of broadest expansion of the business. The partners who founded such limited companies in one locale were, generally, *condotta* holders in other places as well, often where they resided. They used part of their profits and substance to join partnerships in the organization of new pawnshops. Some wealthy men invested their money in a wide network of pawnbanks spread throughout various provinces. One pawnbroker from Rimini whose origin was Rome and who lived for some time in Ancona, was a partner in pawnshops in Padua, Montagnana and San Marino. Bankers of this type could be found in other places as well.[2] The general insecurity of the banking business impelled the financiers to diffuse rather than concentrate their capital despite two obvious disadvantages: the impossibility of direct supervision and the necessity of paying the manager's salary.[3] Rarely do we find a case of the uninterrupted existence of a pawnshop business for decades,[4] since the *condotta* was generally granted for short time periods and it was impossible to know whether or not it would be renewed by the city administration. There was

---

[1] For specifics of such companies see Luzzatto, *Urbino*, p. 29 ff.

[2] *Ciscato*, p. 19; Colorni, *Il prestito, etc.*, p. 47; Cassuto, *Florence*, p. 125 ff.

[3] The manager of a pawnshop that was opened in Padua in 1380 received an annual salary of 185 ducats. See *Ciscato*, p. 20.

[4] In Rimini one man held a pawnshop for thirty six years. See Sonne, *Hatekufah*, p. 649.

a constant threat of unforseen taxes that would be levied, or the possibility that some excuse would be found to nullify the payment of obligations. As a remedy pawnbank partnerships were created to save at least part of the capital in the event of the loss of the main investment. Thus, the partnership pattern was a kind of mutual protection society of the Jewish bankers that was rooted essentially in political rather than economic conditions.

There were several forms of the banking transaction.[1] Most were small loans against securities which were returned to the borrower upon payment of the debt. In the event of non-payment the pawnbroker was permitted to sell the pledge and use the money to repay the debt, the interest and his expenses. If any balance remained, it was returned to the pledge owner. The *condotte* contained detailed provisions regarding pledge selling, in order to prevent cheating by the lenders and inter-ference by the borrowers at the sale of the pledge objects. The sources mention various kinds of pledges including precious stones and books. However, most of the plegdes were men's garments. This was probably one of the causes of Jewish involvement in the used clothes business, *strazzaria* (see next chapter). Large, long term loans that were extended to repu-table merchants were bonded by notes. Such notes were strongly binding and the government gave full support to their collection by effective action against the borrower's property. There were rare instances of mortgage loans against real estate.

Pledge loans were recorded in special ledgers and these were accepted by the courts as valid evidence. The notation included the name of the borrower, the date of the transaction, a description of the pledge and the amount of the loan. Such ledgers were generally kept in Hebrew. However, in the middle of the sixteenth century governments began to insist that records be kept in Italian.[2]

---

[1] This description in Luzzatto, *Urbino*, p. 31 ff. is typical of many banks.

[2] *Ibid.*, p. 33 ff. Cf. Cassuto, *Florence*, p. 160 ff. for a very interesting description of two pawnshop ledgers written in Hebrew.

The management of a pawnshop was a quite complicated matter. On the one hand a thorough knowledge of the *condotta* was necessary, and in addition Jewish moneylenders strove to follow the Pentateuchal laws against usury. Another important factor was the administration of the pawnshop including the evaluation and selling of pledges. It is, therefore, not surprising to hear of a pawnbroker who sent his son to a neighbor's pawnbank to learn "the ways of the pawnshop".[1] Moreover, professional management manuals for bankers were authored by Italian Jews. The book *Eternal Life* by Jehiel Nisim da Pisa [2] described various lending methods and their relationship to the Jewish usury ban. We also find a technical handbook that endeavored to guide "the moneylender who was the chief manager, whether the capital belonged to him alone or was in partnership". This book, found in manuscript,[3] is called *Tractate of Lender and Borrower*, and teaches the moneylending business by way of positive and negative commandments that the lender must fulfill.

e.

The preceding survey underscores the fact that the money lending business was one of the most important phenomena in the life of Italian Jewry during the Renaissance. Although the lending of small sums against pledges and charging high interest were a grave social affliction, we encounter only few voiced protests against it during most of the tri-century Period. Moreover, famous rabbis were also moneylenders and, according to Isaiah Sonne,[4] most of the North Italian rabbis were bankers even at a time when they functioned as heads of rabbinical schools. Leon da Modena in 1584 [5] charged that

[1] Marx, *Louis Ginsberg Jubilee Volume*, Hebrew section, p. 276. Cf. *Ibid.*, Note 28.

[2] See Cassuto, *Ibid.*, p. 429 and Marx, *Ibid.*

[3] *HUCA*, 26:46 ff. (Hebrew section). In another part of the manuscript the date 1634 is mentioned indicating that the *Tractate of Lender and Borrower*, was written prior to that date.

[4] Sonne, *Kobez al jad*, N. S. 3:155.

[5] In his essay against gambling entitled *Sur mera*. The treatise first appeared in Venice in 1595 and was later re-published several times. See chapter 4.

"in our generation all interest lenders are regarded honorable and not only are they not ineligible to testify and to judge, it is quite the reverse, namely, their word is (considered) as reliable as a hundred witnesses, they are our leaders and judges".

This fact is partially explicable by the weakened religious life that stemmed from a serious lack of religious leadership and the unfortunate belief in fatalism that claimed all human events were to be determined by the stars (see below, Section V). The fact that their Christian neighbors, the Lombards and Florentines, were in the front rank of international banking, undoubtedly legitimized the business in Jewish eyes. Moreover, despite the great poverty of its masses, Italy was then one of the more economically advanced countries and many loans were floated for commercial ends rather than life necessities. Thus, interest payments did not always have the character of usury. But one of the crucial factors that led Jews into money-lending, especially emigrants from Germany in search of residence places, was the fact that this business opened the gates of many cities that otherwise would have remained closed to them.

Nevertheless, the moneylending business did evoke opposition. In addition to Leon da Modena's plaint, we hear the biting words of Rabbi Abraham Jaghel Gallichi [1] who was once himself one of the moneylending rabbis and subsequently personally experienced the deplorable results of the venture. His experience led him to the conclusion that interest lending brought no benefit to the community and caused only economic damage. The rabbi-poet Samuel Archivolti [2] also spoke in this mood, that usury is "an occupation that engenders the pursuit of plunder, alienation of relatives, hatred of friends, enmity of the masses, a torrent of woe". These sentiments were expressed at the end of the Period when Italian Jewry experienced a religio-moral renascence. Two generations earlier, however, Rabbi Abraham Farissol in his book *Magen Avraham* [3] vigorously defended the Jewish moneylenders.

[1] *Ge ḥizzayon*, Alexandria, 1879, p. 4b.
[2] *Maayan ganim*, Venice 1532, p. 22b.
[3] Chapter 73, published in *Haẓofeh lehokmat Yisrael* 12:290.

He was aware that Christians regarded moneylending as a despicable occupation and he even conceded "that may he who flees from an evil reputation and chooses to pursue a good one by engaging in suitable occupations and proper businesses warrant endless blessing". But he was also aware of the fact that the pope and other Christian rulers assented to the practice of usury and received through taxation a large share of Jewish profits. In these circumstances, a large part of interest money reverted to the states' treasuries thereby benefiting the entire country. In his opinion, there was also some advantage in the actual process of extending loans to Christians.

Some measure of tension arose over the collection of interest from Jewish borrowers that was a by-product of the money-lending business with Christians. There was an urgent need for capital by the *condotta* holders in the period prior to the Franciscan attack on the Jewish loan business. The scarcity of capital created a dearth of money available to Jews for free loans, (*gemilut ḥasadim*). Thus, it sometimes happened that Jews borrowed on interest from co-religionists. There were incidents of tricking unwilling Jewish lenders into interest transactions with fellow Jews by sending a Christian intermediary who ostensibly borrowed money for himself when, in reality, he was merely an agent for his Jewish friend.

The Florence Congress of 1428 [1] acted to eliminate the practice of accepting interest from Jews and especially the aforementioned deception. It decreed that whenever a Jewishly owned pledge was deposited with a Jewish lender through a Christian intermediary, the Jewish borrower had to pay the entire interest claim on his debt to the Jewish charity fund for distribution to the poor. An additional fine of two ducats for the charity fund was also levied upon him for such a transgression.

It is difficult to ascertian whether the effort to eliminate this practice was successful. No further complaints of this kind were heard in a later period. This, however, may reflect the effects of Franciscan propaganda against Jewish money-

[1] The decision is found in Cassuto, *Florence*, p. 363 ff.

lending practices that seriously reduced its scope, rather than the efficacy of the Florence Congress decision. The limitation of the business created an excess of idle Jewish capital and automatically eliminated usurious credit to Jews.

CHAPTER TWO

TRADE

a.

A study of the character and scope of Jewish trade in Renaissance Italy reveals that unlike the usury business trade lacked a unified line of development. Even prior to the start of the Period the Christian merchants' guilds succeeded in ousting Jews from the field in many places. Nevertheless, throughout the entire Period we do encounter all possible varieties of trade among Jews, from petty merchandising of used clothes to large international enterprises. In fifteenth century Urbino, for example, we find coexistent with the bankers who also conducted ramified trade and manufacturing projects, a small group of petty, impoverished shopkeepers.[1] At the end of the Period we hear that in Ferrara "most of the city's businesses are in the hands of wealthy Jews".[2] There were also places where a far greater proportion of Jewish residents than might be reasonably expected were engaged in trade. In a list of the year 1527 containing the names of 104 Roman Jews, we find forty merchants of all types.[3] The information we have regarding the number of Jewish merchants in Padua [4] is even more significant. By the beginning of the sixteenth century they had become so numerous that Christian merchants began to fear their competition. In 1571 the city had

---

[1] Luzzatto, *Urbino*, p. 23, p. 25 ff.
[2] *Hamagiha*, p. 188.
[3] L. Livi, *Gli Ebrei alla luce della statistica*, vol. 1, 1918, p. 136. It is difficult to draw definite conclusions from this list since it represents only about one fourth of the total Jewish population and we do not know whether or not the pawnbrokers are included among the forty merchants.
[4] The figures are found in *Ciscato*, p. 99. Cf. *Ibid.*, p. 97.

fifty-five Jewish merchants and in 1615 their number rose to
eighty-four. When we consider that the entire Jewish population at that time was only 665, or roughly one hundred and
twenty families, it means that two thirds of the Jewish
population earned their livelihood from various forms of
trade.[1] Moreover, the Jews constituted ten percent of the
city's merchants while they were only two percent of the total
population. However, this situation applied only to Padua
and, perhaps, several other places, and was not typical in the
composite portrait of Jews in trade. The overall situation
reveals isolated merchants here and there, with each one
involved in a different area of trade. It seems that the only
trade categories that drew a large concentration of Jews were
textiles and precious stones, as well as export and import.

Legally, Jewish trade was based upon two fundamentals. It
existed partly by virtue of traditional tolerance and partly by
special licenses that were granted during the Period. Many
condotte specifically granted the Jewish moneylender the
right to engage in trade as well,[2] and there were even permission grants to carry on trade prior to the agreement on money
lending.[3] Urbino, as we have seen, offers a classic example.
The legal rights of the shopkeepers were rather vague and
probably rooted in tradition. Conversely, the bankers came to
the city through a contract with the prince to open pawnshops
and to engage in trade and manufacturing.

Wherever Jewish trade reached substantial proportions,
we encounter the common accompanying manifestations of
consolidation and competition. In mid-fifteenth century
Padua the Jewish trade in used articles [4] became so significant
that Jewish and Christian merchants agreed to organize a

---

[1] Further verification can be derived from the fact that in 1533
the community's two directors were dealers in used merchandise.
See Morpurgo, *Padua*, p. 13.

[2] *JQR*, 4:225; *Romagna*, 1908, p. 269.

[3] L. Ottolenghi, *Brevi cenni sugli Israeliti casalesi*, Casale Monferrato 1866, p. 7.

[4] *Strazzaria*. This term has a dual meaning. In many places it
refers to the used clothing trade, in most cases it indicates trade in
used luxury articles, such as furniture and books that were sold by
the aristocracy and were still usable.

common association. The agreement [1] called for the organization of two parallel sections, Jewish and Christian, with equal rights. It was also agreed that the association's decisions regarding religious matters [2] were not binding upon the Jews. This organization was obviously formed to prevent uncontrolled competition among the merchants. That such action became essential is clearly evident from the fact that in 1571 the *Capitoli* of the Florence community introduced special procedures to prevent competition among the merchants. [3] In Padua, about 1583, Jewish merchandising middlemen so increased in numbers, and competition between them became so fierce, that the *kehillah* was compelled to set up a special committee to deal with their problems. [4] Competition sometimes even forced merchants to turn to peddling. Such was the case in Rome early in the Period and in Florence close to its end.[5] Peddling was quite widespread among the Jews in the middle of the sixteenth century and since women also entered this field, Maharam of Padua considered it appropriate to warn against the dangers involved. He rebuked one community for "you see and remain mute and do not rebuke Jewish daughters, the women among you who go out alone to the market places and to every fair like peddlers, who wander from place to place to sell their merchandise".[6]

However, most of the Jewish merchants were regular shopkeepers. In their stores they sold most of the necessities of daily life and even the Christian community sometimes acknowledged their useful social function. This was especially the case in Padua where the gentiles readily admitted that Jewish merchants imported articles previously available only in Venice or in certain places abroad. Even more the students of the University of Padua appreciated the Jewish mercantile function and did all in their power to protect it.[7]

[1] The document was published in *Ciscato*, p. 255 ff.

[2] Merchants and artisans guilds generally marched as separate groups in religious processions.

[3] Cassuto, *I piu antichi capitoli del ghetto di Firenze*, p. 7.

[4] Morpurgo, *Padua*, p. 16.

[5] *Vogelstein-Rieger*, vol. i, p. 302 ff.; Cassuto, *Ibid.*, p. 4 ff.

[6] *Responsa of Maharam*, par. 26.

[7] *Ciscato*, pp. 109, 111.

The most important contribution of the Jewish merchants everywhere in Italy was in the clothing trade. First and foremost they controlled a significant share of the used clothes business, which before the mass production of garments provided most of the clothing necessities. To begin with, this business was linked with Jewish pawnbroking, since most of the pledges were garments. Unredeemed pledges thus streemed directly into the Jewish clothing trade. In addition, this branch of business encountered little opposition from Christian merchants because of its undesirability. Jews had engaged in this business in Padua early in the Period,[1] and it expanded greatly in the course of time. There were even places where this was the customary Jewish occupation. [2] When the persecution of Jews in the Papal States began in the second half of the sixteenth century, this business—*strazzaria*—was the only one by which they were permitted to earn a livelihood.[3]

There were also Jewish merchants who sold new clothes throughout the entire Renaissance. [4] Moreover, many sources that cite Jews who were in the *strazzaria* business, refer to the sale of both old and new clothing. [5] We also have extensive information on Jewish trade in textiles that suggest a special preference to this field. Early in the Period we find Jewish peddlers in Rome who sold silk, and later we learn that Jewish pawnbrokers in Urbino opened a store specifically for the sale of textiles. [6] Their stock consisted mostly of velvet, brocade, and silk. One source tells of Jews who engaged in the sale of

---

[1] *Ibid.*, p. 12.

[2] A document of 1584 issued by the doge of Venice stated with regard to the Jews of Asolo that *strazzaria* was ,,*il solito exercitio suo*". Cf. M. Osimo, *Narrazione della strage etc.* p. 28, Note E.

[3] See *Tarbiz* 2:345: "And they will not be permitted to engage in any business except *strazzaria* and *cenciaria* (rag trade)."

[4] Rome (*Vogelstein-Rieger*, vol. 1, p. 303); Padua (*Ciscato*, p. 255 ff.); Florence (Cassuto, *Capitoli*, p. 4 ff.).

[5] An agreement between Jewish and Christian *strazzaria* merchants in 1448 contains specific reference to "*tutti strazzaroli si de l'arte vecchia come della nova*" (*Ciscato, Ibid.*).

[6] *Vogelstein-Rieger, Ibid.*; Luzzatto, *Urbino*, p. 25; A. Medini e G. Tolomei, *Per la storia anedottica dell' universita di Padova*, 1911, p. 94 ff.

leather as well.[1] It is noteworthy that some Jewish merchants in the fifteenth century advanced payments to silkworm growers against the anticipated product that the growers were obligated to sell them.[2] There was thus a fusion of the loan business and trade, which was possibly far more widespread than is apparent from the sources. In contrast, we have only sporadic information about Jews who dealt in furniture, iron, soap, and various food staples. It is thus difficult to determine their relative significance within the framework of Jewish economic life.[3]

Although Jewish trade did not penetrate the Italian economy very extensively, there were, nevertheless, periodic complaints by Christian merchants that they were unable to withstand Jewish competition. These complaints resulted from the temporary concentration in Jewish hands of a specific branch of a trade in a given city. In Mantua, for example, in 1477 there were so many Jews who dealt in textiles that Christian merchants considered themselves imperiled. In Rome too, Christians complained that Jews held monopolies in several branches of trade and had too much influence in price fixing.[4] In the city of Venice all sorts of devices were utilized to restrict Jewish trade. Jews were forbidden to sell their wares retail outside of the ghetto or to bring them to market places or fairs. Even the Jewish trade in used articles was periodically attacked. Ultimately, however, the *strazzaria* was recognized as a Jewish "business," but only Ashkenazim and Italiani were permitted to deal in it. Levantine and Sephardic Jews were permitted to deal only in the wholesale trade.[5] Matters were far more serious in Padua, the only city wherein a substantial part of its Jews earned its livelihood from trade. As early as 1502 the city council complained that

[1] *Ciscato,* p. 106.
[2] See R. Strauss, *Die Juden im Koenigreich Sizilien,* Heidelberg 1910, p. 37, Note 57.
[3] See Morpurgo, *Padua,* p. 6; *Ferorelli,* p. 127; Ferorelli's information is based upon sources that refer to sporadic cases. See *Ibid.,* Notes 8-17.
[4] Colorni, *Magistrature maggiori,* p. 11; Milano, *Roma,* pp. 7, 12.
[5] Roth, *Venice,* pp. 173, 176.

Jewish merchants were so numerous that the position of the Christian merchants was being undermined. With the advance of the sixteenth century and the further development of Jewish trade, propaganda by Christian merchants increased. As a result, in 1558 Jews were forbidden to engage in trade except for the *strazzaria*. The Jews did not despair but petitioned the central government of the Venetian Republic to annul the ban. The Jewish merchants had powerful allies in Christian society. The many students of the university in Padua strongly demanded that the ban be annulled. And the ban was, indeed, revoked.

A new attempt to ban Jewish trade in Padua was launched in 1571, when a wave of anti-Jewish feelings and demands for the expulsion of the Jews had swept over the Venetian Republic. We have no exact knowledge how long the trade ban was in effect this time. However, when the *condotta* was renewed for all Jews of the Venetian Republic in 1581, Jewish trade was again permissible in Padua. An attempt one year later to bar Jews from dealing in new furniture was not successful, and with the close of the Period, Jewish trade in Padua was flourishing.[1]

The local Paduan authorities who in 1558 decreed the ban upon Jewish trade were probably inspired by the anti-Jewish bull promulgated by Pope Paul IV in 1555, which, among other things, forbade the Jews to engage in trade. To be sure, when the pope's wrath abated he qualified his intent by disclaiming any effort to deprive Jews of all sources of livelihood; he only meant to remove them from trade in primary staples to prevent the cultivation of ordinary relationships between them and the Christians. After ten years the bull was modified somewhat and Jews were permitted to engage in peddling and several other minor areas of trade, and in some crafts.[2] But Jewish trade never completely recovered from the blow it received from the bull, at least in the Papal States.

[1] *Ciscato*, pp. 97, 111-115; Morpurgo, *Padua*, p. 6.
[2] Milano, *Ibid*.

b.

Against this changing background, Jewish merchants
succeeded in establishing a firm hold over two specific areas of
trade, import and export and precious stones and metals.
The reawakened social life and the efforts by the many
Renaissance princes to refine their daily life created a great
demand for jewelry and precious stones. The rising participation of women in court life further intensified the quest for
jewels. The demand for jewelry among Jews, too, reached such
proportions that special communal ordinances had to be
issued to limit it.

A certain quantity of precious stones came into the possession of Jewish moneylenders in the form of unredeemed
pledges. This, incidentally, led to the development among
them of a high degree of expertise in this field. We have a
great deal of information regarding Jews in Urbino, Florence,
Padua, and Mantua who dealt in precious metals and stones.
Most prominent in the trade, however, were Venetian Jews.
Four times during the sixteenth century attempts were made
to bar Jews from the precious stones trade in Venice. The
fact that the ban had to be reinstituted indicates the impossibility of eliminating the Jews from this field. During the entire
second half of the sixteenth century Mantua Jewish merchants
were sent by the dukes to Venice to purchase precious stones
in their behalf. Jews also imported precious stones from the
Orient into Italy and broadened this aspect of the trade
immensely. The Volterra family of Florence who engaged in
this business amassed in the mid-fifteenth century a fortune
of one hundred thousand ducats. Once, we are told, they
were visited by "a great dealer (a Jew) in precious stones"
from Egypt.[1]

In response to the need of Jewish merchants, guides to the
jewelry business were written in Hebrew. In 1571 Meshullam

---

[1] Luzzatto, *Urbino*, p. 26; Cassuto, *Florence*, p. 407; *Meshullam
da Volterra's Travelogue*, ed. Yaari, Jerusalem 1949, pp. 54, 58;
L. Schiavi, *Gli ebrei in Venezia*, p. 506; Medini e Tolomei, *Ibid.*;
Ciscato, p. 100.

da Volterra of Pesaro [1] wrote a book that included "coin
tariffs and the value of precious stones and pearls and many
kinds of gold and silver coins". This book, highly regarded by
experts, also described in detail the procedure of silver and
gold casting.[2] Several decades later the renowned scholar
Abraham Portaleone devoted a part of his remarkable work
Shilte hagibborim to lengthy descriptions of precious stones,
their lands of origin, and their "special qualities". This was
accompanied by a kind of catalogue of all precious stones with
detailed information about each of them. The author "carefully
searched in many cities" for the price lists that he published
and which served as a guide to the purchaser and the seller in
their negotiations. To make his price lists truly accurate and
practical he listed the prices of diamonds as they were on the
first day of the month of Shebat, 1606.[3] Much of his information the author borrowed from Meshullam da Volterra's book,
but he also conducted his own investigations in the entire
relevant literature and among diamond dealers, and gave a
complete description of all aspects of this trade.

Jewish wholesale trade, especially importation from foreign
countries, achieved truly grand proportions. Not only was
there no resistance to Jews in this field, but they were, on the
contrary, officially invited to some places on condition that
they engage in foreign trade. As we have seen, many pawnbroking combines were also involved in the wholesale trade.[4]
There were, however, several big merchants who were exclusively engaged in the wholesale and import business. When
Spanish and Portuguese Marranos came to Venice, they were
permitted to settle there only on condition that they conduct a
wholesale trade.[5] In Southern Italy many large scale Jewish
merchants maintained warehouses in the seaports and had
business contacts with many cities. They controlled so many

---

[1] *Shilte hagibborim*, beginning of Chapter 56.
[2] Abraham Portaleone considered him a great expert in precious
stones. See *Ibid.*
[3] *Ibid.*, p. 49b; p. 59.
[4] Luzzatto, *Urbino*, p. 25 ff.
[5] Roth, *Venice*, p. 67.

enterprises that numerous officials and agents [1] were continuously in their employ. There were also Jewish purveyors
who accompanied the Italian armies. When we consider that
this was a period of many wars that were waged throughout
the peninsula, this business obviously was of significant scope.

The following details will further illuminate the scope of the
Jewish import and export trade. Isaac Abravanel of Ferrara,
grandson of Don Isaac, used to keep merchandise in Alexandria, Egypt and had a special overseer there to supervise his
affairs.[2] The right of the Levantine Jews in Venice to engage
in foreign trade was expressly guaranteed in 1541 when they
entered the "old" Ghetto. The Venetian Senate also formally
resolved that most foreign imports were to be managed by
Jewish merchants.[3] Significantly, Mantuan Jewish merchants
had contacts with the German imperial court and had received
a permit from the king of France "to travel (through) his
kingdom's cities to trade".[4]

The good reputation of the Jewish merchants saved them
from expulsion from the port city of Ancona when Jews were
expelled from the Papal States in 1569, "...because they are
all businessmen... and there is business and trade in all
lands, and especially in Turkey, and where merchandising is
carried on Jews have great repute".[5] In 1572 Prince Emmanuele Filiberto of Piedmont granted permission to Jews to
come and settle in his land to develop trade, although he
hated them.[6] As far as we know no new Jewish community
was established in Piedmont on the basis of this invitation,
probably because of its distance from the sea. However, the
new Jewish settlement that was established in the port city of
Leghorn in Tuscany on the basis of the charter known as *La
Livornina*,[7] became a major Jewish community. The glorious

[1] *Ferorelli*, p. 128.
[2] *Responsa of Rabbi Isaac de Lattes*, p. 24 ff.
[3] Roth, *op. cit*, pp. 62, 176.
[4] *Shalshelet haḳabbalah*, p. 70 and *Emeḳ habaka*, p. 123.
[5] *Hamagiha*, p. 159.
[6] *REJ* 5:231 ff.
[7] See G. Sonnino, *Storia della tipografia ebraica in Livorno*, Turin
1912, p. 3.

Leghorn community began to develop after the close of the
Renaissance Period. But its foundation was rooted in the
economic policy of the Italian states which evolved during the
Renaissance.

Finally it should be noted that a part of Italian Jewry
earned its livelihood in the book business, as a book market
of major proportions developed among both Christians and
Jews. A detailed description of this business area will be given
below in a chapter dealing with books and libraries.

CHAPTER THREE

CRAFTSMEN, WORKERS, AND MANUFACTURERS

In addition to moneylenders and merchants the Jewish
population also had a working class. Although the paucity of
sources makes it hard to fully determine its scope, it was
apparently significant. Numerically the workers class approxi-
mated that of the merchants. In some places the laborers and
artisans constituted an important part of the Jewish population. As in trade, the Jews tended to concentrate in specific
branches in the labor field too. A geographical survey reveals
that Jewish laborers were numerous in Sicily and Southern
Italy, and also quite significant in the center of the peninsula.
In Northern Italy, however, their number was small.

As early as the thirteenth century there were so many
Jewish craftsmen in Southern Italy that a prominent historian [1] concluded from the sources that they constituted the
bulk of the kingdom's working class. A similar situation
prevailed in Sicily. Rabbi Obadiah da Bertinoro who visited
the island in 1488 reported that in Messina all four hundred
Jewish family heads were craftsmen.[2] This situation explains
why the island's high officials petitioned king Ferdinand to
postpone the expulsion of the Jews decreed by him in 1492.
They argued that virtually all craftsmen were Jews and their
exodus would create a grave shortage in manpower.[3]

[1] See Strauss, *Ibid.*, p. 93.
[2] See *Iggerot Erez Yisrael*, p. 108.
[3] *Guedemann*, vol. 2, p. 259 ff.

Important information regarding Jewish craftsmen in Rome and its environs is available as well. In 1449 a German knight visited Rome and in his travelogue he noted that there were craftsmen among Roman Jews.[1] Obviously they were numerous enough to attract the attention of a foreign visitor. A partial list of the Jewish population in 1527 [2] also reveals a relatively large number of craftsmen among them. A similar situation apparently prevailed in the small towns in the vicinity where there was a relatively large Jewish population. The Jews of Cori, numbering several hundred souls, tried to emigrate to Palestine in accordance with the emigration plan of Don Joseph Nasi. They justified their request on grounds that as artisans they were eligible for his settlement program.[3] At the beginning of the sixteenth century the city council of Padua complained that "soon" every craftsman in the city will be Jewish.[4] Even allowing for the usual exaggeration of opponents, the complaint indicates that also in Northern Italy the number of Jewish craftsmen was significant. The craftsmen class was further augmented by a number of Spanish-Jewish artisans who came to Italy in the 1492 expulsion.[5] There were some craftsmen among the German immigrants as well.[6]

Like the moneylenders and businessmen, the Jewish artisans also were subjected to a changing policy on the part of the governments. Governmental interest manifested itself when in 1492 the king of Naples ordered his officials to register the craftsmen among the Spanish exiles who entered his domain.[7] When in 1572 Duke Emmanuele Filiberto invited the Jews to settle in Piedmont, he explicitly promised to

[1] M. Stern, *Stellung der Paepste*, Part 1, p. 49.
[2] Livi, *Ibid.*, p. 136, Cf. Note 3 on p. 133 that Livi's conclusions are not fully reliable.
[3] *JQR* 2:306. Also published in *Graetz-Rabinowitz*, vol. 7, p. 420.
[4] *Ciscato*, p. 98.
[5] Ferorelli, *Immigrazione etc.*, p. 7 published a document in which the king of Naples instructed his officials to register the occupations (*artificio*) of the Spanish exiles who entered his land.
[6] *Responsa of Rabbi Ḥayim Or Zarua*, Leipzig 1860, p. 41.
[7] See Note 5.

allow them to engage in all crafts.[1] Curiously, however, opposition to Jewish craftsmen appeared in the Republic of Venice which was generally friendly to its Jews. Periodic orders were issued banning Jews from working as weavers, printers, and goldsmiths. Venetian authorities were especially adamant regarding tailoring by Jews,[2] and Padua concurred.[3] The Jewish crafts came under fire in Central Italy when Pope Paul IV started his anti-Jewish policy and banned Jews from all occupations. The Jews of Cori specifically asserted that not only were they not permitted to engage in the trade of new garments and food staples, but "(we) are not even able to pursue our work as craftsmen". The pope's decree was later revised and Jews were permitted to engage in a fairly wide variety of crafts.[4]

Governmental opposition to Jews in the tailoring craft was especially serious, because Jews controlled a substantial part of the used clothes business and the Christians feared lest the Jews dominate the garment industry completely. Jewish tailors were very numerous and could be found everywhere.[5] Many Jews were also engaged in weaving[6] and dyeing,[7] which was a "Jewish" craft in virtually every Mediterranean country.[8]

---

[1] *REJ* 5:231 ff.

[2] See Roth, *Venice*, pp. 172, 173, 182, and J. Bloch, *Venetian Printers of Hebrew Books*, New York, 1932 p. 21. The ban of 1571 on Jewish printing was part of the anti-Jewish policy occasioned by the Cyprus War which, the Venetians suspected, was launched by Turkey at the instigation of influential Jews.

[3] *Ciscato*, p. 108. All the *condotte* of the second half of the sixteenth century persistently reiterated the ban on the tailoring trade.

[4] See Milano, Roma, pp. 11-12.

[5] Jewish tailors were found in the Papal States (Livi, *Ibid.*), in Southern Italy (*Ferorelli*, p. 125), Urbino (Luzzatto, *Urbino*, p. 26), Venice (Roth, *Venice*, p. 173), and Padua (*Ciscato, Ibid.*).

[6] There were Jewish weavers in the Papal States (Milano, *Roma, Ibid.*), Southern Italy (*Ferorelli, Ibid.*), Venice (Roth, *Venice, Ibid.*, p. 172).

[7] Jewish dyers worked in Southern Italy (*Ferorelli, Ibid.*, p. 129) and in Padua (*Ciscato*, p. 128).

[8] Cf. for example, Benjamin of Tudela's report about Jews of Jerusalem who annually "purchased" the dye works from the king "to assure that no one but Jews should do any dyeing in Jerusalem"

Most Jewish apprentices evidently learned the craft from Jewish tailors. In the Roman archives many agreements are still kept in which Jewish parents of the Renaissance Period apprenticed their sons to Jewish tailors. One of these agreements stipulated [1] that the boy had to spend with the master a period of 3 years. The tailor received no compensation for his instruction and even obligated himself to provide most of the pupil's needs. The pupil's chief obligation was to accompany the tailor to any place that he desired to go. Apparently this was a case of an itinerant tailor who journeyed through villages and towns to sew in the homes of his customers. Curiously, an artisan could be found even in the family of a famous scholar and author. In 1605, we learn, Judah, the son of Abraham Portaleone, began "to perfect his hands in the silk craft".[2]

Jewish involvement in the jewelry trade was accompanied by the entrance of many Jews into the profession of gold and silversmiths.[3] We find Jewish gold and silversmiths all throughout the Period in diverse places, in large cities and small ones. In some places they were quite numerous. Such must have been the case in Mantua where in 1612 we find "a street of Jewish goldsmiths", or in Turin where the guild of Christian goldsmiths in 1623 resolved to bar Jews from membership. There were also many Jewish goldsmiths in the Papal States. Their work, too, was banned by Pope Paul IV and made legal again after his death. In contrast, the Venice government systematically harassed Jewish gold and silversmiths, as it generally opposed the Jewish jewelry trade. Jewish achievement in the jewelry craft is further demonstrated by the reputation of various Jewish masters and by the employment

(ed. Asher, vol. 1, p. 34 ff.). An Ashkenazic Jew who lived in South Italy in 1446 taught the dyeing craft to someone who, to judge by his name, was apparently a Christian.

[1] See Berliner, *Rome*, vol. 2, part 1, p. 102. He published the text in *Kobez al jad*, 1893, Section *Sarid meir*, p. 5.

[2] *JQR* 4:337 ff.

[3] The description of the Jewish metal craftsmen is based upon the following sources: *RMI* 9:238; Osimo, *Ibid.*, p. 28, Note 9; *Ferorelli*, pp. 73, 125; Anfosi, *Ibid.*, p. 49; Milano, *Roma*, p. 12; Roth, *Venice*, p. 182.

of some of them in princely courts. Some Jewish craftsmen also produced beautiful Passover plates of majolica.[1]

Jews were represented in various other crafts as well. To be sure, the available information is sparse and fragmentary. For example, the Medici in Florence were involved in a plan to bring Jewish experts to the city to produce saltpeter, needed for explosives. We also know that South Italy had Jewish *"mastri de arte mechanica"*. [2] In Sicily and in Central Italy Jewish blacksmiths and carpenters were numerous, it seems. In the middle of the fifteenth century the government even appointed a chief of the Jewish carpenters in Palermo.[3] In 1488 Rabbi Obadia da Bertinoro found Jewish blacksmiths in the same city. In Rome too, there was a sizable number of Jewish carpenters and blacksmiths. A solitary carpenter was also found in the tiny community of Asolo where less than forty Jews lived.

The Italian publishing houses, Jewish as well as Christian, provided considerable opportunities for Jewish workers. In Italy Hebrew printing developed early and flourished. The Jewish publishers printed large quantities of books to provide for local needs and to fill part of the demand for Hebrew books in other countries as well. All this provided work opportunities in a number of areas such as typesetting, proof reading, and binding. Christian publishers, too, who printed Hebrew books needed Jewish workers for typesetting and proofreading. A sort of class of Jewish printing workers [4] began to emerge, whose members would travel to distant places to work in newly established printing houses. Even when the Venetian government banned Jews from engaging in printing,[5] the ban in effect applied only to publishers. Jewish typesetters and

---

[1] See the article by F. Landsberger, *HUCA* 16:373.

[2] See Cassuto, *Florence*, p. 416; *Ferorelli*, p. 127.

[3] The description of the iron and wood crafts is based on the following: Milano, *Roma*, p. 12; Livi, *Ibid.*; *Iggerot Erez Yisrael*, p. 104; Osimo, *Ibid.*, p. 28, Note 9; Cf. *Lagumina*, vol. I, pp. 504, 505.

[4] See J. Bloch, *Hebrew Printing in Riva di Trento*, New York 1933, p. 8, Note 27.

[5] See J. Bloch, *Venetian Printers of Hebrew Books*, New York 1932, p. 21 and Roth, *Venice*, p. 261.

printers continued to work in Christian publishing houses, since publication was impossible without them.[1]

Another area in which a large number of Jews earned their livelihood was food production where dietary laws necessitated their exclusive employment. Jewish bakers and butchers are mentioned among the many occupations of South Italian Jews. In Rome there was even a *capo degli azimatori*, probably the head of a guild of *mazot* bakers. [2] In Northern Italy we find Jews who distilled liquor and owned dining places.[3]

Although most Jews lived in cities and towns, farming as an occupation was practiced among them throughout the Period. A number of Jews were owners of farm land.[4] In Padua at the end of the fourteenth century several Jews purchased land to work it. We encounter a Jewish farmer in Southern Italy, and the 1527 roster of Roman Jewry lists one farmer among the one hundred and four families enumerated. Fishing is also mentioned as one of the occupations open to Jews in the Papal States in 1566.[5] Among Sicilian Jews farming was pursued by the refugees of the island of Djerba. They cultivated palm trees and various other plants.[6]

Besides the crafts, industrial enterprise occupied a certain, though limited, place in the economic life of Renaissance Jewry. Silk production was one area in which Jews were prominent. In Calabria they virtually monopolized the industry and also had a substantial share of it in other districts of the Kingdom of Naples. The group of sixteenth century Jews in Bologna that called itself "the partners who do silk work", and the Roman family Della Seta ("of the silk") no doubt were involved in the manufacture of silk. Most prominent in silk production was the Venetian Jew Magino di

---

[1] See Roth's article in *Journal of Jewish Studies* 4:116.

[2] *Ferorelli*, p. 125; *Vogelstein-Rieger*, vol. 2, p. 119.

[3] *Israel*, of March 17, 1932; *Invernizzi*, p. 23; Moses A. Shulvass, *In the Grip of Centuries*, p. 103 ff.

[4] For example, see the Introduction of David dei Pomis to his work *Ẓemaḥ David*, available in *Neppi Ghirondi*, p. 86.

[5] *Ciscato*, p. 21; *Livi*, p. 136; Milano, *Roma*, p. 12; *Ferorelli*, p. 126, Note 1.

[6] *Guedemann*, vol. 2, p. 287.

Gabriele to whom Pope Sixtus V granted permission to manufacture silk by his own secret formula which produced a silk harvest twice a year. A year later Magino published a book that dealt with the benefits of cultivating silkworms.[1] An unsuccessful attempt at manufacturing textiles was made by a Paduan Jew in the beginning of the fifteenth century.[2] But clothing and leather factories founded by Jewish financiers of Urbino about the same time were quite successful. A true contribution to Italian industry was made by Jews in Leghorn late in the sixteenth century. They founded two prospering soap factories and laid the foundations for the coral industry that made Leghorn famous in a later period.[3]

CHAPTER FOUR

THE HUMANISTS

The humanists constituted a separate class within Jewish society. Jewish society, reflecting the Christian pattern, had many men who were obsessed with the new zest for learning that captivated the people of the Renaissance. They did not fit into any class in Jewish society, and they were perpetually plagued by economic instability. Their material existence depended mainly upon the support given by the wealthy to research and to literary creativity.

Among the Jews the humanists were patronized primarily by the bankers. Early in the Period Immanuel of Rome spoke explicitly of the "magnate" under whose protection he lived and whose friendship served as a backdrop for his great literary work. The insecurity of the humanist and his perpetual wanderings from place to place were clearly painful to Immanuel, as we see in his complaint: "And I destined myself to walk at the head of wanderers and to diligently (knock) at

[1] Strauss, *Ibid.*, p. 70 ff.; Guedemann, *Ibid.*, p. 68; Preface of the proofreader to the *mahazor* with the commentary *Ḳimḥa deabishuna*, Bologna 1541; Milano, *Roma*, p. 15; Berliner, *Rome*, vol. 2, part 1, p. 23.

[2] *Ciscato*, p. 121.

[3] Luzzatto, *Urbino*, p. 25 ff.; Sonino, *Ibid.*, p. 15.

the gates of aristocrats..." [1] His contemporary Kalonymos ben Kalonymos, the celebrated humanist who came to Italy from Provence, also deplored his unstable life in a hymn to "Those who dwell in houses". [2] The humanists were not only compelled to wander about; they were despised by many people who regarded them as a troublesome, unstable crowd. Even a famous scholar from whom sympathy might be expected referred to them as "completely corrupt, not one of them does any good...they are all like lost sheep...their ways are twisted and devious". [3] Their social position was further worsened by their constant need to flatter "the patrons." The prefaces that the humanists wrote to their books contain many pages of servile flattery. Elijah Baḥur reports the "generally accepted custom [that] requires any author to dedicate his book to one of the great magnates". Leon da Modena who lived about a century later reports the same custom of dedicating a book as a gift "to one's magnate". [4] Even a scholar who served as regional rabbi in the Marche district was completely dependent upon his patron's favors. With great servility and strong pleas he besought him to recommend to the regional *waad* the renewal of his appointment.[5] Relations with the "patron" were so important in the life of the humanists, that they were reflected everywhere in their writings and especially in their beautifully composed letters.

And yet, despite a marginal social position, constant wandering, and lack of economic security, the humanists cherished their calling. Even Kalonymos ben Kalonymos once vigorously defended "the wanderlust that came over him". [6] For there was much in the humanists' life style that was attractive. First and foremost they were drawn into aristocratic circles where a brilliant and free new life was developing. Contemp-

---

[1] *Maḥberot Immanuel*, p. 21.

[2] *Kobeẓ al jad*, N. S., 1:101.

[3] Samuel Archivolti, *Maayan ganim*, p. 26b.

[4] See the Introduction to Elijah Baḥur, *Sefer zikronot*, Paris 1875 and Leon da Modena's Introduction to *Midbar Yehudah*, Venice 1602.

[5] Sonne, *Hatekufah*, p. 655 ff.

[6] *Kobeẓ al jad*, *Ibid.*, Note 20a.

orary rabbis took under consideration the fact that Jewish
humanists frequented the courts of princes and kings and,
therefore, generally permitted them to wear the *cappa*, which
was ordinarily worn by Christian scholars.[1]

The group that supported Jewish humanists included the
wealthiest families such as Da Pisa, Rieti, Sullam, Abravanel,
and Norsa. The humanist's formal position was generally that
of private tutor to family members. However, he received
approximately double the wages paid to a teacher in a middle
class Jewish home. When Joseph da Arli accepted a position in
the home of the magnate Menahem da Monte del Olmo, he
joyfully informed his friends that "my wages are one hundred
scudi, two loads of wheat and wine, and a proper home for my
wife, and my dear only son and I are his (the patron's) dinner
guests."[2] Joseph's predecessor in Menahem's service was Rabbi
Isaac de Lattes, one of the great scholars of the Period. Among
the humanists employed by other Jewish magnates we find
Jacob Mantino, Jochanan Treves, Solomon dei Rossi, Jochanan
Alemanno, and Rabbi Azriel Diena.[3] They were all famous
scholars and authors.

Jewish humanists achieved great success in princely courts
as well. The men of the Renaissance realized that the success
of their efforts at reconstructing the culture of the Antiquity
depended upon their knowledge of the classical languages.
Thus, in addition to the wide demand for teachers of Greek
and Latin there arose a genuine, if limited, need for teachers
of Hebrew and ancient Hebrew literature. Obviously, the
majority of such teachers came from among the Jewish
humanists, who in typical Renaissance fashion easily overcame the doubts over the permissibility of teaching Torah to
non-Jews (see below, Section VIII, Chapter 3). There was also

[1] *Responsa of Rabbi Joseph Colon*, par. 68; Cf. Moses A. Shulvass,
In the Grip of Centuries, p. 56 ff.
[2] These names appear in most of the sources relating to the humanists; Sonne, *Hatekufah*, p. 677.
[3] Responsa of Rabbi Isaac de Lattes, pp. 121, 141; Marx, *Moses
Schorr Memorial Volume*, p. 205; Solomon dei Rossi, *Hashirim
asher lishelomoh*, new ed., Frankfort 1925, Introduction; *Pahad
Yizhak*, entry *haliza kodemet*, p. 22a; *Tarbiz* 8:176; *EJ*, entry on
Jochanan Alemanno.

a great demand for Latin translations from the Arabic literature, which preserved essential parts of classical culture during the Middle Ages. Here, too, Jewish humanists performed a major task. To begin with, even before the start of the Period Jewish translators occupied an important position in the court of Emperor Frederic II in Sicily. Somewhat later several Jewish translators were employed in the court of King Roberto the Wise in Naples, among whom were Judah ben Daniel of Rome and Kalonymos ben Kalonymos. Similarly, Jochanan Alemanno and Abraham Farissol were seen in the courts of North Italian rulers, like Luigi III Gonzaga of Mantua (1444-1478), Lorenzo the Magnificent, and Federico II of Urbino. Pope Nicholas V also used the services of a Jewish scholar, Enoch of Ascoli in his efforts to collect old books. Cardinal Egidio da Viterbo achieved special renown in this respect by keeping in his palace for a number of years Elijah Bahur, the most popular teacher of the Hebrew language to gentiles. It is noteworthy that Germany's most celebrated humanist Johann Reuchlin studied the Hebrew language and literature in Rome under the tutelage of Rabbi Obadiah Sforno, known for his commentary to the Bible. He paid one ducat daily as a tuition fee, a handsome sum in those days.[1] Some Jewish scholars received financial aid from Christian philanthropists even without having rendered to them any specific service in return. Such was the case with Joseph Hagri who was supported by Cardinal Egidio and the priest Magliano.[2]

A certain number of Jewish scholars served as professors in various Italian universities.[3] Although only about ten names

[1] According to Melanchthon in one of his addresses. See *Vogelstein-Rieger*, vol. 2, p. 78.

[2] Catalogue Kaufmann, p. 101; the Introductions of Elijah Bahur to *Sefer habahur* and *Masoret hamasoret* (both books have been published many times). Strauss, *Ibid.*, p. 91; *Kobez al jad*, N. S. 1:96; I. Perles, *Beitraege zur Geschichte der hebraeischen und aramaeischen Studien*, Munich 1884, pp. 200, 203; *Natali*, p. 186; Cassuto, *Florence*, pp. 189, 303, Note 5. Cf. below Section VIII, Chapter 5.

[3] For Jewish professors in Italy see: *Shalshelet hakabbalah*, p. 92 (Abraham de Balmes); *EJ*, vol. 6, p. 959 (Abraham Zarfadi); *Natali*, p. 189 (Jacob Mantino); *Cenni storici*, p. 53 (Magister Elia, who was a professor in Pavia in 1440); C. Roth, *A History of the Marranos*, Philadelphia 1941, p. 77; Marx, *Ginsberg Jubilee Volume*, Hebrew

of such professors are known of the entire three century period, their number was undoubtedly much larger. The majority were teachers of medicine, which is readily under-standable in view of the large Jewish role in the Italian medical profession (see below, Section VIII, Chapter 8). Their number increased sharply after 1500 when many Jewish physicians among the Spanish and Portuguese exiles were appointed as teachers in various universities, in Padua, Ferrara, Pavia, Rome, Pesaro, and Naples. The Jewish professors seem to have been held in great esteem. When Abraham de Balmes, who was a professor in Padua, died, "all his Christian students joined the funeral procession". [1] According to local tradition, Rabbi Judah Minz served as a philosophy professor in Padua. A nineteenth century local rabbi asserted that Judah's Christian students "made their teacher's statue for the university", and that it was still standing in its place.[2] It seems that a professorship was worth attaining from a financial viewpoint as well. One sixteenth century scholar who was trying to obtain an appointment in the University of Pisa was assured by his sponsors that "his wage would equal that of the other *dottori*". [3]

The lack of economic security forced the humanists to engage in many unrelated occupations. Abraham Farissol, for example, who was a noted author, earned his livelihood as a copyist and cantor.[4] Solomon of Poggibonsi was first a pawnbroker, later a clerk in a pawnshop, and finally a teacher and copyist.[5] Jacob Marcaria, a physician and noted rabbi, owner of a Hebrew printing house in Riva di Trento, also

section, p. 30; it is likely that Messer Leon also served as a professor in various universities. He wrote boastfully of himself "and who is the one who lectures in the great houses of learning among many nations . . ." (See Moses A. Shulvass, *In the Grip of Centuries*, p. 61).

[1] *Shalshelet hakabbalah, Ibid.*

[2] Mordecai Samuel Ghirondi who (Neppi-Ghirondi, p. 122) gives the information, states explicitly "I myself have seen it (the statue) placed there (in the University of Padua) on the stairway, with an inscription of high praise".

[3] Marx, *Ibid.*

[4] See Simḥah Bamberger's Introduction to Farissol's commentary on *Ecclesiastes, Kobez al jad*, N. S. 2:3 ff.

[5] See Cassuto, *Florence*, p. 335 ff.

engaged in matchmaking for a livelihood.[1] In a more effective manner the talents of the humanists were used in the service of the Jewish community, especially as scribes and secretaires.[2]

The most multi-employed of all humanists was Leon da Modena, the last and most articulate of the breed. His memoirs list the twenty-six occupations that he practiced,[3] including all humanistic vocations described above. He tutored both Jewish and Christian children, and served as a preacher, cantor, and judge. He wrote all types of legal documents, letters, approbations, occasional poems, and amulets.[4] He also sold nostrum books and worked as a broker and matchmaker. Such conduct, naturally enraged the more "stable" humanists. Perhaps Samuel Archivolti's [5] sharp rebuke of tutors who also engaged in writing phylacteries and *mezuzot*, editing books,[6] and writing all kinds of documents were directed against his pupil Leon da Modena, in whom most of the humanists' virtues and faults blended.

The multiple occupations of the humanists led to frequent strife resulting from competition. For example, the many arguments between Elijah Baḥur and Hillel Kohen resulted

[1] Tarbiz 8:65.
[2] See *Maḥberot Immanuel*, p. 658 ff., p. 689 ff.; Leon da Modena's Introduction to *Midbar Yehudah*; *HUCA* 1:605 ff.; Sonne, *Kobez al jad*, N. S. 3:167.
[3] *Sepher Chaje Jehuda*, p. 64 ff.
[4] Leon da Modena's grandson Isaac Levita, who generally followed in his grandfather's footsteps, was disturbed by the stories of his grandfather's involvement in amulet traffic. In the Introduction to *Magen waḥereb* he claims that his grandfather "was expert in amulets and mysteries but did not make use of them". Regarding amulets there is an interesting note by an anonymous in the manuscript of the book *Belil ḥamiz* (by Joseph Chamiz, a pupil of Leon da Modena) which is kept in the library of the Jewish Theological Seminary in New York: "I knew this man (apparently Joseph Chamiz) in 1620 in Venice, may the Most High protect her. He made use of the *hayot ḥakodesh* to write amulets for non-Jews to be encased in copper containers that they might have their way with harlots". This note hints at the sad results of the readiness by the humanists to place their knowledge at the service of any person or purpose.
[5] *Maayan ganim*, p. 26b ff.
[6] This refers to Jewish censors who were employed by publishers to "expurgate" Hebrew books that they might pass the scrutiny of official Church censors. See below, Section VIII, Chapter 2.

from the fact that both were tutors in Venice. Elijah Baḥur vanquished his foe who apparently lacked the crucial weapon of the humanist, a sharp, biting tongue. Elijah wrote calumnies against his opponent in which he publicly revealed intimate details of his life and appended them to a wall for the widest possible audience.[1] Quite illuminating is a quarrel between Leon da Modena and his teacher Samuel Archivolti. Leon argued that he was about to publish a textbook "to teach our people how to write in Hebrew" and that he had revealed his plan to his teacher ten years earlier. Suddenly he was informed that Archivolti was also preparing such a textbook. He was, therefore, trying to prevent his teacher from carrying out his project. He also used the occasion to accuse his teacher of having copied his (Modena's) ideas in the work *Arugat habosem*.[2]

The main humanistic occupations were teaching and book copying, the latter especially in the first half of the Period. Although the upper social strata preferred written to printed books for a long time,[3] the number of Hebrew manuscript copyists diminished appreciably from about 1500.[4] A recently prepared list of Italian Jewish copyists who lived prior to 1500 contains about five hundred names, of which about four hundred and fifty belong to the period of 1300-1500.[5] Such a list is by necessity incomplete, and the actual number of copyists was much larger. Information regarding the remuneration paid to copyists is scarce.[6] It appears, however, that the sum of 37 florins and food paid in North Italy to a copyist who was engaged to transcribe the Talmud, was the

---

[1] Such as the poem *Hamabdil, Tsaytshrift* 1:150.

[2] *Leo Modenas Briefe*, Number 159. Leon da Modena's plaint was not justified, since Samuel Archivolti published the guide for letter writing *Maayan ganim* in 1553, eighteen years prior to Modena's birth.

[3] *Burckhardt*, p. 151.

[4] See Aaron Freimann in *Alexander Marx Jubilee Volume*, English section, p. 232, that upon the invention of the printing press many copyists turned to new occupations.

[5] Freimann, *Ibid.*, p. 231 ff.

[6] It is difficult to estimate the compensation paid to copyists because they generally were engaged to copy a given volume at an agreed price, and if they worked faster their earnings were naturally larger.

customary wage. In return the copyist had to work seven hours a day from Sunday through Wednesday and four hours on Thursday. He was apparently free of work on Friday.[1]

The compensation paid to tutors ranged from thirty-four to sixty ducats per year.[2] Teachers who received less than forty ducats, generally also received food. These wages, it seems, were paid in quarterly installments. The obligation of a certain tutor to teach four hours daily except on Fridays in return for an annual salary of 37 ducats and meals, seems to have been typical. Most tutors accepted one year contracts, although we know of one case with an engagement for three years. The number of pupils varied from one to five. We know of one tutor who lived at his pupils' home all week and returned to his family for the Sabbaths. Another tutor obligated himself to leave the city with his pupils if they had to move. A fifteenth century author asserted[3] that Jewish teachers were paid more than their Christian colleagues. According to him this was due to the fact that Christian humanists were supported by the magnanimous aristocrats to a greater degree than their Jewish counterparts. Jewish humanists thus had to earn a livelihood through a variety of unrelated and often bizarre occupations.

CHAPTER FIVE

CONCLUSIONS

In the preceding chapters we have described the economic character of the four classes of Renaissance Italian Jewry: moneylenders, merchants, craftsmen, and humanists. Numer-

---

[1] *REJ* 79:44.

[2] For teacher's working conditions see: Cassuto, *Florence*, pp. 187, 415; *Sepher Chaje Jehuda*, p. 32; *REJ, Ibid.*, p. 42; David Kaufmann in *Steinschneider Jubilee Volume*, p. 129; Rabbi Jacob Alpron (Heilpron), *Naḥalat Yaacob*, par. 14; Bernheimer, *Catalogue Leghorn*, pp. 55, 56; Berliner, *Rome*, vol. 2, part 1, p. 100. Since the information regarding tutorial earnings comes from various times and places throughout the Peninsula, we may assume that it reflects the average salary of humanists engaged in teaching.

[3] Rabbi Jacob Provenzal in *Ḳobeẓ dibre ḥakamim*, edited by Eliezer Ashkenazi, Mayence 1849, p. 73.

ically the humanists constituted the smallest group. In addition, there were also groups of physicians and artists, who will be discussed below. Obviously, these groups were also numerically limited. In general, it is difficult to arrive at firm conclusions regarding the proportionate position occupied by the various economic groups within Jewish society. We have seen above (Chapter 3 of this Section) that in Southern Italy there was a very large number of Jewish craftsmen and that the center of the peninsula also had a fairly strong working class. In Northern Italy, on the other hand, there were few artisans, since most of its Jews were German immigrants, whose majority were pawnbrokers. Jewish labor received a heavy blow when the great Jewish center in Naples was destroyed early in the Period. The number of Italy's Jewish craftsmen was further drastically reduced by the expulsion of the Jews from Sicily in 1492. Thenceforth Jewish labor centered mainly about Rome and its environs. The reduced number of Jewish craftsmen in the second half of the Period is manifested by the absence of Jewish artisans guilds and religio-cultural organizations.

Further examination indicates that there was also a number of Jews, possibly quite substantial, who belonged simultaneously to both the craftsmen and merchant classes. The fact that the greatest concentration of Jewish merchants was in retail clothing, and the greatest concentration of craftsmen was in tailoring, suggests that there were many tailors who themselves marketed their wares. Padua, for example, that in the North had the largest number of both Jewish merchants and craftsmen, may be indicative of such a situation. Jewish occupational dualism in Sicily is inferred in the report of Obadiah da Bertinoro that there were four hundred Jewish family heads "all craftsmen, some of whom were (also) merchants". [1]

Another problem that eludes clarification is the amount of capital in Jewish hands. We have seen that most of the loan bankers had modest resources. Nevertheless, information is available regarding great Jewish wealth in various cities.

[1] *Iggerot Erez Yisrael*, p. 108.

On the eve of the Period, in 1299, Pope Boniface VIII stated that the Roman Jews were wealthy.[1] Later in the Period Elijah Capsali, who arrived in the Republic of Venice a short time prior to the War of the League of Cambrai, was greatly impressed by the wealth of the Ashkenazic pawnbrokers. Yet, the wealth of the entire Del Banco family apparently did not exceed one hundred thousand ducats.[2] The same figure applied to the Da Pisa family, and the Volterra family, the largest dealers in precious stones.[3] At the end of the fifteenth century Jewish wealth increased as a result of the fortunes that Spanish exiles brought with them.[4] Less than twenty years later the wealth of Ashkenazic Jews in Northern Italy decreased sharply. The sacking of Padua during the War of the League of Cambrai caused a loss of one hundred and fifty thousand ducats to the Jews of that city.[5]

Jewish wealth reached its highest point during the sixteenth century, primarily as a result of the broadened international trade of the Sephardic Jews and the accumulated profits of the loanbank business that was more than two centuries old at that time. Jews of Bologna were known for their exceptional wealth, and the real estate alone of the Jews in the Papal States was assessed at a half a million florins.[6] The fact that Jews of Piedmont, Milan, Ferrara, and Mantua were prepared to expend ten thousand florins to obtain permission for the printing of the Talmud [7] also attests to their great wealth. The

[1] *Vogelstein-Rieger*, vol. 1, p. 280.

[2] Mendlin left an inheritance of fourteen thousand ducats in cash (exclusive of precious stones). His brother Ḥayim used to pay communal taxes based on an oath of wealth figured at twenty three thousand ducats (see *REJ* 79:36). Counting Anselmo, who was the wealthiest of the brothers, and other family members, their estate amounted to about one hundred thousand ducats.

[3] Roth, *History*, p. 111; *Meshullam da Volterra's Travelogue*, ed. A. Yaari, Jerusalem 1949, p. 58.

[4] Milano, *Roma*, p. 7.

[5] Morpurgo, *Padua*, p. 4, Note 3.

[6] *Hamagiha*, p. 158: "He (Pope Pius V) also had wicked designs upon the holy community of Bologna and coveted their money, for they were wealthy". *Shalshelet hakabbalah*, p. 174: ". . . and a reckoning was made that Jewish possessions in the state (the Pope's) then amounted to more than five hundred thousand crowns".

[7] M. Stern, *Stellung der Paepste*, vol. 1, p. 154.

wealthiest Jews were probably Samuel Abravanel and Elhanan of Fano, each of whom possessed about two hundred thousand florins.[1] However, in measuring these factors against what we have seen above regarding Jewish economic life, it must be concluded that Jewish wealth was concentrated in the hands of the few, while most Jews belonged to the middle class and had only modest resources.

There were also many poor Jews. The Sicilian Christians, who in 1492 petitioned the government to annul the expulsion decree against the Jews, explicitly wrote that there were very few rich Jews, not too many in the middle class, and that the rest of the Jewish population was composed of paupers.[2] Rabbi Obadiah da Bertinoro's description of the Jews of Palermo "who were porters and farm hands, despised by the non-Jews for their tattered and filthy appearance" [3] further indicates that most Sicilian Jews belonged to the proletariat. Several decades later it was reported that the Jews of Otranto, in the Kingdom of Naples, were poor. At the same time David Reubeni related that, except for Jehiel da Pisa, all other Jews in Pisa were poor.[4] In the second half of the sixteenth century the Jews of Cori stated that "we are all impoverished and indigent, we eat by the toil of our hands, and we earn bread by the sweat of our brow". [5] Only in the Ashkenazic North where most of the Jews were pawnbrokers or their agents and employees, was poverty not as widespread as in Southern or Central Italy.

---

[1] *Shalshelet hakabbalah*, p. 97. However, it must be considered that in the fifteenth and sixteenth centuries the value of money decreased. The fortunes of extremely wealthy Jews were more or less similar to those of their Christian peers. The banker Agostino Chigi who left an inheritance in 1520 of eight hundred thousand ducats was an exception. See Burckhardt, *Die Kultur der Renaissance in Italien*, 10-th edition, Leipzig 1908, Vol. 1, Appendix X, p. 324 ff.

[2] Guedemann, vol. 2, p. 264.

[3] *Iggerot Erez Yisrael*, p. 104.

[4] *HUCA*, 1:621; *Sippur David hareubeni*, p. 54.

[5] *JQR* 2:306.

SECTION IV

FAMILY AND SOCIAL LIFE

CHAPTER ONE

FAMILY LIFE

a.

The general picture of Jewish family life which emerges from the sources reflects the characteristic dualism that pervaded all facets of Renaissance Jewish society. On one hand, the Jewish family steadfastly clung to deeply rooted traditional patterns. On the other hand, throughout the entire Period we encounter individuals who attempted to destroy accepted family patterns to satisfy their romantic desires. They battled both the Jewish community and state law and often brought upon themselves untold suffering. They became victims of the Renaissance drive to tear down the barriers that separated man from man. Just as many Jews transgressed the law requiring the wearing of a Jewish badge despite harsh fines, so many Jews broke the traditional barrier between themselves and Christians in the area of sexual life despite the stiff opposition of both communities.

Dowry was an important factor in contracting marriages. Most of the Jewish community earned a livelihood as pawn-brokers and every young man who sought to establish a family needed a certain amount of capital. This fact is amply reflected in the Period's responsa literature which is replete with arguments over the financial aspects connected with the establishment of new families. These conditions naturally evoked complaints in various circles which looked upon marriage from a more idealistic point of view. Rabbi Judah Moscato, an outstanding preacher, once devoted a special sermon to the subject of "how to select a suitable wife who will help you achieve perfection".[1] Financial considerations in

[1] *Nefuẓot Yehudah*, Warsaw 1871, p. 63b, Sermon 26.

arranging marriages were even more disturbing to Rabbi
Aaron Berechiah of Modena, who represented the religio-moral
conscience of Renaissance Jewish society. In his book *Maabar
Jabbok* [1] he voiced bitter feelings over the practice that "a man
of wealth who had a daughter sought to have her marry the
son of a wealthy man; his immediate concern is money and
he marries off his daughter to money, not to a man..." He
further complained that "the daughter of a poor scholar would
remain (unmarried) until her hair turned white" since she
lacked a dowry. But these arguments could not overcome the
inevitabilities of life and the dowry became a crucial factor
in forming a family. A custom even arose to pay a promised
dowry in small installments over a long period of time.[2] It is
difficult to ascertain what could have been considered an
average dowry. The sums that are known vary widely, from
one hundred and sixty to one thousand ducats. It appears,
however, that the customary dowry figure ranged from three
hundred to five hundred ducats.[3]

Special problems included the betrothing of minor girls and
polygamy. Although Rabbi Judah Minz stated that the
Romaneschi (Italianic Jews) did not marry minor girls,[4] the
issue of marriages of minors appears quite frequently in the
responsa literature. It seems that the problem became more
acute in the sixteenth century. The Ferrara congress of 1554
forbade the performance of a marriage of a minor without a
quorum of ten and the consent of her relatives.[5] The fact that
the decision was accompanied by a threat of "excommunication against the groom and the witnesses", clearly indicates the
seriousness of the problem of minor girls who were married
without parental consent.

Cases of polygamy occurred periodically among the Italiani

[1] Lemberg 1876, p. 155b.
[2] *Responsa of Rabbi Joseph Colon*, par. 82: "In accordance with
our custom of obligating the parties to pay the dowry over a period of
time".
[3] See Vittore Colorni, *Annuario di studi ebraici*, 1:178; *Responsa
of Rabbi Judah Minz*, par. 2; *Kirjath sepher* 22:266 ff.
[4] *Responsa of Rabbi Judah Minz, Ibid.*
[5] *Finkelstein*, p. 302.

and Sephardim,[1] while the Ashkenazim abided by Rabbenu Gershom's ban on polygamy. To be sure, the Italiani also tried to limit the practice by explicit reference to the ban.[2] An eighteenth century historian of Sicilian Jewry theorized that the relatively large Jewish population on the island resulted from the practice of polygamy.[3] There is no proof, however, that this is correct. On the contrary, the fact that a Jew who wanted to take more than one wife had to receive special permission from the viceroy [4] indicates that there were very few incidents of polygamy. With regard to Italy proper Leon da Modena stated in his book *Historia de gli Riti Hebraici* that "only rarely does a man marry two wives, and then only after he has lived with his first wife many years without offspring".[5] A case of bigamy for the purpose of fulfilling the precept of natural increase is known to have occurred in 1555.[6] Isolated incidents of bigamy also occurred as a result of the Italianic custom permitting levirate marriages. One rabbi attests that this was an established Italianic practice, and others relate that they personally witnessed several such cases.[7]

Insufficient source material does not afford us a detailed description of betrothal customs, relations between the betrothed couple, or the marriage ceremony. However, some general pattern can be discerned. Relations between the betrothed couple were rather formal, tinged by the general esthetic trend of the Renaissance Period. Several love letters written by an ordinary man to his fiancee at the end of the Period are indicative of the esthetic character of this type of correspondence.[8] Samuel Archivolti in his letter writing guide

---

[1] A Sephardic groom obligated himself in the marriage contract neither to take another wife nor to forcibly divorce his first wife (see *Kirjath sepher, Ibid.*, p. 269). That is, the wife was assured of the same status a wife received among the Ashkenazim in accordance with Rabbenu Gershom's bans.

[2] Ferrara Congress. See *Finkelstein, Ibid.*

[3] *Giovanni de Giovanni*, p. 21.

[4] *Lagumina*, vol. 2, p. 469. Such permission was granted in 1490.

[5] Part 4, Chapter 2, par. 2.

[6] S. Assaf, *Meḳorot letoldot haḥinuk beyisrael*, vol. 4, Jerusalem 1943, p. 114, Note 4.

[7] See *Paḥad Yiẓḥaḳ*, entry *ḥaliẓah*, p. 21b and p. 24.

[8] *RMI* 1:40 ff.

Maayan ganim [1] devoted a special section to such correspondence. It was also an accepted practice in Italy for the fiancé to send his fiancée gifts,[2] despite the possible halakhic difficulties involved. That the wedding ceremony was a joyous and festive occasion is indicated by the fact that all Jewish shops would be closed on a wedding day.[3] A description of Sicilian marriage practices in all their exaggerated southern festivity is found in a letter of Rabbi Obadiah da Bertinoro:[4] "They brought out the bride after the seven benedictions and led her upon a horse through the city streets and the entire community preceded her on foot with the groom surrounded by the elders; preceding the bride, who was the only one on a horse, (were) lads, children, and young men with burning torches in their hands, shouting boisterously...leading her by the crossroads and through all Jewish neighborhoods while the non-Jews looked on and rejoiced with them and no one mocked".

Most Italian weddings were celebrated on Friday, the eve of holidays, and on holidays. Italian Jews did not observe the ban on marriages during the *sefirah* period which explains why Lag Baomer did not become a favored wedding date.[5] The Italiani, like most Renaissance people, were very superstitious and would, therefore, "always perform the marriage ceremony in a room in the presence of witnesses without a quorum of ten...and then repeat the ceremony before a quorum".[6] The illuminated Italian *ketubah*, marriage contract, became common in the sixteenth century. The twelve zodiac signs and the four seasons were the most popular themes of embellishment. The *ketubah* was usually appended by a "Christian contract" written in Latin or Italian which detailed the pecuniary arrangements.[7]

Renaissance Jewish families were not generally large. They

[1] *Maayan ganim*, Venice 1553, p. 36a ff.

[2] *REJ* 10:191; *Responsa of Rabbi Joseph Colon*, par. 171.

[3] Marx, *Studies in Jewish History and Booklore*, p. 114.

[4] *Iggerot Erez Yisrael*, p. 108. A picture of a Jewish wedding in North Italy in the fifteenth century is found in F. Landsberger, *A History of Jewish Art*, Cincinnati 1946, p. 213.

[5] See *Kirjath sepher, Ibid.*

[6] *Responsa of Rabbi Joseph Colon*, par. 170.

[7] See Isaiah Sonne, *Zion*, N. S. 17:154 and *Kirjath sepher, Ibid.*

averaged two or three children per family. In a small eight family community, five of the eight had two children each, only one had five children, and one had three. The average number of children in a family in Rome in 1520 was three. The same held true for a group of Sephardic families who arrived in Italy in 1492.[1] Circumcision rites were celebrated with great joy, and in addition to the customary godfather, another one, generally a minor boy, related to the newborn infant, participated in the ceremony. These godfathers were called *baale berit*, sponsors of the circumcision ceremony.[2]

b.

The stable family life of the masses was often disturbed by the disgraceful behavior of individuals. Such individuals were relatively numerous and they appeared throughout the Period in every region of the peninsula. To be sure, these manifestations within the Jewish fold were only a pale reflection of the moral corruption prevalent in Italian society. But the vulgarity and the bizarre fervor displayed in the pursuit of sexual pleasure indicate the existence of a severe social malady even among the Jews.

Aberration in the area of the relations between man and woman was expressed in various forms. A quite frequent phenomenon was marriage without parental consent. In the comedy *Zaḥut bediḥuta deḳidushin* the servant counsels Jedidiah to follow "the lover's law... to achieve (the fulfillment of his) desires clandestinely".[3] But this theoretical advice is mild compared to the strange case discussed in a responsum by Rabbi Jehiel Trabot,[4] of a young Jewish man of Urbino who tried to marry his fiancée aginst the will of her parents. His actions indicate that nothing could deter him and that in the process he had lost all sense of decency. Similarly,

---

[1] See Osimo, *Ibid.*, p. 27; *RMI* 12-271, Note 1; Ferorelli, *Immigrazione etc.*, p. 14.

[2] For example see the text from the year 1603 published by Kaufmann, Gesammelte Schriften, vol. 3, p. 315.

[3] *Zaḥut bediḥuta deḳiddushin*, p. 65.

[4] See part of the responsum published by A. H. Freimann, *Seder ḳiddushin wenisuin*, Jerusalem 1945, p. 134.

it was not infrequent to find a man who was ready to ruin the life of his family from the moment "that he set his eyes upon another woman". Rabbi Joseph Colon who reported this,[1] hinted that detestable deeds of husbands against their wives occurred frequently and complained bitterly of that generation's licentiousness. A striking example is the case of Don Samuel Abravanel, an important leader of Italian Jewry in the sixteenth century, who had a "natural son, that is, a bastard".[2] Women, too, indulged in immoral behavior, although to a far lesser extent than men.[3]

Sexual relations between Jews and gentile women were common throughout the entire Period and in practically every locale, except Sicily where such indicents were rare.[4] In Florence forty per cent of the criminal indictments against Jews were for such offenses.[5] All governmental efforts, however, seem to have been unsuccessful. When heavy fines, even as high as four thousand ducats,[6] failed to stop Jewish-Christian romantic relations, the Jewish transgressors were even sentenced to death.[7] This matter caused the Jewish community a great deal of woe. Sexual relations between Jews and nuns [8] were especially painful to the Christians and were bitterly denounced in the sermons of the preachers. Also some local expulsions of the Jews were justified as a measure against romances between Jews and nuns.[9]

There were also cases of young Jewish women indulging in sexual relations with Christians. It appears that nearly always the Christian partners belonged to the aristocracy.[10] Such relations sometimes resulted in the conversion of the Jewish

[1] *Responsa of Rabbi Joseph Colon*, par. 63.
[2] Marx, *Moses Schorr Memorial Volume*, p. 218.
[3] *Responsa of Rabbi Joseph Colon*, par. 160: Case of a woman who deserted her husband and wanted to convert to Christianity; *Catalogue Kaufmann*, p. 42.
[4] *Giovanni* de Giovanni, p. 349.
[5] See Salo Baron, *PAAJR* 12:11.
[6] Cassuto, *Florence*, p. 46. *Ibid.*, Note 1.
[7] *Invernizzi*, p. 6.
[8] *Ciscato*, p. 164, Note 1.
[9] L. A. Schiavi, *Gli ebrei in Venezia*, p. 319; *Ibid.*, p. 315; Wolf, *HB* 6:66.
[10] *RMI* 12:378; *Natali*, p. 143.

woman to Christianity.[1] No doubt, at the root of this phenomenon lay the perpetual craving of the people of the Renaissance for glamour and wealth. Nevertheless, one will have to
accept with reservation the assertion [2] that during the ponti-
ficate of Pope Alexander VI (1492-1503) more than fifty
Jewish women were burned at the stake for the sin of sexual
relations with Christians. Unimpeachable sources [3] also speak
of well educated Jewish courtesans who mingled with high
society and yet practised professional prostitution.

This distressing situation periodically aroused the Jewish
community, especially the rabbinate, to take corrective
action. The rabbinic courts investigated all cases that came to
their attention [4] and the Paduan community even sought to
enlist the aid of the Venetian government in curtailing
licentiousness. Rabbi Judah Minz complained bitterly over
the widespread licentiousness in Padua: [5] "The power of
lawless men dominates us and they terrorize the people...
often men of action have wanted... to stand in the breach and
repair the damage secretly through an investigation by the
state courts, but were unable because non-Jews considered
it advisable to place prostitutes in marketplaces, streets, and
every corner to prevent the more serious transgression of
relations with a married woman". An attempt by the Paduan
community in 1599 to forbid Jews to dance with Christian
women [6] indicates that almost a century later, at a time when
Italian Jewry experienced a great religio-moral revival, the
problem of romantic relations between Jews and Christians
was still acute. In addition to local efforts in various cities,
there was also an all-Italian attempt to deal with moral
corruption. The Forli congress of 1418 issued a harsh warning
against licentiousness and imposed very severe fines upon the

---

[1] *RMI, Ibid.*; Cassuto, *Florence*, p. 203.

[2] *Natali*, p. 142.

[3] C. Chledowski, *Rom: Die Menschen der Renaissance*, Munich 1919,
p. 379; *Letterbode* 11:62-65 (a Jewish writer reproves the women
for practicing prostitution and spreading serious diseases among the
men); Cassuto, *Florence*, p. 229.

[4] *Catalogue Kaufmann*, p. 42.

[5] *Responsa of Rabbi Judah Minz*, par. 5.

[6] Morpurgo, *Padua*, p. 17.

transgressors.[1] This effort, too, was ineffective, for the struggle was waged against men and women totally captivated by modes of Renaissance life which emerged from the disintegration of medieval society.

c.

In contrast to the Middle Ages when the position of the woman in society was barely recognized, the Renaissance produced a type of woman who, like the man, strove to achieve fulfillment in all of life's aspects. Women in the Jewish community too, attained a more prominent position. Bienvenida Abravanel, wife of Don Samuel, who, like her husband had access to royal courts, or the enlightened women of the Da Pisa family who, in their summer homes entertained princes and people of high station,[2] were representative of this new type of Jewish woman. The new situation found expression in a literary debate on the role and character of the woman in which authors, rabbis, and kabbalists participated.[3] Although the debate was often uninhibited and even cynical, it was nevertheless quite serious. The true opinion of that generation's scholars on the Jewish woman is reflected clearly in a statement by Rabbi Jacob da Fano:[4] "I know that many daughters have done valiantly in contemporary times". Contemporaries were undoubtedly amazed and sometimes concerned, over women involved in managing pawnshops, providing cloth for the Pope's troops, and venturing

[1] *Finkelstein*, p. 286.

[2] See *Rivista Israelitica*, 3:97 ff., p. 147 ff. and *Sippur David hareubeni*, pp. 53, 55.

[3] Such as Rabbis Elijah Hayim of Genazzano, Raphael of Faenza, Eliezer of Volterra, Leon da Somi Portaleone, and Jacob of Fano. Most of these poems were published in *Letterbode* 10:97 ff. Cf. Kaufmann, *Gesammelte Schriften*, vol. 3, p. 303 ff. and *MGWJ* 42:466 ff., p. 577 ff. Cf. *Zahut bedihuta dekiddushin*, p. 149. The treatises on the criteria of womenly beauty also belong to this genre. The historian Joseph Hakohen enumerated thirty three "conditions", i.e. qualifications of womanly beauty following the lead of the vast literature by gentile writers, especially Firenzuola. See *Burckhardt*, p. 260 ff. Joseph Hakohen differs from him in only a few details.

[4] *Shilte hagibborim*, Ferrara 1556.

into fairs to engage in trade.[1] Jewish women-physicians drew even more attention.[2] The fact that several Mantuan women were authorized by the rabbinate to practice ritual slaughter[3] may, possibly, surprise us more than it did the people of that era. Female authors who wrote in Italian and attained widespread popularity were equally representative of the Period.[4] To what degree women mastered the Hebrew language, the main vehicle of literary expression, is hard to say due to conflicting information. But it is worth noting that women who did not possess the knowledge of Hebrew deplored their lack of education.[5]

The Jewish Renaissance woman manifested courage and ability to act in times of crisis. Thus, it is not surprising that when her family was in trouble, Leon da Modena's mother "girded her loins like a man and traveled to Ferrara and Venice to speak to princes and judges".[6] Tragically courageous was the act of Leon's unfortunate fiancée who when sensing the approach of death "called me, (the fiancé) embraced and kissed me and said, I know that it is insolence, but God knows that during one year of betrothal we did not even touch one another, but now on the verge of death I have the privilege of the dying..."[7] The courageous and enterprising Jewish woman was equally a good and faithful wife and mother, as is clearly reflected in the contemporary literature dealing with the role of the Jewish woman. Messer Leon was of

---

[1] *Finkelstein*, p. 310. From a decision of the Cremona community it may be inferred that women frequently served as managers of pawnshops. The literature on Jewish pawnbroking contains many items on women who owned pawnshops. See Colorni, *Prestito etc.*, p. 34 for a case of a woman who had a *condotta*; cf. *Vogelstein-Rieger*, vol. I, p. 328; *Responsa of Maharam of Padua*, par. 26.

[2] Roth, *History*, p. 240; Luzzatto, *Urbino*, p. 27.

[3] See *Responsa of Rabbi Isaac de Lattes*, p. 139 ff. Cf. Mortara, *Indice alfabetico dei rabbini e scrittori Israeliti*, Padua 1886, p. 54, Note 2.

[4] Debora Ascarelli and Sarah Copia Sullam who will be discussed in Section VI.

[5] Rabbi Jehiel Manoscrivi in his *Ḥokmat nashim*. Cf. the text published in *MGWJ* 47:179.

[6] *Sepher Chaje Jehuda*, p. 16.

[7] *Ibid.*, p. 22.

the opinion that "the three main virtues of the woman are fear of sin, love of morality, and love of work".[1] Abraham Jaghel Gallichi, one of the more sensitive thinkers of the Period, had many ideas regarding a woman's role. In a small pamphlet entitled *Eshet hayil* he dealt with the woman's comportment in her home and toward her husband. In a verse by verse interpretation of Proverbs 31:10-31 ("A woman of valour" etc.) he speaks of the duty of the woman to strive towards harmony with her Creator and her husband and to concern herself with her household and family. In his remarkable work *Ge hizzayon* [2] he presents the ideal woman. He compares the good woman with the evil one, and the good one describes herself as follows: "I am not proud nor haughty ...and I follow his (the husband's) instructions...and my conduct with the manservants and maidservants and my entire household is so polite that they all love me...and I always perform tasks for my husband quickly and diligently ...and I constantly pay heed to his word to satisfy him, and he would not have to address me twice, and my awe of him is like my awe of Heaven...and I appear before him with a radiant face". Even Ashkenazic writers, who were primarily interested in the esthetic aspects of the Renaissance,[3] stressed the importance of teaching women to fulfill their religious duties, to conduct with serenity their households, and to give generously to charity.[4]

CHAPTER TWO

EDUCATION

Education among Renaissance Jews reflected the Period in both choice of curriculum and organizational structure.

---

[1] *Nofet zufim*, p. 101.

[2] The pamphlet was published in Venice in 1605; *Ge hizzayon*, p. 36b.

[3] See the author's study "Ashkenazic Jewry in Italy", *Between the Rhine and the Bosporus*, Chicago 1964, pp. 158-183.

[4] See Erik, *History*, p. 32 ff.; see *HB* 19:82. Steinschneider's remarks on the small volume *Frauenbuechlein* (*Mizwot nashim*), written jointly by a God fearing rabbi and *"eine koestliche Rebbetzin"* (rabbi's precious wife), which was published in Venice in 1552 and in 1558. Comp. also *MGWJ* 47:179.

The course of study represented a typical blend of Jewish and general elements, and its organization was a striking example of individualism in action.

The *kehillah*, which was institutionally weak, could not do very much for the education of the children. It nevertheless made an effort to employ the rabbis as teachers, especially for the children of the poor. Even a leading head of a yeshivah like Rabbi Judah Minz of Padua was obliged to perform this duty.[1] Rabbi David Ibn Jachia mentioned that among his multiple tasks as chief rabbi of the Jews of the Kingdom of Naples he also had to be "a tutor of small children".[2] But there was no fundamental communal educational effort similar to that of the Spanish or Polish Jews. The required means for communal education came from study funds that were collected through voluntary contributions.[3]

Well to do people would send their children to a private school or would keep a private teacher in their homes. A private school which also provided food and housing for its students existed in the first half of the sixteenth century.[4] But the Period's most characteristic educational feature was the employment of the private tutor. There were two principal reasons for this: The aspiration for a well rounded education for the children, and the fact that there were many towns with only one Jewish family. Virtually every *condotta* contained a paragraph granting the Jewish pawnbroker permission to bring a teacher for his children. There was no organized Jewish school in an important city like Urbino even a century after the establishment of a *kehillah*.[5] Moreover, in the large communities which had communal educational facilities, the wealthier classes still tended to engage private tutors in order to direct the education of their children towards goals desirable to them. All this explains why a number of the greatest humanists lived as private tutors in the homes of the wealthy.

[1] *REJ* 79:34.

[2] *HUCA* 1:617.

[3] Sonne, *Kobez al jad*, N. S. 3:153.

[4] The source is available in Assaf, *Meḳorot letoldot haḥinuk beyisrael*, vol. 4, Jerusalem 1943, p. 20.

[5] Luzzatto, *Urbino*, p. 24.

Generally, however, the private tutor's status was deplorable. He was a wanderer perpetually in search of work and a home, and his instability earned him a bad reputation. Samuel Archivolti, who severely criticized the conduct of his fellow humanists (Section III, Chapter 4), was especially worried by the fact that "many people entrust their sons in their care to learn righteousness and wisdom and they mislead them into a wilderness where there is no right way". Forgetting that he was personally more fortunate than most of the *melamdim*, he concluded his attack with the insulting remark: "the jackass tutors are a disgrace to us".[1]

The composite character of the curriculum (see below) also required the engagement of Christian teachers for Jewish children. In Sienna Jewish children went to the home of a Christian teacher to study *grammatica*, that is, Italian grammar. When a *yeshibah* was established there, the Christian teacher taught grammar in the *yeshibah*.[2] Undoubtedly, the kind of education that Abraham Colorni[3] received also required Christian teachers. The widespread acceptability of Christian teachers by Jews is further evident from the fact that in 1429 Pope Martin V granted the Jews explicit permission to study in Christian schools.[4]

The course of study followed both in the school and by the private teachers consisted of sacred and secular subjects, music and dancing. The Period's cultural program obliged the student to receive instruction in "both God's perfect Torah and philosophy". In a letter of recommendation in behalf of a candidate for the position of *rosh yeshibah* in the home of one of the wealthy, a rabbi assured the employer that the teacher was fluent in both "Hebrew and Italian (or: Latin)".[5] But the sources clearly reveal that the emphasis was upon sacred

---

[1] *Maayan ganim*, p. 26b ff.

[2] Marx, *Louis Ginzberg Jubilee Volume*, pp. 278, 285 (Hebrew section).

[3] A contemporary Christian termed Abraham Colorni's education, which also included a course in fencing, "well rounded". See G. Jare, *Abramo Colorni*, Ferrara 1891, p. 6.

[4] M. Stern, *Stellung der Paepste*, Part 1, p. 41.

[5] Cassuto, *Florence*, p. 404 (text of the letter); Marx, *Ibid.*, p. 294.

lore. Rabbi David Ibn Jachia labeled grammar, poetics, logic, and all-Ghazali's a work which he taught, as "dessert". The core of instruction was the Talmud, which was studied daily.[1]

There was a clearly unified curriculum of sacred studies despite the lack of a uniform educational framework. All writers who reminisced about their school years [2] asserted that as soon as youngsters could study the Bible with commentaries, they started to learn Mainomides' Code of Laws. When they became familiarized with this text they moved to the Mishnah and thence to the Gemara and Tosafot. This program was described by Leon da Modena in his book *Historia degli Riti Hebraici*,[3] which was composed at the end of the Period and constitutes a sort of summary of Jewish life at the time. We find this course of study taught in the second half of the sixteenth century in a three level school: "Some of you will spend the morning studying Maimonides' Code of Laws..., and some of you will study the Mishnah, and the older ones will study Alfasi's Code".[4] A note in a holiday prayer book manuscript of the mid-sixteenth century offers the following details of a boy's education: "At the age of three he knew his Creator. Praised be the Lord that on the first day of Iyar 1560 he began to study. At the age of four and a half he recited the *haftarah* in the synagogue... He started to write at the age of five and a half. At six and a half he, thank God, started to put on *tephillin*. At eight and a month...he began the study of Alfasi...At twelve and a half he started to read the Torah in the synagogue..."[5] It is difficult to determine whether this was the normal educational program or whether this was a case of an exceptionally gifted youngster. That not every child was able to complete the entire educational program is indicated by the fact that Abraham Jaghel Gallichi composed

[1] *HUCA, Ibid.*

[2] Such as Abraham Portaleone in his Introduction to *Shilte hagib-borim.* Cf. *Neppi-Ghirondi*, p. 43.

[3] *Historia de gli Riti Hebraici*, Section 4, Chapter 10 (Hebrew translation).

[4] Marx, *Ibid.*, p. 289, Note 91. Alfasi replaced the Talmud when the latter was burned in 1553 and further publication was banned.

[5] Published by Assaf, *Ibid.*, vol. 2, p. 114. The text follows that of Nedarim 32a.

the abbreviated primer of religious fundamentals *Leḳaḥ tob*, which, he hoped, "children would learn easily by heart". Such a book was especially needed for pupils from wealthy families who in their youth became absorbed in business and did not complete their course of study.[1]

The secular studies generally included Italian, Latin, singing, and dancing. Sometimes philosophy or other subjects were added. Proper deportment, an important aspect of Renaissance social life, was also cultivated. As a rule they sought to inculcate in the children "Torah and good manners that they might acquire proper intellectual and civil virtues".[2]

CHAPTER THREE

DAILY LIFE

a.

The Renaissance trend toward refinement of daily life also influenced the architecture and interior of the house. Houses were often surrounded by gardens, were built spaciously, and had decorated walls. Housing conditions of the Jews were also generally good.[3] Sometimes even families that were not especially affluent lived in homes with separate rooms for each of their children. One old woman had such a large home that she was able to sublet four rooms.

Renaissance Jews had a clear concept of a beautiful home. Leon da Modena's father who was not wealthy, purchased "a lovely palace" in Ferrara. The son also had such a "beautiful and comfortable" home in Venice that he lived in it for seventeen years despite his perpetual inclination for change.

---

[1] Assaf, *Ibid.*, vol. 4, p. 22. The statement regarding non completion of a course of study indicated that there was a standardized curriculum as a minimum requirement for the education of a Jewish child. *Leḳaḥ tob* was published many times. The edition used by the present writer was published in Piotrkow in 1913.

[2] From the program of a Jewish "university" prepared by Rabbi David Provenzal. See *Halebanon*, 5:434. Information regarding the study of secular subjects is available in most of the sources cited in this chapter.

[3] *Maḥberot Immanuel*, p. 32; *Sippur David hareubeni*, pp. 36, 37, 40.

When he was compelled to move to another home, he complained of its darkness and ironically dubbed it the "cave of Machpelah".[1] The truly wealthy class lived in palaces. Ishmael da Rieti owned a very large home in Sienna, and Jehiel da Pisa's home was even larger. David Reubeni remarked that it was "an exceedingly large home".[2]

Very little is known of the interior decor of Jewish homes. A picture of the second half of the fifteenth century [3] portraying a Passover seder shows a rather spacious room with a large table covered with a white tablecloth in the center. There are no pictures upon the walls, pursuant to the ban of painting figures (see below, Section VII, Chapter 1). But the ceiling is decorated with square coffers in a pattern common in aristocratic homes. The homes were framed by gardens and in Pesaro even the synagogue was surrounded by a garden.[4]

The Renaissance custom of maintaining a country home was very popular among the wealthy Jews. Information about such homes is available from the middle of the fifteenth to the middle of the sixteenth century, mainly from Tuscany. Jews in Ferrara at the end of the Period also had "rural estates".[5] The summer residences were handsomely furnished and had many rooms, in each of which were a bed, a table and various household articles. The spacious courtyards and gardens surrounding the summer homes formed the backdrop of the summer's social life.

The practice of keeping pet animals and birds seems to have been quite widespread. A description by Immanuel of Rome of a wealthy man's home included "birds and animals". In a fifteenth century picture of a Passover *seder*, a small dog is seen playing beside the table. Similarly, in the comedy *Ẕaḥut*

[1] *Sepher Chaje Jehuda*, pp. 14, 16.
[2] *Sippur David hareubeni*, pp. 51, 52. "An exceeding great home" (comp. Jonah 3:3).
[3] Published in Elkan N. Adler, *Jewish Travellers*, London 1930, facing p. 156. Cf. *Moses Gaster Jubilee Volume*, p. 43 and facing p. 44.
[4] *Emeḳ habaka*, p. 126; *Meor enayim*, Part 1, p. 20; *Sepher Chaje Jehuda*, p. 25.
[5] *Meor enayim, Ibid.*; *Tarbiẕ* 4:272: "Also in the country home"; *Sippur David hareubeni*, p. 55; Cassuto, *Florence*, pp. 228, 422; *Meshullam da Volterra's Travelogue*, p. 58.

bedihuta dekiddushin an infant plays with "his precious dog", and one of the household members even believes that "the dog is more intelligent than the servants".[1]

Wealthy Jewish families generally kept male and female slaves, mainly negroes. There is substantial information on the subject from the second half of the fifteenth century until the end of the Period. Since there were no large landowners among Renaissance Jews, it can be assumed that the slaves were used as domestics. While the Church disapproved of Jewish slave owners and encouraged the slaves to escape, provided that they converted to Christianity,[2] Jews continued to keep slaves. Whenever Jews sought permission from an Italian ruler to settle in his domain, they explicitly included the right to bring along their slaves.[3] Jewish slave ownership also became a subject of rabbinic discussion,[4] since following the pattern of Christian society,[5] sexual relationships between Jewish masters and their female slaves were not infrequent. To be sure, rabbinic concern did not alter the situation. In 1472, for example, the wife of Don Isaac Abravanel sent a negro female slave as a gift to the wife of Jehiel da Pisa.[6] Obviously, the male and female slave were a part of the wealthy Jewish household.

b.

In the framework of the elegant home of the wealthy, a rich social life unfolded with all the refinements introduced by the Renaissance. David Reubeni's travelogue and the comedy *Zahut bedihuta dekiddushin* abound in descriptions of this life and its amenities. Azariah dei Rossi described with visible pleasure how a wealthy man in Ferrara, on Sabbath eve, would sit "with his esteemed wife and nine children... and other

---

[1] *Mahberot Immanuel*, p. 42; *Zahut bedihuta dekiddushin*, p. 135; Adler, *Ibid*. Cf. *Moses Gaster Jubilee Volume, Ibid*.

[2] *Ferorelli*, p. 109.

[3] Ibid., pp. 72, 73; *Balletti*, p. 65. *REJ* 5:231 ff.; E. Loevinson, *Le basi giuridiche della communita Israelitica di Livorno*, Livorno 1937, p. 5.

[4] *Catalogue Kaufmann*, p. 65, responsum 70; *Responsa of Rabbi David Ibn Zimra*, par. 68.

[5] *Burckhardt*, 10-th German ed., Leipzig 1908, vol. 2, p. 298.

[6] *Ozar nehmad* 2:69.

members of the household in a room around the fire, in accordance with the custom".[1] Ovbiously, pleasant talk at the fireside was an accepted practice.

One of the main ways of spending leisure time was reading for pleasure. Books both Jewish and non-Jewish were available in abundance,[2] and their entertaining character is evident from the frequent statements of the authors that they composed their works "to drive away sorrow and sadness".[3] Besides belles-lettres we find in the literature collections of riddles and tricks for play and entertainment".[4] To be sure, tricky formulas were also used for such pragmatic purposes as exchanging of coded letters and communicating in secretive language. The author of the comedy *Zaḥut bediḥuta deḳiddushin* stated that as non-Jews "have found an appropriate manner of pleasing people by composing words that are recited before princes and notables of the land", he too wrote his play, since Jews as yet lacked this literary genre.[5] From the very beginning of the Period Jews adopted the custom of the Christian intelligentsia of sitting together in a group and being entertained by reading and storytelling. The background of the *Decameron* and of Straparola's *Le Piacevoli Notti*, a group of people passing the time in the countryside, is also the framework of the stories, debates, and anecdotes of Immanuel's *Maḥbarot*.[6]

The tendency to celebrate a wide variety of occasions added excitement and color to life. The Forli congress of 1418 noted the fact that "those who make weddings extend themselves beyond their financial capacity and are more lavish than

[1] *Meor enayim*, Part I, p. 11.

[2] See below, Section VI.

[3] Such as the Hebrew translation of the Arthurian legends (see *Ozar tob*, 1885, p. 1 ff.); the Introduction of Abraham Farissol to *Iggeret oreḥot olam*, Venice 1587.

[4] *Shoshanat Yaakob* by Jacob Heilpron, Venice 1591; Rabbi Jacob Landau in *Sefer ḥazon*, printed at the end of *Sefer haagur*. To be sure, he is somewhat concerned over his preoccupation with such light fare and prays "that I be not regarded as a fool".

[5] *Zaḥut bediḥuta deḳiddushin*, p. 22.

[6] See the Preface to *Maḥberot Immanuel*: "We went strengthened by the food, the wine, and (the meat of) the fowl, and we gathered in a large meadow and told many stories". (p. 13)

wealthy non-Jews".[1] However, despite the limitations imposed by the congress, the Jewish masses found many occasions
for feasts and entertainment. It was customary in Piedmont for
yeshibah heads to make a feast on Lag Baomer for their students and local scholars. The numerous descriptions by Immanuel of Rome of wine drinking and gluttony, despite their
obvious exaggeration, attest to the general trend. All these
desires were satisfied on Purim and Simhat Torah.[2] The
apostate Giulio Morosini described the noisy festivities on
Simhat Torah in the synagogue of the Venice ghetto and
called them carnivals. These celebrations even attracted many
Christians. The custom of selecting a "Purim king" or "prince"
was generally practiced. Rabbi Judah Minz upheld the right
of "wearing masks that the boys and the girls, the aged and
the young donned on Purim". They used to present theatrical
plays on that day and acted as though it were indeed a Jewish
carnival. A number of books of the *Maseket Purim* type were
widely read. The poet Joseph Zarfadi composed a special song
in praise of this literary genre, and another writer praised in
a poem the man chosen to be the "Purim King". Immanuel
too presented many of his stories on drinking revelry within
the framework of Purim. Similarly, singing and dancing were
almost a daily routine and were an important part of the
educational curriculum.[3] We have seen that it was customary
to dance and to present musical selections in honor of important visitors.[4]

Young people, especially among the wealthy, participated
in all sorts of sport activities to which they devoted a large
proportion of their time.[5] In 1511 young Roman Jews

[1] *Finkelstein*, p. 286.
[2] *REJ* 10:185 ff., Note 3; *MGWJ* 47:174; *Responsa of Rabbi Judah Minz,* par. 17; several manuscripts of *Ẓaḥut bediḥuta deḳiddushin* state that the comedy was written for presentation on Purim (see *MGWJ* 75:115); Cassuto in *Gaster Jubilee Volume*, p. 59. Cf. the fragment of *Maseket Purim* in *Vogelstein-Rieger*, vol. 1, p. 339, Note 1; G. Morosini, *Via della fede*, Rome 1683, p. 789 ff.
[3] See above, this Section, Chapter 2 and below, Section VII, Chapter 2.
[4] *Sippur David hareubeni*, p. 53.
[5] Regarding the following see Roth, *History*, p. 387; Sonne, *Hateku-fah*, p. 678.

arranged a race under the supervision of Messer Rabi, who might possibly be identical with the famous physician Samuel Zarfadi. They raced from Saint Peter's square to the Saint Angelo fortress. A hundred armed young men rode horses and alongside them fifty others marched, carrying olive branches and banners. It is difficult to ascertain the purpose of this festival, but it shows that large numbers of young people participated in games. Joseph Arli spoke with fatherly pride of his son who was the "commander" of the young men of noble descent in Macherata and whom "they all followed wherever he went".

Ball playing was very popular with both Christians and Jews.[1] In the comedy *Zahut bedihuta dekiddushin* a boy asks the woman who took care of him to give him a certain garment "so that I can move more easily when I play ball today". The popularity of tennis was reflected in rabbinic deliberation over whether or not it should be banned as a form of gambling since "the only reason they come to the game is to win money". Another question which agitated Venetian rabbis was whether to permit ball playing on the Sabbath. Various people also complained over the time wasted upon ball playing and warned the youth not to become overly absorbed by it. It is therefore not surprising to hear Rabbi Immanuel da Benevento, under the terrifying impact of the burning of the sacred books in 1553, complain that in the morning hours when the mind is most attuned to study, the young men "arise (and go) to the vineyards to see whether the vine-blossom opened... and the harp and psaltery, the tabret and the pipe, are in their feasts...[2] and at noon like valiant men they race...in the streets in pursuit of pleasures...or waste their time over books of history and politics[3]... or they gamble with dice..."

---

[1] *Zahut bedihuta dekiddushin*, p. 130; the article by Isaac Rivkind, *Tarbiz*, 4:372; Assaf, *Ibid.* 4:27; Marx, *Louis Ginzberg Jubilee Volume*, p. 276 (Hebrew Section). For the spread of ballplaying in Renaissance Italy see *Burckhardt*, p. 290 and the remarks of Hiram Peri, *Ibid.*

[2] Comp. Song of Songs 7:13 and Isaiah 5:12.

[3] He was certainly referring to the well known book *I reali di Francia*, which was, perhaps, the most popular book in Italy.

The practice of hiking in the countryside and of living in summer homes introduced Italian Jews to the non-Jewish custom of hunting.[1] An invitation from a summer resort in Vignone by a group of young Jews to their friends in Florence described how they "spread nets and lay snares to capture... crows". The well known merchant and traveler Meshullam da Volterra, after hunting in the vicinity of Florence sent the game as a gift to Lorenzo the Magnificent. To be sure, he hunted only deer, permitted for consumption by the Jewish dietary laws.

c.

We have seen how Rabbi Immanuel da Benevento complained with bitterness that the youth gambled with dice. This complaint was certainly not exaggerated, for the sources attest that Renaissance Italian Jews were seriously affected by this social affliction. One gets a clear impression that dice and card playing were an important part of social life during the entire Period. Especially shocking was the fact that it spread to all strata of society and that it flourished under all conditions. Efforts by individuals, by the organized Jewish community, and by the authorities to arrest the spread of gambling were virtually all in vain.

Testimony regarding the widespread popularity of gambling in the early part of the Period comes from Immanuel of Rome and Kalonymos ben Kalonymos. Immanuel placed the dice gamblers in Gehenna, and in *Maseket Purim* the unsavory social types, such as Mr. Thief, Mr. Lusty and Mr. Extortioner are joined by Mr. Gambler.[2] The matter became extremely grave in the beginning of the fifteenth century and the Forli congress of 1418 attempted serious measures to root it out (see below). However, at the end of the century Don Isaac

---

[1] The sources are published in Cassuto, *Florence*, p. 422 and in *REJ* 76:143.

[2] *Maḥberot Immanuel*, p. 797; *Maseket Purim*, according to *Vogelstein-Rieger*, vol. 1, p. 338, Note 3. For the spread of dice and card playing see: *Kirjath sepher* 14:551; *Ẓaḥut bediḥuta deḳiddushin*, pp. 47, 131; Sepher Chaje Jehuda, passim; *Sur mera*, Prague 1515, p. 15.

Abravanel again had to deplore the proliferation of gambling.[1]
Italian Jewry's addiction to gambling reached its peak at the
end of the Period, despite the wave of religious enthusiasm
that then passed over the Jewish community. At that time
even children played cards. Leon da Modena gambled all his
life and lost enormous amounts of money. To be sure, Leon da
Modena was not the only Jewish gambler. But he was more
candid than others and related in his memoirs some terrifying
details of his misery and his absolute failure to free himself
from the gambling plague. His remarks in the pamphlet
Sur mera were surely true that scholars and wise men did not
abstain from gambling. "I will not mention their names since
it is not proper, but daily do I see learned men who are not
concerned over this and take to gambling"... This, incidentally, was written by Leon da Modena when he was still a young
man, before his frightful gambling career had started.

Perhaps the interesting remarks of Abraham Jaghel Gallichi
in his work *Ge ḥizzayon* regarding gambling [2] could shed some
light on this bizarre situation. He tells us that Renaissance
people believed that the stars foreordained man's destiny over
which he had no control (see below Section V), and that
this belief was somehow linked to cards and the "mysteries"
they concealed. "The stars—we read—are divided into twelve
constellations and forty-eight forms, and the cards also
contain forty-eight forms, and each one of the four kings has
including himself, at his table (comp. The Song of Songs 1:12)
twelve pieces (cards) which correspond to the twelve constellations..." This statement is followed by an explanation:
"...the function of the stars is like the function of a card
game. As the stars (i.e. fate) sometimes raise man from the
dungheaps into the heights and then he is suddenly lost forever
and observers seek him in vain, so do the cards elevate a man
by endowing him with an abundance of luck...and no sooner
do you look at him, and he is gone..."

Bearing all this in mind we can understand why gambling
was so popular and why such vast sums of money were involv-

[1] See Introduction to his commentary on Sayings of the Fathers.
[2] *Ge ḥizzayon*, p. 8a.

ed.[1] The effort of the Forli congress to limit the play to small
sums failed completely. A Jew who played cards with the
Duke of Ferrara in the course of one evening lost three
thousand ducats, the equivalent of the average resources of a
Jewish pawnbroker. More details about Leon da Modena's
gambling career should prove very illuminating. Fragmentary
figures indicate that he lost twenty-six hundred ducats at
dice tables, but in reality his losses were at least ten times
higher. On Hanukah 1595 he lost one hundred ducats, and
more than three hundred ducats on Hanukah 1599. In the
month of Iyyar 1601 he won five hundred ducats, but soon
lost them and an unknown amount of additional money.
Leon da Modena's gambling career lasted almost fifty years
and from his own accounts it may be surmised that he lost an
average of five hundred ducats a year. He gambled on Hanukah to celebrate the holiday. In 1620 he gambled to drown his
anguish over the death of his oldest son, and he gambled in the
fall, winter and summer for no apparent reason. Even when
he had no money he gambled and paid his losses from his
income as a teacher and preacher. In the end, he believed, that
the stars ("fate") "forced me to err in the foolishness of
gambling all my life, while my soul knew its faults and evil
quite well... Had it not been for this I would have rejoiced
and been happy with my lot all my days..."

The feeling that gambling was a social plague that must be
vanquished was not limited only to the communal agencies,
but was similarly prevalent among individuals, including
many who were themselves deeply enmeshed in gambling.
Leon da Modena proudly related that his father "did not like
to gamble".[2] A famous rabbi "took an oath not to gamble,"
and an ordinary man of Ferrara scrawled a pledge on the
flyleaf of his prayerbook not to gamble. A Jewish group with
outspoken religio-moral goals forbade its members to gamble.
Curiously, it still offered a rather ample list of days and occa-

---

[1] For the sums involved see *Finkelstein*, p. 284; *Ẓaḥut bediḥuta
dekiddushin*, p. 47. *Menorah Journal*, Spring 1946, p. 92.
[2] *Sepher Chaje Jehuda*, p. 24. For information on the following
see: *Kirjath sepher* 14:551; *Heasif* 3:214 ff. *Menorah Journal*, *Ibid.*

sions on which gambling was permitted, such as *Ḥol Hamoed*, Hanukah, a circumcision, and the seven days of festivity following a marriage. Moreover, the society's head was authorized to grant dispensation for gambling on other days. The example of Leon da Modena illustrates that despite self imposed limitations there was enough opportunity for self-destruction.

The Hebrew literature also entered the fight against gambling.[1] Immanuel of Rome placed gamblers in hell because their heavy gambling losses drive them to curse God. In his journey to the world of the spirits Abraham Jaghel Gallichi also encountered the soul of a man who had been a cardplayer during his lifetime and was being punished after death. To be sure, the sincerity of these attacks will have to be questioned. The preacher Moses ben Joab in one of his poems attacked the evil man who gambled, while admitting at the same time somewhat unabashedly that he wrote another poem during a gambling party. Similarly, the true purpose of the dialogue *Sur mera* written by Leon da Modena is still not clear. It purportedly aimed at discouraging gambling, as its title implies. But the arguments of the defender of gambling are stronger than would be expected. The debate ends with the conclusion that gambling is evil because it causes a person to neglect his affairs and the study of Torah. But the moral corruption inherent in gambling is not rendered clear and without reservations in the debate. Apparently a struggle raged in the mind of the youthful author between a rejection of gambling in principle, and the recognition that a person could not break free of it.

Communal struggle against gambling was much more determined.[2] When, for example, it was learned that a

[1] Cf. *Maḥberot Immanuel, Ibid.*; *Ge ḥizzayon*, p. 7 ff; Cassuto, *Florence*, p. 229; Leon da Modena's *Sur mera* first appeared in Venice in 1596. The printer Solomon Ḥayim Ḥaber Tob in justifying the publication claimed "that the gambling plague had spread throughout the entire Jewish world".

[2] Cf. *Kirjath sepher, Ibid.*; decisions of the Forli congress, *Finkelstein*, p. 284; the responsum of Leon da Modena against the ban on gambling is available in *Paḥad Yiẓḥak*, in the entry entitled "ban on gambling," pp. 53 to 55.

renowned rabbi had violated his oath not to gamble, "Israel
cried out to him" with indignation. The attitude of the organized community was adequately expressed by the harsh
language of the decision of the Forli congress: "And anyone
who will transgress this decision regarding gambling shall be
denounced as a sinner and transgressor and shall also pay a
fine of one ducat to the community's treasury each time that
he transgresses, in addition to a fine to be imposed on the
homes in which the gambling took place. And if he refuses to
pay the aforementioned fine, the community must refuse to
allow him to be included in a quorum (*minyan*) for public
worship or to be called to the Torah..., and anyone who
knows... a Jew who has violated this decision must publicly
reveal it or be fined in the manner indicated". But, how could
such decisions be properly enforced then and later, if even a
member of the Venetian rabbinate (Leon da Modena) denied
in a brilliant opinion the authority of that community's
executive council to ban dice playing.

Governmental attitude to Jewish gambling was ambiguous.[1]
In Florence many Jews were punished for violation of the ban
against gambling. Similarly, Jews were punished there for
the manufacture and sale of cards and for their importation
from Sienna. The government of Lombardy instead, whose
only concern was that Christians should not gamble at cards,
in 1479 permitted card playing in a Jewish tavern in Pavia,
provided that only Jews shall be admitted. In view of all this
it is hardly surprising that the Jewish community could not
rid itself of the gambling plague. It was a social evil that
Renaissance Jewry transmitted to the succeeding generations.

d.

The similarity of daily life patterns created a genuine
closeness between the Jewish and Christian populations. The
new regard for the individual removed many prejudices and
created a hospitable climate for mutual relationships. The
closeness of Jew and gentile was expressed primarily in

[1] See Cassuto, *Florence*, pp. 194, 228; C. Roth, *Gli ebrei a Firenze
sotto l'ultima republica*, Florence 1924, pp. 11, 13; *Invernizzi*, p. 23.

increased personal and social contacts. A wide variety of such
interrelationships are reported in the sources.[1] In 1542 many
Christian guests, including the nobility, were invited to a
Jewish wedding in Modena. Many Christian nobles used to
visit Jehiel da Pisa at his summer residence, and his wife would
entertain them by playing the harp. In 1484 a Sicilian Jew
even invited his Christian friend to act as the godfather at his
son's circumcision. Jews also served Christians as dance and
song instructors, and sometimes as matchmakers. Relations
between Jews and Christians in the city of Scandiano were so
friendly that they provoked the public ire of the local priest.
He complained that Jewish and Christian women visited each
other in their homes, and that Christian and Jewish children
played together. Joseph Arli even boasted over the fact that
his son cultivated close social relationships with Christians.

These developments created an atmosphere of mutual trust
between Jew and Christian.[2] When a conflict arose in Mantua
between the Jewish pawnbrokers and the *kehillah*, two Jewish
judges were selected to adjudicate their differences, and a
Christian was invited to serve as arbitrator to decide the issue
in the event that the Jewish judges could not agree. The
friendly attitude of Christian officials to Jews during the
persecutions of Pope Paul IV is truly moving. A police
officer in Terni who treated Jewish prisoners from Civitanova
well, remarked: "And I love you all as myself, and I want to
treat you well, for the Holy One, blessed be He, has never
forsaken you, and you, although in exile, are beloved by God
and He constantly performs miracles and wondrous acts in
behalf of the Israelite nation". In another city (Ascoli) "the
local residents had compassion with the Jews". When during
disturbances in Rome a rumor spread of the Pope's death and
a mob attacked the Inquisition prison to free its inmates, one
of the mob remarked to the Jewish prisoners: "Do not fear,
for I like Jews since my youth". Such sentiments were

---

[1] Cf. *Balletti*, p. 123 f.; *Sippur David hareubeni*, p. 55; *Giovanni
de Giovanni*, p. 341; *Foa*, p. 109; Sonne, *Hatekufah*, p. 678.

[2] Colorni, *Magistrature maggiori*, p. 21; *Tarbiẓ* 2:481, 486, 489;
Alim 2:50.

expressed many times in various places and situations. An
official delegated by the Pope to confiscate Hebrew books,
apologized that "he was forced to do what he was doing".

This mutual friendship was so rooted in both Jewish and
Christian hearts, that combined efforts of the Church and the
Jewish communal authorities to keep the two groups apart
were not successful.[1] The great Christian preachers of the
fifteenth century were the first ones to oppose in their sermons
Jewish-Christian rapprochement. In addition to such propaganda, Church authorities formally proclaimed social contacts
with Jews as forbidden. In 1522 a synod banned "intimate
conversation with Jews at a party or dance". This was rather
mild in comparison to the recommendations of Pope Paul IV
in his bull of 1555. A contemporary Jewish writer stated that
the Pope commanded "that non-Jews must not break bread
with Jews, must not play any games with them, must not
enter into partnerships or engage in anything that would
lead to closeness, such as *conversazioni*. But even these efforts
were ineffective. In 1592 it was still necessary to reissue a ban
in Rome forbidding Jews to teach Hebrew, singing, dancing,
and other arts to Christians. Similarly, the Jewish community
in Padua in 1599 had to forbid the Jews to dance with Christians. The social contacts between Jews and Christians endured
throughout the first half of the seventeenth century. In the
middle of the century Christians, including priests, were still
coming in large numbers to the synagogue in the Venetian
ghetto to listen to the sermons of Leon da Modena.

e.

The menu of the Jewish family was generally similar to that
of the Christian neighbors, insofar as the Jewish dietary laws
were not affected. There were, however, various foods that
were especially favored by Jews, particularly certain varieties

---

[1] *Ferorelli*, pp. 189, 226; H. Hildesheimer, *Simon von Trident*,
Berlin 1903, p. 3; *Tarbiẓ, Ibid.*, p. 345; A. Bertolotti, "Gli ebrei in
Roma", published in *Archivio storico*, 1879, p. 262; Morpurgo, *Padua*,
p. 17.

of vegetables.[1] Both Christians and Jews devoted great
attention to the preparation of meals. A dinner lasted several
hours and included numerous courses. Kalonymos ben Kalonymos enumerated twenty-four food varieties in *Maseket
Purim* [2] that a Jew presumably had to consume on Purim.
Most of these foods bore Italian names indicating that they
were common to both Jews and Christians. Wine drinking
was widespread, with little concern over the ban on wine
made by non-Jews.[3] Jews also followed the custom of
toasting one another with the word *brindisi*.[4] In the beginning
of the fifteenth century, with the rising affluence of Italian
Jewry, the Forli congress felt compelled to limit excesses that
had become the rule at weddings and feasts, for "we have
seen... (that Jews) tend to go beyond their means, even more
than wealthy non-Jews..."[5]

The trend toward luxury expressed itself in dress as well.
Jewish moneylenders possessed many garments given to them
as pledges and never redeemed, and could therefore easily
dress well. Since these garments were all pledged by Christians,
a debate arose whether it was permissible for a Jew to wear
such clothing, or would he be transgressing the injunction
"not to follow their statutes". Community intercession
manifested itself periodically when it became necessary to
restrain the craving for luxury or to stress the need for
decency in dress. Both motives are apparent in the detailed
decrees regarding permissible garb for Jewish women that
were issued by the Forli congress in 1418.[6] Even harsher
warnings and threats were included in an anti-pomp decree

[1] Roth, *History*, p. 359.

[2] According to the material in I. Davidson, *Parody in Jewish
Literature*, N.Y. 1907, p. 22, Note 36.

[3] See *Responsa of Maharam of Padua*, par. 76 and *Historia de gli
Riti Hebraici* by Leon da Modena, Part 2, Chapter 8, par. 1. It should
be noted, however, that fifteenth century Sicilian Jewry adhered
strictly to the ban on non-Jewish wine. Cf. *Iggerot Erez Israel*, p. 104.

[4] *Shalshelet hakabbalah*, p. 40: Rabbi Akiba's toast "wine and health
to the mouth of our teachers and their disciples" (Shabbat 63b)
was explained by Gedaliah as referring to "*brindisi*, the toast currently
proposed at banquets".

[5] *Finkelstein*, p. 286.

[6] *Ibid.*, p. 284 ff. Comp. Leviticus 18:3.

that was adopted by the Venetian executive council in 1543. This decree was reenacted in 1584.[1] It may be assumed that the custom of issuing anti-pomp decrees became common in a much earlier period. To be sure, such decrees did not achieve their purpose. They were contrary to the depply rooted esthetic aspirations of the age. In the second half of the sixteenth century the complaint was still heard "that this is the evil path chosen by all of our women in this wicked generation to pour out endless sums of money for such worthless and utterly useless things (i.e. clothes)". As late as 1612 the English traveler Thomas Coryat observed that Jewish men in Venice were elegantly dressed and that the clothes and jewelry of their wives were no less magnificent than those of the women of English aristocracy.[2]

Decrees regarding clothing included limitations on the wearing of jewelry. That the Jewish women exhibited their jewels excessively is apparent from the decree of the Venetian executive council of 1543 that permitted each woman to wear jewels worth up to three ducats. To be sure, many of the jewels may have been pawns deposited by gentile debtors. True, important community leaders in the fifteenth century like Rabbi Joseph Colon and Messer Leon defended "those who wore jewelry and bands of gold".[3] But most communal leaders sharply opposed this rabbinic view and compared those who bedecked themselves to "believers in witchcraft".

f.

We have seen that periodic opposition arose to the wearing of clothes similar to those worn by Christians. To be sure, a number of Jews, especially those who had contacts with governmental circles, wore the *cappa*, the garment of Christian scholars, with rabbinic permission. Furthermore, according to Rabbi Joseph Colon the clothes of most Jews were not much different from those of their gentile neighbors. But about

[1] Sonne, *Kobez al jad*, N. S. 3:159 ff.

[2] *Zahut bedihuta dekiddushin*, p. 24; T. Coryat, *Coryat's Crudities*, Glasgow 1905, vol. 1, p. 372.

[3] *Responsa of Rabbi Joseph Colon*, par. 88, at the end of the responsum.

sixty years later when Solomon Molkho traveled through Italy in non-Jewish garb, it evoked the ire of certain circles, and the rabbis were compelled to defend his behavior with the argument that he was meeting with princes and kings for the sake of all Jewry. There were similar disagreements over the matter of covering the head. Apparently, most Jews were not very meticulous in the observance of this practice and did uncover their heads when in Christian company or because of the heat.[1]

The tendency of most Jews to eliminate a distinctive Jewish garb was vigorously opposed by the Church.[2] In Rome and Palermo harsh laws existed as early as the fourteenth century, compelling Jews to wear a specifically designed mark upon their clothing. Men were obliged to wear short red jackets as outer garments and women special outer skirts over their dresses. Other Italian states also strictly supervised Jewish distinctness in dress, even if the form varied in different locales. In Milan the Jews had to wear "yellow hats in the Muscovite style". In Venice the Italiani and Ashkenazim wore yellow or red hats, while the Levantines wore yellow turbans.

Jewish dress was thus fashioned by both internal and external factors. It varied in different times and places during the three century period and cannot be described in detail, since only a few portraits of contemporary Italian Jews are extant. The portraits that we do have [3] generally depict the men wearing garments of varying lengths and the women garbed in long dresses reaching to their shoes. All garments are

---

[1] *Ibid.*; *MGWJ* 75:132 f.; I. Rivkind, *Louis Ginzberg Jubilee Volume*, p. 401 ff. In the Notes Rivkind assembled ample material bearing on the question of uncovering of the head.

[2] *Vogelstein-Rieger*, vol. I, p. 335; *Emek habaka*, p. 111; *Lagumina*, vol. I, no. 53. The order issued for the purpose of enforcing the law on the distinctive badge in Mantua in 1577 also described the badge in great detail. For the text of the order see L. Carnevali, *Il ghetto di Mantova*, Mantua 1884, p. 9 ff. Cf. Coryat, *Ibid.*, p. 371.

[3] Such portraits can be found in: Adler, *Ibid.*, opposite the frontispiece; Roth, *History*, opposite pp. 174, 175; Roth, *Venice*, opposite pp. 123, 174; S. Muntner, *Rabbi Shabetai Donnolo*, Jerusalem 1949, opposite p. 16; Landsberger, *A History of Jewish Art*, p. 213.

closed about the neck, sometimes with ties among the men. All the men wear hats which are sometimes broad-rimmed and sometimes as small as skullcaps, and the women's heads are also covered.

g.

One of the striking characteristics of daily life during the Renaissance was the concern over health and cleanliness. Jewish appreciation of cleanliness was even generally stronger than that of their Christian neighbors. Children were admonished to observe rules of personal cleanliness and seem to have been punished for not doing so. Communal action was equally vigorous. The 1571 constitution of the Florence community contains a paragraph specifically obligating everyone to keep his home clean and to refrain from discarding garbage in the streets.[1]

The concern for hygiene and health was aided by the publication of health manuals.[2] The famous publisher Gershom Soncino printed upon a large sheet the fourth chapter of Maimonides' *Hilkot deot* which contains instructions for the preservation of physical health. The sheet had a decorative border and was evidently designed to be hung upon a wall. Much advice in matters of health is found in Abraham Portaleone's encyclopedic work *Shilte hagibborim*. The preacher Judah Moscato believed that the smoke of incense could be used as a disinfectant of the air in time of an epidemic. The most interesting work in the entire literature on health is the pamphlet *Moshia ḥosim* by the brilliant and many-sided author Abraham Jaghel Gallichi. In this truly popular health manual he concerned himself particularly with the bubonic plague, which was frequently recurring in those times. He tried to clarify the causes of this desease and indicated

---

[1] Cassuto, *I più antichi capitoli del ghetto di Firenze*, 1915, p. 4.

[2] Sonne, *Alexander Marx Jubilee Volume*, p. 223 ff. (Hebrew Section); *Shilte hagibborim*, Epilogue; *Moshia ḥosim* first appeared in Venice in 1587. It was reprinted in 1604; *Ibid.*, on p. 18a is quoted Rabbi Judah Moscato's opinion on the nature of incense. The opinion on "Jewish" maladies was expressed by Rabbi Abraham Jaghel Gallichi in his book *Ge ḥizzayon*, p. 33a.

preventive measures. He recommended moderation in every situation and avoidance of spicy food and alcoholic beverages. He also listed prescriptions and foods that were effective in the prevention of a variety of other diseases. Curiously, with all his belief in preventive medicine, he still was sure that there were specific Jewish maladies which occurred because "of their (i.e. the Jews') fate".

SECTION V

RELIGIOUS LIFE AND MORALITY

a.

The question of the relationship between Renaissance culture and religion has not, as yet, been adequately explored. It may be stated with certainty that the Renaissance fostered a positive attitude toward religion as a fundamental value in the spiritual life of mankind. But it did not identify itself with religion per se as the only basis for human life on earth. Consequently, the Renaissance limited the scope of religion in human affairs. The religious life was further influenced by the aspiration of Renaissance man to reproduce the Antiquity and by the individualistic inclinations of the people.[1]

The religious and moral life of Renaissance Jewry was also influenced by the new cultural stream. However, since the Renaissance among the Jews was not the result of an inner development but came essentially as an external influence, its impact on Jewish religious life was not all pervasive. It must also be stressed that religion served as a kind of barrier against excessive absorption in Renaissance culture and generated definite opposition to the intrusion of alien mores. Not only were the periodic disputes over the legitimacy of one practice or another on the basis of the ban against "following their statutes" (Leviticus 18:3),[2] but voices in various quarters were heard expressing genuine remorse over absorption in an alien culture. Nor is this plaint heard only at the end of the Period that was characterized by a great swell of religious feeling among Italian Jews. Even Moses Rieti the refined

---

[1] See *Burckhardt*, pp. 321 ff., 341 ff., 367.

[2] See *Responsa of Rabbi Joseph Colon*, section 88 and section 149 on the subject of permitting the wearing of the *cappa* and *REJ* 79:40 for the opposition in Padua to the elaborate funeral of Rabbi Judah Minz; *Responsa Abukat rokel* by Rabbi Joseph Karo, section 65 regarding Rabbi Judah Minz's fight against an ark cover in the synagogue that bore an embroidered family seal in bas-relief.

humanist who lived at the high point of the Renaissance, regretted that he occupied himself with secular wisdom and had incorporated it in his work *Miḳdash meat* (*The Lesser Sanctuary*): [1] "during my youth I built gossamer structures on emptiness, I increased endlessly my guilt of wasting (time)".[2]

Yet, despite this, Jewish religious life and attitudes tended to be influenced by the Renaissance. Merely to recall the assertion of Azariah dei Rossi [3] that Rabbi Obadiah Sforno explained the *urim wetummim* as "comparable to the auguries pronounced by idolatrous priests in ancient times and known as oracles"; or the belief of Rabbi Johanan Alemanno that Plato "received (his teachings) from the prophets", [4] is enough to indicate how the Renaissance affected religious views. Religious practice was narrowed down by the trend toward an affluent life pattern and an education that strove to impart the arts of music, dance, and the composition of elegant letters. Obviously, the study of Torah and serving one's Creator were no longer considered the only way of life to be pursued by the Jew. In effect, the religious life of Renaissance Jewry was a complex resultant of these opposing factors and must be evaluated and understood in this light.

b.

The absence of a strong communal organization further contributed to the weakening of religious life. With its influence curtailed, the community had to limit its activities to giving meager support to Torah study [5] and maintaining the central religious institutions such as the synagogue. That some communities possibly lacked even the main religious institutions is indicated by the refusal of a large portion of the Treviso Jews

[1] *Iggeret ḥamudot* by Elijah Ḥayim of Genazzano, London 1912, p. 4 and p. 23 ff.
[2] *Ibid.*, p. 24.
[1] See *Meor enayim*, section *Yeme olam*, p. 64. I checked Sforno's commentary to Exodus 28:30, Leviticus 8:8, and Numbers 27:21, and did not find this interpretation. Regrettably, I could not check the first edition of the commentary.
[4] *Shaar haḥesheḳ*, Leghorn 1790, p. 34a.
[5] See Section VIII, Chapter 3.

to maintain a ritualarium.[1] The existence of many synagogues in various cities [2] should not be misconstrued as an indication of any special desire to build houses of worship. The multiplication of synagogues was primarily the result of the multigroup communities, [3] and wherever there was a mixed Jewish population there were Italianic, Sephardic, Ashkenazic, and Levantine synagogues. Many synagogues were also founded by wealthy individuals [4] whose maecenean aspirations accorded with the spirit of the age.

Moreover, the position of the rabbinate was weak and its activity in strengthening religion was limited. We have seen (Section II, Chapter 5), that the rabbi was not a leader who supervised the religious life of the community and its moral standards, but was essentially a functionary utilized by the community for its administrative and educational needs. The complaint which Rabbi David Ibn Jachia filed against the Union of Communities in the Kingdom of Naples [5] stressed his role as a judge, elementary teacher, secretary of the community, a calligraphy instructor, and a scribe of letters and documents. Not a word is mentioned about the Association's concern over strengthening religion or raising the community's moral level.

The limitation of the authority of the rabbi in the Renaissance community was not the only factor diminishing his role as a religious leader. The Italian rabbinate of the Period did not generally supply the type of spiritual leadership common in the age of the "Pious Men of Ashkenaz" or in Eastern Europe. Numerous complaints by contemporaries were leveled against rabbis which were also echoed by outstanding

[1] See *Responsa of Rabbi Judah Minz and Maharam of Padua*, par. 7.

[2] There were ten synagogues in Ferrara in the mid-sixteenth century (*Meor enayim*, part 1, p. 20). The same was the case in Mantua. Cf. *Responsa of Maharam of Padua*, par. 64: "Thank God there are plenty of synagogues there".

[3] In 1524 there were in Rome even special synagogues for the immigrants from Catalonia and Sicily: see *RMI* 10:326.

[4] Such as the Canton family synagogue in Venice that was founded in 1532 (see Adolfo Ottolenghi, *Rivista di Venezia*, 1929, p. 480, Note 1) or the Meshullamim synagogue (see Roth, *Venice*, p. 141).

[5] *HUCA*, 1:617 ff.

men in the rabbinate. In connection with the excommunication of a woman by leading rabbis, Maharam of Padua complained that "a group of rabbis whom I do not know and with whose names I am not familiar rose to her aid and annulled the decree of the leaders who had previously excommunicated her". [1] When Rabbi Judah Minz prohibited the placing in the Paduan synagogue of an ark cover with protruding figures, the donor, Herz Wertheim, "through his wealth found rabbis who aided him and made available to him proof from the Talmud permitting it". [2] Similar complaints were voiced by another great sixteenth century rabbi, Azriel Diena who protested against the custom of granting ordination too easily, based only upon erudition, without probing whether or not the ordainees were also God fearing. He argued that such rabbis "do not know God in their hearts, will be corrupt, and will use their knowledge as a tool to amass wealth and power..." [3] This type of Italian rabbi appeared as Rab Ḥamdan ("The Greedy") in the comedy *Zaḥut bediḥuta deḳidushin*.[4] He used his legal knowledge to pervert justice and to advise transgressors how to evade the law. Small wonder that rabbinic ordination was often revoked in sixteenth century Italy. The situation is illuminated glaringly by a statement of one of the friends of the humanist Joseph Arli in connection with a legal suit against him. Joseph Arli was summoned before a court composed of rabbis from Padua, Venice, Mantua, Ferrara and Bologna, the five leading communities of Northeastern Italy. Nevertheless, the writer believed that his friend was vindicated only because of the power of his able plea. "And lo"—he writes—"the rabbis could not pervert judgement against him although they were biased, and there is no doubt that if the forementioned distinguished scholar (Joseph Arli) were naive and simple-minded he would have been hopelessly trapped by their

[1] *Responsa of Maharam of Padua*, par. 73.
[2] *Abuḳat roḳel, Ibid.*
[3] Fragment of a responsum published in *Kirjath sepher* 14:550.
[4] Mentioned frequently in *Zaḥut bediḥuta deḳiddushin*. He is an important figure in the play.

corruption. But since the forementioned rabbi was a fighter from his youth and knew how to separate the fine flour from the chaff, he emerged vindicated and they were compelled to restore the rabbinic crown to his head..." [1]

Such testimony indicates beyond doubt that unqualified individuals entered the Italian rabbinate of the time and that a great deal of mutual suspicion prevailed among the rabbis regarding the legitimacy of their counterparts. Moreover, a number of North Italian rabbis, and possibly a majority of them, engaged in business while simultaneously serving as rabbis.[2] Although a broadly tolerant attitude to such a situation was typical of the Period, it did not add stature to the rabbi's role as spiritual leader.

One inevitable result of this situation was Jewish patronage of non-Jewish courts, against which leading rabbis fought a losing battle.[3] There was no use in taking a case to a rabbinic court if a counter opinion by another rabbi was easily obtainable after a decision. To be sure, patronage of non-Jewish courts during the Italian Renaissance need not be viewed as a breach of Jewish communal loyalty. The fact that many social barriers between Jew and Christian fell, led Jews to trust the judgements of a gentile judge. At the close of the Renaissance period when religious sentiment mounted among Italian Jews (see below, this Section, part 8), they began to regard the patronage of non-Jewish courts as incompatible with religious life. It was then that the *Yeshibat Shalom* society in Ancona whose bylaws reflected the new moralistic and pietistic direction of the age, resolved to forbid its membership to settle their differences in non-Jewish courts.[4]

The extent of the rabbi's influence is difficult to ascertain. Indications are that it was quite limited. Even the Verona community, which had a definite religio-moral orientation, limited its rabbi's influence in communal affairs. In a contract with Rabbi Menahem Cohen Porto, a renowned scholar, the

---

[1] See the article by Marx, *Tarbiz* 8:184.
[2] Sonne, *Kobez al jad*, N. S. 3:155.
[3] Marx, *Studies*, p. 122.
[4] See *Haasif* 3:214 ff.

community obligated him to attend meetings of the community administration whenever summoned. However, they also stipulated that "if he is not asked he cannot attend". With another rabbi they made a proviso that he was not permitted to introduce any ordinance even on ritual matters, without the agreement of two other rabbis, and even then he must obtain the concurrence of the *parnasim* with regard to the timing of its promulgation.[1] Against the background of such limitations the actual influence of the rabbi was mostly determined by his personal qualities and devotion.

Throughout the Period a certain number of rabbis, mostly men of outstanding character, attained great reputation and influence as regional religious leaders. We have seen that on the basis of the *condotta* many sparsely populated communities arose, sometimes even lacking a quorum of ten adult Jews. Such tiny communities obviously could not employ a rabbi to minister to their needs.[2] Therefore, when religious guidance was needed such communities turned to a well known rabbi in the city closest to them. This is why many of the responsa of Rabbi Joseph Colon and Rabbi Judah Minz were addressed to ordinary people or lay community leaders. Such frequently consulted rabbis were ultimately accepted informally, and often even formally, as chief rabbis of entire regions.

c.

Rabbinic failure to guide religious life led to religious doubt even in circles that were close to the rabbis, and especially among students of the yeshibot. The sources indicate the existence of this phenomenon during the entire sixteenth century. A startling incident took place in 1502 in the *yeshibah* of Rabbi Judah Minz in Padua: "...He himself (Rabbi Judah Minz) saw and felt that some of his students whom he had nurtured rose up without provocation to swallow him

[1] Sonne, *Kobez al jad, Ibid.*, pp. 170 and 176. These contracts are dated 1584 and 1592.
[2] For example, the community of Asolo numbered 37 souls, and in the detailed population list that we have no one is designated as a rabbi.

alive and they maligned him terribly and testified falsely in public against him, some personally and others through accomplices, each one according to his capacity, and all because he, who had never been partial to anyone reproved them over their evil acts that he considered improper... and because of his reproof they threatened him, but he controlled himself and spoke freely of the strong heresy that some of his students manifested when they assembled at the invitation of Rabbi Simmelin, may Heaven protect him, in Padua the sixth of Shebat, 1502..." [1] In the middle of the sixteenth century one of the disciples of Joseph Arli praised him not only for having taught him Torah but also for having dispelled all his doubts regarding matters of faith.[2] Shortly thereafter Rabbi David Provenzali promised in the first paragraph of his program for a Jewish university that he would attempt "to remove from their (i.e. the students') hearts any root sprouting false knowledge if it should, God forbid, be present". [3] That this was not a superfluous promise is evident from the fact that the burning of the Talmud in 1553 was regarded as a punishment for widespread freethinking. Rabbi Immanuel da Benevento who in his work *Liwyat ḥen* complained about this matter also alluded openly to hostility toward the Talmud: "And there can be no doubt that the Talmud was burned only because of the sin of those who derided it and the many ignorant who took pride... in false opinions... and attacked the masters of the Talmud..." [4] The rampant religious skepticism apparently undermined the belief in the immortality of the soul as well. Rabbi Samuel Judah Katzenellenbogen, son of Maharam of Padua, devoted a eulogy over one of the most prominent rabbis to a demonstration of proofs for the soul's immortality: "...I have seen fit to bring these proofs as refutation of the ideas of the irresponsible skeptics".[5]

---

[1] *Sefer pesakim*, Venice 1519, p. 28a.

[2] See Marx, *Louis Ginzberg Jubilee Volume*, pp. 20-21 (Hebrew Section).

[3] *Halebanon* 5:434. Cf. M. Guedemann, *Abraham Berliner Jubilee Volume*, p. 164 ff.

[4] p. 109a.

[5] *Derashot harab Shemuel Yehuda Katzenellenbogen*, Venice 1594, p.

In addition to such skepticism current mainly among the intellectuals, religious apathy and a frivolous attitude toward ritual observance and religious institutions prevailed among ordinary people. In the second half of the fifteenth century an incident occurred where a large group of Jews came to a small town to participate in a wedding and "in the group were both young and old" and all of them carried "their baggage and their staffs on the Sabbath in the streets without any restraint". Rabbi Joseph Colon was extremely agitated over this and remarked to them: "Has the Sabbath been annulled?". [1] Even at the end of the Period when a religious awakening stirred Italian Jewry, the Venetian Rabbinate felt compelled to write a letter upbraiding the Jews of Capodistria [2] for the infrequent attendance at synagogues which were empty mornings and evenings for want of a prayer quorum. Similarly, the rabbis were not successful in enforcing the ban on drinking wine made by non-Jews. Maharam of Padua complained that the rabbis had no power to oppose this practice. Years later Leon da Modena stated explicitly that all Italian Jewry does not abide by the ban on non-Jewish wine.[3]

Another striking failing lay in the fact that even those religious duties that were practised, were performed with laxity. The contemptuous attitude toward prayer was bitterly resented by Samuel Archivolti: "Nothing can justify the practice of some present day cantors who chant the sacred prayers in secular folk melodies and thus obscenity and shame invade the minds (of the worshippers) in the midst of the sanctified word". [4] Such testimony regarding isolated events is buttressed by a general complaint over excessive surrender

28a. Cf. *Burckhardt*, p. 404 ff. for the weakening of the belief in the soul's immortality among Christians as well.
[1] *Responsa of Rabbi Joseph Colon*, par. 46.
[2] *Leo Modenas Briefe*, p. 19, no. 19.
[3] See *Responsa of Maharam of Padua*, par. 76 and Leon da Modena, *Historia de gli Riti Hebraici*, part 2, chapter 8, par. 1. However, Sicilian Jews prior to their expulsion did abide by the ban on non-Jewish wine. Cf. *Iggerot Erez Israel*, p. 104.
[4] *Arugat habosem*, Venice 1603, p. 110b. Rabbi Solomon Alami also complained in his *Iggeret hamusar* that Spanish cantors had followed this questionable practice. See *Ibid.*, Jerusalem ed., 1946, p. 25.

to non-Jewish patterns. Venice took the lead in this respect and its fame as a hotbed of sinners even reached the Holy Land. In *Shibḥe Rabbi Hayyim Vital* there is a story of a *dibbuk* that entered a girl's body in Damascus in 1609 and called upon the people to repent. The *dibbuk* spoke of the evil behavior of Damascene Jews and predicted that disaster will also come to the sinful Jewish community of Venice.[1] Other communities followed the lead of Venice. The grandiose funeral of Rabbi Judah Minz arranged by his son Abraham [2] is illustrative of the extent of Jewish acceptance of Renaissance customs.

To be sure, strong discontent did develop in Padua over this funeral, and Rabbi Abraham Minz was compelled to bring Talmudic proof validating a lavish funeral. In fact, virtually every violation of religious life was accompanied by protest and resistance. Not only do we encounter protest but a positive call to repentance as well. A book of sermons *Bet moed* by Rabbi Menahem Raba (Venice, 1604), meant to be a resource volume for preachers, included a complete grouping of forty sermons on the subject of repentance. Obviously, repentance was a topic widely discussed by the preachers. Here and there, moreover, communities retained a thoroughly pious mode of life. The Jews of Macerata, for example, "were reared in our holy Torah, poring over it constantly, day and night". [3]

d.

What then was the reason that virtually until the end of the Period no signs of universal repentance were apparent, and that the weakness of religious life, which also engendered widespread moral laxity, prevailed? The answer to this question may be found through a closer look at the psyche of the Renaissance Jew. Renaissance man's effort to liberate himself from the shackles of the Middle Ages failed because of his

---

[1] Acknowledged by Rabbi Azriel Diena in a responsum. *Shibḥe Rabbi Ḥayim Vital*, n. p., 1862, p. 9a.
[2] *REJ* 79:40.
[3] Sonne, *Hatekufah*, p. 653.

belief in the decisive power of the stars over his destiny.[1] This belief served also to justify man's evil inclinations and to free him from responsibility for his actions. Fatalism and blind belief in the power of the constellations were equally widespread among the Jews, and especially among the intellectuals. Immanuel of Rome was convinced that "if the decree was promulgated on high, human endeavor was of no avail". Kalonymos ben Kalonymos also felt the same when he asserted "that when God acts...his decree is firm and human effort is futile". [2] These early Jewish men of the Renaissance were joined in their belief in fatalism not only by a man like Leon da Modena, but even by such distinguished moralists as Rabbi Raphael Norsa, and Abraham Jaghel Gallichi. They went as far as to attribute everything to the force of the stars. Abraham Jaghel Gallichi was of the opinion that certain maladies "were common among them (i.e. the Jews) because of their constellation, which affects them all". While Rabbi Raphael Norsa acknowledged the power of the stars, he did at least assert that the Torah was given to the people of Israel as a means of overcoming astral influence. But Abraham Jaghel Gallichi believed that only the patriarch Abraham succeeded through his exceptional deeds and devotion to God to neutralize planetary decrees. However, "...there is no power in average deeds to change for good or ill that which has been ordained".[3]

To people with such a fatalistic outlook, repentance appeared to be futile and devoid of efficacy in changing fate or man's character. We can thus also understand why Rabbi Menahem Raba's sermons dealt with the need for penitence rather than its ways, so that the people would become convinced that there is benefit in repentance and that ultimately it leads to a reconciliation between God and man.

---

[1] See *Burckhardt*, p. 342 ff.

[2] See *Maḥberot Immanuel*, p. 31; I. Sonne's introduction to *Iggeret hamusar* by Rabbi Kalonymos ben Kalonymos, *Kobez al jad*, N. S. 1:102, Note 32. The 27th *maḥberet* in Immanuel's *Maḥbarot* deals with the constellations. Cf. *Dibre ḥakamim* edited by Eliezer Aschkenazi, Metz 1849, p. 37 ff.; J. L. Zlotnik, *Research of the Hebrew Idiom* (Hebrew), Jerusalem 1938, p. 59 ff.

[3] *Ge ḥizzayon*, p. 11b.

A result of the belief in fatalism and of the lack of confidence in the value of average good deeds, was the emergence
of extensive corruption among the Jewish population. To
begin with, a considerable part of the Italian Jewish community, including rabbis, engaged in moneylending and
virtually no one was concerned over its negative moral, social,
or political aspects. As eminent a writer as Abraham Farissol
discussed usury in virtually complete equanimity and justified
it, adding merely a brief note that "he who shuns an evil name
and prefers a good one through his choice of an honest occupation and proper business ventures...merits many blessings". [1] He was thus aware of more suitable economic
pursuits but did not consider it necessary to urge the people
to turn to respectable professions. Clear statements against
engaging in moneylending were heard only at the close of the
Period with the general heightening of moral sensitivity.
Abraham Jaghel Gallichi arrived at an opposition to usurious
lending only after having personally experienced the dismal
consequences that can result from it. [2] Then he became convinced that this business was not a social asset and only led to
general debasement. It was, in addition, the chief factor in
expulsions and other afflictions that beset Jews in all lands of
their dispersion. At approximately the same time Samuel
Archivolti also expressed sharp opposition to the loan business
claiming that "it leads to the pursuit of robbery, alienation of
family, hatred of friends, animosity of the masses, and an
overwhelming anxiety..." [3] Until then no such voices were
heard during a period of almost three centuries.

Other social evils, more grave than usury, although not as
widespread, plagued Renaissance Jewish society as well. [4]
Especially shocking is the large number of informers and
murderers. There were Jews who murdered in the act of
robbery, and others who hired themselves out as murderers.

[1] See *Magen Abraham*, Chapter 73, published in *Hazofeh* 12:290.
[2] *Ge ḥizzayon*, Ibid., p. 4b and passim.
[3] *Maayan ganim*, Venice 1553, p. 22a.
[4] Such as the bizarre case of parents who wanted to exhibit for
money siamese twins born to them. See *Zera anashim*, Husiatyn
1902, p. 50 ff.

There was even a Jewish physician who murdered a colleague because the latter was more successful. Solomon Molko complained that in Venice he was given poison by Jews and Rabbi Azriel Diena accused David Reubeni of plotting to murder him.[1]When Padua was sacked after its conquest by the Austrians during the War of the League of Cambray (1509), Jews also participated. Elijah Capsali described it as follows: "And many of the Jewish populace also donned armor and weapons and joined non-Jews and they also looted in the aforementioned sacking. These ruthless Jews did more harm to their fellow Jews in Padua than did the gentiles, for they invaded the homes of wealthy Jews... and engaged in looting from their fellow Jews". [2]

Such incidents and many other available examples indicate the serious corruption that penetrated all strata of Jewish society. It should be noted, however, that the corruptness of Jewish society was relatively mild in comparison with the violence and depravity that were prevalent in Renaissance society at large.

e.

Renaissance Jewry was also beset with many superstitious beliefs, although they were not as harmful as its blind fear of the power of the stars. Such tenets as, for example, belief in the efficacy of witchcraft and in demons weighed heavily on the Jew's coul and blurred his view on matters of faith, Thus, religious reaction to critical situations in the life of man was rarely expressed in the form of a silent and heartfelt prayer. It assumed highly emotional forms, and its dramatic exaggeration appealed strongly to the Renaissance imagination. There was a case where a Torah scroll was placed in the lap of a woman to ease her intense labor pains.[3] The rabbi who sharply protested this practice stated that in Hungary it sufficed to bring the Torah scroll into the room of a woman in labor. But

[1] See Solomon Molko's letter included by Joseph Hakohen in *Dibre hayamim*. See the Amsterdam edition of 1733, p. 93b and Rabbi Azriel Diena's letter in *REJ* 30:307.

[2] *REJ* 79:51.

[3] See *Kirjath sepher* 14:543.

in Renaissance Italy more dramatic action was demanded. Rabbi Obadiah da Bertinoro told that when he was in Palermo en route to the Holy Land, people wanted parts of his clothing as amulets, and remarked: "They treated me like the gentiles do their saints..." [1] Vows and oaths were numerous in Renaissance Italy, and the Responsa literature is filled with questions from people who regretted impulsive religious actions and sought means of evading their consequences.[2] The large number of reports regarding belief in the existence of demons, *dibbukim* and other spirits, coupled with the fact that numerous scholars of the period professed their belief in them, leaves little space for surprise that even an enlightened humanist of first rank, Rabbi Yohanan Alemanno wrote a book attempting "to establish this discipline (i.e. magic and witchcraft) theoretically and thereby also validate all the talismanic practice connected with it". [3]

And yet, these same Jews were also able to perform regular *mizwot* quite devoutedly, especially in the face of challenge. An entire Jewish community once had the courage to refuse to stand with heads uncovered in a church, despite the king's demand.[4] This is particularly noteworthy when we recall that the Jews of Italy were not overly concerned with the matter of head covering (see above Section IV, Chapter 3). Similarly, in one of the small towns Jews courageously removed an apostate from the synagogue who had entered under explicit instructions of Pope Paul IV.[5] When a local fast was decreed in a time of stress, the entire Jewish population fasted in solidarity throughout all of Italy.[6] It should also be noted that

---

[1] *Iggerot Erez Israel*, p. 107.

[2] See *Responsa of Maharam of Padua*, passim, also *Kirjath sepher*, *Ibid.*, passages of various responsa printed there. See *Responsa of Maharam*, par. 69 regarding the community of Monopoli, whose inhabitants left the city because one of its rabbis "excommunicated the entire community" in the preceding generation. "The hearts (of the people of the community) still pounded . . . and (they were) frightened at the rustle of a driven leaf".

[3] *Kirjath sepher* 5:273.

[4] See *REJ* 10:184.

[5] *Emek habaka*, p. 137.

[6] See *Meor enayim*, Part 1, p. 20 and *Hamagiha*, p. 162.

once a *miẓwah* was performed, it was done wholeheartedly and without hypocrisy. Religious hypocrites were virtually non existent. We can safely believe Leon da Modena when he assured us that he was sincere and that he more frequently avoided clandestine wrongdoing than public sin.[1]

f.

The composite character of the Jewish community resulted in a multiplicity of religious customs and rites. In the life of the ordinary man this manifested itself primarily in the area of prayer ritual. Other areas of the religious practice, such as laws dealing with what was permitted or prohibited, were primarily the concern of the rabbis, who adhered to different legal traditions. The existence of several prayer rites was reflected in the large number of synagogues we find in various places. The multiplicity of synagogues was so striking that Pope Paul IV in his anti-Jewish legislation permitted the maintenance of only one synagogue in a community.[2] At the beginning of the Period there was only one order of prayer in all of Italy, the Italianic, also known as *minhag bene Romi* or *minhag Loez*. The Italianic daily prayerbook generally resembles the Ashkenazic and Sephardic prayer orders, differing from these versions approximately in the degree that they differ from each other. Basic differences, however, are found in the Italianic order of prayers for the holidays.[3]

The Ashkenazic prayer order began to take root in Italy with the beginning of German Jewish immigration. We have seen (Section I, Chapter 1) that the Ashkenazic immigrants moved into cities with no Jewish population. Thus, in a large part of Italy areas of German Jewish settlement arose where the prayer order was, naturally, Ashkenazic. When the German immigration reached districts near the Po River, it encountered communities of Italianic Jews. Whenever a small number of Ashkenazim settled in an Italianic community, they

[1] *Sepher Chaje Jehuda*, p. 69.
[2] Sonne, *Tarbiẓ* 2:345.
[3] *Iggerot Shadal*, Przemysl 1882-Cracow 1891, pp. 434-464 where a detailed description of the Roman *maḥazor* is available.

prayed in the Roman ritual. However, as soon as they increased to parity, they would establish a synagogue for themselves and follow the Ashkenazic rite. There were not many
incidents of strife between the Italiani and the Ashkenazim
over the prayer order.[1] Such was not the case with the Sephardim. When they came to Italy they settled generally in
cities with Italianic communities. Nevertheless, even when
small in number they established Sephardic synagogues. They
also protected their prayer version far more zealously than the
Ashenazim.[2] Thus, only in two areas did a unified prayer order
exist. In a substantial part of North Italy the Ashkenazic
rite was followed and in the region of Rome whith its old
Italianic communities the Roman usage dominated. In all
other parts of the peninsula the three rites existed side by side.
In the first half of the Period, until the expulsion in 1492,
there was also an independent prayer order in Sicily, which
leaned toward the North African rite.[3]

The differences among the three groups were not limited to
the prayer order but manifested themselves in the entire
synagogue service. Rabbi Obadiah da Bertinoro found an
entirely different form of service in Sicily than what was
customary on the Italian mainland.[4] He was surprised by the
large number of cantors who participated in the service.

At the end of the Period Leon da Modena observed that the

[1] Very interesting is the example of the relations between Ashkenazim and Italiani in Ferrara. When the Ashkenazim started to
arrive in that city at the end of the fifteenth century, it had one
Italianic synagogue which the Ashkenazim frequented for prayer.
In 1532 a separate Ashkenazic synagogue was established as a result
of their increasing numbers. In 1573 after the destruction of Ferrara
in a violent earthquake the Ashkenazim and Italiani reunited in one
synagogue while the Sephardim, even then, remained apart. (See
above, Section II, Chapter 3).

[2] See the preceding Note and I. Sonne, *Zion*, N. S. 3:154 regarding
the Aboab family's plea before the Venetian government to prevail
upon the Ashkenazic community of Verona to permit them to pray
according to the Sephardic rite.

[3] See Leopold Zunz, *Zur Geschichte und Litteratur*, p. 524 and
Simon Bernstein, "Fragments of Poetry from the Golden Age",
HUCA 16:99 ff.

[4] See his letter, *Iggerot Erez Israel*, p. 106.

Ashkenazim sing more than the others and that the Levantines and Sephardim chant in a style resembling the Turkish
mode. But Italianic prayers, he thought, were most beautiful
and sweet and it was delightful to listen to them.[1]

The various prayer versions have persisted in Italy up to the
present and have withstood external pressures. Pope Paul IV's
order limiting Jews to only one synagogue in a city did not
lead to the creation of a unified rite. The various rites also
withstood the natural assimilationist trends prevalent among
the diverse Jewish groups, even though they all used the
Hebrew pronounciation common in Italy for many generations. There is evidence from the end of the Period[2] that
"some people in the latter generations have changed the
prayer order from Italianic to Sephardic or vice versa". However, the various groups fought stubbornly against any
change. Somewhat later the leaders of the Italianic synagogue
in Venice forbade any visiting Italianic Jew to worship at a
Sephardic or Ashkenazic synagogue. When an Italianic Jew
arrived in the city the sexton was sent especially to invite
him to the Italianic synagogue. The other two synagogues with
differing rites naturally responded by issuing injunctions.[3] A
similar situation existed in Ancona and Florence,[4] and undoubtedly in many other cities as well. The large number of
editions of prayerbook translations into Italian, Yiddish and
Portuguese[5] shows that there was a tendency to encourage
loyalty to the specific rites of the different groups.

As indicated, matters dealing with laws of what is prohibited
and what is permitted also reflected group diversity. In this
area custom played an important role in Italy, because

[1] *Historia de gli Riti Hebraici*, Part i, Chapter ii, par. 6.
[2] *Maabar Yabbok* by Rabbi Aaron Berechiah of Modena, Lemberg
1867, p. 96b.
[3] See *Ozar tob*, 1885-1886, p. 13.
[4] See the list of documents from the archives of the Ancona community published in *Corriere Israelitico*, 1914 and Cassuto, *I più
antichi capitoli del ghetto di Firenze*, p. 19. In Florence a decision
was made to prohibit any changes in the Italianic order of prayers
as found in the Bologna edition of the *maḥazor*.
[5] See Cassuto, *REJ* 89:260 ff.; *Yivo Annual of Jewish Social
Science* 1:272.

Italiani and Ashkenazim, as opposed to the Sephardim, stressed the validity of the *minhag*, as practiced by the people (see below, Section VIII, Chapter 3). A decisive factor was the avowed effort to preserve the ancient Italianic *minhag*. With the emergence of the composite Jewry, the Italiani constituted at most only one third of the Jewish population and thus found themselves on the defensive. They therefore clung to the two *minhagim* collections, *Shibale haleket* and *Tanya*, that were composed at the beginning of the Renaissance period and incorporated the customs of Rome, the ancient center of uninterrupted Italianic tradition. One of the rabbis explicitly endorsed *Shibbale haleket* as "a book designed to maintain our Italianic custom". [1] The Italianic *minhag* tended to avoid extremes in the fulfillment of *mizvot*. Rabbi Joseph Colon stated "that in all Italian lands they followed the rulings of Maimonides who tended to be lenient", and almost two centuries later Leon da Modena too attested to this fact. [2] Similarly the Ashkenazim, Sephardim and Levantines followed their own forms of observance with the result that in this area, as in prayer, a multi-faceted pattern emerged. We have seen (Section II, Chapter 7) that Messer Leon opposed such multiplicity and attempted to impose a central rabbinic authority to enforce halakhic unity. About eighty years later an eminent rabbi again made a powerful appeal: "Would that our scholars unite for the sake of God's service and decide to follow one recognized codifier of their own choice and agree to abide unqualifiedly by his decisions in all matters. Strife would then cease to exist in Israel and there would be no more a multitude of groups..." [3] These efforts were largely unsuccessful, and Italian Jewry remained fragmented with each group bent upon its ways.

---

[1] *Kebod ḥakamim* by David son of Messer Leon, Berlin 1899, p. 39.

[2] See *Responsa of Rabbi Isaac ben Sheshet*, Munkacs 1901, par. 34 p. 104 (responsum of Rabbi Joseph Colon) and the responsum of Leon da Modena regarding uncovering the head, published by Isaac Rivkind in *Louis Ginzberg Jubilee Volume*, p. 419 (Hebrew section).

[3] See *REJ* 32:132 and Moses A. Shulvass, *In the Grip of Centuries*, p. 56 ff.

g.

The period of the Renaissance was an era of harmony and rapprochement between Jews and their gentile neighbors. The anti-Jewish propaganda of the fifteenth century Christian preachers [1] only slightly and very briefly disturbed this harmony. Moreover, even then many humanists sided with the Jews. A statement by Antonio di Ferrari, known as Galateo [2] is typical: "The Jews are an ancient and noble people. Everything in Christian culture is derived from Judaism, for their religious writings are read in Christian churches, not those of Livy or Aristotle". Such views also made an impact in the area of religious life.

To begin with, there existed a mutual theoretical interest of both religions in each other, accompanied by mutual respect. Christians, including the clergy, visited synagogues to hear sermons of rabbinic preachers. Similarly Leon da Modena was visiting a Catholic church. This interest seems to have spread to the ordinary people as well. When Bernardino da Sienna, one of the great preachers, came to Aquila in Southern Italy in 1438 and preached before the king and large crowds, many Jews also came to hear him speak.[3] Missionary sermons which Jews were compelled to hear were only instituted late in the Period as part of the open anti-Jewish policy of Pope Paul IV.[4]

An attitude of mutual esteem was also apparent in the many religious dialogues which, in contrast to the disputations conducted in Germany and Spain, were motivated by efforts at understanding and clarification rather than compulsion.[5] In these debates which extended through the entire Renaissance period and somewhat beyond, participated some of the most outstanding rabbis and scholars, such as Abraham

---

[1] See *Ferorelli*, p. 189.
[2] See *RMI* 12:378.
[3] See Alexander Marx, *HUCA* 1:617; *Sepher Chaje Jehuda*, p. 34; G. Pansa, *Gli ebrei in Aquila nel secolo XV*, Aquila 1904, p. 203.
[4] See A. Milano, *RMI* 18:517 ff.
[5] Abraham Farissol translated part of his book *Magen Abraham* into Italian in order to give his Christian opponents an opportunity to answer him. See *Ḥayim Michael Catalogue*, p. 319.

Farissol, Solomon Molko, Azariah dei Rossi, Azriel Alatini, and Leon da Modena.[1] Ferrara was a center of such discussions, for its enlightened dukes manifested a genuine interest in deliberations upon religious matters. Encouraged by them, Abraham Farissol wrote his *Magen Abraham*, one of the greatest Jewish polemical works. One Ferrara debate attracted Giovanni Pico della Mirandola, the well known philo-Semite and scholar.[2] At a debate held in 1617 with the participation of Rabbi Azriel Alatini, approximately two thousand people were present, "many of whom were the most important people of the city".[3] The contemporary polemical works offer a clear picture of the issues under discussion. Elijah Levita, known as *Baḥur*, summarized them in his work *Sefer zikronot*. He listed among the book's advantages that "this book can be used as a polemical reference work and will be very effective in debating those who oppose our faith... It is well known that most of the differences between us and them are over the question of the Messiah whether he has come or will come, and over the length of the exile and the time of redemption, over paradise and hell, and whoever may debate these subjects should study (the book) and find arguments".[4] Elijah's remarks indicate that such debates were widespread in Italy. Abraham Farissol stated indeed that "he debated with them (i.e. the Christians) many, many days".[5]

The religious toleration of the Catholic clergy allayed Jewish suspicions and Jewish teachers readily taught Rabbinic

---

[1] See Joseph Hakohen, *Dibre hayamim*, p. 91b (Solomon Molko); *Meor enayim*, section "Imre binah", p. 130 (Azariah dei Rossi); *Wikuah al niẓḥiut hatorah*, edited by Giuseppe Jarè, Leghorn 1876, p. 1, (Azriel Alatini); *Leo Modenas Briefe* no. 47 (Leon da Modena); *Hazofeh* 12:283 (Abraham Farissol).

[2] See Heinz Pflaum (Hiram Peri), *MGWJ* 72:348.

[3] See *Wikuah al niẓḥiut hatorah*, Ibid.

[4] *Sefer zikronot*, Frankfort 1875, p. 6.

[5] *Hazofeh, Ibid.*; Cf. Cassuto, *Florence*, p. 271 for the debate before Prince Sigismondo Malatesta in Rimini in 1477, and *Vogelstein-Rieger*, vol. 2, p. 5 for the invitation of Aaron Abulrabi by Pope Martin V to speak before him and the cardinals on the subject of the *cherubim*.

literature to Christians despite the reservations of some rabbis. Some Jewish scholars even went much farther. Abraham Portaleone, for example, recommended that Jews should purchase Christian prayerbooks and use them as textbooks for the study of the Greek language.[1] Another rabbi employed a gentile as teacher of Italian in his *yeshibah*.[2] Also it was not uncommon to invite gentile friends to serve as godfathers at circumcision ceremonies.[3] It is thus not surprising that sometimes a genuine friendship developed between rabbis and Christian clergymen.[4] Jewish concern over friendly relations with Christians in religious matters is amply manifested by the fact that during the first half of the sixteenth century the rabbis sifted the penitential prayers and deleted those sections that might offend Christians.[5] Somewhat ambiguous, to be sure, was the rabbis' attitude to Christian religious literature. Like Abraham Portaleone, Abraham Jaghel Gallichi was unconcerned over its impact upon Jews, and modeled his manual of religious instruction *Leḳaḥ tob* after catechism books used by the Catholics. But when Leon da Modena translated from Italian into Hebrew the Christian ethical tract *Fior di virtù*, he eliminated all purely Christian material and replaced it with passages and ideas from Rabbinic literature.[6]

The social rapprochement between Jews and Christians had a twofold result. On the one hand it brought about a loosening of religious observance, but on the other hand it removed many factors that historically had led Jews to conversion. It now became possible for Jews to have social

[1] *Shilte hagibborim*, p. 9b.

[2] See Marx, *Louis Ginzberg Jubilee Volume*, p. 285 (Hebrew section).

[3] Such an event occurred in 1484 in Castrogiovanni, Sicily (see *Giovanni de Giovanni*, p. 341). A similar case in Venice is recorded in the chronicle "Sipur haẓarot sheabru beitalyah", published in Moses A. Shulvass, *In the Grip of Centuries*. The story of the godfather is found on pp. 96-97.

[4] See *Meor enayim, Ibid.*, for the friendship of Azariah dei Rossi with Dominican friars. Cf. *REJ* 30:311.

[5] *Iggerot Shadal*, p. 1142.

[6] *Leḳaḥ tob*, Venice 1587; Leon da Modena, *Ẓemaḥ ẓaddiḳ*, Venice 1600 (new edition, Tel-Aviv 1949) which is an adaption of the Christian Italian treatise *Fior di virtù*. Cf. *Sepher Chaje Jehuda*, p. 42.

contacts with society at large without abandoning the Jewish faith. Aside from cases of conversion resulting from strong political pressure which will be discussed below, incidents of baptism were generally not very numerous. An English traveler who visited Italy in 1612 complained bitterly over the paucity of Italian Jewish converts.[1] Most of the recorded conversions occurred among Jewish women who wished to marry upper class Christians.[2] Most male converts were also motivated by the desire to marry gentile women. No evidence is available that social pressure was openly applied to induce Jewish apostasy. On the contrary, an incident recorded in great detail by Rabbi Joseph Colon[3] indicates that a Catholic bishop showed concern for the feelings of Jews in a case of conversion. The numerous voluntary religious debates did not result in many incidents of Jewish apostasy or Christian conversion to Judaism, although several conversions to Judaism are recorded. There was only one serious incident of mass Jewish conversion that followed a messianic disappointment. According to an account in *Shalshelet hakabbalah,*[4] disappointment over "messiah" Asher Lemlein who appeared in 1502 in Northern Italy, caused "mass conversions, for when the fools saw that the Messiah did not come they then converted".

During the Period there were three incidents of mass Jewish conversion as a result of governmental pressure toward this end. The first one took place early in the Period when the kings of the Anjou dynasty succeeded in forcibly converting the Jewish community of the Kingdom of Naples.[5] When a

---

[1] Some cases of divorce and *halizah* involving converts are mentioned in the responsa of Rabbi Judah Minz and Maharam of Paduda. But generally the available information indicates that conversion incidents during the Renaissance Period were few in number. The number of conversions increased during the seventeenth and eighteenth centuries due to intensified political and religious pressure. See T. Coryat, *Coryat's Crudities*, vol. 1, p. 373.

[2] For example, see *RMI* 12:378: a Jewess converted to Christianity in order to marry a son of the duke of Neri.

[3] In his *Responsa*, par. 160.

[4] *Shalshelet hakabbalah*, p. 64; *Graetz-Rabinowitsch*, vol. 7, p. 157.

[5] See Cassuto, *Hermann Cohen Jubilee Volume*, p. 389 ff. and

new Jewish settlement was formed in that kingdom in the
ensuing two centuries and was further augmented by the
immigration of Spanish exiles in 1492, Naples was conquered
by Charles VIII, king of France, and once again most of the
community were transformed into Marranos. In 1504 there
were only a few isolated Jews in the Kingdom of Naples and
virtually the entire Jewish community was composed of
Marranos.[1]

The third great wave of conversion resulted from the policy
of Pope Paul IV which with one stroke deprived the Jews of
their newly won contacts with gentile society. The blow was
so great that many Jews submitted to conversion and there
was "no town without an apostate".[2] In the town of Cori, in
the vicinity of Rome, conversion was a daily occurrence.[3]
Such was, no doubt the situation in other locales as well.

h.

While thus a certain number of Jews converted to Christianity following the introduction of Pope Paul's new anti-Jewish
policies, the bulk of the Jewish community considered them
a mere indication that the time had come to re-appraise its
position within society at large. It became obvious that the
entire social structure of the Renaissance was beginning to
totter and that they must re-shape their life according to new
principles. The Jewish community as an institution was not
seriously affected by Pope Paul IV's policies. It was the
individual Jew who was deeply hurt, and he was compelled
again to resort to Jewish content in order to fill the vacuum
that developed about him following the severance of his
contacts with the larger society.

These factors that forced the Italian Jew to alter his way
of life and his attitudes were buttressed by the comparatively
large immigration into Italy of Jews from the Holy Land and

Asher Gulak and Samuel Klein Memorial Volume, p. 138 ff. Cf. Joshua
Starr, *Speculum* 21: 203 ff.
[1] *Register of the Jewish Theological Seminary of America*, 1940,
p. 65 ff.
[2] See Sonne, *Tarbiz* 2:347.
[3] *Graetz-Rabinowitsch*, vol. 7, p. 419 ff.

other Levantine countries.[1] These Jews represented a conservative religious element who advocated a more rigid way of observance.[2] They were also deeply interested in the teachings of the kabbalists. During this era the *Zohar* was published several times in Italy. Rabbi Israel Sarug, a Palestinian kabbalist, traveled all over Italy and founded "academies" of Palestinian mysticism. In addition to Rabbi Israel Sarug who taught the mystic doctrine of Rabbi Isaac Luria, the disciples of Rabbi Moses Cordovero were also actively engaged in spreading their master's kabbalistic teachings in Italy.[3] The number of kabbalists increased, and Rabbi Menahem Azariah da Fano became their inspired and enthusiastic leader. Such developments endowed life with a more ascetic and serious direction and strengthened adherence to the performance of religious duties. These trends even invaded a "modern" community like Venice. The English traveler who visited Venice in 1612 was very much impressed by the strict observance of the Sabbath and by the fact that the synagogues were filled with men, women, and children during Sabbath morning services.[4]

The drive to create the movement of *Shomerim laboker* (Watchmen for the morning, comp. Psalms 130:6) [5] also emerged in the circle of Rabbi Menahem Azariah da Fano. This was a movement of kabbalists who undertook the task of hastening the coming of the Messiah by infusing new significance into the rite of midnight prayer for Israel's restoration. Simultaneously the people who were involved in this move-

---

[1] See Moses A. Shulvass, *Roma wirushalayim*, Jerusalem 1944, p. 85.

[2] See the aforementioned responsum of Leon da Modena on the subject of head covering, *Ibid.*, p. 419.

[3] See *Zion*, N. S. 5:214 ff. and Moses A. Shulvass, *Ibid.*

[4] Coryat, *Ibid.*, p. 372 ff.

[5] See Moses A. Shulvass, *Ibid.*, p. 110 ff. After publication of *Roma wirushalayim* I found in the Introduction to the prayerbook *Ashmoret haboker* by Rabbi Aaron Berechiah of Modena a statement that the founder of the movement was Rabbi Menahem Azariah da Fano when he was a young man. Since Rabbi Menahem Azariah was born in 1548 we may assume that the first society was founded close to 1570.

ment began to deepen their religious consciousness, and their viewpoints and their behavior acquired a religio-pietistic coloring. One young man rose for forty consecutive nights to recite the midnight prayer for Israel's restoration. Moreover, he was so enthusiastically dedicated to the performance of good deeds that his strength failed and he died of brain fever.[1] The movement produced its own liturgical and theological literature which attests to the deep religious experience of those who were involved.

A kindred religio-pietistic aspiration was shared by associations of men who, unlike the *Shomerim laboker* movement, stressed the study of Torah rather than prayer. Torah study during most of the Renaissance period had an essentially cultural and scholarly character. This is obvious from an examination of the activities and behavior of Torah study societies in the sixteenth century.[2] However, such groups that were established at the end of the century [3] demonstrated through their by-laws that they regarded the essence of Torah study as fulfilling a *mizwah*. These societies also placed many obligations upon their membership that were designed to improve their religious and moral behavior. Members were obligated not to include God's name in their oaths, not to patronize non-Jewish courts, and not to gamble. The religious significance of Torah study was considered so great that a contemporary chronicle regarded the closing of the *yeshibah* in Cremona as the cause of persecutions and expulsions.[4] This also explains why Italian Jewry for decades spent money and pleaded to attain the revocation of the ban on publishing the Talmud.[5] The scope and zeal of these efforts so obviously transcended normal human endeavor for a purely cultural goal, that it is apparent that Torah study became for the community leadership a matter of self-sacrifice.

[1] According to an account by the physician Ḥabib, known as Amatus Lusitanus, in his famous work *Centuriae*. Cf. H. Friedenwald, *The Jews and Medicine*, Baltimore 1944, p. 381.
[2] *Meor enayim*, section *Yeme olam*, p. 93 ff.
[3] *Heasif* 3:214, 220.   [4] See *Hamagiha*, p. 158.
[5] See M. Stern, *Stellung der Paepste*, part 1, p. 153 ff.; *Hamagiha*, p. 175; *Sepher Chaje Jehuda*, p. 12.

The positive effort at reforming human conduct was based upon a new trend of critical self evaluation and repentance which was virtually non existent till the last decades of the Period. Blame for the burning of the Talmud in 1553 was placed upon those Jews who manifested a critical attitude to it.[1] Abraham Portaleone composed an extremely harsh confessional formula "in order hat every sinner might be able to easily recite what he has done. . . ." In fact, his magnum opus *Shilte hagibborim* was written chiefly as a penitential act to atone for cultivating "foreign soil" during his long life.[2] Even Leon da Modena was concerned and besought God that he should not die prior to atoning for his sins.[3] In a moment of despair, buffeted by life's adversities he went as far as to exclaim: "I shall change my way of life, I shall withdraw into a life of isolation, for all my joy is gone". Such attitudes were characteristic of many Italian Jews whom the changed social and political status had propelled toward a more ascetic life. The establishment of ghettos in the Italian towns at that time greatly facilitated the Jewish withdrawal from the larger society. It now became common to include in the program of Torah study the reading of "a pietistic book",[4] and this literature as represented by the writings of Rabbi Raphael Norsa[5] was now in great demand. Thus, some Jews carried the mood to extremes. By and large, however, Italian Jewry knew how to adjust to the new situation and live a fuller Jewish life without losing the many values which it had acquired during the height of the Period.

[1] Rabbi Immanuel da Benevento, *Liwyat ḥen*, p. 109a.

[2] See the Introduction to *Shilte hagibborim* and p. 126b.

[3] *Sepher Chaje Jehuda*, p. 34. To be sure, he expressed such feelings very rarely in his writings, while statements regarding the power of the constellations occur quite frequently.

[4] *Midbar Yehuda* by Leon da Modena, Venice 1602, p. 58a.

[5] See H. G. Enelow, "Raphael Norzi: A Rabbi of the Renaissance", *Hebrew Union College Jubilee Volume* (1875-1925), pp. 333-378.

SECTION VI

LITERATURE

INTRODUCTION

The love of the book evoked by the Renaissance and the invention of the art of printing (see below, Section VIII, Chapter 2), created a close bond between Renaissance man and literature. Reading became a pastime to a much greater degree than heretofore, and all social and cultural phenomena found colorful expression in literature.

The same factors also created multifarious literature among Jews. It was written in every language spoken by the composite Italo-Jewish community and incorporated many old and new literary genres, whether native or borrowed from elsewhere. The following discussion does not purport to be a systematic literary history. Rather than present here a comprehensive description of the literature, I have preferred to deal with its various branches in connection with a portrayal of the diverse areas of life. For example, Rabbinic literature will be discussed in conjunction with a description of Torah learning. Similarly, the political literature will be linked with the portrayal of Renaissance Jewry's aspirations to full participation in life. The ensuing chapters deal especially with poetry and belles lettres whose primary aim was amusement and the improving of man's nature. Only a general outline will be drawn emphasizing their character, their sources and their role in the life of the individual and the society.

CHAPTER ONE

HEBREW LITERATURE

a.

Renaissance Jewry's main vehicle of literary expression in Hebrew was poetry. Here too, we note the general phenomenon in Jewish life of the Period: Great quantitative and qualitative creativity far beyond the small proportional size of the Jewish community. Our attention is also drawn to the wealth of forms of poetic expression. Early in the Period Hebrew poetry had borrowed the sonnet from the Italians. About a century later the *terzina* appeared and we also encounter the octave by the start of the sixteenth century. In addition to these literary forms regularly used by such poets as Immanuel of Rome, Moses Rieti and Joseph Zarfadi, Italian Hebrew writers also periodically employed other Italian poetic forms, the *sestina*, the *canzona*, the *canzonetta*, and the *madrigal*.[1] Spanish Hebrew poetry also exerted a strong influence upon its Italian sister. It appears at times that this influence was even greater than that of Italian Renaissance poetry. The greatest poet of the period, Immanuel of Rome, followed its patterns in most of his writings. The Arabic meter appears in Hebrew poetry throughout the Period. The Italian Hebrew poets even made an important contribution in its use through their custom of constructing each line with a definite number of syllables regardless of whether or not they were long or short. Metaphors used by poets of the Golden Age are common in the works of fifteenth and sixteenth century Italian Hebrew poets. This phenomenon was due to the close relations between the Kingdom of Naples and Spain during the entire fifteenth century, and to the settlement of about ten thousand Spanish exiles in the various parts of Italy.[2] The majority of Hebrew poets were Italiani and thus we find them in Rome and central Italy, especially the Marche region and Tuscany. Ashkenazic North Italy did not produce Hebrew poets until virtually the end of the Period. The influence of the Spanish exiles was most apparent through an important group of poets in Ferrara [3] during the second half of the sixteenth century.

In addition to multiple literary forms, there was a striking

[1] See the Introduction to Jefim Schirmann, *Anthologie der Hebraeischen Dichtung in Italien*, Berlin 1934, p. 26 ff.
[2] Cassuto, *Florence*, p. 343; S. Bernstein, *Mishire Yisrael beitalyah*, Jerusalem 1939, p. XXIII.
[3] Their poems were published by Bernstein, *Ibid.*, nos. 44-90.

multiplicity of topics. Religious hymns, elegies, poems of reproof, epics, love songs and occasional poems were composed with a great deal of talent. Yet except for the work of Immanuel of Rome, religious poetry predominated. It was written with idealism and dedication and was an important vehicle of expression of the Jewish community bent upon protecting its Jewish essence within the stormy reality of the Renaissance.

The greatest Renaissance Hebrew poet was Immanuel of Rome. His poetic talent, linguistic buoyancy, and prolific output place him above all his contemporaries. He was highly alert and quickly reacted to the events of the day. In his latter years he assembled all his poems in the framework of a story written in rhymed prose (*mahbarot*), and modeled after the works of Judah Alharizi. Here he used his wide erudition in the Scriptures, Rabbinic Literature and the moralistic and philosophic writings of the Middle Ages to create a new, independent style that flows smoothly and allusively, for the sole purpose of entertainment. Immanuel's frivolity led to mixed opinions in ensuing generations. When the *Shulhan aruk* banned the reading, printing, and copying of "rhymes of idle talk and lust", it cited Immanuel as an example.[1] Immanuel also provoked the anger of Italian Hebrew poets of a later period who, while admiring his vast talents, could not tolerate the obscenity in his writings. The remarks of Immanuel Franzes are characteristic [2]: . . . "There arose Rabbi Immanuel ben Solomon of the Marche region, who was most adept at versification but who corrupted his ways by composing prurient poems which are forbidden to be heard, and may God forgive him and those who published everything without rooting out the thorns from the vineyard (for) his work contains many worthwhile poems". Even Moses Rieti, himself a Renaissance poet, refused to mention Immanuel in his renowned poem *Mikdash meat* written to immortalize the names of the sages, writers, and poets.[3] Nevertheless, most Renaissance Jews

[1] *Shulhan aruk, Orah hayim*, section 307, par. 16.
[2] *Metek sefatayim*, Cracow 1892, p. 43; Hezekiah David Abulafia, *Ben zekunim*, Leghorn 1793, p. 35: "Immanuel has no God".
[3] *Mikdash meat*, p. 106, Note: "And I did not mention Immanuel in my poem . . . because of his language and the lustful writings".

reacted indulgently to Immanuel. Obscene language was
common in the poetry and prose of the Renaissance, and
sexuality and sensual pleasure were the central theme of its
countless short stories. Jews accepted this type of literature
and read it despite sporadic protests. It is not, therefore,
surprising that one of the great rabbis of the sixteenth
century interspersed within his legal responsa metaphors that
were borrowed from Immanuel's *Maḥbarot*. Elijah Baḥur, who
introduced a typical Renaissance novel into Yiddish literature
(see the following chapter), repeatedly copied Immanuel's
style, while the poet Moses ben Joab followed Immanuel like a
disciple. Leon da Modena's admiration of Immanuel was
boundless. He desired to resemble his hero and called him the
poet par excellence.[1]

The number of Hebrew poets was quite large.[2] The tendency
of Renaissance education to teach youth the skill of writing
elegant letters and of oratory, led many to study the art of
versification. Immanuel of Rome repeatedly praised the poet
Judah Siciliano stating that "the reason for Judah's poetic
aptitude lies in the fact that he was being hired to teach it to
young lads and worked at it all the time".[3] Quite a number of
poetry manuals were very popular. It is likely that the manual
Darke noam by Moses ben Shem Tob Habib became known in
Italy at the time its author lived there. Even better known
were *Liwyat hen* by Immanuel da Benevento (the last section)

---

[1] See Sonne, *Kirjath sepher* 15:267; the second Introduction to
Masoret hamasoret by Elijah Baḥur; Cassuto, *Florence*, p. 342 ffff.;
Divan Modena, p. 145, no. 115 and Leon's Introduction to *Hashirim
asher lishelomoh*, new ed., Frankfurt 1925.

[2] Many compositions of approximately forty Renaissance poets
were published by J. Schirmann, *Ibid*. According to the introductory
remarks regarding his selections (p. 28), it can be surmised that
we know of at least one hundred and fifty Hebrew poets during the
Renaissance Period. About ninety poems of the Period were published
by Simon Bernstein in the collection mentioned above. Leo da Modena's
Divan should also be included among Renaissance Hebrew poetry.
Numerous poems by many Renaissance poets have been published in
various volumes and periodicals, and others have been discovered
in manuscripts. The most important unpublished poems, undoubtedly
are those by Joseph ben Samuel Zarfadi.

[3] *Maḥbarot*, p. 373 ff.

and Samuel Archivolti's *Arugat habosem*. A good portion of the latter volume deals with a theoretical clarification of the problem of poetry through many examples illustrating meters and rhyming patterns. These works were all surpassed by the last chapter of *Meor enayim* by Azariah dei Rossi entitled "On Hebrew Poetry", which discusses the meter problem in Scriptures and the connection between various meters and the inner character of the poem. The widespread involvement in the theoretical aspect of poetry was underscored by Rabbi Azariah when he remarked that while he was writing his work he consulted "many contemporary scholars" regarding the biblical meter.[1]

b.

The Hebrew belles lettres also enjoyed great popularity, although to a lesser degree than poetry.[2] The novels and short stories that have come down to us demonstrate craftsmanship that recalls the best in Italian fiction. The wondrous book *Ge ḥizzayon* by Abraham Jaghel Gallichi[3] is truly outstanding and can be read today with genuine interest. The author interwove two stories in his book with a great deal of talent: One, a true story that described his trials when he became involved in financial deals and ended in prison, and

[1] *Darke noam* was first published in Constantinople, n. d., then in Venice in 1540 in a collection of several grammatical works. The tract also appeared with the sixtieth chapter of *Meor enayim* by Azariah dei Rossi, Roedelheim 1806; *Liwyat ḥen* appeared in Mantua in 1551; *Arugat habosem* appeared in Venice in 1596 and in Amsterdam in 1930; Chapter 60 of *Meor enayim* is found in the Benjacob edition, p. 206 ff.

[2] Several novels and short stories were translated into Hebrew from Italian and other languages; they will be discussed in a chapter below. Some scholars also regard the chronicle *Shebet Yehudah*, written in Italy in the 1520's, as a collection of short stories. However, despite the recognizable influence of the Italian short story, the work is clearly historical, not designed to amuse or moralize but, rather, to clarify the political, social, and religious position of the Jewish people in the Christian world.

[3] Part of the book appeared in 1882 in Alexandria (Egypt) from a manuscript that was discovered in Tiberias. The book is very rare and a new edition is much needed. The short stories are found on pp. 12b, 13b to 15b, 30a. For a discussion of the entire book see *Hebraeische Bibliographie* 21:76 ff.

the other, imaginary, that depicted how the soul of his deceased father visited him and took him on a journey through the other world. Between the autobiographical and fictional parts, several beautiful short stories are interspersed with all the exciting traits of their Italian models. In one of them a man falls in love with a married woman who wants to remain loyal to her husband. Through trickery, a typical motif of the Renaissance short story, he murders the husband in order to attain his desire. However, the widow also knew how to exercise trickery to avenge the murder of her husband. It ends as in a true love tragedy with the widow's suicide, and as in the Italian short story, everybody sympathized with the virtuous woman and she "was buried with great honors next to her husband". A story about a young girl from Egypt told to him by Job on his visit to the other world, is reminiscent of Arienti's famous story about Francesco Sforza.[1] The many short stories included in the chronicle *Shalshelet hakabbalah* were a concession to the widespread demand for belles-lettres. They are full of wondrous things and here too, through trickery the good conquers evil and the clever one dupes the fool.[2] A perfect short story is found in Immanuel's *Mahbarot*; the poet told it to his "patron" in order to entertain him and to lift him from a depressed state of mind.[3]

c.

The greatest influence upon Hebrew literature was exercised by Dante, even though he is not regarded as a Renaissance poet. Dante dominated Renaissance literature and thus put his imprint upon the Period's most important Hebrew literary works. Three of the greatest Hebrew writers tried to imitate him, hoping thereby to produce the *magnum opus* that would captivate the Jewish world: Immanuel of Rome, Moses Rieti and Abraham Jaghel Gallichi. Much has

---

[1] A German translation of the short story is found in F. Blei, *Frauen und Mænner der Renaissance*, Hellerau 1927, p. 94 ff.

[2] *Shalshelet hakabbalah*, pp. 33, 52, 58, 62, 65, 66, 70, 80, 82 ff., 87, 93.

[3] The fourteenth *mahberet*.

been written [1] on the relationship between Immanuel and Dante and we are still not certain whether or not they knew one another. As a rule, when Dante's influence on Immanuel is cited, reference is made to the twenty-eighth *Maḥberet* and Dante's *Comedy*. And, indeed, Immanuel, like Dante, meets many of his acquaintances in the nether world, speaks to them and explains their fate as a consequence of their deeds in this world. This lends the same realistic character to the *Maḥberet* that Dante's *Comedy* has. And yet, Immanuel felt free to judge the great figures of the world by a different norm than did Dante. Dante generally placed the great figures of the pagan world in the limbo, which is a sort of borderland of Gehenna. Limbo dwellers were not chastised with the afflictions reserved for the wicked. Dante merely denies them hope for salvation. Immanuel justly chose a different path and had no compunction in actually placing men like Plato, Aristotle, Galen, and Avicenna [2] in Hell, considering their misguided views that contradicted the idea of God's unity and *creatio ex nihilo*. The twenty-eighth *Maḥberet* thus became an important vehicle of enhancing the value of pious deeds and wholesome views among the contemporaries.

The other poet who tried to imitate Dante, Moses Rieti, stated explicitly that his motive in composing his great poem *Mikdash meat* was:

"For I saw that the Christian nation
has a book laden with imagination".[3]

He composed his poem in *terzine* and opened it with a prayer to God: "strengthen my hand on the day when I sing my song", much in the way Dante upon his entry to Paradise turned to Apollo with the plea *"Fammi del tuo valor"*.[4] Like Dante, who

[1] See the entry in *Encyclopaedia Judaica*, vol. 8, p. 402 ff., written by Umberto Cassuto where the pertinent literature is listed. Cf. Cecil Roth, *RMI* vol. 17 for the historical background of Immanuel's poetry.

[2] *Maḥbarot*, p. 796.

[3] *Mikdash meat* by Moses Rieti, Vienna 1851, p. 3a.

[4] *Ibid.*, p. 2a. See Dante Alighieri, *La divina commedia*, ed. Camerini, Milan 1938, p. 299. This also proves that Moses Rieti intended to write a Hebrew work akin to the third part of Dante's work.

marked the start of his journey in the nether world in astrological terms, Moses Rieti too, fixed the day of his birth by
the stars.[1] Linguistic borrowings from Dante's *Comedy* and
Vita nuova abound throughout the work. As Dante, in
describing Paradise, parades the most prominent religious
thinkers and philosophers before his readers, so Moses Rieti
presents all the great Jewish spiritual and lay leaders in the
part of his poem entitled "The Palace". Although a lesser
talent than Immanuel, Moses Rieti was closer to Dante
through his noble style, lofty spirit, and the fact that he
wrote his poem in *terzine*, as did Dante.

The third attempt to imitate Dante was made at the end of
the Period by Abraham Jaghel Gallichi in *Ge ḥizzayon*. We
have seen that like Dante, Gallichi visited the world of the
spirits and was accompanied there by a "guide". The people
whom Dante encountered in the other world were mere
shadows. Abraham Jaghel Gallichi, too, when he met his dead
father realized that he was in the world of the shadows: "And
I sought to embrace him and to kiss his hands, and lo I was
embracing the wind". [2] He too asked the souls whom he met
on his journey what they did while still alive and what was
their fate after death. Like his great predecessor, the author of
Ge ḥizzayon lends a realistic contemporary aura to his story
by inviting the reader to follow him on his "journey".

CHAPTER TWO

YIDDISH LITERATURE

The existence of a large Ashkenazic population in North
Italy led to the emergence of a body of literature written in
Yiddish that occupies an important position within the
framework of old Yiddish literature. While this literature was
not quantitatively large, it was important because of the
talent of its authors and the Renaissance character of its
principal works.

---

[1] *La divina commedia*, p. 28, *stanza* 38 of the first *canto*. See Camerini's explanation, *Ibid.*; *Miḵdash meat*, p. 4b.

[2] See *Ge ḥizzayon*, p. 1. The leader is his father.

Northern Italy became a center of Yiddish literature in the second half of the fifteenth century,[1] the period of climactic numerical and economic development of this Ashkenazic settlement. The importance of the center grew with the development of the printing craft, and during the ensuing sixteenth century Yiddish books were published in at least four North Italian cities, Venice, Cremona, Mantua, and Verona.[2] The principal works of North Italian Yiddish literature were written in the first half of the sixteenth century. However, by the middle of the century unmistakable signs of an eclipse began to be noticeable. The deterioration was primarily due to the cessation of mass immigration from Germany and the process of forgetting the Yiddish language by the Ashkenazim (see above, Section II, Chapter 3). An additional factor in the decline lay in the clearly secular character of the principal works of Yiddish literature with their Renaissance share of obscene language. Gumprecht of Szczebrzeszyn, who at that time composed a Yiddish poem in Venice on Hanukah and Purim, assured his readers that his book will contain "no unclean word...as can often be found in other Yiddish books".[3] In that period religious renewal among Italian Jewry started to assert itself vigorously, resulting in the emergence of a disdainful attitude toward the frivolous elements of Renaissance literature. Religious literature in Yiddish, to be sure, continued to flourish in Italy for at least sixty to seventy years longer, until due to the process of forgetting the Yiddish language, Yiddish readers had all but vanished.

[1] See Erik, *History*, p. 13 ff. A detailed description of North Italian Yiddish literature is also available in I. Zinberg, *The History of the Jewish Literature*, vol. 6, Vilna 1935.

[2] The first bibliography of old Yiddish books was prepared by Moritz Steinschneider and was published in instalments in *Serapeum*, 1848-1869. A great deal of information regarding Yiddish books published in Italy is available in the works listed in Note 1 and in Eleazar Schulman, *Sefat yehudit-ashkenazit wesifrutah*, Riga 1913.

[3] Gumprecht's poems were published by Moritz Stern from a manuscript. See Moritz Stern, *Deutsche Sprachdenkmaeler in hebraeischen Schriftcharakteren I : Lieder des venezianischen Lehrers Gumprecht von Szcebrszyn* (Szczebrzeszyn), Berlin 1922. Cf. p. 1.

During its heyday Yiddish literature had quite a large reading public. Elijah Baḥur wrote Yiddish epics [1] while living in heavily Ashkenazic Venice, but none during his sojourn in Rome. Obviously, he wrote for an audience that needed his works in Yiddish. To further satisfy the need of literature in Yiddish, it became customary to prepare for the women handwritten volumes which contained a melange of religious and secular works.[2] The Yiddish reading public was, of course, constantly augmented by new arrivals from Germany who could not yet satisfy their need for entertainment by reading the great Italian epics of the Renaissance.[3] The entertainment function of Yiddish literature was clearly stressed by Elijah Baḥur in the introduction to *Bovo d'Antona*: "that they might find delight in it, and read it on Sabbaths and holidays".[4] Even more readers were attracted to Yiddish literature by the then fashionable occasional poems which adressed themselves to events of everyday life. To this category belong such works as Elijah's well known satiric poem *Hamabdil*, his poem *Haserefah*,[5] as well as the anonymous

[1] Scholars agree that Elijah Baḥur is the author of *Paris un Wyena*. This writer believes, however, that in view of the striking differences between this work and *Bovobuch* it is impossible to reach a final conclusion until *Paris un Wyena* will be comprehensively studied for inner proof regarding its author and his milieu.

[2] N. Shtif gave a detailed description of such a manuscript in *Zeitschrift* 1:140 ff. and 2-3:525 ff. The literary pieces in the manuscript are listed by Shtif, *Ibid.*, 1:142. The manuscript was copied by the scribe Kalman ben Simon of the well known Pescarol family. The number of Yiddish manuscripts from Italy is very large. See Erik, *Ibid.*, p. 15.

[3] It is evident from the Introduction to *Maareket haelohut* that Italian Jews used to read "Boccaccio or the history of kings" i. e. *Il Decamerone* and the well known story *I reali di Francia*. The quotation is available in *Sinai* 5:361.

[4] The text was published in a simplified style approximating modern Yiddish by N. B. Minkoff, *Elye Bokher and his Bove-Bukh*, New York 1950, p. 59.

[5] The poem *"Hamabdil"* was published with a commentary by N. Shtif in *Zeitschrift* 1:150 ff. He also published parts of the poem *"Serefah"*, *Ibid.*, p. 177 ff. An Analysis of the first *stanza* indicates that the poet is referring to a plague, rather than a fire and speaks of the plague as "the fire by which God consumed", which is the Hebrew expression generally used to indicate a plague or some other

dirge upon the death of the renowned Rabbi Abigedor Cividali, composed almost a century later.[1]

A major aspect of Italian Yiddish secular literature is the impact exerted on it by the Renaissance epic. About the year 1500, when the octave appeared in Italian Hebrew poetry, Elijah Baḥur initiated its use in the Yiddish epic. A careful study of his style reveals great resemblance to the style of Ariosto,[2] the greatest Renaissance poet. In *Bovo d'Antona Elija* simply "judaized" the Italian epic, thereby bringing it closer to the life sphere of the Jewish reader and endowing it with a great deal of humor. However, in *Paris un Wyena* he periodically interrupted the story in order to impart to his Jewish readers his own opinions, which were those of a Renaissance Jew. In these remarks "the sarcastic and skeptical wit of the Renaissance is combined with elements of practical wisdom and behavior patterns found in the writings of the Jewish moralists".[3]

Bovo d'Antona and *Paris un Wyena* concluded the period of the *Spielmann*, the minstrel in Yiddish literature. Much as the Yiddish *Spielmann* poetry in earlier times was borrowed primarily from medieval German literature, Elijah's two Yiddish epics are translations of Italian romances. They became original Yiddish epics through the translator's changes and additions. Elijah was a great poet. It is no simple matter [4] to compose a stanza of octaves in Yiddish, and a major talent is needed to compose a poem of six hundred and fifty stanzas (*Bovo d'Antona*) or of eight hundred stanzas (*Paris un Wyena*). Not only did Elijah know how to give his works unusual artistic beauty, but he also understood how to

calamity. The few selections published by Shtif clearly reveal that the poet is dealing with events that occurred during the war of the League of Cambray. "Ḥ. Anshel" is perhaps identical with Ḥayim Meshullam, the well known leader of Paduan Jewry and of the Paduan refugees in Venice.

[1] For the dirge in memory of Rabbi Abigedor Cividali see Shulman, *Ibid.*, p. 138.

[2] Detailed information on the subject is available in Erik, *Ibid.*, p. 197.

[3] Zinberg's remarks, *Ibid.*, p. 98.

[4] According to Minkoff, *Ibid.*, p. 17.

hold the reader in suspense to give him the greatest possible enjoyment." Sometimes he evokes the reader's participation through a pious sigh, sometimes by a vivid description, and sometimes by an arrogant jest".[1]

While there is no absolute certainty that Elijah Baḥur is the author of *Paris un Wyena*, it is certain that in addition to *Bovo d'Antona* and the occasional poems, he wrote other works in Yiddish. In the introductory poem to the first edition of *Bovo d'Antona* [2] which he wrote as an old man, he expressed concern lest all his books and poems be forgotten after his death. He therefore, promised to publish all of them to save them from oblivion.

Despite the artistic quality of the secular Yiddish poetry and the genuine need for it, it did not gain a dominant position within the framework of Yiddish literature of that time in Italy. Most Yiddish works belong in the various literary categories that served religious needs, especially those of the Jewish woman. In one of the handwritten volumes mentioned above, which includes more than twenty literary pieces, two thirds represent religious writing and only one third is secular. The core of the Yiddish religious literature consisted of translations and paraphrases of various Scriptural books. During the sixteenth century seven Yiddish editions of biblical books appeared in Italy.[3] These books included a translation of the Pentateuch (Cremona, 1560) and the Psalms by Elijah Baḥur (Venice, 1545). About this time the *Shemuel Buch*, an excellent paraphrase of the biblical *Book of Samuel* was published in Mantua. This book may have possibly been written in North Italy.[4] In addition to the printed books, many manuscript volumes were in use, including translations from Scriptures, some of which were rhymed.[5] These books were translated into Yiddish mainly to serve the needs of the North Italian Ashkenazic school where the pupils were taught to interpret

[1] M. Weinreich, *Studies in History of the Yiddish literature*, Vilna 1928, p. 169.

[2] Published by Minkoff, *Ibid.*, p. 59.

[3] Erik, *Ibid.*, p. 14.

[4] Weinreich, *Ibid.*, p. 86.

[5] *Ibid.*, p. 126.

the Scriptures in Yiddish.[1] In 1548, also, Yiddish translations of several Apocryphal books appeared in Venice.[2]

In addition to biblical books, Italian Ashkenazic Jewry had at its disposal a variety of manuals and treatises that served to guide the daily religious life, such as *Mizwot nashim*, or *Frauen Buechlein*. The prayerbook, the Passover Haggadah, and The Sayings of the Fathers were also available in Yiddish translations.[3]

CHAPTER THREE

JEWISH LITERATURE IN ITALIAN

We have seen (Section 1, Chapter 4) that all the Italiani, as well as many Ashkenazim and Sephardim, knew Italian well. Consequently, there was no urgent need for Jewish books in the Judeo-Italian dialects, and the demand for belles-lettres could be filled by the Period's rich Italian literature. Italian Jewry nevertheless aspired to have its own literature in Italian and the Judeo-Italian dialects. An anonymous defender of the Judeo-Italian literature argued that just as Rabina and Rab Ashi wrote the Talmud in Aramaic because Jews spoke that language at the time, similarly Italian in his time served as the principal language of Italian Jewry.[4]

Some Jewish writers had a predilection for composing bilingual poems. Like their gentile colleagues who wrote Italian-Latin poems,[5] they wrote verses in which Hebrew and Italian words appeared side by side. This device which may

[1] Cf. the portion of the Introduction by Elijah Baḥur to his Yiddish translation of the Psalms, published by Zinberg, *Ibid.*, p. 112. A facsimile of a page from a manuscript Yiddish glossary to the Pentateuch can be found in Weinreich, *Ibid.*, before p. 9.
[2] Shulman, *Ibid.*, p. 49.
[3] Most of this literature is listed in Steinschneider's bibliography, *Ibid.* More information about these manuscripts is available in Schulman's work.
[4] See David Kaufmann, *Gesammelte Schriften*, vol. 3, p. 306; a great deal of bibliographical data regarding the Italian literature of the Jews are available in Steinschneider's article in *MGWJ*, vol. 42.
[5] Such as Teofilo Folengo (1492-1543) who wrote the famous parody *Baldus*.

appear bizarre to us, enjoyed great popularity among the people of the Renaissance. A literary debate over women (see Section IV, Chapter 1), was conducted mainly in rhyme, half Hebrew and half Italian. Azariah dei Rossi composed a poem in honor of a duchess in Hebrew, Aramaic, Latin, and Italian. Leon da Modena demonstrated his skill by writing a Hebrew-Italian poem where the Italian rhymes matched the Hebrew in both meaning and sound.[1]

The literature in Judeo-Italian consisted mostly of translations of the Scriptures and the Prayer book. In addition it also contained original works offering religious direction, especially to women. In the Hebrew introduction to the Italian guide *Ḥokmat nashim* dealing with religious laws that apply to women, the author explicitly stated that he wrote in Italian because most women did not understand Hebrew. Some of the Bible translations or portions thereof which are known today date back to the early Renaissance. They are generally written in various dialects that were spoken in Central and South Italy. They began to approximate literary Italian only at the close of the Period. The translation of about one third of the Psalms by Leone da Sommi[2] offers a striking example. Another example is a remarkable Italian translation of Sayings of the Fathers from the end of the Period.[3]

Quite prolific was the Judeo-Italian liturgical literature, the "*volgare* prayers". At least twelve translations of the prayer-book, mostly of the Roman rite, were made in the fifteenth and

---

[1] See the list of bi-lingual poems prepared by D. Blondheim, *REJ* 82:386 ff. A good part of the poems on women were published by Neubauer in *Rendiconti della Academia dei lincei*, 1891, vol. 7, second semester. Leone da Sommi's composition of fifty stanzas of eight verses, four in Hebrew and four in Italian, were republished by Jefim Schirmann in his edition of *Ẓaḥut bediḥuta deḳiddushin*, p. 151 ff. Cf. *Ibid.*, p. 147 ff. Leon da Modena's poems were published in *Divan Modena*, pp. 51, 212 ff. Cf. *Meor enayim*, Zunz's Introduction, p. 18.

[2] Cf. Cassuto in *Miscellanea di studi ebraici in memoria di H. P. Chajes*, p. 25; *Aron Kaminka Jubilee Volume*, p. 129 ff.; Schirmann, *Ibid.*, p. 5; *MGWJ* 47:179. The author of *Ḥokmat nashim* was Jehiel Manoscrivi. The book was written in 1565.

[3] See Steinschneider, *General Introduction*, p. 66.

sixteenth centuries. Some of the prayerbooks that are extant in manuscript were explicitly prepared for women, and most copies of the printed prayerbooks were probably owned by women. Important parts of the prayerbook, such as the "Reproof" of Rabbi Baḥya, the "Great Confession" of Rabbenu Nisim, and the Sephardic *Abodah* were translated by the celebrated poetess Deborah Ascarelli. She also translated *Meon hashoalim* by Moses Rieti, which because of its lofty style was regarded as akin to religious poetry and was recited in the synagogue. It was characteristic of the Period that translations of prayers by a woman were recited in the synagogue.[1] Sermons were mostly preached in the synagogue in Italian, although generally published in Hebrew. However, we do known of sermons that were written originally in Italian, with Hebrew script. Undoubtedly, many pamphlets dealing with laws applicable to women, in the vein of *Miẓwot nashim*, were written in Italian or translated into Italian. The latter was translated into Italian by Jacob Heilbronn, a writer who lived at the end of the Period.[2] Most of these guides, like those in Yiddish, were lost because they were widely used and small of size.

Leon da Modena's *Historia de gli Riti Hebraici* occupies a unique position in the Judeo-Italian literature. This work [3] was composed at the suggestion of an English scholar. The book was not written for the Jewish reader, but was intended to acquaint the Christian public with the Jewish people and its way of life. The book was quite effective in disseminating information about Jews among non-Jews. Of course, it also was of great use to Jews who did not have direct access to the sources of Judaism.

[1] See Cassuto, *Aron Kaminka Jubilee Volume*, p. 139 ff.; *REJ* 89:266 ff.; *Encyclopaedia Judaica*, vol. 2, column 163; Goldenthal's Introduction to his edition of *Miḳdash meat*, Vienna 1851, p. XXV ff. "*Meon hashoalim*" is the second section in the second part of the poem (*Ibid.*, p. 42 ff.). Cf. Steinschneider, *Ibid.*, p. 65.

[2] *MGWJ* 42:521, Italian sermons of Rabbi Mordecai Dato; cf. Steinschneider's bibliography of old Yiddish literature, *Serapeum*, no. 200.

[3] The book appeared in 1637 in Paris and later in Venice. It was translated into Hebrew by S. Rubin under the title *Shulḥan aruk* and was published in Vienna in 1865.

Some Jewish writers who are mainly known for their literary contributions in Hebrew, also wrote Italian poetry and prose for the general reading public. The degree of actual Jewish participation in Italian literature exceeds that which is implied by the available sources. Immanuel's sonnets and poem describing the court of Cangrande della Scala are surely only a part of his contribution to Italian literature. Likewise, Leone da Sommi composed numerous Italian poems in addition to his many plays and the famous theoretical essay on the theatre. To the group of Jews who wrote in Italian belonged also Messer Leon's son David, who composed "many verses in Hebrew and in the Christian tongue (Italian or Neo-Latin?) in his spare time", and David Guido of Rome who in 1499 authored a lovely poem "Sponsali della luna".[1]

CHAPTER FOUR

NON-JEWISH LITERATURE AMONG JEWS

The fact that most Jews understood the Italian language, together with their general closeness to Renaissance culture, evoked among them a great interest in the literary works of the Period. This is quite apparent from the concern that it aroused in rabbinic and Jewish literary circles. The rabbis clearly recognized the powerful attraction of such literature and were afraid that it would infringe excessively upon the reading program of the average Jew. To counteract such tendencies, Abraham Farissol wrote his book on geography *Iggeret orhot olam*. He wanted to give his Jewish audience serious reading matter and wean it from reading "lewd poems and stories of ancient wars which...were never fought and were only written as fiction". Rabbi Immanuel da Benevento reacted with harsher words to the tendency of reading alien literature. He wrote under the depressing impact of the burning

[1] Four sonnets and the poem were republished by Habermann in his edition of the *Mahbarot*, p. 992 ff.; *Ibid.*, p. 1004 ff. a verbal Hebrew translation of the five poems is available; for Leone da Sommi's poems see Peyron's catalogue of manuscripts in the library of Turin, p. 9; for David, son of Messer Leon see *Hebraeische Bibliographie* 12:33; for David Guido see *Natali*, p. 71.

of Hebrew books in 1553 and complained bitterly that many people "driveled over chronicles and the nature of kings and states", instead of engaging in serving God and studying Torah. He believed that the Talmud burning came as a punishment for the excessive absorption in the Renaissance and its literature. He recommended an increased preoccupation with *kabbalah* literature in lieu of Talmud study, which had become impossible after the burning of its volumes. With an aching heart he cried out: "What should he (the Jew lacking Talmudic books) read and study in order to know the glory and majesty of God, perhaps the books of Boccaccio or the stories about the kings?" [1]

On the other hand, there were rabbis and writers who did not see any peril in the popularity of non Jewish literature among the Jews. Moreover, they even helped to make it more accessible. At the time Abraham Farissol sought to wean his contemporaries from reading "lewd poems", the poet Joseph ben Samuel Zarfadi translated the comedy *La Celestina* into Hebrew from Spanish specifically "to sweeten the suffering of the poor and the anxiety of the human heart". Decades earlier Daniel ben Samuel da Rossena translated the Italian novel *Bernabo e Luciana*, and Messer Leon attempted to explain to his Jewish audience Petrarch's love for Laura. Paralleling this was the widespread dissemination among North Italian Ashkenazim of popular German love poems. [2] Similarly, the poem about Theoderic the Great was popular among them. To an even greater degree the Italiani and Italian speaking Ashkenazim and Sephardim indulged in reading the works of the great poets of the Renaissance,

[1] See the beginning of the Introduction to *Iggeret orehot olam*, Venice 1587; Introduction to the third chapter of *Liwyat hen* by Rabbi Immanuel da Benevento, Mantua 1557 and the Introduction to his edition of *Maareket haelohut*, Mantua 1558; "Boccaccio" refers to Boccaccio's *Il Decamerone*; "the story of the kings" or: "the history and character of the kings" no doubt refers to the famous book *I reali di Francia*.

[2] See Cassuto in *Jewish Studies in Memory of George A. Kohut*, Hebrew section, p. 121 ff. Steinschneider, *MGWJ* 42:422; the Introduction of Cornelio Adelkind to the Yiddish translation of the Psalms as quoted in *Zinberg*, vol. 6, p. 112; *REJ* 10:94 ff.

Boiardo, Ariosto, and Tasso. That Abraham Portaleone, for example, was familiar with this literature is evident from the fact that he described the warriors in the court of David and Solomon as *paladini*, a term very frequent in the Italian Renaissance epic. Quite revealing is the fact that Leon da Modena, at the age of twelve, translated into Hebrew the first *canto* of Ariosto's great epic *Orlando Furioso* as well as the notoriously lewd twenty eighth *canto* which is omitted in many of the work's published editions.[1]

In addition to the epic which during the Renaissance period performed the function of today's novel, there existed a vast literature in other genres. Its primary function was to inspire the reader and guide him toward perfection rather than to entertain him. It is not yet possible to depict fully the extent of the penetration of this literature, in the original or in translation, within Jewish society. Only a thorough analysis of the Period's Hebrew literature will demonstrate how Jewish writers tried to adapt the alien literature to the needs of the Jewish community. We might cite as an example the small moralistic book by Leon da Modena *Ẓemah ẓaddiḳ* which, according to the author's admission, was a translation of *Fior di virtù* written by an unknown gentile author. This work aimed at clarifying the essence of man's inner inclinations and instincts and to teach him how to live the right life. It is filled with quotations from ancient writers and the Church fathers. When Leon da Modena decided to translate this work into Hebrew he knew that it could not be presented to the Jewish reader in its original form. He therefore expurgated a large portion of the quotations and replaced them with passages from rabbinic literature ("and I exchanged all quotations from their teachings and from the writings of their saints

[1] See *Shilte hagibborim*, p. 34b; *Zinberg, Ibid.*; Leon da Modena's translation is available in *Divan Modena*, p. 33 ff. There are different opinions regarding the origin of the Hebrew translation of a part of the Arturian legends made in 1279 (published by Berliner in *Oẓar tob*, 1885, p. 1 ff.). See M. Gaster, *Studies and Texts*, London 1925-1928, vol. 2, p. 942 ff. It would be worthwhile to study the degree of the influence of the Renaissance epic on the first part of David Hareubeni's autobiography (pp. 7-18 in the Aeskoly edition, Jerusalem 1940).

with words of our rabbis of blessed memory.") We can see that this procedure was commonly followed from the fact that even earlier Elijah Baḥur tried to "judaize" various parts of the epics that he translated into Yiddish.[1]

At the end of the Period which was characterized by a withdrawal from Renaissance culture, apparently opposition to alien literature also heightened. Leon da Modena tells about it in his derisive plaint against "those who boast about their piety and disdainfully refrain from reading a book that is not written in Hebrew".[2] However, the attraction this literature exerted upon the Italian Jew never completely waned. It was indeed an integral part of his life.

[1] *Ẓemaḥ Ẓaddiḳ* first appeared in Venice in 1600. A new edition appeared in Tel-Aviv, 1949. Cf. *Sepher Chaje Jehuda*, p. 42 and *Zinberg*, vol. 6, p. 95.

[2] The responsum by Leon da Modena on head covering was published by Isaac Rivkind in the *Louis Ginzberg Jubilee Volume*, Hebrew section, p. 413.

THE FINE ARTS

CHAPTER ONE

THE VISUAL ARTS

Painting and sculpture which were the most important cultural expression of the Italian Renaissance did not attract Jews in the same degree as did its other aspects. Apparently the negative attitude of the Jewish religion toward these art forms operated as an effective barrier. Several isolated incidents, which will be discussed below, will demonstrate that religious circles mounted a powerful protest when they felt that Jews had become so immersed in the art of the figure that they ran the risk of transgressing the ban on making images. A scrutiny of Jewish creativity in the visual arts shows, indeed, a rather modest volume with no especially great artistic quality. There is, however, great historical significance in Renaissance Jewry's artistic experience. They were the first Jews to demonstrate an interest in art a long time prior to the Emancipation period.[1]

Ambiguous as it was, Renaissance Jewry's interest in art was unmistakable. The sixteenth century artist-writer Vasari tells us [2] that when Michelangelo was working on the statue of Moses, many Jews came to observe his work. The Jews of Florence used to climb into Brunelleschi's famous dome of *Santa Maria del Fiore* until this practice was banned toward the end of the Period.[3] Moreover, the Jews of Siena erected in their ghetto a statue of Moses that was sculptured by a Christian artist.[4] The financial support given by a well known Jew to several Christian artists was a similar expression of Jewish interest in the arts. There were also statements by

---

[1] See F. Landsberger, *HUCA* 16:374.
[2] *Vogelstein-Rieger*, vol. 2, p. 122.
[3] *Ciscato*, p. 140, Note 1.
[4] Landsberger, *Ibid.*, p. 366.

certain leading Jewish scholars reflecting their high regard of art. Curiously, the appreciative Jewish statements were made at the very end of the Period when a negative attitude toward art began to be manifested by the Counter-Reformation. Samuel Archivolti who opposed adorning the synagogue with murals, wrote an enthusiastic poem in praise of a Christian artist in which he stressed the eternal value of art. All living beings of the world, even the mightiest of the princes, descend to the grave says the rabbi. Only the artist's work stands for eternity. Leon da Modena was evidently certain that the congregation present at his first sermon in the great synagogue of Venice knew a great deal about art when he compared the difference between a great writer and a speaker to that between the painter and the sculptor. Elaborating on this felicitous comparison, he spoke at length about the equalities of sculpture and drawing and the various procedures of the artist and sculptor.[1] He also asserted that many Italian Jews displayed portraits and pictures in their homes. To be sure, most of the portraits did not show a figure in relief.[2]

A liberal interpretation of the Second Commandment combined with Renaissance man's aspiration for self-perpetuation was responsible for the preservation of a number of portraits of Renaissance Jews. There were also a number of medallions with protruding images. A portrait of Leon da Modena was made by a Christian artist, but an accident occurred and the portrait was lost as it was about to be completed. This did not deter Leon and he succeeded in perpetuating his likeness in another portrait that was preserved in one of his books. Portraits were also made of Maharam of Padua, his son Samuel Judah Katzenellenbogen and Rabbi Menahem Azariah da Fano. Reliable information has it that there was a statue of Rabbi Judah Minz in the University of Padua where he served as a teacher.[3] While it may seem

---

[1] *Vogelstein-Rieger, op. cit.*; Samuel Archivolti's poem was published by Simon Bernstein, *Tarbiẓ* 8-62; this sermon by Leon da Modena is found in the collection of his sermons *Midbar Yehudah*, Venice 1602, p. 5a.

[2] *Historia de gli Riti Hebraici*, Part 1, Chapter 2, paragraph 3.

[3] See: *Sepher Chaje Jehuda*, p. 54; *Hebraeische Bibliographie* 3:109

strange that an Ashkenazic rabbi who fought for years to have a *paroket* removed from a synagogue because it had images embroidered in relief, would consent to have a statue sculptured of himself, it is not beyond the realm of possibility. Also Rabbi Samuel Archivolti who wrote a poem in praise of the artist's craft, objected to paintings within the synagogue. Italian Jewish artists it seems, sometimes tried to perpetuate their memory through self-portraits. In a manuscript that was written in Parma in 1387 by the copyist Elijah ben David we find a portrait depicting the copyist as he was presenting the book to his employer.

All doubts vanished with regard to the legitimacy of book artistry. In this area the Italian Jews made a real effort to reach a high degree of artistic perfection. Many manuscripts copied in Italy, that are found in the great collections of Hebrew manuscripts, contain illuminations of rare beauty. In comparison to Spanish manuscripts "the Italian (manuscripts) are superior in execution and artistry, the pictures more beautiful and the decorations floriated, with lovely initials and capitals, occasionally introducing coats of arms, especially on the first page". [1] Artistic motifs were drawn from all areas of nature and life including animals and people. Illuminations

(Maharam of Padua); *Palge mayim*, Venice 1608, p. 6b (Rabbi Samuel Judah Katzenellenbogen). The portrait of Rabbi Menahem Azariah da Fano was published in *REJ* 39:115 and republished in Judah Wojdyslawski, *Sefer toledot rabbenu Menahem Azariah mifano*, Piotrkow 1904, facing the title page. See *Ibid.*, p. 74, a letter by Rabbi Joseph Jaré of Ferrara for the source of the picture. The information regarding Rabbi Judah Minz's statue is found in *Neppi-Ghirondi*, p. 122. Ghirondi claims that he saw the statue and its identifying inscription. Cf. the article by Elkan Adler cited below in Note 1. For Jewish medallions see *Landsberger*, p. 366 ff. Landsberger's argument, p. 367, that the medallion "Eli Romi" depicts the portrait of Elijah Beer himself seems reasonable. A picture of the medallion appears there in the portraits section, no. 7 (*Ibid.*, following p. 396). A medallion depicting Elijah Lattes is reproduced in *MGWJ* 38:239.

[1] See Cassuto, *Florence*, pp. 188, 192. See the basic article by David Kaufmann on the history of illumination of Hebrew manuscripts in *Gesammelte Schriften*, vol. 3, p. 173 ff. See especially p. 217, also *Catalogue Kaufmann*, p. 99 ff. Cf. *Landsberger*, p. 211 and the article by Elkan Adler in the *Gaster Jubilee Volume*, pp. 37-49. See especially pp. 38-39.

are found in manuscripts from all areas of literature, such as prayerbooks, Scrolls of Esther, other biblical books and even halakic literature. Elijah Baḥur complained over the exaggerated effort to enhance a book artistically, which reached such proportions that they affected textual exactitude: "...For scribes were not concerned with the text, their only aim was to enhance their script, and to keep the lines uniform and equal on every page and, moreover, to decorate them with paintings and drawings, with curlicues and bows, with buds and flowers".[1] Nevertheless, his contemporary, the wealthy Joseph Castelfranco of Brescia had no compunction about commissioning an artist-scribe to copy for him the volumes of the Talmud. An eyewitness reported that the copyist produced a work of art like "never done before". "I have seen their beauty", he added, and he expressed his regret that the fine artist could not complete his work because of the war that broke out at the time.[2] Beginning with the early sixteenth century, when printed books began to seriously displace manuscripts, the Scroll of Esther became the principal work on which artistic efforts were concentrated. The religious usage required that it be written on parchment, and thus it remained the only object on which illuminators could still show their prowess.[3]

The custom of artistic book decoration also penetrated the printing craft. Many of the Hebrew books that appeared in Italy during the Period contained drawings. Here too all doubts were eliminated and we find many pictures of animals and humans alongside the traditional decorations. The most common motif was that of *cherubim*. The drawings or coats of arms were often incongruous, and sometimes totally unfit to decorate sacred works. There were also many non-Jewish motifs in the illustrations.[4] Christian printers published many

[1] In the second Introduction to *Masoret hamasoret* which first appeared in Venice in 1538.

[2] *REJ*, 79:44.

[3] *HUCA* 16:363.

[4] See *Minḥah belulah* by Rabbi Abraham Porto, Verona 1594, at the beginning of each book of the Pentateuch and at the end of the volume; *HUCA, Ibid.*, p. 362; Joseph Reider's article in *Freidus Memorial Volume*, p. 150 ff.; *Zion*, N. S. 17:154 (Isaiah Sonne's article).

Hebrew books and used cuts of non-Jewish drawings to enhance Hebrew books. There are many illustrations in the Yiddish novel *Paris un Wyena* that appeared in Verona in 1594. The Christian publisher of this novel also published it in Italian several years later and again used all the illustrations in the Italian edition that were in the Yiddish edition.[1]

Renaissance man's involvement with the visual arts furthered their introduction into the synagogue. Externally, Italian Jewish houses of worship were rather modest, for governments opposed the construction of magnificent synagogal structures. A good example is the striking difference between the simple exterior of the Sephardic synagogue in Venice and its rich interior. When the Paduan magnate Naphtali Herz Wertheim tried to build a gold-plated synagogue for himself, the government of Venice forced him to stop half-way through.[2] For this reason the artistic effort centered on the holy ark, the pulpit, and the pews.[3] A Roman synagogue had very beautiful silver vessels made by Benvenuto Cellini. The ark curtain in Herz Wertheim's unfinished synagogue was embroidered with pearls and entranced the viewers with its exquisite beauty. There was an ark in a synagogue in Ascoli that was built of wood from a nut tree with engravings in gold. It was resting on two reclining lions, and ascent to it was by stairs built between the lions. The workmanship was so fine that the lions gave the impression of being alive. When the Jews were expelled from Ascoli in 1569, the ark was transferred to Pesaro and stood in the Sephardic synagogue for decades. A holy ark from Modena, built in 1472, and now kept in the Musée Cluny in Paris, is reminiscent of Brunelleschi's doors in Florence.[4] The practice of painting murals in synagogues seems to have been common. In 1620 a Jew in Carpi received permission from the government to enlarge the synagogue. He also asked to be allowed to decorate the walls

[1] See *Erik, History*, p. 437.

[2] See Roth, *Venice*, p. 140 and *REJ* 79:43.

[3] See *Menorah Journal*, Spring 1946, p. 76; *REJ, Ibid.*; *JQR,* 9:254; *Kaufmann, Ibid.*, p. 98; a picture of the holy ark in a synagogue in Modena is available in *Landsberger*, p. 189.

[4] *Balletti*, p. 86.

with paintings, arguing that "all synagogues have many beautiful paintings of all kinds". An example of such a house of worship is the Ashkenazic synagogue in Venice, which had murals depicting birds and flowers.[1]

Although art within the synagogue was an accepted fact, periodic attacks on its legitimacy were made. We have seen that at the end of the Period Rabbi Samuel Archivolti [2] who appreciated the visual arts, expressed an opinion in opposition to paintings within the synagogue. His opposition was not based upon the fear of transgressing the Second Commandment. Transgression occurs, according to him, only when one depicts objects that were worshipped by pagans. Consequently, birds may be depicted in synagogue murals. He opposed illustrative art in the synagogue, especially flowers, only because their beauty might distract the worshipper's attention and thereby weaken his devotion, without which prayer is meaningless. He was also afraid that the synagogue would take on the appearance of a theatre if there were too many paintings. "How can synagogue walls become like the walls of a theater of *comedianti*", he argued. He also feared other pitfalls. It is possible, he claimed, that Appio could accuse the Jews of worshipping the image of an ass [3] because there might have been a picture of an ass in one of the synagogues.

The only serious strife over the subject of art within the synagogue that we know of was in connection with Herz Wertheim's beautiful ark curtain.[4] He tried to have the curtain displayed on holidays despite the opposition of rabbi Judah Minz. The rabbi considered the curtain objectionable because of the Wertheim family coat-of-arms that was embroidered upon it with the letters in relief. But Wertheim, who was one of the rabbi's antagonists, did not want to submit "and through his wealth found rabbis to aid him and they supplied him with Talmudic evidence that it was permitted". When Wertheim placed the curtain in the synagogue "by

[1] See Samuel Archivolti's responsum in *JQR* 9:266 ff.
[2] *Ibid.*
[3] See Josephus, *Against Appio*, Hebrew translation by Y. N. Simchoni, Tel-Aviv 1938, p. 61 ff.
[4] See *Responsa Abuḳat roḳel* by Joseph Caro, par. 65.

force, ...the old man (Rabbi Judah Minz) left in a great rage
and the dispute became intensified..." The war surrounding
this ark curtain lasted a long time and there were efforts to
settle the differences by granting permission to use it with
the provision that the family coat-of-arms would not be in
relief. The dispute was finally settled about fifty years later,
when Wertheim's heirs acceded to the request of Maharam of
Padua that the protruding family seal be covered up.

Information regarding Jewish artists is very sparse even
though they probably were fairly numerous. Most of them
presumably were classed as professional copyists.[1] To them,
as we have seen, is due credit for the many beautiful handwritten books that excelled in artistic script, illustrations, and
bindings. Evidently there were not very many Jewish artists
who actually painted. Among the few names that we do know
we find Angelo d'Elia and Jacobe di Vitale, but their works
are unknown. The two greatest Jewish artists Francesco
Ruschi, a painter, and Salomone da Sesso, an expert sword
engraver, both converted to Christianity. Several wood engravers are also known,[2] as well as a substantial number of
Jewish silversmiths. The Jewish artists who worked in majolica
were discussed above (Section III, Chapter 3).

The most popular Jewish artist seems to have been Moses
Castelazzo of Venice.[3] A son of an immigrant from Germany,
he worked all his life as a painter, especially of portraits.
Late in his life he planned to publish with the assistance of his
sons, skilled engravers, an illustrated edition of the Pentateuch. Hoping for a great commercial success for his venture,
he attempted to obtain protection of his rights from the
Venetian government. There is reason to assume that the
project was carried out even though not a single copy of the
work has been found. Moses was also active in Jewish communal
affairs.

[1] Jewish artists may possibly be found in a list of copyists published
by Aaron Freimann in *Alexander Marx Jubilee Volume*, English
section, p. 231 ff.

[2] *HUCA* 16:373.

[3] See Kaufmann, *Gesammelte Schriften*, vol. 1, p. 169 ff.; *REJ*
22:290; *Sippur David hareubeni*, p. 31 ff.

CHAPTER TWO

MUSIC AND DANCE

a.

Renaissance Jewish society had a genuine interest in music and in the art of dancing. Music appreciation and its expression, however, were far more extensively cultivated than dancing. The widely known writer Abraham Farissol, who was also a musician, once signed his name on a manuscript that he had copied as though it were composed of three musical symbols "fa-re-sol".[1] Musical education was very popular. A recommendation for a candidate for the position of a rosh yeshibah stressed his proficiency in music. When David Reubeni stayed in the home of Jehiel da Pisa, the women of the household tried to lift his spirits with dance and music. Song, music and dance were a preferred pastime of the Jews in Monferrato. This resulted in such a close social contacts between Jews and gentiles that the government was moved to proclaim a ban on Jewish visits to Christian homes.[2] Against this backdrop we can appreciate Leon da Modena's enthusiastic attitude toward music:[3] "I lack the space to include what the sages have reiterated regarding the glorious beauty and usefulness of music, for all the beauty in the lower, middle, and upper worlds is an order of voices and exquisite music, and how the soul, through music and song, becomes awakened and is elevated from matter into the heavenly dwelling place of its Creator".

The great centers of Jewish music were Mantua and Venice. In Mantua musical life enjoyed the support of the dukes of the House of Gonzaga who employed many Jewish musicians, and no other Jewish community had in its midst so many professional singers and dancers.[4] When the Mantuan com-

---

[1] *Kobez al jad*, N. S. vol. 2, p. 3, Note 1.

[2] See Marx, *Louis Ginzberg Jubilee Volume*, p. 294 (Hebrew section). *Sippur David hareubeni*, p. 53; *Foà*, p. 109.

[3] *Bet Yehuda* (also called *Haboneh*), Arakim 11. Quoted according to *Libowitz*, p. 95 ff. (see below, Note 1, p. 242).

[4] For Jewish musicians in Mantua see d'Ancona A., *Origini del teatro italiano*, Turin 1891, vol. 2, pp. 398-401.

munity was destroyed following the occupation of the city
by the Emperor, many Jewish musicians fled to Venice. In
Venice, too, they found an atmosphere appreciative of their
talents. Aided by Leon da Modena "who was himself a tenor
with a pleasant voice", [1] they founded a musical society [2]
patterned after the "academies", cultural associations, which
then proliferated throughout Italy. The society existed for
several years and its members used to meet twice weekly to
sing and to play under the direction of Leon da Modena.
Shortly after its establishment, however, the academy was
compelled to severely limit its activities since many of its
members perished in an epidemic in the autumn of 1630. It
seems that another musical academy was organized in the
Venice ghetto several years later. This academy was also
founded by a recently arrived immigrant.

Jewish interest in music was based upon the conviction that
this art is a genuine part of Jewish culture. Immanuel of Rome
stated simply: "What does the art of music say to Christians?
I was stolen away out of the land of the Hebrews!" [3] Several
sixteenth century Italian Jewish scholars who wrote studies
on music, disputed the tradition that Pythagoras discovered
the art of music. They argued that "Jubal was the father of all
such as handle the harp and pipe". Consequently, it was even
considered permissible to listen to women's singing. Mixed
dancing of both sexes was an accepted pattern. To be sure,
there were also derogatory remarks directed at "those who
danced". But even those who banned mixed dancing did
permit male dancing teachers to dance with women. [4] An

[1] From the Introduction by Isaac Levi to *Magen waḥereb* as quoted
in Nehemiah S. Libowitz, *Leon Modena*, 2nd ed., N. Y. 1901, p. 97.
[2] Most of the information regarding the musical academy in
Venice is available in Roth, *RMI* 3:152 ff.
[3] *Maḥberot Immanuel*, p. 185 (6th *canto*). Comp. Genesis 40:15
and Immanuel's commentary to Proverbs 26:13.
[4] Comp. Genesis 4:21. See the list of documents in the archives
of the community of Ancona, *Corriere Israelitico*, 1914. A poem
deriding dancers was published by Simon Bernstein in *Mishire
Yisrael beitalia*, Jerusalem 1939, p. 33. In the Introduction to *Hashirim
asher lishelomo* Leon da Modena sadly related that since the murder
of his son Zebulun he no longer listened to "the voice of male or
female singers".

attempt to attack a synagogue choir that sang in conformity with musical scales aroused Leon da Modena to write a spirited responsum in defense of music. [1]

The interest in music was the source of a considerable literature on the subject of music and dancing. For example, Guglielmo da Pesaro wrote an important work on the history of dancing, *Trattato della danza*,[2] in which he presented an idealistic approach toward dancing in protest against those who dance merely to satisfy their lust. More abundant are the works dealing with the history of music and descriptions of various musical instruments. Here too, Mantua was in the forefront. The famed Mantuan preacher Rabbi Judah Moscato devoted the first sermon in his book *Nefuzot Yehudah* to the subject of music and its history. He demonstrated a basic knowledge of music and musical instruments. His fellow Mantuan Abraham Portaleone devoted about ten chapters of his great work *Shilte hagibborim* to music.[3] He dealt at length with the music of the Temple service, discussed the instruments, and explained how they were used. His remarks indicate that there was a debate among Jewish musicologists in Mantua over the place of music in ancient Judaism. Rabbi Samuel Archivolti likewise dealt with this question in a poem in his book *Arugat habosem*.[4] He speculated that music was created through "rotation of the heavenly spheres" and was transmitted to mankind through Jubal. Music was then forgotten because of the flood and was rediscovered by Pythagoras. King David also understood its subtleties. However, music will attain its true fulfillment in the future with the coming of the Messiah and the resurrection of the dead.

The Jewish interest in music understandably influenced the

---

[1] Leon da Modena's responsum on music was published at the beginning of *Hashirim asher lishelomo*. Excerpts from it are available in *Libowitz, Ibid.*, p. 96.

[2] See the detailed study by Otto Kinkelday in *Freidus Memorial Volume*, p. 329 ff.

[3] Chapters 4-13. Information regarding the debate of the Mantuan scholars is at the end of Chapter 13, p. 10a.

[4] p. 118a. The writer overlooked the fact that King David lived about five hundred years before Pythagoras.

synagogue service. Leon da Modena tells [1] that the Ashkenazim in Italy sang in their synagogues more than others. The Levantines and Sephardim sang in a particular style similar to the singing of the Turks. But Italiani prayer was most beautiful and sweet and was a pleasure to hear. Rabbi Obadiah da Bertinoro noted that Sicilian synagogues had many cantors. He probably meant that the cantor sang with a choir. Leon da Modena believed in the usefulness of the choir and fought zealously for its legitimacy. The greatest impact on sacred music was made by the composer Solomon dei Rossi who was also essential in introducing choirs into the synagogue. His book *Hashirim asher lishelomo* [2] contains melodies for a number of important prayers. To be sure, musical enthusiasm led to some distressing results within the synagogue. Samuel Archivolti complained bitterly "over some contemporary cantors who chanted the sacred prayers to the tunes of secular folk songs which mingled the sacred words with obscene and licentious thoughts". [3]

b.

The composers and musicians known to us by name were not too numerous. Even the membership of the two Jewish musical societies in Venice is known only in part. Most of these artists attained wide renown, especially in high Christian society. The dei Rossi family in Mantua [4] stood in front rank. In addition to Solomon, his sister Europa attained distinction and played regularly before royalty, as did her son Anselmo (Asher). Solomon's creative period fell between 1587 and 1628.

[1] *Historia de gli Riti Hebraici*, Part I, Chapter 11, paragraph 6; Rabbi Obadiah da Bertinoro (see *Iggerot Erez Yisrael*, p. 105) praised the five cantors in Palermo and assured that he had not heard anyone like them in any of the places that he visited. Apparently, the custom of maintaining in a synagogue a choir emerged in Sicily about a century earlier than on the Italian mainland.

[2] The book appeared in Venice in 1623 and was republished in Frankfort in 1925. Cf. *Vogelstein-Rieger*, vol. 2, p. 310.

[3] *Arugat habosem*, p. 110b.

[4] For the dei Rossi family see: the Introduction to *Hashirim asher lishelomo*; E. G. Birnbaum, *Juedische Musiker am Hofe zu Mantua*, Vienna 1893, pp. 13-28; L. Carnevali, *Il ghetto di Mantova*, p. 30, Note 1; Cf. *HUCA*, vol. 23, part 2, p. 383 ff.

In 1589 he published a collection of compositions, *Il primo libro delle canzonette a tre voci*. Later he resided in Rome where he composed several other important works. At the turn of the century he and his sister were on the payroll of the ducal court in Mantua. Solomon also enjoyed steady patronage from the wealthy Sullam family. The compositions of his nephew Anselmo were likewise well known. Other artists who achieved renown in Mantua were the performers Abraham dell'Arpa and Isacchino Massarano, who was also a dancer. Outstanding composers were David Civita, author of *Premitie armoniche* that appeared in Venice in 1616 and Allegro (Simhah) Porto whose musical compositions were collected in a three volume work.[1] Jewish artists were also prominent in Rome. Jacob of San Secondo was famous as a violinist during the times of Pope Alexander VI. He played at the wedding of the Pope's daughter Lucrezia Borgia. A few other Jewish artists in Rome converted to Christianity, probably to further their careers. One of them, an expert flutist, was knighted by Pope Leo X.[2]

The passion for music led to the inclusion of music and dance in the educational programs for the young, especially among the wealthy families. In a letter to his pupil a teacher urged him to practice the violin and lyre daily at dusk. Leon da Modena who in his youth learned to play, to sing, and to dance, hoped that Solomon dei Rossi's work *Hashirim asher lishelomo* would encourage many to study music.[3] Music and dance were widely taught by private Jewish teachers and in schools established for this purpose. Quite revealing is the fact that Rabbi Jacob Levi, Leon da Modena's son-in-law, continued to teach dancing and music even after his ordination.[4]

It seems that Jewish schools and teachers of music and

[1] *RMI* 3:154; Birnbaum, *Ibid.*, p. 12 ff.; *d'Ancona, Ibid.*, p. 400 (especially for the activities of Massarano as an expert in dancing).
[2] *Vogelsteiner-Rieger*, pp. 119-121, 439; Marx, *Moses Schorr Memorial Volume*, p. 213; Birnhaum, *Ibid.*, p. 8.
[3] S. Asaf, *Mekorot letoledot hahinuk beyisrael*, vol. 4, p. 26; *Sippur David hareubeni*, p. 53; *Sepher Chaje Jehuda*, p. 17; Solomon dei Rossi, *Hashirim asher lishelomo*, Introduction.
[4] *Sepher Chaje Jehuda*, p. 33.

dance enjoyed a good reputation among the Christian population. During the entire Renaissance period we encounter
both Church and government efforts to prevent Christians
from studying music and dance from Jews.[1] The famous
Christian preacher Bernardino da Feltre, in a sermon delivered
at Parma, criticized upper class Christian women who studied
dancing under Jewish instructors. In the Republic of Venice
in 1443 Jews were forbidden to maintain schools of art,
dancing, singing, and music. Despite this, the daughter of
Filelfo the Younger was the pupil of the famous dancing instructor Guglielmo the Jew. As late as 1592 it became necessary to ban Roman Jews from teaching singing and dancing to
Christians, even though the policy of complete separation
between Christians and Jews initiated by Pope Paul IV had
been in effect about forty years.

CHAPTER THREE

THE THEATER

a.

The theater of the Renaissance developed quite late in the
Period. At first the *sacre rappresentazioni*, sacred plays,
dominated the Italian stage. A genuine Renaissance drama,
and especially the pastoral play, began to appear in the sixteenth
century. The ducal court in Mantua played an important role
in the process of developing the secular theather. It was here
that the first attempts were made to stage Guarini's *Il pastor
fido*.[2]

When the secular theater came into being, the drama
emerged among the Jews as well. Mantua served the Jews too
as a theatrical center during the entire sixteenth century and
most of the first half of the seventeenth century. There was

---

[1] *Menorah Journal*, Spring 1946, p. 77; G. Wolf, *Hebraeische Bibliographie* 6:66; Baron, *Samuel Krausz Jubilee Volume*, p. 34, according
to Zagata, author of a history of the city of Verona, which appeared
in the eighteenth century. *Freidus Memorial Volume, Ibid.*, p. 368;
A. Bertolotti, *Gli ebrei in Roma*, Spoleto 1879, p. 262.

[2] This is discussed at length in d'Ancona, *Ibid.*, especially p. 535
and p. 576 (the concluding chapter).

also a Jewish theater in Venice. Undoubtedly, Jewish theaters also played in other cities, although the available information refers only to theatrical or quasi theatrical productions on Purim (see Section IV, Chapter 3).

There were two aspects to Jewish theatrical life in Mantua.[1] On one side there existed a Jewish theater that even tried to obtain permission to maintain a special building for regular performances. On the other side, the Mantuan community was obligated to bear the expenses for performances by Jewish actors in the ducal court. There is evidence that as early as 1525 the Jewish community paid this tax and kept on paying it uninterruptedly to the very end of the Period.[2] This suggests that there were among the Jews of Mantua such talented actors, that the duke preferred to accept their artistic services in lieu of a regular tax. Once, during great festivities in the ducal court, two performances were presented, one by the Christian company and one by the Jewish, the *istrioni Ebrei*. The plays presented by the Jews included comedies by Ariosto and Bernardo Tasso. The Jewish performances strongly impressed foreign guests visiting Mantua who wrote specifically about it in their travelogues. They were especially impressed with Simon Basilea, one of the actors who could play many, varied roles. They also liked the intermezzo, the Jewish troupe's original contribution to the play. Emissaries of other countries even informed their governments, in accordance with the custom of the time, about the play of the Jewish company. Contemporary Christians attested that the Jewish actors did not perform on Sabbaths

---

[1] The description of the Jewish theater in Mantua is based on the important archival material published by d'Ancona in a special chapter, *Ibid.*, p. 398 ff. A summary of the material in Hebrew is available in Schirmann's Introduction to *Zaḥut bediḥuta deḳiddushin*, and in Yiddish in Ignacy Schipper, *Geschichte fun idiszer teater-kunst un drame*, vol. 1, Warsaw 1923, p. 38 ff.

[2] Cecil Roth theorized (*HUCA*, vol. 23, part 2, p. 154) that this "tax" grew out of the custom to force the Jews (in Rome, for example) to entertain the masses with buffoonery. The fact that Mantua occupied a special position not only in Jewish theatrical life but in the general history of the Italian theater, seems to disprove Roth's theory.

and Jewish holidays, and on days preceding holidays they hastened to complete their performances prior to the advent of the festival.

The Mantuan Jewish company was at the height of its success in the second half of the sixteenth century. It was then led by Leon Sommi da Portaleone. An excellent actor, he also wrote many dramas and undertook a study of the theoretical aspects of the theater. When the famous playwright Muzio Manfredi wanted to stage his tragedy *Semiramis* in Mantua, he approached Leon. He was full of praise for the Jewish actor and relied upon him in preparing the performance since he was aware that Sommi was a *"Maestro di quest'arte"*.[1]

In addition to the theatrical troupe that performed regularly, Mantua had, as we have seen, numerous Jewish musicians and choreographers such as Abraham dell'Arpa and Isacchino Massarano. The latter was asked by Manfredi to direct the dancing in *Semiramis*. Massarano was also in charge of the choreography in other plays that were performed in Mantua and Padua, including *Il pastor fido*.[2] The famous engineer Abraham Colorni served as a technical advisor in the theater of the Mantuan court.[3]

Although Jewish theatrical achievements in Venice were rather modest, there too various plays were staged. A Christian resident of the city recorded in his diary that on March 4, 1531, which was Shushan Purim, the Jews performed a very lovely comedy in the ghetto.[4] In 1559 and again in 1592 they performed *Esther*, a drama written by Solomon Usque and Eleazar Halevi.[5] In 1605 we again encounter a number of Venetian Jews, amateur actors, preparing the presentation of a comedy.[6]

There were also playwrights among the Renaissance Jews, again primarily in Mantua and Venice. In the first quarter of

[1] See the letter published by d'Ancona, *Ibid.*, p. 424 Note 1.
[2] See *Ibid.*, and pp. 400, 541, 542, 552.
[3] Schipper, *Ibid.*, p. 49, who borrowed this information from an Italian monograph that discusses engineers in the Mantuan court.
[4] The text is in d'Ancona, *Ibid.*, p. 429, Note 1.
[5] See Roth, *JQR*, N. S. 34:77-78.
[6] *Leo Modenas Briefe*, pp. 113-115.

the sixteenth century the physician-poet Joseph Zarfadi
translated into Hebrew the Spanish play *La Celestina* by
Fernando de Rojas, which first appeared in 1499.[1] In 1525
one of the Mantuan Jewish actors wrote a play that was then
performed by the Jewish acting troupe in the ducal court.[2]
The play *Esther* that was written and performed in Venice,
was mentioned above. Other plays, especially pastorals, were
written at the end of the Period: Leon da Modena wrote a
pastoral *Jacob and Rachel*, and Angelo Alatini wrote a similar
play entitled *I trionfi*.[3] Leon da Modena also attempted to
revise the drama *Esther* to make it conform to the changed
theatrical taste of the times.[4] All these plays were written and
presented in Italian.

The most prolific Jewish playwright of the Renaissance was
undoubtedly the actor Leon Sommi. His plays outnumbered
those written by all other Jewish playwrights of the Period.
As the secretary of the academy *degli Invaghiti* he was
obligated to write plays for the society. Apparently most of
the dramas that he wrote were performed at meetings of the
society. One of his manuscripts that contained eleven plays
was in the Turin library and was destroyed by fire. Most of
these plays were pastorals, while others were comedies.
Mythological figures abounded in all of them in accordance
with the Period's taste.[5]

There is no trace of Sommi's Jewishness in any of his plays,
as they were written for non-Jewish audiences whose literary
taste was then completely geared to the classical world with
all of its mythological elements. Some years ago a Hebrew
comedy was discovered with all indications that its origin was
mid-sixteenth century Italy. Manuscripts of this comedy
which was given the bizarre title *Zahut bedihuta dekiddushin* [6]

[1] See Cassuto, *Jewish Studies in Memory of George A. Kohut*, p. 123.
[2] The play presented by the Jews was *per loro composta* (see d'Ancona, *Ibid.*, p. 401).
[3] *Sepher Chaje Jehuda*, pp. 44-45.
[4] *JQR, Ibid.*, p. 78.
[5] The list of plays by Somo is available in d'Ancona, *Ibid.*, p. 404.
[6] The name indicates that it is a comedy (*Zahut bedihuta*) centering
upon the subject of marriage (*kiddushin*). The play was edited by
Jefim Schirmann, Jerusalem 1946.

by a later copyist, name the author as Judah. The name
Judah, as well as certain passages in the text, led several
scholars [1] to ascribe the comedy to Leon Sommi. The play
was written in prose and is currently the only Hebrew comedy
that we have from a period prior to the eighteenth century.
There is no doubt that it is an original Hebrew comedy. The
Jewish motifs are the decisive factors in most of the involved
action and the plot is borrowed from the Midrash Tanhuma.[2]
However, the comedy's structure is a faithful replica of the
Period's Italian plays. In order to lend the comedy an authentic Jewish character, the author lets the action develop against
a Palestinian, biblical backdrop. But the characters that
appear in it, the marital intrigues that constitute the focus of
action, and especially the manner in which they were solved,
are clearly contemporary. The Period's responsa literature is
replete with the kind of situations that we encounter in this
comedy.[3] The play is divided, in the fashion of that era, into
five acts ("parts") and is written in a felicitous blend of
biblical, talmudic, and contemporary Hebrew style.

Leon Sommi, as we have seen, was also the author of a
dialogue that dealt with the fundamentals of the theater.
Written in Italian, the dialogue was entitled *Dialoghi in
materia di rappresentazione scenica*, and was one of the earliest
of such works.[4] Three men are engaged in the dialogue with
one of them Veridico "the truth speaker", representing the

[1] Umberto Cassuto (in a personal conversation) and Schirmann.
Schirmann admits (in his Introduction to the play, p. 7) that there
are certain contradictions between the structure of the comedy and
Leon Somo's theoretical views on the drama (see below). Schirmann
tries to explain the contradictions by the assumption that Somo
altered his ideas on the theater in the period between the composition
of the play and his book *Dialoghi*.

[2] Portion *Lek leka*, Chapter 8: A story about a man who traveled
overseas, etc.

[3] See above, Section IV, Chapter 1. Slaves that were passed on as
inheritance or who were freed by their masters were, contrary to
Schirmann's view, not uncommon during the Period. See above,
Section IV, Chapter 3.

[4] A fairly detailed description of *Dialoghi* is found in d'Ancona,
Ibid., p. 410 ff. Valuable details are also found in Schipper, *Ibid.*,
p. 47.

author's views. Veridico the Jew asserts that the Hebrews preceded the Greeks in introducing the drama, since *The book of Job* was written in the form of a dialogue. This was one of the manifestations of a general trend in Renaissance Jewry to prove that the ancient Hebrews had a decisive role in the development of human culture. Sommi's work discusses the history and rules of the drama, the need to divide it into five acts, and technical problems of staging. His technical advice is very significant and appears almost modern. He recommends that costumes be made to accord with the time and place in which the play is set. He also advised changes of scenery to reflect different situations in the various acts. He demanded the elimination of obscene language which was typical of Italian comedy of that time. This counsel grew out of his recognition that the main purpose of comedy was not to entertain the audience, but to cure human shortcomings by exposing them in public.

SECTION VIII

THE WORLD OF SCIENCE

CHAPTER ONE

INTRODUCTION

All through the Period of the Renaissance the Italian Jews
were dominated by a passion for inquiry. Early in the Period,
when Jews were prominent as translators of scientific works from
Arabic into Latin, Italian Jews believed that their proficiency
in the sciences was superior to that of their gentile neighbors.[1]
However, soon scientific research began to pick up momentum
also within Christian society. A race then started to obtain old
manuscripts and to study the classical languages, in which
both Christians and Jews participated. The thirst for knowledge and the passion for inquiry were so strong that the problem of investigative legitimacy and the limits of research became
a topic of perpetual discussion. Inherent in the principle of
scientific involvement was an infringement on the place of
religion in man's life. Engagement in scholarship and research
seriously limited the time that might have been devoted to the
study of Torah. In the first part of the Period Torah study
was mainly regarded as an intellectual activity, and the
religious aspect was not emphasized. Only a minority felt that
a broadened concern with other disciplines curtailed Torah
study. The majority regarded both Torah study and the
sciences as two necessary areas of knowledge for a Jew's
total fulfillment. An anonymous Jewish humanist of Florence
wrote in 1490 to his patron: "And you should continue
learning both God's perfect Torah and philosophy..."[2] In

[1] This assertion by the learned poet Judah Romano is found in
Guedemann, vol. 2, p. 134.
[2] Cassuto, *Florence*, p. 404. The author of *Ẓaḥut bediḥuta deḳiddushin*
(p. 31) also maintained that pleasure, benefit, and honor are gained
"through the knowledge of the mysteries of the true Torah and its
commentaries and the familiarity with the nature of all species of
the creatures", that is to say through the study of both the Torah
and natural sciences.

this statement he clearly formulated the enlightened Renaissance Jew's cultural program. Only at the end of the Period when religious sentiment heightened among Italian Jewry, and Torah learning was under attack by the Counter-Reformation, did Torah study assume a religious dimension. At that time repentant voices bemoaning the involvement in secular studies were heard in far greater volume than previously.

The scientific interests of the Renaissance Jews were of a very wide scope. Not only were Jews involved in medical studies, a field that was cultivated by Jewish scholars in every age,[1] but all areas of research came within their purview out of pure humanistic interest. Samuel Archivolti sang a hymn of praise to secular wisdom with an enthusiasm that merits attention: "I will sing a song to God, I will sing to the God of Israel, He has awakened me from slumber of negligence, has transformed darkness into light for me, He has given me a heart to know and eyes to see how goodly are the tents of Edom's wisdom, and the dwelling places of his glorious greatness".[2] The great admiration for "Edom's wisdom" often led Jewish scholars into forms of free inquiry which placed them in an antagonistic position toward the established religious tradition. Azariah dei Rossi's *Meor enayim* with its array of historical and chronological investigations, often critical of sanctified statements by the ancient sages, was the most drastic expression of the emergent trend. Although Rabbi Azariah spoke in profound admiration of the Talmudic sages, he clearly stressed his viewpoint that their statements were based on human reasoning and could, therefore, be subjected to rational analysis.[3] His remarks at the conclusion of a lengthy analysis of the story of Titus' gnat are a striking example: "From all that has been mentioned, I believe that it should be *very clear* that this story of Titus recounted by

---

[1] See, for example, the lengthy discourse of Rabbi Jacob Provenzal published in *Dibre ḥakamim* by Eliezer Ashkenazi, p. 63 ff. See especially *Ibid.*, p. 73 ff.

[2] In the Introduction to his book *Maayan ganim*, Venice 1553.

[3] See, for example, *Meor enayim*, section *Imre binah*, p. 164 ff. See *Burckhardt*, p. 376 for a similar trend among Christian scholars, especially the higher clergy.

our teachers was not that way at all in any part of it". And he adds: "I cannot refrain from informing you, my dear reader, that when my remarks about Titus' gnat became known, some of our scholars raised a clamor against me arguing that I had flawed the holiness of our sages' remarks... Despite this I have not refrained from recording it in a book..." Abraham Portaleone followed a similar course. He first asserted that "I have not, Heaven forbid, undertaken to dispute my teachers...", but added: "However, if it is permitted to question from time to time statements of the sages..." And in conclusion he specifically stated: "I shall later feel free to question these remarks by the sages and shall clarify them, for it is difficult to believe..." The lure of research was so intense that several of the greatest authors quoted in their writings long passages from unorthodox *Meor enayim* without indicating the source. Abraham Jaghel Gallichi did this in his book *Bet yaar halebanon*, as did Gedaliah Ibn Jachia in *Shalshelet hakabbalah*. Even though the latter ordinarily mentioned his sources in connection with every small bit of information, he copied long passages of *Meor enayim* without any mention of their origin. Cases of textual criticism this writer found only regarding the Mishnah and the Midrashim.[1]

The drive to inquiry was accompanied by a strong desire to disseminate basic information in all areas of knowledge. To begin with, this desire found expression in the great Hebrew literary works of the epoch, such as *Maḥberot Immanuel* and *Mikdash meat*, which abound with descriptions of various scientific subjects. Similarly, the many discourses on nature included in a popular volume like *Shalshelet hakabbalah* helped immeasurably to dispense the knowledge of the world among broad circles of the Jewish population.

The interest in general knowledge also found expression in the attempt at establishing Jewish universities in Sicily and in Mantua. The plan of a Jewish university in Sicily was conceived by the organization of Jewish communities on the

---

[1] See *Meor enayim, Ibid.*, pp. 103, 105; *Shilte hagibborim*, p. 95a and all of Chapter 87; *Shalshelet hakabbalah*, p. 17.

island, and was very important because of its official nature.[1] In 1466 the plan was submitted to the king and approved by him. According to the plan courses were to be conducted in the subjects generally offered in a university, such as medicine and law. The university was also explicitly granted the privelege of conferring academic degrees. There is no information as to whether the plan materialized.

Much more is known about the Jewish university in Mantua. Rabbi David Provenzal and his physician-son Abraham in 1564 conceived the idea of founding a private school in which students would receive a higher education simultaneously in both Jewish and general subjects. They hoped to receive proper remuneration for their efforts [2] through providing the students with room and board. To be sure, they wished to make it possible for the poor to enroll, and besought the kehillot to send them qualified students on communal scholarships. Father and son were prepared to devote all their time to the establishment and administration of the school. A great scholar was to be hired as instructor for the senior class. If the enrollment will be large, they asserted, additional teachers will be appointed, experts in their respective fields.

The curriculum was based on the principle that the Jewish and secular subjects were equally important. In the Jewish studies area a great deal of time was to be devoted to the Talmud and codes. Ashkenazic scholars were to teach these subjects, since they surpassed their Italianic colleagues in the

[1] The document is published in R. Starabba, *Ricerche Storiche su Guglielmo Moncada*, Palermo 1878, p. 47 ff. Guedemann also gives a description of the subject, *Ibid.*, p. 261.

[2] The program was published from the only remaining copy of the prospectus in *Halebanon*, vol. 5. An English translation is available in J. R. Marcus, *The Jew in the Medieval World*, Cincinnati 1938, p. 381 ff. It was generally believed that the plan was never activated. However, Isaiah Sonne correctly argued (*Expurgation of Hebrew Books—the Work of Jewish Scholars*, New York 1943, p. 20 ff.) that there are many allusions in a variety of sources to indicate that it did materialize. Further proof may, perhaps, be seen in the fact that Abraham Portaleone called Abraham Provenzal "head of the academy" (*Shilte hagibborim*, p. 185b). Were Abraham not the head of an educational institution, he would have merely referred to him as a sage and physician.

Talmudic disciplines (see below, Chapter 3). Other Jewish subjects to be taught were the Bible with its commentaries and Hebrew grammar. General studies were to include Latin, logic, philosophy, and medicine, so that Jewish medical students would need to study in a non-Jewish medical school only a short time. Arithmetic, geometry, geography, and astrology would also be offered, apparently to students who were interested in obtaining knowledge in the liberal arts rather than in medicine. The third group of subjects, stylized letter writing, and debating proficiency, aimed at teaching the students the special skills which an educated Renaissance man was expected to possess. The program was outlined in a circular which was sent to communities and individuals. The college was indeed opened in Mantua and existed ten years, and perhaps, even longer. We do not know how many graduates the school produced.

Enthusiasm for study and free forms of inquiry that led several Jewish scholars to develop attitudes contradictory to the religious tradition, evoked a protest in certain circles. As early as the middle of the fifteenth century Messer Leon attempted to ban Gersonides' commentary on the Pentateuch in which he believed to have found heretical ideas.[1] Of a more decisive nature was the attack launched about a century later against Azariah dei Rossi's *Meor enayim*. The ban on the book was proclaimed by the rabbis of such important communities as Venice, Pesaro, Ancona, Padua, Verona, Rome, Ferrara, and Siena.[2] In order to gain community support for the ban, they preached extensively on the subject in the synagogues. They also published the proclamation on a broadsheet for public distribution. The rabbis understood the far reaching consequences that would emerge from the analyses in *Meor enayim* if they were to produce a radical revision of biblical chronology. If Azariah was right, one of the rabbis argued, it will follow that all divorce decrees ever issued were wrongly dated and invalid.

[1] See Moses A. Shulvass, *In the Grip of Centuries*, pp. 56 ff.
[2] The material is published in Kaufmann, *Gesammelte Schriften* vol. 3, p. 83 ff.

The Jewish public generally heeded the bans on free inquiry. Messer Leon's ban on Gersonides' Torah commentary was effective for a long time. Similarly, the ban on *Meor enayim*, proclaimed in 1574, was still in effect in 1619. Such bans and doubts regarding the legitimacy of scientific research led a part of Italian Jewry, including some rabbis, to oppose preoccupation with science. One example are the rabbis of the Naples region of the late fifteenth century, who were known as having no interest in the sciences. About a century later the humanist Judah Moscato complained that the Jews' degradation "can be attributed to their amazing descent into the profound depths of foolishness...which is very obvious in our generation".[1] Moreover, certain scholars consciously abandoned scientific research in order to devote themselves exclusively to Torah study. The preacher Azariah Pigo tells [2] that in his youth "I was captivated by the brood of aliens (comp. Isaiah 2:6), the secular disciplines". Even after he overcame his infatuation and devoted himself to the study of Torah, he was still strongly attracted by the secular studies and he "worried over the future lest the lust for an alien bosom overtake me".

It is thus evident that Italian Jewry's relationship to science paralleled its approach to the entire range of Renaissance culture: Many of them dedicated themselves wholeheartedly to research and science, with some even going to extremes. But there were also opponents of excessive absorption in science. As a result, Italian Jews contributed significantly to the sciences, but at the same time remained basically a religious community.

CHAPTER TWO

BOOKS AND LIBRARIES

a.

One of the outstanding characteristics of Renaissance culture was the love of the book. The thirst for knowledge

---

[1] Shulvass, *Ibid.*; Kaufmann, *Ibid.*; *Dibre ḥakamim, Ibid.*, p. 75; *Nefuẓot Yehudah*, sermon 33.
[2] See the Introduction to his book *Giddule terumah*.

that pervaded the Period made the book an object of necessity and admiration. Libraries ceased to be institutions available only under the aegis of the Church. Private libraries were created and expanded. Not only did professional scholars collect books, but even laymen increasingly began to introduce books into their homes.

The admiration for the book and the desire for broadening the boundaries of knowledge inspired Renaissance men to search fervently for old manuscripts. They wanted to reacquire for the European cultural world the scientific treasures of the Antiquity that lay neglected and forgotten during the Middle Ages. Kings and princes no longer considered it feasible to expend all their wealth on construction and warfare, and devoted a sizable share of their income to the acquisition of books and to their copying. The wealthy followed their lead and also allocated part of their earnings for this purpose. At their disposal was a multitude of humanists with their bibliographical expertise, perpetually ready to travel in search of manuscripts and to copy them. Through their travels in Greece, Italy, and the Rhine region in order to find and purchase books, they laid the foundation for many great collections that have survived till our days. This activity, especially vivid during the fifteenth century, is responsible for the fact that when the Renaissance reached its apex, the idea of book collecting became universally accepted.

The invention of the printing press was, naturally, the most significant factor in book distribution. It brought about a sort of democratization of the world of books. Although hand-written volumes were still highly favored even decades after printed books had begun to be widely distributed, a realization emerged of the enormous importance of books that could be purchased at a modest price. Scholars who heretofore had great difficulties in gaining access to scientific sources now found them readily available. Jewish involvement with the book paralleled that of non-Jewish society. To begin with, Jews fully participated in the endeavor to discover manuscripts, to import them to Italy,[1] and to copy them. They also

[1] Enoch of Ascoli was sent by Pope Nicholas V to purchase for

developed a ramified printing industry, which published
books in many languages both for Jews and gentiles.

b.

Jewish interest in books was primarily manifested through
the establishment of valuable libraries housing many volumes.
As early as 1231 a Hebrew library of twenty eight volumes
existed in Genoa. Occasional information tells also of Jewish
libraries that have existed during the fourteenth and fifteenth
centuries.[1] About 1450 the Finzi family of Bologna possessed a
library of some two hundred manuscripts; the Finzis were very
wealthy and were able to expend the money required to
purchase such a large and valuable library. The largest library
was built by the da Pisa family of bankers. They started their
collection as early as the end of the fourteenth century and
kept expanding it during the fifteenth century and beyond.
This library achieved its maximal size and importance during
the lifetime of Jehiel Nisim da Pisa who was himself a writer.
When he died the library was liquidated and sold as part of his
estate. Azariah dei Rossi related that he too was one of those
who purchased books "from the estate of Rabbi Jehiel Nisim
of Pisa, may his memory prove a blessing".[2] That there were
many other Jewish libraries is indicated by the fact that in a
community like Florence virtually every Jewish family had a
book collection.[3]

With the growing distribution of the printed book during
the sixteenth century, the Jewish libraries became larger and
more numerous. The sources know of many books and book
owners who were affected by the laws of expurgation of
Hebrew books passed by the Council of Trent.[4] In Cremona,

him ancient books in Greece, France, and Germany. Cf. *Natali*,
p. 186.

[1] See: *Mahberot Immanuel*, p. 250 ff.; *Speculum*, 25:192 ff.;
Berliner, *David Hoffmann Jubilee Volume*, p. 286. The catalogue of
books is also found there.

[2] See: *EJ*, vol. 6, column 1010 (Cassuto); Cassuto, *Florence*, p. 223,
224, 263; *Meor enayim*, section *Imre binah*, p. 78.

[3] Cassuto, *Ibid.*, p. 223.

[4] The subject of the attack on the Jewish sacred books in Italy
is treated by Abraham Berliner in *Censur und Confiscation hebraeischer*

for example, whose Jewish community numbered about four hundred souls, twelve thousand books were destroyed by the Church at one time,[1] and there can be no doubt that the Inquisitors did not succeed in confiscating every Hebrew book in the city. We encounter similar figures in other places as well. The apostate-censor Domenico Hierosolymitano singlehandedly "purged" more than fourteen thousand printed books and twenty seven hundred manuscripts in Mantua and 1764 books in the neighboring town of Viadana.[2] The countless names of owners that appear in Jewish books from Italy indicate that virtually every Jewish home had books. These names, as well as other details, show that the love for books was commonly shared by all Jewish groups —the Italiani, the Ashkenazim, and the Sephardim, but most of the book owners in the fifteenth century were Italiani. In the sixteenth century names of Sephardic library owners begin to appear. Especially extensive and valuable was the library owned by Samuel Abravanel, later still augmented by his sons Joseph and Judah.[3] The incident described above regarding twelve thousand books that were destroyed in Cremona attests to the extent of book ownership among the Ashkenazim.

Renaissance Jewry's love for books sometimes assumed exaggerated forms. Azariah dei Rossi speaks frankly of his lust for ancient books.[4] The brothers Don Jacob and Don Judah Abravanel in 1558 purchased Maimonides' *Code of Laws* and prepared a bill of purchase that was written so meticulously[5] as if the transaction involved a large estate. We also encounter those characteristic phenomena of bibliophilism

Buecher im Kirchenstaate, Berlin 1891. Cf. *Hamagiha*, p. 180 for the confiscation of books in Pavia and Lodi.

[1] See Berliner, *Ibid.*, p. 6.
[2] See N. Porges, *Abraham Berliner Jubilee Volume*, p. 284.
[3] See *Meor enayim*, section *Imre binah*, p. 68 and *Encyclopaedia Judaica*, vol. 1, column 587.
[4] *Meor enayim*, *Ibid.*, p. 43.
[5] Published in *REJ* 36:71. It apparently was a manuscript, even though it was purchased after the work had been printed. Such a bill of sale was also published by Cassuto in the *Aaron Freimann Jubilee Volume*, p. 23.

like the zealous concern that no outsider should learn the contents of rare volumes. Gedaliah ibn Jachia related some very interesting incidents about this in *Shalshelet hakabbalah*. He had heard that there were many manuscripts that contained Maimonides' responsa and medical essays. But these writings remained unknown because "their owners were unwilling to make them accessible". One story that he recorded in his chronicle was taken from a manuscript. "But", Gedaliah added, "I was unable to copy many other lovely stories that were in this manuscript because the scholar who showed it to me was unwilling".[1]

c.

The Renaissance period that began early in the fourteenth century and ended in the early seventeenth century, first depended exclusively upon manuscripts. The first Hebrew printed books began to appear in Italy in the last quarter of the fifteenth century. In fact, printed books did not begin to circulate until the last decade of the century.

To satisfy the demand for manuscripts a large corps of copyists and vast sums of money were needed. Fortunately for Renaissance Jewry these resources were available. This was an era of economic prosperity in which, as we have seen, the Jewish population fully shared. Thus it became possible, for example, for the Brescia banker Joseph Castelfranco to have the entire Talmud copied on parchment at the expense of an enormous sum of money.[2]

About four hundred and fifty names of scribes are known to us who copied Hebrew books during the period of the Renaissance prior to the year 1500. Many of them came from among the ranks of the humanists who, as we have seen, were in perpetual search of a livelihood. A good copyist was required to be learned both in Jewish and general subjects, and the humanists were therefore most suited for this type of work. In addition, there were a multitude of mediocre copyists whose existence is attested to only by the manuscripts they copied.

[1] *Shalshelet hakabbalah*, pp. 63, 88.
[2] *REJ* 79:44.

It is safe to assume that in the many Jewish manuscripts from
Italy not yet described by the bibliographers, many other
names of Jewish Renaissance copyists are hidden. Curiously, a
thirteen year old copyist who later became a famous scholar,
also perpetuated his name in the manuscript upon the completion of his task.[1] The habitual wandering of the humanists
made it possible to have Hebrew manuscripts copied even in
remote areas with a scarce Jewish population.

d.

Beginning with the last quarter of the fifteenth century
printed books began to be available to the Jews of Italy. Italy
was the birthplace of Hebrew printing and here the first
editions of the Jewish classical literature were published.
The Italian Hebrew presses also printed many contemporary
works and so fully provided for the reading needs of Renaissance Jewry throughout the sixteenth century.

The admiration for the book had a great impact on the
development of Hebrew printing. To begin with, great
concern was given to the preparation of a correct text. To
accomplish this, recognized scholars were engaged as editors
and provided with a large number of manuscripts of the book
to be published. The Soncino printers related that when they
prepared for publication David Kimhi's *Sefer hashorashim*,
they used manuscripts from Spain, France, Germany, and
Italy. [2] The famous Christian publisher Daniel Bomberg did
likewise when he prepared the printing of Rabbi Joseph
Colon's *Responsa* (1519). [3] The text of *Amude golah*, published
in Cremona, was based upon seven manuscripts, and for the
edition of *Tikkune Zohar* (Mantua, 1558) no less than ten
manuscripts were utilized. The effort to give the reader a
correct text that could be read easily is also manifested in
Abraham Portaleone's attempt to introduce punctuation

[1] See Aaron Freimann, *Alexander Marx Jubilee Volume*, English
section, p. 239 ff. The young copyist was David ben Abraham Provenzal. See *Catalogue Kaufmann*, p. 21.
[2] Cited in J. L. Zlotnik, *Maḥbarot mini ḳedem*, vol. 1, p. 2.
[3] Cf. the detailed table of contents of the *Responsa of Rabbi Joseph
Colon*, Venice 1519.

marks in his work *Shilte hagibborim*, "in accordance with the usage of the Latin scholars".[1]

The printing of correct texts began to encounter great difficulties about the middle of the sixteenth century when the Church started its campaign against Hebrew sacred books. At first all Hebrew books were under indictment. However, the Jews convinced the Church that it would suffice to eliminate from the Jewish sacred books all that might be considered an insult to the Christian faith, and to permit the publication of purified texts. Thus a system of purging Jewish books arose that employed many expurgators, including a large number of apostates. Inevitably, book censorship was periodically entrusted to unqualified men who despoiled a text wherever, in their ignorance, they suspected a derogation of Christianity. To remedy this situation the publishers began to engage genuine experts to do the censoring. On one hand these experts had to be rabbinic scholars in order to make sure that the texts remained unmutilated by the expurgation. On the other hand they had to know the dogmas of Christianity in order to be able to find in Jewish writings the passages that directly or indirectly offended Christianity. Thus many leading Italian rabbis were engaged in the expurgation of Hebrew books. [2] A good example is Azariah dei Rossi who related [3] that "some time ago...I expurgated a number of books". The delicate position of the sacred books also resulted in efforts to impose communal supervision over the printing of previously unpublished Hebrew books. [4] The communal

---

[1] I. Sonne, *Expurgation*, p. 27; *Encyclopaedia Judaica*, vol. 4, column 97 (Cassuto); *Shilte hagibborim*, p. 184b.

[2] This is treated at length in I. Sonne's forementioned study *Expurgation*.

[3] *Meor enayim*, section *Yeme olam*, p. 204. Cf. *Maayan ganim* by Samuel Archivolti, p. 26b ff.: "they (the teachers) make corrections in the books".

[4] See the decision of the Ferrara congress of 1554 regarding the printing of books in *Finkelstein*, p. 301. On the back of the title page of a copy of *Elleh hadebarim*, Mantua 1566, kept in the Library of the Jewish Theological Seminary of America, I found a handwritten note containing an endorsement by the rabbis of Ferrara dated 1587, lending renewed affirmation to the decision of 1554. Rabbi

leaders and the rabbis-censors worked under the harsh circumstances of ecclesiastical persecution of the Hebrew book, and their achievements constituted a great act of salvation of Jewish cultural values.

To facilitate the use of the printed books, the Renaissance publishers provided them with elaborate reference guides and indices. The Jewish publishers adopted the innovation, often outdoing their gentile colleagues. The Hebrew publishing house in Cremona used to supplement its books with all sorts of indices, tables, and references. The edition of *Sefer ḥasidim* that appeared in Bologna in 1538 has a table of contents stretching over some fifty pages. Elijah Baḥur praised the Christians for having divided Scriptures into chapters, thereby making them easier to read. [1] He, too, divided his books extensively to facilitate their use for the reader.

The output of the Jewish publishing houses was quite impressive. A good example is the Bomberg press which in 1521 published twenty three works, twenty titles in 1522, and twenty four in 1523. Five hundred was probably the number of copies printed in an average edition of a Hebrew book. [2]

e.

The trade in books occupied a significant place in Jewish economic life during the entire Period. The number of Jewish booksellers was quite large and included some wealthy merchants. Here and there a bookseller even employed agents to help him in the selling of books. The wide scope of the Jewish book trade is indicated by the fact that the permit granted to Paduan Jews to deal in used merchandise also included books. The Jews understandably wished to have a share of the book market in a city with a famous university

Abraham Joseph Solomon Graziano who had this copy attests that this note was already in the book when it came into his possession.

[1] Sonne, *Ibid.*, p. 22 and p. 25, Note 70; *Encyclopaedia Judaica*, vol. 1, column 515; Elijah Baḥur's remarks regarding the advantage of dividing the biblical books into chapters are found in the Introductions of several of his books.

[2] See Moses Marx' article on Gershom Soncino, *HUCA* 11:484, Note 108 and *Alim* 2:81 ff.

and thousands of students. [1] Sporadic information is available regarding the prices of books. Book prices soared at the end of the fourteenth century due to increased demand. A manuscript prayer book of the Roman rite was sold in 1475 in Foligno for seven ducats, which was a very high price in those days. A Pentateuch in Yiddish, printed in Verona in 1560, sold for only one ducat. [2] The Jewish book traders were also active in the export and import of Hebrew books.[3]

f.

An inventory of the libraries clearly reflects the cultural attitudes of the Period's Jews. With all the interest in the secular sciences and in the belles-lettres, the number of sacred works that were kept in libraries far surpassed all the other book categories. A good example is a library from the close of the fifteenth century that had been collected over two generations. [4] It contained mostly Scriptures, Biblical commentaries, the Talmud, and Talmudic novellae, a great deal of responsa, and prayer books. In addition there were the works of the great Spanish and Provencal grammarians and the philosophical writings of Rabbi Levi Gersonides. The da Pisa family library was more balanced. [5] In addition to the Bible and its various commentaries, prayer books, *mahazorim*, and halakic literature, it contained many books on philosophy, astronomy, geography, and history. Non Jewish belles-lettres

[1] See J. Bloch, *Hebrew Printing in Naples*, New York 1942, p. 6; *Ciscato*, p. 104, Note 1.

[2] See: *Vogelstein-Rieger*, vol. 1, p. 331; *REJ* 105:73; Erik, *History*, p. 34. Lists containing prices of various books are available in *Vogelstein-Rieger, Ibid.*; *HUCA, Ibid.*, p. 433, Note 10 (prices current in the year 1498) and *Reshumot* 1:309 ff.

[3] See: J. Bloch, *Ibid.*, p. 7, Note 13; *HUCA, Ibid.*; the prices that Reuchlin paid for Hebrew books printed in Italy were quite high. Cf. Perles, *Beitraege*, etc., p. 158 and Max Erik, *Vegen alt-yiddishn roman un novele*, Vilna 1926, p. 243; *Alim* 1:70 ff.

[4] *Alim, Ibid.*

[5] Cassuto, *Florence*, p. 223. An entirely different kind of book collection we find in the catalogues published by Nehemiah Allony in the *Simhah Asaf Jubilee Volume*, p. 35 ff. To be sure, until it can be ascertained whether these books belonged to the author of the catalogues or were held by him merely as pawns, no definite conclusions can be drawn.

in Italian and in Yiddish translations were also part of the
average Jewish Renaissance library (comp. Section VI, Chapter
4). A thorough scrutiny of the Jewish Renaissance libraries
will, no doubt, manifest their basically Jewish character. The
thousands of books confiscated and expurgated by the
censors beginning with the middle of the sixteenth century
(see below) further attest to it. The censors were, of course,
interested in religious literature; they were not concerned
with books on astronomy or history.

g.

In the middle of the sixteenth century the Hebrew book in
Italy was gravely threatened. An important element in the
strategy of the pope's war against the Reformation included
an attack upon Jews and Judaism. One aspect of the battle
was the burning of Hebrew books and a ban upon the printing
of the Talmud. Italian Jews regarded this policy as a severe
blow and sought ways of nullifying or circumventing it.

There is evidence that all over Italy Jews kept volumes of
the Talmud illegally despite the personal danger that it
involved. Abraham Portaleone tells with a sense of satisfaction
that during his studies "...through God's favor we had in our
meeting place all volumes of the Talmud".[1] Rabbi Azariah
Pigo also related that he possessed three volumes of the Talmud. Moreover, when he lived in Pisa he used to borrow
various tractates from nearby villages. Undoubtedly, a great
deal of further information regarding books that were kept in
Italy in defiance of the law of the Church is scattered in the
Period's literature.

The organized Jewish community obviously was not satisfied by the illegal possession of books by individuals. It therefore made strenuous efforts to obtain permission for the Jews
to keep their books. These endeavors lasted for decades and
were only partially successful. Jewish emissaries were sent
to the Council of Trent to seek permission for the printing of

[1] Abraham Portaleone, *Shilte hagibborim*, Introduction (available
also in *Neppi-Ghirondi*, p. 43); Azaria Pigo, *Giddule terumah*, Introduction.

the Talmud. In 1581 a delegation headed by the famed scholar Abtalyon da Modena interceded with Pope Gregory XIII in behalf of the Jewish books. Similar repeated actions were undertaken by the Mantuan community. The communal efforts culminated in the convocation of special congresses (*waadim*) in an attempt to gain permits for the printing of the Talmud.[1] Permission to print the Talmud was not granted, however. To be sure, the appointment of censors made the existence of Jewish libraries possible. Although henceforth a large proportion of the Jewish books were filled with erasures and emendations, they continued to satisfy the main religious and cultural needs of Renaissance Jewry.

CHAPTER THREE

TORAH LEARNING

a.

The place which Torah learning occupied in the life of the Jew was determined by his desire to harmonize the religious and cultural values of Judaism with Renaissance values and its life style. This dualistic orientation is strikingly apparent in the spiritual makeup of many Italian rabbis who attained a high level of general culture and were, simultaneously, outstanding Talmudic scholars. Such a cultural program created the basis for the longed for harmony, but did not protect the individual from difficult practical pitfalls in its attainment. Abraham Portaleone was afraid that his sons would be prevented from studying Torah properly by the tempo of daily life. He therefore prepared a minimum program of Torah learning which, to be sure, called for four hours of daily study. "And know my dear sons that you should not be concerned over the length of my plan, for I am certain that God will grant you the strength to follow it...for the regular curriculum with the extra programs should not take two hours, and half an hour of study should follow the afternoon

---

[1] See *Hamagiha*, p. 157 and Colorni, *Magistrature maggiori*, p. 16; *Sepher Chaje Jehuda*, p. 12; M. Stern, *Stellung der Paepste*, part 1, p. 153 ff.

service, and no more than an hour and a half every evening which amounts to a total of four hours".

Similar conditions led Rabbi Jacob Landau to compose his book *Haagur*, as a concise compendium of the Jewish law. The pupil for whom he wrote the book was involved in general studies "and the few hours left would not suffice to study these (original rabbinic) texts..." [1] Obviously, Jacob Landau's pupil was a typical representative of his period.

b.

At the end of the thirteenth century, with the start of the Renaissance Period Torah study and Jewish law in Italy were strongly influenced by Franco-German Jewry. Italian scholars did not compose systematic legal codes, but like the Ashkenazim, concentrated, rather, upon compiling collections of laws and customs. Close to the start of the Period the collection of customs *Shibale haleket*, and its abbreviated version *Tanya* were compiled in Rome. A fifteenth century scholar [2] stated in reference to *Tanya* that "the Italiani follow its decisions in all matters..." About a century later Gedaliah Ibn Jachia [3] similarly asserted that *Tanya* "is a guide to Italy's (religious) practices". Rabbi Menahem Recanati's *Piske halakot*, written at the beginning of the Period, further emphasizes the closeness of Italian and German Jewries. The vast majority of his references were borrowed from German and French scholars, primarily the Tosafists. In contrast, he limited his borrowing from the Spanish School almost exclusively to Alfasi. Of the other Spanish scholars, Maimonides was accepted in Italy because of his tendency toward a lenient interpretation of the law. Rabbi Joseph Colon attested that "in all Italian lands they follow the practices according to Maimonides who is one of those who decide leniently..." [4] A few decades later the author of *Haagur* also stated that "...the Italiani rule that it

[1] *Shilte hagibborim*, p. 2b; p. 133a; *Sefer haagur*, Introduction.
[2] *Responsa of Rabbi Joseph Colon*, paragraph 144.
[3] *Shalshelet hakabbalah*, p. 81.
[4] *New Responsa of Rabbi Isaac ben Sheshet (Perfet)*, Munkacs 1901, par. 34 (p. 104).

(the matter under discussion) was permitted, following the opinion of Maimonides, for they abide by his rulings in most of their practices".[1]

The influence of German Jewry upon Torah study in Italy was largely due to the immigration of German Jews into North Italy during the fourteenth and fifteenth centuries. Significantly, the Italianic scholars enthusiastically welcomed the Ashkenazic influence. Messer Leon's son David, who studied in the *yeshibah* of Rabbi Judah Minz in Padua,[2] stated: "... all this we Italiani received from our French and German teachers from whom Torah issues forth and from whose mouths we live..." (i.e. on whom we rely). When he once became involved in the study of Nahmanides' *Novellae*, he apologized: "And here I have entered the domain of the Spanish scholars to discuss Naḥmanides' *Novellae* even though such is not our practice in the *yeshibot* of Germany and Italy, for all our study centers about the *Tosafot*, especially the profound, short ones of Touques, and just as they (the Sephardim) study their novellae, such is our practice with regard to the Tosafists..." We have further testimony of special interest in the *Tosafot* at a later period, the middle of the sixteenth century. The prominent position occupied by the Franco-German Torah school was also expressed in the wide popularity of *Sefer mizwot gadol* by Rabbi Moses of Coucy. The *Arbaah turim* of Jacob ben Asher enjoyed a prominent position, particularly among the Ashkenazic and Sephardic immigrants. To the former he was the son of Asher ben Jehiel, the distinguished German rabbi, while the latter appreciated him as a scholar who lived most of his life in Spain and was familiar with Sephardic practices.[3]

The acceptance of Ashkenazic authority by the Italiani was not limited to the classical Ashkenazic teachers, Rashi, the

[1] Sudylkow 1834, p. 92a.
[2] *Kebod ḥakamim*, Berlin 1899, pp. 63, 64, 129.
[3] See Sonne, *Kobez al jad*, N.S. 3:152, the minutes dated 24th of Elul, 1539. The letter of Rabbi Joseph Arli to Johanan Treves was published by Marx in the *Moses Schorr Memorial Volume*, p. 201. Cf. also I. Sonne's study in the *Alexander Marx Jubilee Volume*, Hebrew section, pp. 210-211.

Tosafists, and Maharam of Rothenburg. They knew that the Ashkenazim who resided in the northern part of the peninsula surpassed them in Torah learning. We have seen that Messer Leon who presided over a large *yeshibah* in Naples sent his son to the North to study Torah under the Ashkenazim. The situation was still the same in the middle of the sixteenth century, as is illustrated by a statement of an Italiani: "...the only thing in which the Ashkenazim are superior to the Italiani is their proficiency in (using the) *pilpul* method in the study of the Talmud..." When a decline in Torah knowledge ensued at the end of the Period as a result of the burning of the Talmud and the other sacred books, it was still possible to point to the *yeshibah* in the Ashkenazic community of Verona as the only remaining center of Torah learning.[1]

Sephardic and Levantine influence in the area of Torah learning (Venice, Leghorn) became evident only after the close of the Renaissance Period. Nor did the Provencal immigrant scholars make any impact on Torah study during the Period. One of them, Rabbi Ḥayim Carmi, who lived in Padua, avoided visiting the *yeshibah* of Rabbi Judah Minz because "he followed a different path and style in learning". An attempt to have him exchange views (in Hebrew) with an Ashkenazic rabbi did not succeed for it was apparent "that they were not halakically compatible".[2]

c.

Public efforts in behalf of Torah study were expressed in a form that was typical of the weak organizational structure of the Jewish community. Among the manifold duties placed upon the rabbi, who received his salary from communal coffers, was the instruction of the young. [3] Rabbi Judah Minz in Padua was obliged to teach students of parents who were unable to pay tuition fees. [4] Rabbi David Ibn Jachia in Naples had to preach on the Sabbath "and had to teach

---

[1] *REJ*, 105:56 and Sonne, *Kobez al jad, Ibid.*, p. 175.
[2] *REJ* 79:35.
[3] See Marx, *HUCA* 1:616 and Sonne, *Zion*, N.S. 3:123 ff. See also *Kobez al jad, Ibid.*, p. 151 ff.
[4] See Elijah Capsali, *REJ* 79:34.

Talmud, Commentaries, and other subjects", and was also "to tutor the small pupils". At virtually the same time we find a similar contract with a rabbi in Verona, in the North, where Johanan ben Saadiah assumed the responsibility of teaching the children in the community and of maintaining a *yeshibah*. [1] This primary function of the rabbi is further attested to by the designation *rosh yeshibah* appended by Gedaliah ibn Jachia in *shalshelet hakabbalah* whenever he referred to Italian rabbis.

Aside from this, sporadic community efforts were made for financial support of Torah study. The Verona community, for example, allocated subventions for students who came from other locales to study with its rabbi, and its leadership became noted for the fact that they "constantly anointed their shields (comp. Isaiah 21:5) to support the study of Torah". At the end of the Period the community of Venice founded a *yeshibah* in Conegliano for young men from all of Italy. Many students at this *yeshibah* received food, lodging, and even clothing.[2] Some communities also established under their auspices special funds for Torah study. In Verona, for example, there was a collection of contributions in the synagogue every Monday and Thursday in behalf of such a fund.[3]

A framework for adult Torah study was provided by societies organized on the basis of private initiative. Such societies appeared for the first time in the sixteenth century. In the 1520's Rabbi David Ibn Jachia related that "societies of devoted men hire (scholars) to read and to preach for them on the Sabbath". [4] A few decades later Azariah dei Rossi tells very interesting details [5] about similar societies in Ferrara. One was an association of scholars that called itself *Accademia*, and the second one was a *midrash-yeshibah* founded by the Sephardim. In both of these organizations Renaissance patterns were followed as a matter of course. The name *Accademia* was adopted following contemporary usage. The

---

[1] Marx, *Ibid.*, pp. 616-617 and Sonne, *Ibid.*, p. 152 ff.
[2] Sonne, *Ibid.*, p. 175 and *Corriere Israelitico* 15:197, Note 2.
[3] Sonne, *Ibid.*, p. 153.
[4] Marx, *Ibid.*, p. 620.
[5] *Meor enayim*, section *Imre binah*, p. 112 and section *Yeme olam*, p. 93 ff.

Sephardic society "elected each day a president from their midst by rotation", a typical democratic procedure in the Italian private scientific institutions that strove to imitate the academic custom of ancient Greece. Of a similar nature was the learned society that was founded in Venice in 1594 by Kalonymos Belgrado with the active participation of Leon da Modena. This institute used to meet in the garden pavilion of its founder.[1] Leon da Modena's inaugural sermon offers detailed information regarding its curriculum and activities: "...And when, with God's help, you come here you will listen to perfect sermons every single Sabbath, and on each and every morning important laws will be interpreted and discussed; and during the winter a moralistic treatise will be read every night". We have here a comprehensive program of daily involvement in every area of Torah study. The reading during winter evenings of a moralistic treatise was a sign of the times, for the end of the Period was characterized by a revival of piety, and a mere intellectual preoccupation with Torah study no longer satisfied the Italian Jews.[2]

While the Belgrado *yeshibah*, although established by an individual, enjoyed the support of the *ẓedaḳah* society of Venice,[3] other similar institutions were maintained wholly by their founders. Such *yeshibot* were maintained by Isaac da Fano, Ishmael Rieti, and Judah Saltaro.[4] Be it noted, that the Rieti academy in Siena attracted young men from other cities, and its activities were conducted in a formal and organized manner.

d.

In the period prior to the Renaissance, *yeshibot*, that is schools of higher Torah study, were found mainly in Southern

[1] *Sepher Chaje Jehuda*, p. 25. This society was also called *yeshibah* and *midrash*. Cf. *Midbar Yehuda*, p. 58a.

[2] The new trend was clearly evident in the programs of many study societies of that time. Comp., for example, the bylaws of the society that was founded in Ancona in 1586, *Haasif* 3:214 ff. and p. 220.

[3] The Introduction to *Midbar Yehuda*.

[4] See: *REJ* 79:44; *Meor enayim*, section *Yeme olam*, p. 184; Alexander Marx, *Louis Ginzberg Jubilee Volume*, Hebrew section, p. 271 ff.; *Miḳweh Yisrael*, Venice 1607, p. 9a.

Italy. Early in the Period this center of study was destroyed
due to persecutions by the first kings of the Anjou dynasty.
True, when Jewish settlement was reconstructed in the
southern cities, new *yeshibot* did arise in various places.
However, the main success of the *yeshibah* institution in the
Renaissance Period is linked to the Ashkenazic immigration
into North Italy. Elijah Capsali told the story of North Italian
Torah study in his work *Dibre hayamim lemalkut Venezia*. [1]
Although he idealized the past in the face of the troubles that
befell the *yeshibot* in the time of the war of the League of
Cambrai, it is generally correct that during the great Ashkenazic immigration into North Italy entire *yeshibot* with their
student bodies and teachers were simultaneously transplanted.

The Ashkenazic *yeshibot* in North Italy reached the peak of
their expansion during the second half of the fifteenth
century and the early sixteenth century. The first school to
attain fame was headed by Rabbi Joseph Colon, following him
to the various localities in which he lived. Equally important
was the *yeshibah* established somewhat later in Padua by
Rabbi Judah Minz. The school existed there more than a
century and developed its own unique tradition of Torah
learning. Many other small and large *yeshibot* existed in other
North Italian cities. The *yeshibot* of Verona and Cremona
attained wide renown in the second half of the sixteenth
century. When a decline in Torah study set in at the end of the
Period, the school of Verona remained famous as the main
center of Torah learning in North Italy. [2] The *yeshibah* of
Conegliano was also, undoubtedly, an Ashkenazic school. [3]
Alongside the Ashkenazic and Italianic *yeshibot* there was
possibly a center of Torah study in Sicily, or at least an
independent local tradition of learning. [4]

[1] *REJ, Ibid.*, p. 33.

[2] See: *REJ, Ibid., Kobez al jad, Ibid.*, pp. 175-176 (Verona), and
Emek habaka, p. 129, in a gloss of the *Magiha* (Cremona).

[3] See above. The two founders Rabbi Israel Conian and Rabbi
David Marcaria were Ashkenazim.

[4] Comp. the postscript to Nachmanides' commentary to the
Pentateuch published in Naples in 1490: "Indeed this holy volume
surpasses all others in its beauty and exactitude, for the texts used
for this publication were edited by the *sages of Messina* . . .".

Typical of the North Italian Talmudic schools was the *yeshibah* of Padua. It was a genuine Ashkenazic institution in which the entire day was devoted to the study of Gemara and the Tosafot, and where the *pilpul*, the argumentative lecture, was the chief contribution of the *yeshibah* head. The sharp-minded student, capable of indulging in *pilpul*, earned the highest praise. One of the scholars used hair-splitting dialectics to such a degree, that he often missed the truth. All this was remarkably similar to what we know of the curriculum and methods of study practiced in the sixteenth century *yeshibot* of Poland.

In a similar fashion Talmudic studies were conducted in the Italianic *yeshibot*. In the school of Siena "one of the students would expound a problem and his classmates would stand near him and pose many questions...and the discussion would be a prolonged one..." Here, too, the basic text was a tractate of the Talmud with the Tosafot commentary. Unlike the Ashkenazic *yeshibah*, however, the Italianic school offered also a curriculum of secular studies devised to give the students the well-rounded education which a man of the Renaissance was expected to have. This included primarily the Latin language, the composition of elegant letters, and rhetoric. The course of study planned for the Jewish university (see above this Section, Introduction), was a logical and ulti-mate expression of the striving for cultural duality by Renais-sance Jewry, especially the Italiani.[1]

The social status of *yeshibah* heads and students cannot be fully described on the basis of the available sources. *Yeshibah* heads generally received their salaries from communal funds or wealthy individuals. But these were not their exclusive sources of support. Rabbi Joseph Arli and Rabbi David ibn Jachia, for example, also received a modest tuition fee from the parents of their students. Rabbi Johanan ben Saadiah, head of the *yeshibah* of Verona, was involved in pawnbroking, as were several other rabbis and heads of *yeshibot*.[2] It is difficult

[1] For the cultural dualism of the Italiani see Moses A. Shulvass, *In the Grip of Centuries*, p. 229 ff.

[2] Cf. the document published by Sonne, *Kobez al jad, Ibid.*, p. 154 ff. and his Note on p. 155.

to determine how such activities affected their position as heads of *yeshibot*. It should be noted, however, that a very tolerant spirit prevailed during the Renaissance Period toward the involvement of intellectuals in commercial affairs.

Two different groups could be discerned among the learners in the *yeshibot*. The first was composed of adult scholars who divided their time between studying and instructing the younger pupils. They generally occupied a mid point between the *yeshibah* heads and the young students. Messer Leon's son David alluded to such scholars when he related that "in Naples, in his great *yeshibah*, my master, my father, may his memory prove a blessing... had under him twenty-two famous ordained rabbis", and that in the Paduan *yeshibah* "all those rabbis who were there ordained me".[1] The bulk of *yeshibah* students were young people who came from the local area and from other places as well. The schools tried to attract the youth who desired to study Torah. The Verona community resolved in 1539 "...to try and bring here young capable students", and allocated for them financial support. Ishmael da Rieti also tried to attract students to the *yeshibah* founded by him: "whoever is for God should join me, let him ascend the mount of our *yeshibah*, may its foundation be strengthened by the study of its pupils and by the community of its scholars..."[2] We know from Rabbi Elijah Capsali's account that students came to Padua from Germany and France, and he himself came from the island of Crete. In Italy, as in Germany and Poland, *yeshibah* students used to wander from one school to another. Elijah of Pesaro, a student in the *yeshibah* of Siena, had been in several *yeshibot* prior to his coming to Siena. He was very critical of the academies and charged that most "employed unwise methods and failed to penetrate to the depth of the (studied) text".[3] Obviously, there existed among the students a sort of "popular opinion" regarding the quality and importance of the various schools.

[1] *Kebod ḥakamim*, p. 64.
[2] Sonne, *Ibid.*, p. 153; Marx, *Ibid.*, p. 284 (letter of the *yeshibah* head Rabbi Joseph Arli).
[3] Marx, *Ibid.*, p. 287.

Ordination in Italian *yeshibot* was described by Leon da Modena as follows: "In Italy the older rabbis ordain a new rabbi and refer to him in writing or orally as *Caver di Rab*, associate rabbi, if the ordainee is young or not sufficiently learned. If they found him properly knowledgeable and fit to be a member of a rabbinic court, they referred to him as *morenu* or *rab*".[1] Many young men sought ordination, as the people of the Renaissance perpetually coveted titles and honors. The pursuit of ordination evoked the ridicule of the Sephardim. Don Isaac Abravanel noted sarcastically: "...after my arrival in Italy I found that the custom of indiscriminate ordination was widespread, foremost among the Ashkenazim. Everyone ordains and is ordained as rabbi. I do not know where this license came from, unless they were envious of the practice of the gentiles of granting doctorates and they did likewise".[2] The desire for the title of rabbi was so great that there were incidents of buying ordination.[3] To be sure, some rabbis acted to curb the questionable practice. Rabbi Judah Minz, for example, never ordained anyone who had not studied at his *yeshibah*. In the same spirit Rabbi Azriel Diena strongly protested against "these ordainees who know not God in their hearts" and suggested measures for denying ordination to unqualified people.[4]

e.

A history of rabbinic literature does not fall within the purview of this work. However, we do want to offer certain general observations emphasizing characteristic features of this literature and describe its place within the Jewish community. We have seen that Italian rabbis mainly composed collections of laws and customs and did not engage in systematic codification of the *halakah*. To be sure, Leon da Modena's grandfather Mordecai undertook "a work like that of *Bet Yosef*",[5] but this attempt did not get very far. Prevailing

[1] In *Historia de gli Riti Hebraici*, Section 3, Chapter 1.
[2] In his commentary on tractate Abot, *Naḥalat abot*, Chapter 6, mishnah 1, New York 1953, p. 377.
[3] See *Dibre ribot bashearim*, Husiatyn 1902, p. 4.
[4] See *Kebod ḥakamim, Ibid.*, and *Kirjath Sepher* 14:550.
[5] *Sepher Chaje Jehuda*, p. 11.

custom was decisive as is indicated by a number of attestations. Jehiel Nisim da Pisa wrote: "And this (i.e. the custom under discussion) is not an appropriate practice to follow, but a stupid custom...just as there are other practices in Italy both in matters of prayer and blessings and other subjects which go counter to the decisions of our teachers, may their memory prove a blessing..." His contemporary, Maharam of Padua wrote in a similar mood regarding a bizarre practice:[1] "I am truly amazed by this custom. However, we are not to rely upon our reason to annul an ancient custom, but we must rather seek with all our strength to find support for its retention, and this is what all our predecessors did when they dealt with a mystifying custom". The situation was summarized at the end of the Period by Leon da Modena in a blunt statement: "Indeed, custom dominates everything".[2]

Within this regime of custom, an explicit trend by the Italiani to protect old Italianic practice was apparent. Nor should this be surprising. With the arrival of large numbers of Ashkenazim and Sephardim, the Italiani, as we have seen, became a minority within the Peninsula's Jewish population. In order to secure the survival of their own *minhag*, they clung to the works *Shibbale haleket* and *Tanya* which represented the authentic religious practice of Italianic Jewry. This is clearly evident from a statement by Messer Leon's son David that *Shibbale haleket* was "a book intended to bolster our practices, the customs of Italy".[3]

The *minhag* that prevailed in Italy, as a rule, had a liberal tendency that would not tolerate the restrictions of Poland or the Levant. In 1453 Rabbi Joseph Colon noted "that in all Italian lands practices follow the decisions of Maimonides who was one of those who ruled leniently". At the end of the Period Leon da Modena vigorously announced: "...Since I have observed that the majority of this community and most Italian Jews do not regard it (uncovering the head) to be

[1] See, Jehiel Nissim da Pisa, *Minhat kenaot*, Berlin 1898, Introduction; *He lakem zera lizedakah*, Venice 1553, par. 78.

[2] In a rhymed approbation to Isaac Tyrnau's *Sefer haminhagim*, Venice 1616. Cf. *Divan Modena*, p. 88 for the sources of this epigram.

[3] *Kebod hakamim*, p. 39.

forbidden, I conclude that it is permitted, as I would act, were I to take a resolute course, regarding many other practices of Italian Jewry which are questioned (by the other communities). And our leaders should prove their validity... so that the Levantines and Ashkenazim would not think that we are heretics and they are the pious Jews, because we too regard both God's written and oral word as eternally binding and pleasant for ourselves and our descendants forever".[1] Despite this, however, there were people who tried to become "establishers of customs" and who strove to indroduce innovations in accepted practices contrary to the opinion of the Italianic rabbis.[2] It is understandable that the religious diversity of a composite Jewish population in Italy would lead to tension in this field. Thus, the strong demand of Rabbi Abraham ben Isaac da Pisa (died in 1554) is not surprising: "Would that the contemporary great rabbis assemble together and serve Him in unanimity by following one of the outstanding decisors whom they would select and agree to adhere rigidly to his decisions in all matters. There would then be no dissension in Israel, nor will it be divided into (differing) groups..."[3] For, indeed, no spot in the world faced the risk of sectarian divisions to the extent of Italian Jewry with its multicommunal structure.

Italian rabbis employed responsa as the principal method of religious guidance. It also became the most popular form of the Period's rabbinic literature. Responsa literature quantitatively exceeded every other literary form that appeared in rabbinic writing to such an extent that it became its most characteristic expression. There were various reasons for this. The dynamic tempo of life did not allow time for theoretical engagement in halakic problems. It presented the rabbis daily with a host of practical problems that related to the

---

[1] Responsum on the permissibility of uncovering the head, published by Isaac Rivkind in *Louis Ginzberg Jubilee Volume*, Hebrew section, p. 419.

[2] See the decision by Rabbi Menahem Azariah da Fano on the subject of shaking the *lulab*, *Yemin Hashem romemah*, Venice, n. d., p. 2a.

[3] *REJ* 32:132. Cf. Moses A. Shulvass, *Ibid.*, pp. 63-64 and Note 27.

character of the Renaissance Jew and his dual loyalty to his
ancestral heritage and the dazzling alien culture in which he
lived. Also the fact that the position of the rabbinate as a rule
was weak, and rebellious individuals could always find another
opinion,[1] compelled the rabbis to seek a colleague's endorsement for their decisions or opinions. Thus responsa literature
flowered and broadened increasingly, and there were even
several cases that gave rise to special collections of opinions.
Most Renaissance rabbis preferred writing responsa because
more than the other literary genres (such as novellae or
commentaries) they expressed the author's individuality. In
the responsa they also could easily demonstrate their talent of
composing beautifully stylized letters, which Renaissance man
truly admired. Rabbi Azriel Diena, for example, used in his
responsa rhymed prose modeled after the writings of Jedaiah
Hapenini and Kalonymos ben Kalonymos. He also interwove
his responsa with metaphors borrowed from Immanuel's
Maḥbarot.[2]

The stylistic qualities of the Renaissance responsa were
partly responsible for their preservation. They were repeatedly
copied and re-copied, much in the way collections of letters
by famous writers were reprinted as stylistic examples of the
epistolary art (see below, Section IX, Chapter 4). The editor of
the first edition of Rabbi Joseph Colon's *Responsa* described
in the foreword how he and the author's other pupils searched
for manuscripts of the work, for it was known that there were
a large number of extant copies. Even more revealing is the
fact that in the Parma manuscript of the work three signatures
of pupils appear after each and every responsum confirming
its authenticity.[3]

There were, of course, other forms of literary creativity. A
good example is the classical commentary to the Mishnah by
Rabbi Obadiah da Bertinoro. There was also much theoretical
discussion of the *halakah* in the *yeshibot*, which often found

[1] See, for example, *Responsa of Maharam of Padua*, par. 73;
In *Elleh hadebarim*, Mantua 1566, Rabbi Joseph Treves labeled Moses
Basola "the rabbi (who is ready) to assist (whomever hires him)".
[2] See *Kirjath Sepher* 15:267, Sonne's article.
[3] *Ibid.*, p. 264.

literary expression in books such as Rabbi Azariah Pigo's
Giddule terumah. A quantitative comparison, however, leaves
no doubt that the responsum was the Italian rabbi's primary
means of literary expression.

f.

In an era as thirsty for knowledge as the Renaissance,
laymen too were drawn into the orbit of Torah study. The
large number of libraries owned by laymen, which contained an
overwhelming proportion of sacred works, is indicative of this
fact. Wealthy individuals pursued their studies under the
guidance of leading scholars. Thus, for example, Anselmo del
Banco studied Torah under as great a teacher as Rabbi Judah
Minz.[1] Adult groups that could not afford the expense, were
provided with teachers by the communal authorities. In
Verona the rabbi was obliged to lecture at the synagogue
every morning after the prayers, and at dusk prior to the
minḥah service "to whomsoever desired to attend". Part of the
year he also had to teach one of the codes of law "chosen by the
majority of the audience". Additional instruction for adults
was provided through rabbinic sermons, which in many
places in Italy were preached regularly every Sabbath.[2]

At the end of the Period, when pietistic sentiment heightened among Italian Jews, the religious obligation of Torah
study began to be increasingly emphasized. A strong concern
for intensifying adult Torah study then became manifest
among the spiritual leaders. We have seen how Abraham
Portaleone regretted late in his life his preoccupation with
secular sciences and his neglect of Torah learning, and how he
then prepared a detailed program for adult Torah study.

---

[1] See Alxander Marx, *Studies in Jewish History and Booklore*,
p. 129.

[2] See the responsum of Rabbi Moses Provenzal on ball playing on
the Sabbath, published by I. Rivkind, *Tarbiz* 4:373. The respondent
states: "And if they should play at the time the sermon is preached,
this too is deplorable, and in any event it is forbidden to schedule
the play for that time". This indicates, of course, that a sermon was
preached every Sabbath. At the end of the Period Leon da Modena
used to preach in Ferrara every Sabbath upon the invitation of the
community's leaders. See *Sepher Chaje Jehuda*, p. 17.

Another scholar to give curricular advice to the adult student was Rabbi Aaron Berechiah da Modena: "And whosoever is not able to reserve fixed periods for the study of the oral law, should train himself (to do so)... He should at least carefully read the twenty-four books (of the Bible) with cantillation every year through his entire lifetime, which has already, through heavenly mercy, become the pattern of many of the laymen here in our city..." [1] He also wrote the treatises *Meil Ẓedaḳah* and *Bigde ḳodesh* for a similar purpose, incorporating in these works a program and a study guide for the entire week. However, the study program suggested by Abraham Portaleone in *Shilte hagibborim* surpassed all others. It included chapters from Scripture, Mishnah, Gemara, midrashim, and the *Zohar* and aimed at inculcating in the student a very broad knowledge of the basic works of Judaism. Both of these study programs were composed about the same time and attest to the laymen's efforts to study Torah and their need for guidance.

It is difficult to ascertain the degree of the knowledge of Torah among Jewish women. Considering women's general position in Renaissance society,[2] it may be assumed that they possessed a fair degree of Jewish knowledge. Certain women are known to have been well versed in the Hebrew language. On the other hand, a complaint [3] was voiced that "due to women's subordination to men they did not know nor understand the sacred tongue". It seems that most of the educated women belonged to the higher classes of Jewish society. David Reubeni noted that the women of the Da Pisa and Abudarhin families knew all twenty-four books of the Bible. [4] The Jewish women in Mantua [5] who were given diplomas as ritual slaughterers and vein removers must have been quite well

[1] *Maabar Yabok*, Lemberg 1867, p. 132a.
[2] See *Burckhardt*, Section 5, Chapter 6. Cf. above Section IV, Chapter 1.
[3] Rabbi Jehiel Manoscrivi in the Introduction to *Hokmat nashim*, published in *MGWJ* 47:179.
[4] p. 39 and p. 57.
[5] See *Responsa of Rabbi Isaac de Lattes*, p. 139 ff. and M. Mortara, *Indice alfabetico dei rabbini e scrittori israeliti*, Padua 1886, p. 54, Note 2. Cf. Charles Duschinsky, *Gaster Jubilee Volume*, p. 96 ff.

versed in at least one area of Rabbinic literature. One of them studied the laws of ritual slaughter from Rabbi Jacob Weil's *Sheḥitot ubediḳot*, a popular handbook for ritual slaughterers. The most learned Jewish woman was Fioretta, the wife of Solomon da Modena; both Rabbi Aaron Berechiah and Leon da Modena spoke highly of her many times. She steadily engaged in the study of Scriptures and Mishnah, the codes of law, especially that of Maimonides, and the *Zohar*.

A special problem was posed in Italy by the desire of many Christians to study Torah with Jewish teachers. Renaissance man's efforts to reproduce the ancient world let to a heightened interest in the Hebrew language and literature as a significant part of classical culture. Also, emergence of the Reformation whose slogan was a return to the Bible, created among the Christians the desire to read it in the original Hebrew. Thus the demand for Jewish teachers was great, evoking a debate among the rabbis as to whether teaching Torah to gentiles was permitted. One of the outstanding teachers of Christian humanists, Elijah Baḥur, soon realized that "because of this a furor was raised against me... and some of the rabbis snub me". But the fighting scholar was undismayed by "some of the rabbis" and dedicated his book *Masoret hamasoret* "to all students, whether Christian or Jew".

The rabbis began discussing this problem even prior to the beginning of the Renaissance. Rabbi Isaiah da Trani the Younger was evidently unhappy with the practice.[1] "And since I have seen some of our evil men mock and degrade the words of the sages and teach the *midrashim* to non-Jewish (priests), falsifying and ridiculing our Torah, I have undertaken to explain the subject of the *midrashim*. It appears to me that a Jew who teaches (a non-Jew) Torah transgresses the prohibition 'thou shalt not place a stumbling block before the blind'". Nevertheless, he was ready for a compromise: "This refers only to the Pentateuch and its precepts which are enjoined upon Israel, but Prophets and the Writings are permitted to be taught to a non-Jew..." The tendency to

[1] See *Meat debash* by David Sassoon, Oxford 1928, p. 42 ff. Cf. S. Asaf, *Meḳorot letoledot haḥinuk beyisrael*, vol. 2, p. 95 ff.

compromise persisted among Italian rabbis during the entire Period, even though opinions varied greatly as to what might actually be taught to gentiles. Thus, two of the greatest sixteenth century scholars, Elijah Menahem Halfon and Johanan Treves, [1] permitted the instruction of Scriptures in Hebrew to non-Jews but insisted that they be denied knowledge of "the mysteries of Torah", among which Johanan Treves included the Talmud and midrashic literature.

To be sure, Jews taught the Christians "mysteries of the Torah" as well. Elijah Baḥur was not the only one to do so, but all Jewish humanists who had close contacts with Christian scholars did likewise. In the many religious debates whose purpose was merely academic and devoid of any tendency toward religious compulsion, Christians also acquired Jewish knowledge. Another way for Christians to acquire Jewish knowledge was to attend Sabbath services in the synagogues where the rabbis preached mostly in Italian. Christians, including priests, used to come to hear Leon da Modena's sermons in the Venetian syanagogues, just as monks a century earlier used to attend the synagogue in Naples to listen to sermons of Rabbi David Ibn Jachia.[2] Moreover, there was a plan to establish a school of Hebraic studies for both Jews and Christians. In 1556, right in the middle of the persecutions of Pope Paul IV, Duke Ercole II granted permission to a Jew Solomon Riva to open in Ferrara *uno studio d'Hebrei*, justifying the permit by the assertion that the school will be very advantageous to *molti Hebrei et Christiani scolari si forestieri come sudditi nostri*. The permit also stated explicitly that they will learn in the school "all the wisdom of Judaism".[3] We do not know whether the plan materialized. But at the time it was a logical expression of the strong desire of many Christians to acquire a knowledge of Judaism and Rabbinic literature.

g.

In the middle of the sixteenth century Torah study in Italy

[1] See *JQR* 9:503, and Alexander Marx, *Moses Schorr Memorial Volume*, p. 197.
[2] See *HUCA, Ibid.*, p. 617.
[3] *Balletti*, p. 82.

received a severe blow due to the attack that the Church made against the Talmud. To be sure, in the beginning the papal decree against the Talmud did not affect all of Italy. The rulers of some Italian states did not feel bound by papal decrees and the Jews continued to possess their sacred books unmolested. Moreover, the ban at first applied only to the Talmud and did not include the codes of law.[1] Thus tens of thousands of sacred works remained in Jewish hands despite the fact that large quantities of books were burned in Rome, the cities of the Romagna region, Venice, Ferrara, and Mantua. When permission was granted to expurgate books about half a year later, this further aided the preservation of many books. Nevertheless, the blow was severe since the areas in which the decree was activated had a large Jewish population and most of the *yeshibot*.

The rabbis and the *yeshibot* tried to remedy the situation in various ways. Some of them kept volumes of the Talmud illegally (see this section, chapter 2). The majority, however, were unable to study Talmud and began to use substitute works. Rabbi Jehiel Nisim da Pisa in the introduction to his book *Minḥat ḳenaot* stated sadly that "...because of our sins ...the rivers of the Talmud have dried up in these lands, and we are unable to cite evidence from the words of the Talmud and must rely upon (quotations from the Talmud as cited in the writings of) Maimonides, *sefer miẓwot gadol*, (the Talmud commentary of) Rabbi Asher ben Jehiel, and (the code of laws of) his son Rabbi Jacob". However, the primary substitute for the Talmud was *Sefer hahalakot* by Rabbi Isaac Alfasi, since he quoted substantial portions of the Gemara text to the point where his work was referred to as "the little Talmud". Rabbenu Nisim's commentary on Alfasi's work occupied the position formerly held by the Tosafot.

Italian Jewry was only partly successful in its efforts to maintain Torah study on the former level. True, literary creativity in the area of Rabbinic literature increased precisely at that time. On the other hand, however, many complaints

---

[1] *Emeḳ habaka*, pp. 129, 130. Comp. the document published by Sonne in *HUCA* 22:33.

were voiced about a general decline in Torah learning. Rabbi David Provenzal, who in 1564 planned the program for the establishment of a university, was the first to proclaim with an aching heart that the *yeshibot* had all but disappeared and explicitly connected the decline with the unavailability of the Talmud.[1] Twenty-five years later an ordinary Jew in Venice complained that "Torah is virtually forgotten in Israel, especially among the Ashkenazim". [2] At the same time the leaders of the Venice *kehillah* also deplored the progressive decline of Torah learning among Italian Jewry. [3] Obviously, the flourishing of Rabbinic literature due to the efforts of a few dedicated authors could not prevent the general drop in the level of Torah learning caused by the confiscation of the Jewish books.

The general picture of Renaissance Jewry's involvement in Torah learning thus presents the following: Torah study did not monopolize the entire intellectual interest of the Italian Jew in the same manner we find in contemporary Germany or Poland. However, it maintained a central position within the context of the Renaissance Jew's dual cultural concern. At times it even exceeded the extent of allegiance given to other disciplines. At first the Italian Jew regarded Torah study essentially as a cultural experience. Later, at the end of the Period, when religious feeling intensified among the people, involvement in Torah study also assumed a religious dimension. Torah learning was transformed into an act that merited great sacrifice in its behalf.

CHAPTER FOUR

HEBREW LINGUISTICS

Various factors combined to give Hebrew language and grammar an important position within the intellectual life of Renaissance Jewry. In addition to an increased interest in the language and its literature as a result of the general quest

---

[1] See *Halebanon*, 1866, p. 418 ff.
[2] *Kobez al jad, Ibid.*, p. 175.
[3] *Corriere Israelitico* 15:197, Note 2.

for knowledge, Hebrew was also universally acknowledged as one of the classic languages. Thus the drive to reproduce the ancient world included the study of the Hebrew language. Some authors even attempted to write books in Hebrew in genres that hitherto were never tried in order to illustrate its fitness for any field. Messer Leon stated specifically that he composed his book *Nofet zufim* to illustrate the possibility of using the Hebrew language rhetorically. Similarly, the Prologue to the comedy *Zahut bedihuta dekiddushin* contains the statement that the author wrote it "to demonstrate to all peoples and princes that ... our holy tongue exceeds in rank and advantages all over which gentile scholars boast..." [1]

The great interest in the language made the study of Hebrew grammar very popular. Italian scholars derided the German rabbis because they did not write a correct Hebrew. They carefully supervised their children's education in grammar, remembering well the admonition given by Kalonymos ben Kalonymos upon his arrival in Italy: "My son, pursue diligently the reading and study of grammar, for it is the fount of all wisdom and the foundation of all science, and whosoever remains ignorant in it will not avoid embarrassment and error in his speech and writing". Even Rabbi Immanuel da Benevento, who regarded the neglect of Torah study as the cause of all woes, composed a book on Hebrew grammar and encouraged his son to study this discipline. Consequently, Italian Jewry attained a degree of knowledge in the Hebrew language that was unequaled in the contemporary Jewish world. A mid sixteenth century letter stated that "the Italiani surpass the Ashkenazim in Hebrew grammar and the proper way of reading the Bible, with all its rules and principles".[2]

The interested public had at its disposal a wide ranging grammar literature, in part composed of the classical works by the great Spanish and Provencal grammarians, and in part of works written by Italian scholars. It appears that the

[1] For the general revival of the study of Hebrew see *Burckhardt*, p. 152; Cf. the Introduction to *Nofet zufim* and *Zahut bedihuta dekiddushin*, p. 119.
[2] See *Kobez al jad*, N. S. 1:106 ff.; *REJ* 105:56.

principal texts for grammar instruction were *Miklol* and *Sefer hashorashim* by David Kimhi. In a sample letter addressed to his father a young man complains that he had not yet purchased these two books for him. In fact, at the end of the fifteenth century *Sefer hashorashim* was published at least three times in Italy. Possibly the most noteworthy publication was an entire series of small grammar books printed by the Bomberg press in Venice. This series included works by Elijah Baḥur, Zedekiah Anaw, Abraham Ibn Ezra, and *Petaḥ Debaray* by an anonymous Spanish writer. All these books appeared in 1546 and were of the same size and form.[1] Obviously, there was a great demand for grammar literature which the Bomberg press filled with this series.

Local linguistic literature included an impressive number of dictionaries. Nathan ben Jehiel's *Aruk* was a unique type of Talmudic dictionary and served as a model for Italian writers. At the end of the fourteenth century the basic dictionary for the study of Bible, *Maḵre dardeḵe* was written. The author offers brief Hebrew explanations to every word in alphabetical order, often followed by additional explanations in Italian and other languages. Numerous other dictionaries were written during the fifteenth and sixteenth centuries, including several in bizarre format. The magnum opus of the linguistic literature was the work *Ẓemaḥ David* by the famed physician David dei Pomis, a Hebrew-Italian-Latin dictionary with very accurate translations. The various detailed indices give *Ẓemaḥ David* the character of a modern dictionary.

The Renaissance scholars with their keen historical sense engaged extensively in the study of the nature and history of the Hebrew language. In *Arugat habosem* Samuel Archivolti tried to formulate a psychology of language and to sketch a portrait of the language of the Mishnah. He also discussed the problem of punctuation and accentuation. Abraham Portaleone too offered in *Shilte hagibborim* a history of the Hebrew language and its script.

---

[1] Sonne, *Zion*, N. S. 17:150; Cf. J. Bloch, *Hebrew Printing in Naples*, p. 19; J. Bloch, *Venetian Printers of Hebrew Books*, p. 11, Note 36.

A variety of aspects of the Hebrew language is discussed in *Mikneh Avraham* by Abraham de Balmes which appeared in Venice in 1523. Here, for the first time syntax appeared as a special aspect of grammar. The author wrote the book in Hebrew and Latin to make it accessible to both Jew and gentile. Although the style lacks elegance, the book exerted a strong influence and several sixteenth century grammarians used it in the preparation of their books. Abraham de Balmes believed that God created the Hebrew language at the time He formed the universe. This is why, he opined, it was called the sacred tongue.[1]

Elijah, known as Bahur,[2] occupies a unique place among Italian grammarians. He was born in Germany in 1469 and came to Italy at the turn of the century when the Ashkenazic community in North Italy was at the peak of its expansion. This was also the time when Christian interest in studying the Hebrew language was at its height. The young immigrant quickly penetrated Renaissance society, acquiring all the virtues and faults of the humanists. In addition, he had a keen perception of the contemporary cultural trends. We have seen (section VI, chapter 2) how he was active in Northern Italy as a Yiddish writer. When the Ashkenazic community began to decline due to the War of the League of Cambrai, Elijah left for Rome and was thrust into the center of the Christian humanistic world. Here too he knew what to offer to the circles in which he lived and concentrated primarily upon literary activity in the field of Hebrew grammar. He wrote so many books on Hebrew language and grammar that

---

[1] See J. Bloch, *Hebrew Printing in Naples*, p. 18; *Meor enayim*, Section *Yeme olam*, p. 93. *Zemah David* appeared in 1587; *Arugat habosem* appeared in 1602. See *Ibid.*, passim, and especially Chapter 24; *Shilte hagibborim*, p. 170b. Samuel Archivolti in *Arugat habosem* and Rabbi Immanuel da Benevento in *Liwyat hen* relied on *Mikne Abraham*.

[2] There are many monographs on Elijah Bahur and the various aspects of his literary accomplishments. A detailed bibliography is found in Jacob Shatzky's *Elye Boher*, Buenos Aires 1949, p. 61 ff. For his activities as a grammarian see especially J. Levi, *Elia Levita und seine Leistungen als Grammatiker*, Breslau 1888.

contemporaries dubbed him "Elijah the grammarian".[1] He was not an original grammatical scholar, like Abraham de Balmes, for example. He drew amply from earlier works of grammar; but he knew how to present the results of earlier researchers to his contemporaries in a simple fashion that was close to their way of thinking and their interest. He wrote his books in a beautiful and clear Hebrew style. He also, as we have seen, overcame more easily than did other scholars the doubts regarding the permissibility of teaching Torah to non-Jews and thus became the great teacher of the Hebrew language to the Christian world. He was quite conscious of his success and wrote in typical humanistic self-glorification: "And in this do I praise myself and I will say truthfully that no writer had been so blessed by God to see prior to his death his books quoted, studied, and reprinted so many times, as God has blessed me during my lifetime, that my name should be known among so many non-Jewish and Jewish students who desire to learn our Torah".[2]

CHAPTER FIVE

KNOWLEDGE OF THE ANCIENT WORLD

a.

The knowledge of the ancient world and the desire to reproduce it in daily life occupied a central place in the mind of Renaissance man. Similar tendencies were alive among the Renaissance Jews as well. These tendencies manifested themselves in a positive attitude to the cultural tradition of the ancient world and in an effort to acquire the knowledge of this world. While the Italian Jews maintained a fully critical attitude towards Christianity, they displayed a pronounced interest in the mythological tradition of the pre-Christian world. They strove to acquire the knowledge of both classical

[1] *Shalshelet hakabbalah*, p. 30; *Minḥah belulah* by Abraham Porto, p. 55b: "and from the mouth of my master Rabbi Elijah the grammarian . . .".

[2] In the second Introduction to *Masoret hamasoret*, quoted in *Zinberg*, vol. 4, p. 68, Note 2.

languages, Latin and Greek, and to master the Greek and
Latin literatures, the history of Antiquity, its religion,
mythology, and way of life.

The interest in the ancient world and its culture is evident
in the Hebrew literature of the Period. To begin with, Abraham Portaleone in *Shilte hagibborim* furnished detailed
descriptions that yield a truly clear picture of the ancient
world and its way of life. Besides, one must not forget that
this work—as the author assures us [1]—was an act of penance
and it aimed to replace his secular studies. Nevertheless, the
writer devoted a considerable part of the book to a description
of the classical world. Obviously, he thought that a Jew who
was repenting did not need to refrain from pursuing classical
studies. Leon da Modena entertained similar beliefs. When he
translated the Christian ethical treatise *Fior di virtù* into
Hebrew, he replaced all passages mentioning the dogmas or
saints of Christianity with passages from Rabbinic literature,
but retained all the legends and tales about Greece and
Rome.[2] The Jews of the sixteenth century evinced a great
interest in the *Dialoghi di amore* of Leone Abravanel because
it offered explanations of many Greek legends.[3] It is beyond
doubt that Gedaliah Ibn Jachia included in *Shalshelet haḳabbalah* [4] the chapter which describes ancient idolatry and the
detailed information about the ancient world and its history
for the purpose of satisfying the deep curiosity about these
subjects among the Jews. The immigrant Don Isaac Abravanel
shared Italian Jewry's admiration for the classical world; in
his commentary on the Pentateuch he had many words of
praise for the Greeks and Romans. He admired their political
wisdom, their heroism, and even their physical appearance.[5]

---

[1] See the Introduction to *Shilte hagibborim*, also published in
Neppi-Ghirondi. See *Ibid.*, p. 44.

[2] See *Sepher Chaje Jehuda*, p. 42. The Hebrew name of the treatise
is *Ẓemaḥ Ẓaddiḳ*. The booklet was published in Venice in 1600.
A new edition appeared in Tel-Aviv in 1949.

[3] See I. Sonne, *Tarbiẓ* 3:287 ff.

[4] *Shalshelet kakabbalah*, p. 140 ff.

[5] *Commentary on the Pentateuch*, Hanau 1710, p. 40a. Cf. *Pesiḳta
derab Kahana*, Section *Parah*: "without blemish—this is Greece".

b.

The interest in the Antiquity brought about a strong desire to acquire the knowledge of the Latin and Greek languages. Although the Jews of the Renaissance were equally interested in both classical languages, the knowledge of Latin was far more widespread than that of Greek. Various factors were responsible for this. To begin with, Jews who spoke Italian found it much easier to learn Latin than Greek. In addition, the knowledge of the Latin language had a practical value in everyday life. The Renaissance had developed an excellent epistolography and rhetoric in Latin in addition to the Neo-Latin literature. Everyone who desired to let his son have a good education was obliged to let him acquire a thorough knowledge of that language. Thus we find among the Italian Jews men who knew Latin, from the beginning of the Renaissance until its end.[1] They acquired the knowledge of the language either by studying with private tutors or in *yeshibot*. Had we compiled a list of Italian Jews of the Renaissance who knew the Latin language, it would have had to include many authors, rabbis, and scholars. Especially widespread was the knowledge of Latin among the Jews in the Kingdom of Naples.[2] The participation of South-Italian Jewish scholars in the major effort of translating scientific works from Arabic into Latin was equally impressive. This effort began in the late Middle Ages and continued all through the period of the Renaissance.[3] At the same time, there appeared in Italy translations from Hebrew into Latin and vice versa.[4] We also

[1] Such as the poet Judah Romano, the friend of Giannozzo Manetti, the Florentine scholar Immanuel (see Cassuto, *Florence*, p. 275), Elijah del Medigo, Azariah dei Rossi, Jacob Mantino, Joseph Zarfadi, Rabbi Judah Moscato, Abraham Portaleone, and others. See *MGWJ* 42:262 ff.

[2] *Ferorelli*, p. 102, particularly Note 8.

[3] See R. Strauss, *Die Juden im Koenigreich Sizilien*, Heidelberg 1910, p. 91 for the special status enjoyed by Jewish translators in the court of Frederick II in Sicily.

[4] See Steinschneider, *Allgemeine Einleitung in die juedische Littera-tur des Mittelalters*, p. 92. Steinschneider incorrectly wrote that translations from Hebrew into Latin appeared in Italy until the middle of the sixteenth century. Actually we also find them later. Rabbi Moses Alatini, for example, translated several books from

find a certain number of Jewish authors who wrote original works in Latin prose.[1]

While most of the scholars had merely a literary knowledge of Latin, some were able to make practical use of it as a spoken language. The physician David dei Pomis, author of the trilingual Hebrew-Latin-Italian dictionary *Ẓemaḥ David*, delivered a long speech in Latin in the presence of Pope Pius IV and the cardinals.[2] Abtalyon da Modena also had an opportunity to address Pope Gregory XIII in Latin. In his speech which lasted two hours Abtalyon pleaded for permission to print the Talmud.[3] It should also be noted that in the middle of the sixteenth century the former Portuguese Marrano Didacus Pyrrus, who was living in Ancona as a Jew, was one of the most famous Neo-Latin poets. [4]

The admiration for the Greek language was equally remarkable. Obadiah da Bertinoro believed that "no language among the descendants of Japheth (i.e. the Europeans) is as beautiful as Greek".[5] Some of the scholars who knew Latin also knew Greek,[6] but, to be sure, rarely reached in it the same degree

Hebrew into Latin at the turn of the seventeenth century. See the Introduction to *Ẓemaḥ David* by David dei Pomis, also available in *Neppi-Ghirondi*. See *Ibid.*, p. 88. Cf. also *Abraham Berliner Jubilee Volume*, p. 272. Among the other translators we find Kalonymos ben Kalonymos, Jacob Mantino, and Azariah dei Rossi.

[1] Such as David dei Pomis and Abraham Portaleone who wrote many Latin works, or Lazzaro da Viterbo who wrote a long Latin tract in which he wanted to prove to Cardinal Sirletto that the Jewish scriptural version was genuine. See *JQR* 7:283.

[2] See his autobiographical introduction to *Ẓemaḥ David*, also available in *Neppi-Ghirondi*. Cf. p. 89.

[3] *Sepher Chaje Jehuda*, p. 12.

[4] See Roth, *History*, p. 300. It is probable that David, the son of Messer Leon was also a Neo-Latin poet. He relates (*HB* 12;33) that he composed "many verses in Hebrew and in *lashon noẓri* . . ." Since the Italian language was generally referred to as *leshon laaz*, I am inclined to assume that *lashon noẓri* ("Christian language") refers to Latin, used by the Church in worship.

[5] Commentary to the Mishnah, tractate Sheqalim, chapter 3, mishnah 2. References concerning the positive attitude of the Rabbis to the languages of the *bene Japheth* may be found in various sources, as for example Genesis Rabbah chapter 36 (ed. Leipzig, p. 64) and Deuteronomy Rabbah, at the beginning of chapter 1.

[6] Such as Elijah del Medigo, Joseph Zarfadi and Rabbi Judah Moscato.

of perfection as in Latin. This can be seen from the fact that
the number of Jewish translators from Greek into Hebrew was
far smaller than of those who rendered from Latin into
Hebrew. We can thus understand why Azariah dei Rossi
deplored the fact that he did not know Greek sufficiently.[1]

There were, however, exceptions. For example, Abraham
Jaghel Gallichi was able to translate a chapter of IV Ezra
from Greek into Hebrew.[2] But it was again Abraham Portaleone who surpassed everyone in the knowledge of Greek and
in his efforts to encourage its study. He knew that there are
five dialects in the Greek language, and was able to classify
the ancient Greek poets according to the dialects in which
they wrote. He printed in his work the Greek alphabet, and
he stated clearly that he was doing it to make it possible for
the Jews to learn the language. He even went to the dubious
extreme of advising them to buy Christian prayerbooks and to
use the Greek parts for the study of the language.[3]

c.

The knowledge of the classical languages was accompanied
by a wide dissemination of the knowledge of Graeco-Roman
literature and the cultural tradition of the ancient world. The
many Italian translations of works of the classical literature
made it possible for everyone to become familiar with the
culture of the Antiquity, even without an adequate knowledge
of its languages. For instance, we find a common man quoting
the Iliad in a letter to a relative.[4] Obviously, some knowledge
of the ancient culture also penetrated into uneducated circles.

A profound knowledge of classical literature was, of course,
found only among the scholars. Here again Abraham Portaleone and Azariah dei Rossi surpassed all others. The starting
point of Portaleone's description of the various fields of
knowledge were the sciences of the Antiquity. When he

---

[1] *Meor enayim, Ibid.*

[2] *Kobez al jad*, 1889, p. 38.

[3] See *Shilte hagibborim*, in the Introduction entitled *Leshonot
hagoyim*, pp. 4a, 8a and b. He had Latin books in his library. See
JQR 4:337 ff.

[4] See *RMI* 1:37 ff.

described the architecture of the Temple in Jerusalem, he referred continuously to the works of Vitruvius, the greatest architect of the Antiquity. His knowledge of the classical literature was broad enough to include the comedies of Terence and Plautus. An almost equally thorough knowledge of the Roman and Greek writers possessed Azariah dei Rossi, who quoted in his work more than one hundred Roman and Greek authors. [1] Judah Moscato, a great writer and preacher, quoted in addition to Plato and Aristotle, Seneca, Ovid, Cicero, Quintilian, and others. [2] In his sermons he liked to use material from the Roman and Greek legends as illustration of his thoughts. [3]

Quotations from the classical literature are frequently found in the writings of other Jewish authors as well. In a poem dedicated to the history of music, Samuel Archivolti wrote about Pythagoras as the "rediscoverer" of music. Judah Moscato likewise knew of him as the restorer of the art of music. [4] Abraham Farissol continuously referred in his *Iggeret orehot olam* to the geographical writings of Ptolemy. Messer Leon and Judah Moscato, who wrote about rhetoric from the theoretical point of view, derived their knowledge from the writings of Aristotle, Cicero, and Quintilian. [5] In his own sermons, Judah Moscato followed Cicero and divided them into four parts: *exordium*, preposition, analysis, and conclusion. Azariah Pigo, another great preacher of the Italian-Jewish Renaissance, composed his sermons in the same manner. [6]

The Hebrew epistolography of the Renaissance imitated both the contemporary Neo-Latin writers and Cicero. [7] Now

---

[1] Cf. Azariah's biography by Zunz, published in the Benjacob edition of *Meor enayim*, and the list of authors in the Cassel edition, Section *Mazref lakesef*, p. 161.

[2] See *Nefuzot Yehuda*, Introduction and pp. 2, 26, 128a.

[3] See Israel Bettan's study in *HUCA* 6:305.

[4] See *Arugat habosem*, p. 118a and the first sermon in *Nefuzot Yehudah* entitled *Higgayon bekinnor*.

[5] Cf. *Iggeret orehot olam*, passim, and *Meor enayim*, Section *Imre binah*, Chapter 11. Cf. *Nofet zufim*, passim and *Nefuzot Yehuda*, p. 78a.   [6] See Israel Bettan's study in *HUCA* 7:467.

[7] See the study by Alexander Marx on Joseph Arli, *Tarbiz* 8:172.

and then we also find Jewish authors who made use of material from the Greek-Roman religion and mythology. Rabbi Obadiah Sforno explained that the *urim wetumim* are "comparable by their nature to the predictions of the pagan priests which in ancient times were called oracles..." The playwright Leone da Sommi introduced many figures from the classical mythology into his Italian plays,[1] and likewise did Judah Moscato in his sermons. Needless to say, almost all authors made use of the writings of Philo[2] and Josephus. Many also quoted Plato extensively. The knowledge of Antiquity was further fostered by a deep interest in its archeological remnants. For example, David Finzi of Mantua was the owner of a collection of ancient coins which Azariah dei Rossi used to study.[3] The physician Enoch of Ascoli was sent by Pope Nicholas V, a great admirer of the ancient world, to acquire old manuscripts for him in Greece, the Balkan countries, France, and Germany.[4] Abraham Portaleone tells us that the Jews had a passion for collecting "gold medals... old bronze figures and other objects, such as vessels..."; to this report Portaleone adds a warning to his Jewish contemporaries not to spend too much money for such acquisitions.[5] Obviously, the passion of the Jews for collecting archeological objects was widespread and assumed dimensions characteristic of the epoch of the Renaissance.

CHAPTER SIX

HISTORY AND GEOGRAPHY

a.

Renaissance society's scholarly interest was vividly reflected in the field of history and geography. A society that strove to

[1] See *Meor enayim*, Section *Yeme olam*, p. 64. I have examined Rabbi Obadiah Sforno's commentary on Exodus 28:30, Leviticus 8:8, and Numbers 27:21 and have not found this explanation. See D'Ancona, *Origini del teatro Italiano*, 2nd ed., Part 2, p. 404.

[2] See R. Marcus, *HUCA* 21:29 ff. that Azariah dei Rossi was one of the first who critically examined Philo's works in a thoroughly comprehensive manner. It was he who suggested the name Jedidiah as a Hebrew translation of the name *Philo*. Philo was very popular among Italian Jews at that time.   [3] *Meor enayim*, Section *Yeme olam*, p. 188.   [4] See *Natali*, p. 186.   [5] *Shilte hagibborim*, p. 60b.

re-discover the world and man and to reproduce the life patterns of the ancient past, understandably evinced a profound interest in social studies. As a result, a widely ramified historiography emerged in fifteenth century humanistic circles that prepared the ground for the researches and teachings of Guicciardini, Macchiavelli, Bembo, and others.[1] The development of Jewish Renaissance historiography paralleled that of the Italians in scope and depth.

The most potent factor that led to the emergence of a Jewish historiography were the streams of Jewish immigration that poured into the Peninsula throughout the Period (see section 1, chapter 1). When the immigrants found a refuge in Italy, for the first time they were able to ponder the problem of their people's strange fate, with themselves as the most recent victims. They were simultaneously surprised to observe that within the frame of Renaissance free society the Jew had ceased to be a passive pawn of history. They noted that the Jew could regain the initiative in shaping his own destiny and revive the rare phenomenon of an active Jewish history, at least for short periods. In addition, the rapprochement between Jews and gentiles and the enhanced importance of the Jewish people as keepers of the ancient Hebrew culture were surprisingly new manifestations. When the immigrants contrasted this portrait of a more free and wealthy Jewish community, socially and economically active, with the oppressed and degraded Jewish community in Germany or the one that was persecuted and exiled from Spain, they perceived that Italian Jewry had truly arrived at a period of great historic moment. This is why a trend emerged, mainly among the immigrants, to re-examine the problem of the Jewish position among the nations.[2] Joseph Hacohen, the least sophisticated among the sixteenth century historians, stated explicitly that "...the expulsions from France and this bitter and hurried expulsion (from Spain) had impelled me to write this book (*Emek habaka*)". Samuel Usque, the poet-historian, also stated in the introduction to his work that when he saw

---

[1] See *Burckhardt*, pp. 64 ff., 180 ff.
[2] See Moses A. Shulvass, *In the Grip of Centuries*, pp. 205-210.

the suffering of his brethren who were driven from Portugal (i.e. the Marranos who left Portugal and were scattered in various European countries) and their spiritual confusion, he decided "to write the history of all the calamities that befell our people, each calamity and its cause". On the other hand, some historians were especially impressed by the great strength and free status of the Jewish community in Turkey. An anonymous author, the "Annotator" (*Hamagiha*) explicitly linked the annulment of the expulsion decree against the Jews of the Venetian Republic in 1573 with a recognition by the government that if the expulsion were effected the exiles would go to Turkey and reinforce its power: "Who has raised the Turks' power and where did they find craftsmen to make battering rams, bows, catapults, swords, small and large shields, to beat down the power of the gentile nations, but the Jews whom Spanish kings had expelled".[1] The chronicle *Shebet Yehudah* was even more representative of the intentions of the contemporary historical literature. Despite the seeming calm with which the book was written, the great penetrating question of the author, a Spanish refugee, runs through it seeking to understand the destiny of the Jewish people and the meaning of the events on its stormy course.

This tendency among immigrant thinkers to use history as a means of probing social problems found a hospitable ground in the general historical interest that seized both Christians and Jews. Rabbi Immanuel da Benevento considered the pre-occupation with history a factor that distracted a Jew from the study of Torah ("they indulge in the vanity of studying books about history and the nature of kings and states"),[2] an indication that it had reached considerable proportions. Even Rabbi Azariah dei Rossi who thought that the Jewish people did not need to concern itself with the past, but to follow the teachings of the Torah, admitted that "...in my spare time I

---

[1] *Emek habaka*, p. 102 and p. 168. To be sure, this passage was copied from his book *Dibre hayamim. Consolation for the Tribulations of Israel*, translated by Martin A. Cohen, Philadelphia 1965, p. 39.
[2] *Liwyat hen*, p. 26a. Comp. Maimonides, Introduction to *Perek Helek*, ed. Rabinovitz, Jerusalem 1961, p. 135.

read all the famous chronicles..." [1] In his responsa Rabbi
Azriel Diena involved himself in historical and chronological
problems, with very few apologies, and in a similar vein
Samuel Archivolti reported about his familiarity with the
writings of Josephus.[2] Additional information about the study
of history is quite frequent in contemporary literature. And
here too, as on many other occasions, Leon da Modena spoke
most frankly when he unapologetically described the keen
delight that he derived from knowing the history of his
ancestors and teachers and important men.[3] The most striking
expression of the interest in history was the book *Shalshelet
hakabbalah*. Written in a poor style with a bizarre multitopical
content, this book was certainly not meant to satisfy the
scholar's intellectual needs. It was written to provide the
folk with reading material in a field which it found most
attractive. The interest in history, finally, stimulated many
writers to record events of autobiographical nature, mostly in
the form of notes inserted in introductions to literary works.
Again, Leon da Modena surpassed his contemporaries in his
autobiography which is amazingly frank and honest.

Most Jewish Renaissance historians discussed in their
works both general and Jewish history. A considerable number
of chapters in the chronicle *Shalshelet hakabbalah* deal with
the past of various nations in an effort to connect them
chronologically with Jewish history. Joseph Hacohen's work
on general history (*Dibre hayamim lemalke Zarephath ubet
Ottoman hatugar, The History of the Kings of France and the
House of Ottoman the Turk*) is much larger than his Jewish
chronicle. He opened the work with a brief description of
the origin of the European nations. He then proceeded to the
history of the Frankish Empire and to a detailed account of
the wars between the Crusaders and Moslems in the Middle
East. He continued to treat at length the political entanglements in Europe and the many changes in various countries
during the Middle Ages. He properly described the struggle

---

[1] *Meor enayim*, Section *Imre binah*, p. 254 ff.
[2] See *Kirjath Sepher* 14:547; *JQR* 9:266 ff.
[3] *Sepher Chaje Jehuda*, p. 9.

between the Christian West and the Moslem East as the
central point of historical happening during most of that
period. In the second part, which is a kind of chronicle of his
time, the author described the events that occurred in Genoa,
where he resided. After the book's publication in 1554, Joseph
Hacohen wrote a sequel describing contemporary events up
to the 1570's. He dealt continuously with contemporary
political problems which preoccupied the Renaissance Jew as
a concomitant of his effort to participate fully in life (see
below, section IX, chapter 5). The concern with contemporary
issues is also present in the *History of Pope Paul IV* by
Benjamin Nehemiah of Civitanova. The author intended to
relate the history of the anti-Jewish policies of this pope.
Nevertheless he digressed periodically to a description of
general events, demonstrating a keen grasp of the political
complexities of the time. He concluded his work with an
excellent description of the events surrounding the pope's
death. At the very end of the Period an anonymous author
wrote a sequel to Joseph Hacohen's *Dibre hayamim.* Joseph
Hacohen had brought the account up to the last war of Emperor Charles V, and the continuator related the events from
the Emperor's abdication until 1605. He followed, and even
exceeded Joseph's method of introducing events of Jewish
life into his accounts of general history.[1]

Among the various historical disciplines, archeology and
chronology attracted much of the attention of the Renaissance
Jew. Archeological interest resulted primarily from the
effort to reproduce the ancient world. A full chapter in
Shalshelet hakabbalah is devoted to explaining ancient Jewish
coins by comparing them with contemporary currency. In
contrast to other parts of the book this chapter presents the

[1] *Dibre hayamim* was first published in Sabionetta in 1554. Part 3,
edited by David A. Gross was published in Jerusalem in 1955. In
this part Joseph Hacohen describes events of the years 1556-1562.
It is possible that Joseph Hacohen was influenced in the selection
of the name of his book by the popular work *I reali di Francia.* The
chronicle of the Magiha was published by S. D. Luzzatto in his edition
of *Emek habaka.* See Moses A. Shulvass, *In the Grip of Centuries,*
pp. 390-393. The chronicle of Benjamin Nehemiah was published by
I. Sonne, *Tarbiz* 2:331-376 and 477-502.

results of independent research done by the author-compiler. The architecture of the Temple and the sacrificial service were of even greater interest to most Jewish readers. The literature of the Period, and especially Abraham Portaleone's *Shilte hagibborim*, satisfied the public's curiosity by offering lengthy descriptions of the Temple, its vessels, and its music.[1]

The author of *Shalshelet hakabbalah* was also concerned with the difficult problem of biblical chronology. He repeatedly noted that he had investigated the chronology of various events and personalities, and regretted that often it was impossible to unravel the difficulties: "And both Christian and Jewish commentators have exerted themselves strenuously to reconcile them (i.e. conflicting dates in the Bible) to no avail, to the extent that one Christian commentator said these words about those who attempt to reconcile (conflicting verses), that it was a wasteful effort because of the wide disparities and the difficulty of reconciling (the verses)".[2] The most substantial treatment the problem of chronology received in Azariah dei Rossi's *Meor enayim*. In this area too Azariah carried his research to the point of conflict with talmudic tradition.

b.

The ramified historical interest was matched by the great contemporary historical works *Shebet Yehudah, Consolacam as tribulacoens de Israel, Emek habaka*, and *Shalshelet hakabbalah*. [3]

---

[1] See *Shebet Yehuda*, p. 128 ff.; *Shalshelet hakabbalah*, p. 19 ff. *Shilte hagibborim*, Chapters 4 to 13 and passim.

[2] *Shalshelet hakabbalah*, p. 26.

[3] It is difficult to give references for all that follows, since the passages used as source material are very numerous and are scattered in all the works under consideration. The following studies on these works merit attention: I. Baer's Introduction to *Shebet Yehuda*, Shochet ed., Jerusalem 1947; Abraham Neuman's study on *Shebet Yehuda* in *Louis Ginzberg Jubilee Volume*, English section, p. 453 ff.; his study on Usque's *Consolation, Rosenbach Jubilee Volume*, p. 180 ff.; Martin A. Cohen's Introduction to his translation of *Consolation*; S. D. Luzzato's Introduction to *Emek habaka* and Moses A. Shulvass, *In the Grip of Centuries, Ibid.*; Salo W. Baron's studies on *Meor enayim* in the *Israel Abrahams Memorial Volume* and in *REJ*, vols. 86-87; Steinschneider, *Die Geschichtsliteratur der Juden*, Frankfurt

These books were written approximately within a sixty year period by writers of varied background and viewpoint. There are thus many differences in their literary structure, content, attitude, and the sources used by the authors. Common to the authors is courage in expressing their opinions and a broad utilization of sources, unknown until that time.

Of these books, *Consolacam as tribulacoens de Israel*, *Emek habaka*, and *Shalshelet hakabbalah* are chronicles, that is, collections of accounts regarding past events or personalities, arranged in a more or less chronological order. In contrast, *Shebet Yehudah* contains fictitious stories and imaginary discussions and debates between Jews and gentiles along with accounts of actual events that were based on solid historical sources.

The author of *Shalshelet hakabbalah*, Gedaliah Ibn Jachia tried to arrange his work in the form of a general history, from the creation of the world until his era. In his detailed description he does not distinguish between political, cultural or literary events, and frequently confuses them. Chronological order is virtually the only frame of his work. He interspersed the book with many descriptions of areas other than history, such as spheres, the origin of languages, witchcraft, and other matters. He concluded his book with a chronicle of the persecutions, libels, and expulsions up to his own days.

The author of *Emek habaka*, Joseph Hacohen excluded from his work the history of the First and Second Commonwealths, for he wanted to relate "the tribulations that befell us". Thus, *Emek habaka* was intended to be a history of the Jewish people in the Diaspora. However, despite his professed goal, the author also described many events in Jewish history that were not calamities. His historical sense did not permit him to limit himself to the narrow confines that he drew.

Samuel Usque's work, written in Portuguese, was also intended by the author to be an account of the calamities that befell the Jewish people. There are three parts to the book. The first two were composed in the form of a pastoral. Three

1905, the paragraphs describing these works. *Greatz-Rabinowitz*, vol. 7, p. 423.

imaginary shepherds, whose names suggest Jacob, Nahum and Zachariah, meet and discuss the sufferings of the Jewish people. In a poetic style Jacob tells Nahum and Zachariah a string of stories from the lives of shepherds which symbolize the fate of the Jewish people. He later reveals his identity and continues in the same lyrical tone his account of the history of the Jewish people from the Patriarchal Age until the destruction of the Second Temple. The third part contains a detailed prose account of thirty seven calamities, persecutions, and expulsions that befell the Jewish people. It starts with the Visigothic persecutions of Spanish Jewry in the early Middle Ages and concludes with acts of persecution in mid sixteenth century Italy. In this section Samuel Usque appeared as a genuine historian. He gave references to his Hebrew, Latin and Italian sources, thus contributing fundamentally to Hebrew historiography. By presenting the story of persecutions in Christian lands, he tried to convince the Marranos, for whom primarily the book was written, that the Jewish people was eternal and that it was able to survive despite oppression.

The stories in *Shebet Yehudah* by Solomon Ibn Verga, insofar as they contain sound historical information, were also related essentially to what had befallen the Jews in Christian lands. At the end of the chronicle the author's son Joseph described a number of historical events which came to his attention at the time of the publication of the book.

The broad utilization of sources was greatly enhanced by the linguistic erudition which included the classical languages. In addition, the leading historians who were immigrants had access to sources in Spanish, Portuguese, and Provencal. Also, the friendly attitude to the general culture helped to overcome all misgivings about the use of non-Jewish sources. Azariah dei Rossi, in a lengthy discourse, tried to prove "the need to buttress some (of his) data with testimony of writers who are not of our people". In his work *Meor enayim* he, indeed, quoted over a hundred Greek and Latin writers, in addition to many authors in other languages.[1]

[1] *Meor enayim*, Section *Imre binah*, Chapter 2. See also Azariah's

Solomon Ibn Verga was the first sixteenth century historian to use parallel Jewish and non-Jewish sources. His Jewish sources included such classics as the writings of Josephus and *Seder haḳabbalah* by Abraham Ibn Daud, as well as short popular writings which related various historical events. In addition, *Shebet Yehudah* contains a great deal of material that was taken from non-Jewish sources, especially Spanish literature. Solomon Ibn Verga was also familiar with the Italian short story and the Renaissance spirit is apparent in his frequent use of humor, parody, and subtle irony.

Consolacam as tribulacoens de Israel resembles *Shebet Yehudah* in many aspects, especially in the employment of parallel Jewish and non-Jewish sources. The format of thirty-seven brief chapters for an account of the various persecutions resembles the structure of *Shebet Yehudah*. To be sure, Usque used only a limited number of sources.[1] In addition to Josephus and varied material from midrashic literature, his principal source was the well known antisemitic work *Fortalitium fidei* by Alfonso de Spina. Contemporary events are related on the basis of what the author saw or heard.

Joseph Hacohen in *Emeḳ habaka* used the sources along a similar line. He collected what he found "in the works of the authors", Jews and gentiles, frequently identifying his sources. Most evident is his dependence upon Usque's work. Among his other sources were official documents and information that he amassed by interviewing various people. His critical use of sources is evident in his remark about Maimonides' treatment of the David Alroy story: "(What) Maimonides, may his memory be a blessing, wrote about this man in

---

biography by Zunz, published in the Benjacob edition of *Meor enayim* and the list of authors in the Cassel edition, section *Maẓref lakesef*, p. 161. Cf. Baron's study in the *Israel Abrahams Memorial Volume*, p. 13.

[1] One scholar is of the opinion that Usque did not use *Shebet Yehuda* directly and he even doubts that Usque knew enough Hebrew to read the book. Most scholars agree that Solomon Ibn Verga and Usque used common sources, which, to be sure, can not be identified. See: Fritz Baer, *Untersuchungen ueber Quellen und Komposition des Schebet Jehuda*, Berlin 1923; Cf. also *Graetz-Rabinowitz, Ibid.*, p. 424.

his Epistle (to Yemen indicates) that he perhaps did not have the correct information".[1]

The largest number of sources were deployed by Azariah dei Rossi in his work *Meor enayim*. He was the greatest scholar among the sixteenth century Jewish historians and was very erudite in the entire realm of Jewish literature. His knowledge of non-Jewish literature was also very impressive.[2] *Meor enayim* is different from the other contemporary historical works. The author was not concerned with transmitting past events in the accepted manner, but rather aimed at examining the trustworthiness of the sources and the chronology of the biblical tradition. He succeeded in producing a work of a true scholarly caliber and literary perfection at a time when the other historians basically remained in the category of chroniclers. The high quality of the work leads us to question the veracity of Leon da Modena's statement that most of *Meor enayim* consisted of "flour that he (Azariah) ground with millstones" of (i.e. borrowed from) Rabbi Abtalyon da Modena, Leon's uncle.[3]

Gedaliah Ibn Jachia, author of *Shalshelet hakabbalah*, was very much influenced by the work *Meor enayim*. In several places he quoted lengthy passages from this book without acknowledgement, probably because of the opposition *Meor enayim* evoked in rabbinic circles. Like its model, *Shalshelet hakabbalah* discusses at length chronology, the Ten Tribes, the list of the high priests, and the Septuagint. Following *Meor enayim* which contains a Hebrew translation of the *Letter of Aristeas*, *Shalshelet hakabbalah* includes an abstract of it.[4] Unquestionably, Gedaliah tried to imitate *Meor enayim* even though he did not absorb very much of Azariah's scholarly approach.

Gedaliah Ibn Jachia used as source material virtually all of ancient Hebrew literature, the Apocrypha, and the works of

[1] See: *Emek habaka*, p. 49; *Ibid.*, p. 142: "I have told you what they wrote to me from Rome"; Moses A. Shulvass, *In the Grip of Centuries*, p. 67 ff.
[2] See Azariah dei Rossi's biography by Zunz, p. 6.
[3] *Sepher Chaje Jehuda*, p. 12.
[4] See *Shalshelet hakabbalah*, pp. 30, 31, 37, 39.

the Church Fathers. He also had at his disposal a number of unpublished manuscripts. With regard to the genealogy of the Rabbis he admittedly drew most of his information from Abraham Ibn Daud's *Sefer haḳabbalah*. Gedaliah's essential methodological contribution was his use of Rabbinic literature, especially responsa, as a historical source. But he failed to extract from the sources the relevant material and to transform it into a reliable historical narrative. He was overly concerned with insignificant events of anecdotal character. Only sporadically did he rise to the treatment of his material with scholarly criticism.[1]

c.

Jacob Burckhardt has shown in his great work that one of the most characteristic phenomena of the Renaissance was the discovery of the world that surrounded man. "When the Italian spirit was liberated from the barriers that held back progress...it turned to the discovery of the surrounding world and showed its acumen in describing this world..."[2] Consequently, descriptions of nature and distant lands and their customs proliferated among the Italians. At the same time a great wanderlust awakened among the Italians, and Renaissance men traveled to a far greater extent than was customary in earlier generations.

The interest in the wide world and its literary and practical discovery was also present in Jewish society. Abraham Farissol composed his geographical work *Iggeret oreḥot olam* explicitly "to satisfy the readers' desire". In addition, the Jews manifested a special interest in the geography of the Holy Land.[3] The geographic awareness of Italian Jewry was further augmented by its position on the Mediterranian coast, which placed it in the very center of the Jewish Diaspora. Most emigrants and tourists to the Holy Land passed through Italy and were to the Italian Jews a living source of informa-

---

[1] *Ibid.*, p. 17 and p. 30.
[2] *Burckhardt*, p. 215.
[3] *Iggeret oreḥot olam*, Cracow 1822, p. 23b and the beginning of Chapter 10.

tion about many lands and their Jewish communities.[1] The
contemporary energetic search for the Ten Tribes also contributed to broadening the geographical interest and the practical
knowledge of distant lands. Isaac Ibn Akrish tells of "an
Italian who spent most of his life" seeking the Ten Tribes.[2]
Many ransomed Jews who were released through the efforts of
the Italian Jewish Society for Redeeming Captives also
appeared in Italy. Finally, the mass immigration of Jews
that flowed into Italy from Germany, France, Spain and the
Middle East (see above Section I, Chapter I) in general
"contracted" the world for the Italian Jew and brought the
hitherto unknown remote lands closer to him.

An awakened awareness of nature and its beauty accompanied the general geographical interest. Florentine Jews
used to visit the dome of the church Santa Maria del Fiore
built by Brunelleschi so often that they were banned in 1595
from further entry. This dome attracted visitors primarily
for the view that it offered of the marvelous landscape
surrounding the city.[3] The beautiful mountain areas of the
country also deeply impressed the Jew. While Immanuel of
Rome early in the Period complained over the hardships he
endured crossing mountains, Elijah Baḥur, about one hundred
and fifty years later, was overwhelmed by the beauty of the
Alps as he crossed them.[4] Small wonder then that Samuel
Usque had a receptive reading public for the marvelous
nature descriptions he sketched in the first two dialogues of
his work. His overwhelming rapture for mountains, fields,
rivers, and birds is particularly striking.

A geographical literature, partially original and partially
translated and adapted to the needs of the Jewish reader,
satisfied the desire to know the world and its wonders. The

[1] Moses A. Shulvass, *Rome and Jerusalem*, 1944, Chapters 4 to 8
(Hebrew).
[2] See *Ibid.*, p. 21 ff. and passim; cf. Isaac Ibn Akrish, *Ḳol mebaser*,
Offenbach 1720.
[3] See *Ciscato*, p. 140, Note 1 and Karl Baedeker, *Italien*, Leipzig
1926, pp. 152-193.
[4] *Maḥberot Immanuel*, p. 678 ff. and the Epilogue of *Sefer hatishbi*
by Elijah Baḥur.

first traces of this literature can be found in the many attempts at identifying localities mentioned in the Bible. It is not surprising to find in the geographer Abraham Farissol's commentary on *Job*[1] a study on the location of the Land of Uz. Similar efforts are also found in Usque's work, in *Minḥa belulah* by Abraham Menahem Porto, and in many other works. Don Isaac Abravanel in his commentary on the Pentateuch went even further and "for the sake of comprehensiveness" he offered a lengthy catalogue of the nations who descended from the sons of Japheth, trying to identify them with European and Asian peoples.[2] Many more geographical notes are found in other parts of his Bible commentary. Abraham Jaghel Gallichi's interest in, and knowledge of, geography is reflected in his remarkable work *Bet yaar halebanon*.[3] He obtained his information from literary sources and from conversations with foreign visitors and ransomed captives. More extensive geographical descriptions are found in the correspondence and travelogues of Italian immigrants and visitors to the Holy Land. Some of these letters and travelogues are models of excellent geographical literature. Meshullam da Volterra, for example, describing Alexandria in Egypt, where he spent some time en route to Palestine, related in detail about climate, housing conditions, clothing, food prices, family life, and political conditions.[4]

The most comprehensive works in geography were written by Abraham Farissol and Joseph Hacohen. Joseph's main contribution consisted of a Hebrew translation of two popular non-Jewish geographical works into Hebrew, John Behaim's *Omnium gentium mores, leges et ritus* and Francisco Lopez de Gomora's *La Historia general de las Indias*. He concluded the

[1] Published in the *Biblia Rabbinica*, Venice 1517-1518 and republished in Amsterdam in 1724-1727.

[2] *Consolation*, pp. 44f. and 47f.; *Minḥah belulah*, Venice 1594, p. 13b; Abravanel's *Commentary on the Pentateuch*, p. 40b. His source is the list of nations found at the beginning of *Yosifon*.

[3] See the chapters published in *Kobez al jad*, 1888, p. 37 ff.

[4] A detailed description of Jewish emigration and tourism from Italy to the Holy Land and the pertinent correspondence is available in Moses A. Shulvass, *Rome and Jerusalem*, passim. Meshullam da Volterra's *Travelogue*, Jerusalem 1949, pp. 45-49.

translations with an original chapter describing certain Mediterranean areas omitted by Behaim, as well as the discovery of America, the conquest of Peru, and the New World in general. These translations, though never published, nevertheless seem to have been very popular among the Renaissance Jews.[1]

The outstanding geographical work was Abraham Farissol's *Iggeret oreḥot olam*.[2] In the Introduction the author defined his work as a cosmography, that is, a description of the world. In the first part he outlined the continents and the seas, the lands of the Old World, the climates, and the methods of measuring latitude and longitude. He then described in greater detail the Mediterranean Sea and the travel routes from Venice to various parts of the world (chapters 11-13). There is evidence that these chapters were used by Italian Jews as a travel guide. The first part concludes with an account of the Ten Tribes and a description of "their land". Mass interest in the Ten Lost Tribes was intense and it was unthinkable for an author to compose a book on geography without introducing the popular rumors regarding Jewish independence in unknown countries. The second part discusses the Portuguese geographic expeditions, the discovery of America and the location of...the Garden of Eden.

Abraham Farissol's main source were the writings of the Greco-Egyptian geographer Ptolemy, whose authority he did not question even at a time of the greatest geographic discoveries. Among his Jewish sources were Eldad the Danite, *Yosifon*, and *"baal hamasaot"*, i.e. Benjamin of Tudela.

[1] For Joseph Hacohen's geographical works see J. H. Gottheil, *Publications of the American Jewish Historical Society* 2:129 ff. The manuscript of *Maẓib gebulot amim* that I have seen is kept in the Columbia University Library. It was copied by Joseph Hacohen himself. The many bizarre errors found in the chapter on the discovery of America in *Dibre hayamim* can be explained by Joseph's ignorance prior to his becoming acquainted with Gomara's work.

[2] For what follows see *Iggeret oreḥot olam*, passim and especially pp. 2a and 28b. See Moses A. Shulvass, *Kirjath Sepher* 23:73 ff. about a copy of chapter 11, in which the anonymous copyist introduced certain changes to adapt it to his needs. Detailed information on Farissol can be found in S. Bamberger's Introduction to Farissol's *Commentary on Ecclesiastes, Kobez al jad*, N. S. 2:3 ff.

Farissol also used to gather information from Near Eastern visitors who happened to come to Ferrara, where he lived.

A by-product of the emergence of a geographical literature was the development of a Hebrew geographical terminology. The initial lack of such a terminology is illustrated by the fact that throughout his travelogue Meshullam da Volterra employed almost exclusively Italian navigational and geographical terminology in Hebrew transliteration. Other writers did use many Hebrew terms. While it has not been possible to investigate whether or not all or some of this terminology had appeared in the Hebrew literature of earlier generations, it is germane to note some of them. Joseph Hacohen, for example, used *megillot malaḥut* for sea charts, while Farissol employed *kelaf baale malaḥim* for the same term. Meshullam called a continent *ereẓ ḳayemet*, and many more descriptive forms can be found among various writers. Joseph Hacohen who was familiar with orderly procedure, appended a Spanish-Hebrew geographical dictionary taken from de Gomora's work to the end of his book.

Geographic names were generally copied phonetically from the Italian. However, in line with what was evidently the style of the time, attempts were made to lend a Hebraic sound and meaning to the Italian geographic names. The name of the peninsula *Italia* was patriotically interpreted as *I-tal-Yah*, the island (blessed with) God's dew. In this manner they referred to Cremona as *Ḳiryah neemanah, Faithful City* (comp. Isaiah 1:21), to Montalcino as *Har-El-Zion*, Mount of the God of Zion. Similarly, Bologna, like *Italia*, was divided into three words: *Bah-lan-Yah*, God dwells there. Such attempts can be found throughout the literature of the Period.

CHAPTER SEVEN

PHILOSOPHY AND PHILOSOPHERS

Contrary to what might be anticipated, philosophical thought among Italian Jews did not attain special significance. The men of the Renaissance were concerned primarily with scientific areas that were pragmatically oriented, philology and the social sciences, insofar as they might enrich everyday life. The moderate attitudes that directed Jewish cultural life could assert themselves without profound philosophical speculation. The contemporary Jew was not troubled by perplexities that would impel him to search for answers through philosophical inquiry.

Although the attitude to philosophy as a discipline was positive in general, some opposition could be noticed. The kabbalist Elijah Ḥayim da Genazzano, who was decisively opposed to any Jewish rapprochement with Renaissance culture, complained bitterly about "those who stuffed their bellies with Greek teachings and changed the words of the living God into vanity". He told his readers that Moses da Rieti regretted having composed his philosophical poem *Mikdash meat*. He also believed that Maimonides abandoned philosophy and turned instead to Kabbalah. According to him the study of Kabbalah must replace philosophy.[1] Jehiel ben Samuel da Pisa, author of *Minḥat kenaot*, held similar views. He suggested Nachmanides' commentary on the Pentateuch "from whose mouth we live", as a substitute for philosophy. On one occasion he advised that "whosoever desires to remove the mask of blindness from his face, should pay heed to the words of Rabbi (Moses) Nachmani".[2] A more conciliatory opposition to philosophy was maintained by Rabbi Obadiah Sforno in his work *Or amim*. He did not believe that the Jewish religion is opposed to philosophical inquiry, but he felt that philosophy could not resolve the doubts within the human soul. Only incessant preoccupation with Torah could guide man in the right and useful direction.[3] Other writers merely opposed the extreme views of some philosophers which, they felt, contradicted the fundamentals of Judaism. An example of this latter view can be found in the ban by Messer Leon, himself a brilliant thinker, upon Gersonides' *Sefer hatoaliyot*.[4]

---

[1] *Iggeret ḥamudot* by Rabbi Elijah Ḥayim of Genazzano, London 1912, p. 4.

[2] See *Minḥat kenaot*, Berlin 1898, p. 26.

[3] *See Zinberg*, vol. 4, p. 126 ff.

[4] See Moses A. Shulvass, *In the Grip of Centuries*, p. 56 ff.

An attempt to prove the legitimacy of philosophical pursuits was made by the celebrated thinker Elijah del Medigo in his work *Beḥinat hadat*. Elijah was opposed to Kabbalah and was critical of the *Zohar*. He tried to demonstrate from the Scriptures that not only was there no prohibition of philosophical speculation, but it was, in fact, commendable and useful. To be sure, he too admitted that such pursuit was not an explicit commandment and whenever Torah and philosophy clashed he too relied upon the Torah.[1] Immanuel of Rome voiced the principal Renaissance motto in praise of philosophy: accept the truth whatever its source. In his commentary on Proverbs he attacked "the fools" who say that "we have no share in philosophy, for it is the fruit of the sophistry of Aristotle and other heretics like him who did not believe in our Torah". He argued that in ancient times the Rabbis were in possession of all wisdom, but their writings were lost due to the Exile. He believed that king Solomon was versed in the natural sciences, in metaphysics, and in the other disciplines later taught by Plato and Aristotle. He was certain that the discipline of logic did not distort man's mind. On the contrary, it sharpened the thought and served as a sort of vestibule into the world of wisdom.[2]

The generally friendly attitude of most thinkers and writers made philosophy a legitimate discipline. Moses Rieti described ancient philosophy in exalted terms in the first part of his great poem *Mikdash meat*. The principal Jewish philosophical work created in Italy during the Renaissance, *Dialoghi di amore* by Leone Ebreo (Abravanel), was written specifically for Jews. Whenever the author referred to Maimonides or Solomon Ibn Gabirol or some other Jewish thinker he added the word "our". Most Jewish libraries of the Period contained many philosophical works, and all Jewish printers

---

[1] For the views of Elijah del Medigo see his work *Beḥinat hadat*, Vienna 1833; Julius Guttmann's study in *Israel Abrahams Memorial Volume*, p. 195 and *Zinberg, op. cit.*, p. 42 ff.

[2] See the interesting selection of Immanuel's commentary on Proverbs in M. Guedemann, *Geschichte des Erziehungswesens und der Kultur der abendlaendischen Juden*, vol. 2, Vienna 1884, p. 110 ff.

published philosophical books. The Riva di Trento publishing house specialized in works of this genre.[1]

The main source of knowledge for Renaissance Italian Jewish thinkers was the philosophical literature of Spanish Jewry. Most of them followed Maimonides and Aristotelian philosophy.[2] Italian Jews particularly admired Maimonides' Book of Knowledge and his introductions to the Sayings of the Fathers and to chapter Ḥelek (of Tractate Sanhedrin). Early in the fourteenth century these writings became an integral part of the Maḥazor, according to the Roman rite. The great admiration for Maimonides was clearly expressed in Immanuel's *Maḥbarot*. He tells his patron that he had studied the writings of Maimonides in his youth "for he (Maimonides) was faithful to wisdom and a light searching out every dark and hidden (problem)". He concludes in his usual way with an epigram:

"The works of the master are like queens,
the works of others (like) concubines".

Simultaneously, broad segments of the Jewish population came under the influence of an ascetic Christian movement that originated in Umbria. While this trend did not nullify the Maimonidean influence, it did strengthen the position of books of an ascetic orientation such as *Ḥobot halebabot* and others of this genre. Immanuel himself was influenced by this literature and drew upon it for many poetic motifs and metaphors. As the Period progressed, the ascetic trend among Italian Jews weakened and did not awaken again until the end of the sixteenth century. Thus Maimonides' influence remained firm in the area of thought, as did his Code of Laws in the halakic field. The fifteenth century philosopher Elijah

[1] See, for example, *Dialoghi di amore*, Venice 1545, p. 96b: *Il nostro Rabi Moise*; also J. Bloch, *Hebrew Printing in Riva di Trento*, New York 1933, p. 7.

[2] For Italian Jewry's interest in Maimonides' philosophy see: Sonne, *Tarbiẓ* 5:326 ff.; the Introduction by Isaac Samuel Reggio to *Beḥinat hadat*; Steinschneider, *Allgemeine Einleitung in die juedische Literatur des Mittelalters*, Jerusalem 1938, p. 66; *Maḥberot Immanuel*, p. 326; Cassuto, *Ibid.*, p. 253 ff.

del Medigo faithfully followed Aristotle and Maimonides. He, like Maimonides, became involved in the problem of religious dogma, and similarly searched for a rationale for observance. There were also attempts made in Italy to write commentaries on the *Guide of the Perplexed*; close to end of the Period the *Guide* was translated into Italian by Jedidiah ben Moses of Recanati.

Also quite popular were the writings of Rabbi Jedaiah Hapenini. His work *Beḥinat olam*, widely read during the fifteenth and sixteenth centuries, was published about ten times before the close of the Period. His other work, *Iggeret hitnaẓlut* was so popular that Jehiel da Pisa made it the main target of his attack on philosophy.[1]

The two chief representatives of Renaissance Jewish philosophy Johanan Alemanno and Leone Ebreo did not follow this pattern and were decided Platonists. [2] Johanan Alemanno referred continually to Plato in his writings, claiming for him a legacy of ideas from the Prophets. Leone Ebreo, too, followed Platonic thought in all essential issues. Their main contribution lay in the stimulation of inquiry into issues that were not previously probed in Spanish Jewish philosophy. The problem of esthetics, which was extremely important for the Period's contemporaries, was central in Leone's thought, while the problem of attaining perfection, an equally significant subject for them, was central in the writings of Johanan Alemanno. Both believed that man's goal is to attain supreme harmony through desire, according to Johanan, or through love, according to Leone. Their works are the most brilliant expression of the Renaissance Jew's yearning for perfection. Of the two, *Dialoghi di amore* was the more popular, due parly to the author's fame, and partly to the

[1] See Sonne, *Kirjath Sepher* 15:267; Encyclopaedia Judaica, vol. 3, column 1215. Cf. *Minḥat ḳenaot*, passim.

[2] For Leone Abravanel and Johanan Alemanno see: *Encyclopaedia of Great Men in Israel* (Hebrew) vol. 2, p. 588 ff. and vol. 3, p. 720 ff.; H. Pflaum, *MGWJ* 72:344 ff.; *Zinberg*, vol. 4, p. 27 ff.; *Shaar haḥeshek*, Leghorn 1790, passim and especially p. 34a; for the influence of *Dialoghi di amore* on Renaissance Italian scholars see Sonne, *Tarbiẓ* 3:291. The Hebrew version of *Dialoghi* appeared in Lyck in 1871.

fact that it was first published in Italian, in the form of a dialogue.

Johanan Alemanno devoted many years to the composition of his voluminous works. *Ḥeshek Shelomoh* is a philosophical commentary on the Song of Songs. The actual commentary is preceded by a lengthy introduction and a discourse which describes the virtues of King Solomon. The work is fundamentally a lengthy treatise on the perfect personality. A sort of continuation to *Ḥeshek Shelomo* is his other work *Ḥe haolamim*, in which Alemanno shows the road leading to perfection. The author follows man's life from birth through maturity and teaches him how to plan in every age and circumstance for the attainment of perfection. He then discusses the means of improving one's dispositions and revealing hidden talents in man's soul.

Johanan Alemanno was not an original thinker. However, he was erudite in medieval Jewish and Arabic philosophy, as well as in the classical literature. He maintained friendly relations with several great Italian humanists and, especially, with Giovanni Pico della Mirandola. In the Introduction to *Ḥeshek Shelomo* he gave a superb description of the "seven precious qualities" of the Florentines which equipped them for the political role that their city-state fulfilled in Renaissance Italy. This description is among the finest political discourses in our earlier literature.

Leone Ebreo was an immigrant from Spain and in his teachings was a last glimmer of Spanish Jewish philosophy. Deeply affected by the Renaissance, Leone turned towards Neo-Platonism, the most genuine philosophical expression of the time. The concept of love was the pivot of his philosophical system and through it he attempted to respond to the quests of the time. Leone believed that from his concept of love would result a clarification of the idea of God and a direction for the relationship of man to his creator and to his fellow man. The idea of immortality was also part of his system, blending well with the admiration of the excellent personality that was so prevalent in the Renaissance.

Renaissance philosophers highly valued the *Dialoghi di*

amore. The book was widely read and exerted a strong influence on sixteenth and seventeenth century Hebrew literature. It was also frequently quoted by rabbinic authors under the name of "Philo" and "Sophia", the two participants in the dialogue. Leone's interpretation of ancient Greek legends was greatly appreciated by his contemporaries. A tradition dating back to the second half of the sixteenth century asserts that another philosophical work by Leone Ebreo entitled *De coeli harmonia* was in the possession of his grandson in Salonica. There are no traces of this work, nor is anything known of its contents.

CHAPTER EIGHT

MEDICAL SCIENCE AND PHYSICIANS

Jewish involvement in the medical sciences prior to the Emancipation is a well-known fact. In general, the number of Jewish physicians rose wherever and whenever a rapprochement existed between Jews and gentiles. Increased Christian confidence in the Jewish physician created favorable conditions for Jews to study the art of medicine.

Renaissance Italy was one of the countries where the Jewish physicians attained a very high professional and social status. The partial acceptance of Jews by the humanists and the existence of a great medical school in Padua were responsible for the relatively high number of Jewish physicians. The practice to exempt medics from the obligation of wearing the distinctive Jewish clothes also drew Jews into the medical profession. Indeed, the physicians were integrated into the Renaissance society more than any other Jewish class.

The number of Jewish physicians on the island of Sicily was even larger than on the Italian mainland.[1] The available statistics indicate that the Sicilian Jewish doctors outnumbered those of the mainland three to one.[2] The phenomenon is the

[1] *Lagumina*, vol. i, pp. 69-77.
[2] Cf. Steinschneider's list, *HB*, vol. 17, which includes the names of 1542 Jewish physicians, of whom more than two hundred and forty are from Italy and Sicily. Steinschneider's information is based on data in *Lagumina* and *Vogelstein-Rieger*. He also added some information from manuscripts.

more remarkable, since the rapprochement of Jews and gentiles on the island was never as significant as on the mainland.[1] It is possible that here old traditions of Jewish involvement in the science of medicine have survived from the times of Moslem domination over Sicily.

Although only two hundred and fifty Jewish physicians are known, their number was no doubt larger.[2] About one tenth of the physicians lived during the fourteenth century and the rest were equally divided between the fifteenth and sixteenth centuries. The number of Jewish physicians diminished rapidly in the latter half of the sixteenth century as a result of Church opposition (see below). The period of greatest expansion in the medical field among Italian Jews thus was between 1450 and 1550, that is, the era in which Jewish-Christian rapprochement reached its peak.

The Jewish physicians practiced in many cities, towns, and villages. Their greatest concentration, however, was in the city of Rome. Most of them were either court physicians of the popes and cardinals or authors of medical works. Municipalities of smaller towns used to invite Jewish physicians [3] to their locales under contracts that resembled the *condotte* between cities and Jewish bankers (see above, section III, chapter 1). In some places a sort of physicians dynasties existed that continued in the medical profession for several generations. Jewish women doctors are also known to have practiced in Renaissance Italy. Jewish dentists are periodically mentioned as well.[4] Jewish physicians were also hired to

---

[1] Cf. the picture of Jewish-Christian relations in Sicily given by Rabbi Obadiah da Bertinoro in *Iggerot Erez Yisrael*, p. 104 ff. No doubt, many more names of physicians are recorded in hitherto unused manuscript sources.

[2] Most of the data regarding Jewish physicians in Italy is found in Harry Friedenwald, *The Jews and Medicine*, Baltimore 1944, pp. 551-612.

[3] See David dei Pomis' Introduction to his *Zemah David*, also available in *Neppi-Ghirondi*. See *Ibid.*, pp. 88-89.

[4] The most prominent medical "dynasty" was the Portaleone family. See Vittore Colorni, *Annuario di studi ebraici* 1:169 ff. The family's genealogical table (*Ibid.*, p. 182) lists twelve physicians among eighteen persons. Female physicians were found in various

accompany armies into the battlefield.[1] The *condottieri* maintained military forces on a permanent basis, and a number of Jewish physicians must have been employed in their service.

The social status and high income of the Jewish physicians, which by far exceeded that of the humanists, did not prevent strife and harmful competition among them. The literary quarrels among the humanists were often noisy, but most of the time rather harmless. Competition among doctors, however, sometimes even lead to bloodshed. In 1408 the physician Moses of Tivoli was murdered by another physician, Elijah ben Shabbetai, who resented his success. Similarly, Leon da Modena's grandfather Mordecai was poisoned by other doctors "because they envied him".[2] Indeed, the corrupt morals of the Renaissance affected Jewish physicians too.

At first Jewish physicians obtained their knowledge by studying medical texts and by serving as apprentices of practicing doctors. Immanuel of Rome in his poem placed practitioners who did not study the medical books in the *inferno* and labeled them "false physicians" (Job 13:4), for they deceived the public and endangered human life.[3] Jewish medical students had at their disposal a fairly rich medical literature in Hebrew (see below). A Hebrew translation of Avicenna's *Canon of Medicine*, one of the principal medieval medical texts, was published in Naples in 1492. Also Vesalius in his work that appeared in 1549 included many Hebrew medical terms in Hebrew characters.

Beginning with the early sixteenth century the majority of Jewish physicians received their training in universities. One of the aims of the Jewish university founded by David Provenzal in Mantua was the preparation of students for study in

places in Sicily, and in Trento and Fano. There were Jewish dentists at the court of the Sforzas, rulers of Lombardy.

[1] See the responsum of Rabbi Azriel Diena published in *Kirjath Sepher* 15:127.

[2] See *Natali*, p. 182 and *Sepher Chaje Jehuda*, p. 11. To be sure, Leon da Modena does not state specifically that those who poisoned his grandfather were Jews. He blamed "the city's physicians".

[3] *Mahberot Immanuel*, p. 826.

medical schools. The leading medical school was in Padua. [1] At first it was difficult for Jews to receive the doctor's degree since it was conferred by the local bishop in the course of a religious ceremony. However, later the Venetian Republic appointed a special official who was authorized to confer the doctoral degree upon candidates of other faiths. Jewish students used to pay a higher tuition fee than their Christian colleagues and were also obliged to give various gifts to Christian student organizations. Nevertheless, more than eighty Jewish students completed their medical studies in Padua in the period between 1517-1619. To be sure, many of them were foreign students. Jewish students also studied medicine at the universities of Siena, Pisa, Perugia, and Ferrara. Many Jewish students, including some from Padua, came to study at the university of Ferrara under its famous teacher Antonio Musa Brasavola. [2] There were only few Jewish professors of medicine, as the number of Jews on university faculties was generally insignificant (see above, section III, chapter 4). Most of the Jewish professors of medicine were Spanish immigrants. [3]

Italian Jewish doctors wrote fewer medical books in Hebrew than did their colleagues in other countries. [4] Most Renaissance Jews understood Italian well and did not need medical literature in Hebrew. Moreover, some Jewish writers wrote medical books in Latin to make them accessible to Jews and gentiles alike. Abraham Portaleone, for example, wrote such a book and included in it a variety of medical instructions, as well as correspondence with Christian physicians. [5] On the other hand, several scholars at the beginning of the Period translated various medical works into Hebrew from Latin. [6] Additional Hebrew medical works

[1] See the important documents published in *Ciscato*, pp. 297-307 and by Friedenwald, *Ibid*.

[2] See Kaufmann, *Gesammelte Schriften*, vol. 3, p. 276.

[3] See *RMI* 7:411; *Cenni storici*, p. 53; *Natali*, p. 189.

[4] This is the impression one obtains from Harry Friedenwald's *The Jews and Medicine*.

[5] See *Shilte hagibborim*, p. 185b.

[6] See Friedenwald, *Ibid.*, p. 179 and *Magazin fuer die Wissenschaft des Judentums* 10:103 ff. and 160 ff.

of the Period are extant in manuscripts. A popular description of the various areas of medicine is found in Gedaliah Ibn Jachia's *Shalshelet hakabbalah*.[1]

The largest category of Hebrew medical literature were the manuals of prescriptions and remedies. Such manuals sometimes included hundreds of prescriptions for all kinds of diseases. One manuscript with more than three hundred prescriptions was arranged by the copyist in alphabetical order. The copyist of another manuscript asserted that he tested his remedies on many patients. Abraham Portaleone also incorporated many prescriptions in his Hebrew work *Shilte hagibborim* and assured the reader that they were drawn from experience and not from (theoretical?) medical science. The nature of these folk remedies is well illustrated by the following: "And whosoever wears (on himself) a salted eye of a wolf will not be afflicted with eye diseases...." Joseph Hacohen, the historian-geographer who was also a physician, is the author of a medical book entitled *Mekiz Nirdamim*. The volume contains a Hebrew translation of a Spanish book of remedies in addition to the author's own medical advice. A special batch of prescriptions is provided for the treatment of venereal diseases, "the French malady" that was very widespread in those times.[2]

The legal position of the Jewish physician in Italy was not clearly defined. On the one hand, Jewish physicians were patronized, as we have seen, by various segments of Christian society, including popes, princes, and municipilaties. On the other hand, however, they were often subject to persecution, mainly by Church authorities. An illuminating example is found in the career of the physician David dei Pomis. He acted as municipal physician in Magliano and was invited by the city council of Chiusi to serve in a similar capacity; he

[1] Comp. *Ambrosiana Catalogue*, p. 26; Cassuto, *Florence*, p. 183 and p. 272. For the physician David da Ossana who wrote many medical works, see *Natali*, p. 189. For Jehiel Rehaviah Alatino see *Neppi-Ghirondi, Ibid.* Cf. *Shalshelet hakabbalah*, p. 113 ff.

[2] See Cassuto, *Ibid.*, p. 183 and pp. 188-189; *Catalogue Kaufmann*, p. 170 (Nos. 526-527); *Magazin, Ibid.*, p. 166 ff.; *Shilte hagibborim*, p. 51b; M. W. Bernstein, *Brands Plucked out of the Fire*, Buenos Aires 1956, pp. 183-185.

was also the private doctor of the Orsini and Sforza families. However, when he came to settle in Chiusi the local bishop began to harass him. David thereupon appealed to Pope Pius IV who responded to his request and annulled the ban that the bishop had issued upon his practice. To the physician's misfortune the pope died about a week later, and Pius V who replaced him "renewed the decrees and ordinances of Paul IV" (against the Jewish medical profession). David dei Pomis remained without a position, and for the rest of his life he was left "as the chased gazelle, and as sheep that no man gather-eth" (Isaiah 13:14).[1] The decrees of Paul IV and the opposi-tion of other churchmen to the Jewish physicians resulted from the fear that they might exert religious influence upon Christian patients. The Church admitted this openly, and in order to discredit the Jewish physicians, it also circulated the false accusation that they had poisoned Christian patients. To be sure, at first the ban of Pope Paul IV was not universally observed and city councils continued to appoint Jews as municipal doctors. There were even popes who did not abide by Paul's ban. Gradually, however, the boycott of Jewish physicians spread more and more and became fully effective when Pope Gregory XIII confirmed it in a special bull in 1581.

David dei Pomis, who had personally experienced the effects of the anti-Jewish policy of Paul IV, thereupon under-took a defence of Jewish medical practice. In a small Latin treatise, De medico Hebreo, published in 1588, he made a literary effort to defend himself and his colleagues. He tried to convince the Christian world that the Jewish physician did not commit all those cruel acts of which he was suspect. He argued that the Jewish religion did not permit its adherents to act unethically; that the Jew, a descendant of the patriarch Abraham, was a compassionate person. He cited the names of Jews who attained widespread fame as personal physicians to popes and as authors of important medical works. He concluded the treatise with a prayer that the Christian

[1] See his autobiography in Neppi-Ghirondi, Ibid. For the campaign against Jewish physicians, see: Tarbiz 2:345 (Sonne); JQR 32:229, 239, 248; Roth, Venice, p. 186.

princes would protect their Jewish subjects who were always loyal to them. The argument of the learned physician and linguist was not very effective. Only where the local rulers stood in opposition to the popes, were Jewish physicians able to continue to practice in Italy without harassment.

CHAPTER NINE

THE SCIENCES

a.

The Jew of the Renaissance evinced a deep interest also in sciences other than medicine. They constituted an important element in his aspiration to know the world about him. One of the characters in the comedy *Ẓaḥut bediḥuta deḳiddushin* asserts that besides the mysteries of the Torah man has also to know the nature of all creation in order to attain happiness, success and honor. A contemporary letter expressed the enthusiasm that gripped a Renaissance Jew when he saw the "wonders" of water jets that were installed on the occasion of a wedding in Ferrara. He was enchanted by the technical devices used to operate the jets. The same enthusiasm for the sciences was expressed in lofty words by Moses Rieti in his poem *Miḳdash meat*. While he presented the pantheon of the Jewish sages in a chapter called "The Palace", the sciences are described in a chapter named "The Vestibule". The implication is clear: In order that a Jew may be worthy to enter the palace of Torah, he has first to attain proficiency in the sciences.[1]

Of the various sciences, mathematic and astronomy were the most popular among Jews. The number of Hebrew manuscripts of mathematical and astronomical works copied for private libraries during the Period is quite impressive. Immanuel of Rome characterized one of his contemporaries Benjamin bar Judah as "the head of all scholars in arithmetic and geometry". Various Jewish scientists prepared astrono-

---

[1] See *Ẓaḥut bediḥuta deḳiddushin*, p. 31; *Zion*, N. S. 17:154; *Miḳdash meat*, p. 11 ff.

mical charts and instructed how to build sundials. More
comprehensive works in these two areas were also composed
during the Period.[1] An interest in chemistry was shown by
Abraham Portaleone. In his work *Shilte hagibborim* we find
a lengthy discourse on the various types of salt and their
origin, as well as a prescription for the production of artificial
salt. He also instructs how to mix the Temple oil and how to
manufacture ink.[2]

b.

Renaissance Jews also had the opportunity to learn more
about vegetation and animal life than earlier generations. To
begin with, dogs and other animals, as well as birds were often
kept in Jewish homes. Even more familiar with the animal
world were the Jewish hunters. The many drawings of animals
and birds that appeared in printed Hebrew books further
contributed to the popularization of the animal world. Leon da
Modena's treatise *Ẓemaḥ ẓaddiḳ* which tried to explain human
qualities by comparing them to those of animals and birds, is
filled with drawings of animal life. Periodically, Italian Jews
had an opportunity to see animals that were brought from
oriental countries for the zoos of the nobility.[3]

Animals and vegetation occupied ample space in Renaissance literature and the same holds true of the Hebrew
writings of the Period.[4] Abraham Farissol's book *Iggeret oreḥot
olam* is filled with accounts of animals and vegetation. Birds,
animals, and the agricultural produce of the Spanish colonies
in the New World are described in Joseph Hacohen's geographical work. Here too, Abraham Portaleone surpassed
all others. Discussing the incense used in the Temple service,

[1] *Maḥberot Immanuel*, p. 354; *Catalogue Kaufmann*, p. 167, No.
508; Cassuto, *Florence*, p. 272 and p. 352; Roth, *History*, p. 200;
Berliner, *Gesammelte Schriften*, vol. 1, pp. 123-124; *Vogelstein-Rieger*,
vol. 2, p. 81 ff.
[2] *Shilte hagibborim*, pp. 77, 97, and 181.
[3] See *Maḥberot Immanuel*, p. 42; *Ẓemaḥ ẓaddiḳ*, Venice 1600.
The drawings found in the first edition are reproduced in the new
edition that appeared in Tel-Aviv in 1949.
[4] *Iggeret oreḥot olam*, Chapter 21 and passim; *Shilte hagibborim*,
pp. 53, 56, 83 ff.

he made an effort to identify many plants mentioned in the Bible. In his research he made full use of the contemporary botanical literature, at a time when other Jewish writers still drew their essential information from ancient authors. Abraham also offered in his book quite a systematic description of the animal world. He catalogued the animals according to their bodily characteristics and then described in detail each family; this was followed by a dissertation on the animal world in remote countries. And again, Abraham concluded his research with an effort to identify certain animal names mentioned in Scriptures.

THE RENAISSANCE IN DAILY LIFE

CHAPTER ONE

RENAISSANCE MAN IN JEWISH GARB

Renaissance man's inner life was very complicated. On the one hand, he liberated himself from many limitations imposed by medieval society. He began to observe reality with open eyes and tried to understand it to the best of his ability. On the other hand, he faced new challenges as he tried to reproduce the ancient world and its way of life. His soul was a battleground of medieval social, cultural, and religious values seeking continuity under new conditions.

Out of the conflict of these contradictory forces emerged the Man of the Renaissance. Renaissance man has been extensively described by students of the Period, and new light is still being thrown on various aspects of his personality. Most scholars see him primarily as a man with extremist inclinations and flaming passions that gave rise to both the good and the beautiful and the evil and corrupt in the Renaissance world. Common to all Renaissance men was a lack of inner serenity and an inability to overcome passions. Although his aspiration was to attain perfection in body and spirit, the Period was filled with deeds of cruelty and crime that are frightening in their extremism. But equally striking were his achievements in statecraft, science, literature, and art. Either way he shunned mediocre accomplishment and strove for the extraordinary, reaching the heights of creativity or sinking to the depths of debasement.

This type of Renaissance man was prevalent among the Jews as well. To be sure, only rarely did a Jew's degradation reach the depth of moral corruption that existed in gentile society. But neither did the Jew's cultural and artistic creativity parallel that of his Christian neighbors. Jews accepted the Weltanschauung and the culture of the Renaissance cautiously. Jewish religious fundamentals and vestiges of Jewish separatistic tendencies prevented the Renaissance Jew from following his gentile comrade to the extreme outer limit. But he too had developed the essential attitudes without which Renaissance man would have been basically impossible: courage, and a readiness to attain the desired goal at any cost.

Throughout the Period a number of men appeared on the Jewish scene whose attitude to individuals and the community was aggressive and violent. Most of them came from the ranks of the bankers and the humanists. Humanists often assisted their patron bankers by providing them with propagandistic and legal materials to be used in their frequent disputes and quarrels with their adversaries and the community. When the great controversy erupted in Padua between the banker Herz Wertheim and Rabbi Judah Minz over the ark cover with figures in relief (see above section VII, chapter 1) "he (Herz Wertheim), through his wealth, found rabbis to assist him... and he forcibly placed it (the ark cover) in the synagogue, and the old man (Rabbi Judah Minz) left in anger, and strife increased greatly because of these events..."[1] The tycoon Immanuel Norsa was notorious for his violent actions during a period of forty years "and even achieved his ends with non-Jews as well". Similarly violent was the banker Jonathan Finzi of Reggio. He conducted his business affairs ruthlessly and was perpetually scheming against his enemies. His sons were also corrupt men. A document relating to two Jewish brothers in Macerata who were engaged in all sorts of shady acts and swindling, tells what motivated them: "And they themselves used to boast afterwards to non-Jews, we did thus and so, so that they should become known as shrewd people and as men who succeed in everything, and they were proud and boastful of their success".[2]

The passion to be the winner perpetually drove people

---

[1] *Responsa Abeḳat roḳel* by Rabbi Joseph Karo, No. 65.

[2] See: *Sefer hapesaḳim*, Venice 1519, p. 7b; Sonne, *Hatekufah* 32-33:651; *Balletti*, p. 20 ff. Balletti's description is based upon documents that he found in various archives.

to become involved in strife and dispute that sometimes extended over decades and caused a great deal of hardship to many of the participants. Leon da Modena relates that his father and uncle quarreled over their father's inheritance for more than thirty-two years. In the town of Montagnana no public religious services were held for years because of strife among the congregants. Abraham Minz, the son of Rabbi Judah Minz, was known to be a quarrelsome man. His actions provoked such anger that once, after he had offended Rabbi Jacob Margalit, he was afraid that Rabbi Jacob's students would attack him physically. Rabbi Judah Minz was thereupon compelled "to assemble all the community leaders and have that son (Abraham)...seek...forgiveness after the death of the forementioned man of piety (Rabbi Jacob Margalit)".[1] Like the individual, a community also sometimes used questionable methods to achieve its ends. When Rabbi Obadiah da Bertinoro arrived in Palermo en route to the Holy Land and preached in the synagogue, the community was so impressed that they were determined to retain him there at any cost. "They hired advisers to mislead me", Rabbi Obadiah relates, "and they lied to me..."[2]

The desire to win at any cost also led Renaissance people into the widespread use of trickery and to a morbid drive for vengeance upon their foes. The vengeance of the Renaissance man, according to Burckhardt,[3] was not simple and crude, but had to result from refined plot and simultaneously evoke the admiration of the people, as in the case of the brothers from Macerata. Immanuel of Rome maintained:

> "When did King David demonstrate astuteness?
> When he acted the fool before Abimelech" (comp. Psalms 34: 1)

He also knew the taste of Renaissance style vengeance and wrote:

[1] See: *Sepher Chaje Jehuda*, pp. 13, 16; *Sefer hapesakim*, p. 29b.
[2] *Iggerot Erez Yisrael*, p. 107.
[3] p. 327. See the section on Religion and Morality, passim.

"And when they say: He is jealous and vengeful,
They mean: He is sharp and knows how to ensnare and
destroy his enemies".[1]

One of the finest short stories written in Hebrew during the Italian Renaissance employed the motif of use of trickery by both the villain and hero. This short story found in Abraham Jaghel Gallichi's *Ge ḥizzayon*,[2] tells of a man who fell in love with a married woman loyal to her husband. He slyly murdered the husband and hoped to win the affections of the widow. However, the woman was also adept at Renaissance style trickery and engineered a refined vengeance upon her husband's murderer.

Resolution and courage led Renaissance Jews to worthy and noble acts as well. David Reubeni found Jews in Rome and elesewhere in Italy who were "strong", and "had lions' hearts in everything". Such courage was demonstrated by Italian Jews even decades later. When the policy of oppression was proclaimed by Pope Paul IV, it was accompanied by acts of provocation and derision by Christian officials and numerous apostates. In those days sheer courage impelled the Jews of Recanati to forcibly eject from the synagogue an apostate who had entered on the Day of Atonement carrying a cross. Equally revealing is the incident involving a group of Jews who were summoned before one of the kings and were ordered to remove their hats. They refused even though Italian Jews were not very strict in observing the practice of head covering.[3]

Individuals, too, stood up fearlessly and courageously to government officials of all ranks. Joseph Hacohen ventured to severely reprimand the doge of Genoa for his refusal to release a captured Jewish lad without ransom. "...Look and see my Lord", Joseph Hacohen told him, "money is only ephemeral, if offers no salvation". During the dire days of Paul IV a poor Jew in a small village knew how to defend himself properly against a papal official who called him a dog. In

---

[1] *Maḥberot Immanuel*, pp. 44, 176.
[2] *Ge ḥizzayon*, p. 13b ff.
[3] See: *Sippur David hareubeni*, p. 43; *Emek habaka*, p. 137; *REJ* 10:184.

Casale Monferrato a Jewish woman, her son, and another man were imprisoned because they dared to protest against the crude behavior of an antisemitic official and refused to address him by his title when they faced him. Finally, when Paul IV died and the Roman mob who disliked him started to desecrate his memory, Jews also participated fearlessly in this act. One of them even placed the yellow hat, which Roman Jews were obliged to wear, upon the head of a statue of the pope.[1]

This unusual courage was rooted in the Renaissance attitude which overlooked an individual's origin and social status and was prepared to accept him on the basis of personal contribution and his human worth. The Jew's sense of pride was also reinforced by the *condotta*. In these contracts between Jews and various governmental bodies, both signatories appear as equal parties. The *condotta* so completely filled Jewish social, religious, and communal needs,[2] that it contributed a great deal to the emergence of a proud Jew, free of any sense of inferiority. The character of this Jew who was fully aware of his strength and shortcomings was clearly expressed in the will of Leon da Modena, the most representative Renaissance figure: "...I ask of you, do not overly praise me, only state that I was not a hypocrite, but always sincere, that I was God fearing and shunned sin in private more than in public..."[3]

CHAPTER TWO

SUPERSTITION AND WITCHCRAFT

Courage and self esteem did not free Renaissance man from the bonds of a complex system of superstitious belief. Elements of ancient and new superstitions joined to implant in his psyche a belief in hidden powers that shaped his fate. We have seen (section V) how superstitions, especially the belief in the stars, muddled the Renaissance Jew's religious outlook and justified for him his transgressions and the evil inclinations in his soul. Superstition was equally potent in other areas of life.

[1] See: *Dibre hayamim*, Section 2, p. 47b; *Tarbiz* 2:478, 487 ff. (Sonne); Foa, *Monferrato*, p. 13; *Natali*, p. 151.
[2] See, for example, *Balletti*, p. 20 ff. and *Ciscato*, p. 26.
[3] *Sepher Chaje Jehuda*, p. 69.

The intensity of Jewish involvement in superstition and magic is indicated by the fact that many intellectuals were among their adherents. Leon da Modena relates that his father "was terrified by the constellation that warred against him and he was never able to make a decision..." In these circumstances it is not surprising that when speaking of himself Leon stated: "From my youth I desired to learn from astrologers what, according to the time of my birth, would befall me during my lifetime and how long I would live". His teacher Samuel Archivolti believed "that all numbers up to ten were lucky", and tried to prove that the letter *bet* contained no evil connotation. The belief in the existence of ghosts was also widespread among the scholars. Abraham Farissol believed that in the Northern countries "satyrs danced" (comp. Isaiah 13:21) and Jehiel Nisim da Pisa asserted that ghosts do exist and that "the facts (told) about them are not a matter of nonsense and fantasy". Farissol also seems to have regretted that the art of witchcraft was not sufficiently widespread among Italian Jewry. Abraham Portaleone propagated the belief that precious stones possessed wondrous properties. He was of the opinion that if, Heaven forbid, Jews did not believe this they would be regarded by Christians as lacking in faith. Portaleone believed that whosoever wore a jewel on his left arm would vanquish his enemies, the mighty giants, and evil beasts, and would also be protected from witchcraft, fear, and trembling. "And it will benefit one who seeks peace and pursues it, and will also help him to attain wealth".[1] It seems that most Jewish intellectuals were only doubtful about the legitimacy of one area—astrology. Very few Jewish scholars served as astrologers for kings and princes of the Italian states. Hebrew astrological literature was quite meager and could in no way compare to the abundant Christian astrological literature.[2]

The reservations about astrology did not deter the Italian

[1] See: *Sepher Chaje Jehuda*, pp. 19, 35; *Arugat habosem*, p. 28b; Mattathias Mieses, *Yivo Bleter* 13:152; *Iggeret orehot olam*, p. 4b and p. 24a; *Minhat kenaot*, p. 50; *Shilte hagibborim*, pp. 46a and 49a.
[2] For Jewish astrologers see *Schiavi*, p. 504 and *Ferorelli*, p. 116, Note 1 and p. 120. Cassuto *Florence*, p. 264.

Jew from trying to learn what the future held for him by
other means, such as palmistry and physiognomy. Gedaliah
Ibn Jachia wrote a special book "to interpret all the various
lines of a person's hands and face". Another historian, Joseph
Hacohen, believed that God revealed to him in a dream the
fate of the emperor's navy that had embarked to battle
against the Turks and "his prophecy" was also fulfilled.
Leon da Modena utilized the occult potentialities of dream
divination for personal needs. When one of his relatives was
proposed to him as a wife, he sought through a dream "to see
the woman who was predestined to be my mate. I dreamed
that an old man held me by the hand and led me to a wall
upon which was a sketched figure with a curtain over it, and
when he removed the cover I saw the image of my cousin
Esther and the color of her garments. As I gazed upon her,
the form changed and another one appeared in its stead,
which I did not clearly see". The latter figure was, of course,
that of Rachel whom Leon da Modena married after her older
sister Esther to whom he was engaged, died prior to their
marriage.[1]

It seems that the most widespread category of superstition
was witchcraft in all its ramifications. Even scholars like
Azariah dei Rossi and Abraham Portaleone believed in the
powers of witchcraft. The fear of witchcraft was so intense
that the Italiani followed a standard procedure of a double
marriage ceremony, first in a closed room in the presence of
witnesses but without a *minyan*, "because of the danger of
witches", and then a second time in public. Gedaliah Ibn
Jachia devoted an entire chapter in *Shalshelet hakabbalah* to
witchcraft, and expressed his conviction that the art of
witchery consisted of "a thorough erudition in the science of
nature and astrology". Even as original a thinker as Johanan
Alemanno wrote a special treatise in which he tried to analyse
this "science" theoretically and to explain and justify the
elaborate system of talismans linked with it.[2]

[1] See: *Shalshelet hakabbalah*, p. 98; *Dibre hayamim*, part 2, p. 38b;
Sepher Chaje Jehuda, p. 21 ff.
[2] See: *Meor enayim*, Section *Imre binah*, p. 80 and Section *Mazref*

The number of Jews suspected of sorcery was considerable. According to Pietro Aretino, Roman harlots learned from female Jewish witches how to seduce men. Ortensio Landi tells of the magic demonstrated by a Jewish sorcerer. The protagonist in Lodovico Ariosto's comedy *The Sorcerer* was a Jewish immigrant from Castile. He operated in all social circles, deceived them all, stole their possessions, and often caused the destruction of entire families.[1] Obviously, such stories convinced Christian society that the Jewish community was full of witches and it sought to protect itself. Pope Pius V justified in part his order of expelling the Jews from the Papal States in 1569 on the grounds that the Jews engaged in magic. In Rome in 1592 Jews were explicitly banned from foretelling the future, while in Mantua, Judith Franchetti was burned at the stake in 1600 for the crime of sorcery, and "her disciple" Jacob Fano was sentenced to galley servitude. Thus, it is not surprising that in 1604 a Venetian Jewess tried to obtain a document from the rabbis attesting that she was not a witch. No doubt, the poor woman was suspected of having engaged in sorcery.[2]

Alchemy was a sort of illegitimate "science" that was closely linked with sorcery. Both Jews and Christians sought a method of extracting gold from cheap metals. Three generations of the da Modena family engaged in it and the results were consistently tragic. Leon's uncle, Shemaiah da Modena experimented in alchemy with a Christian. The Cristian duped him, stole his possessions, and finally murdered him. But this did not frighten Leon and he pursued "the foolishness of alchemy", enticed by a physician who later became a rabbi in Rome. Leon da Modena's most gifted son Mordecai met a tragic end when he "learned" from a priest how to extract silver from lead. The poisonous fumes of arsenic and the other

lakesef, p. 51; *Shalshelet hakabbalah*, p. 122 ff.; *Responsa of Rabbi Joseph Colon*, Cremona 1558, p. 141a (No. 170); *Kirjath Sepher* 5:273.

[1] See *Yivo Bleter*, *Ibid.*; Ariosto identifies the sorcerer as a Jew at the beginning of the second act.

[2] See: A. Bertolotti, *Gli ebrei a Roma*, Spoleto 1879, p. 262; *RMI* 9:236; *Leo Modenas Briefe*, p. 132 (No. 141).

chemicals that he used caused a severe sickness and subsequent death. But Leon da Modena persisted in the belief that his son knew how to extract silver from lead. Johanan Alemanno searched for the elixir through which it would be possible "to secure man's physical immortality". He, too, sought this through the aid of a Christian scholar.[1]

The belief in *dibbuḳim* and demons was also widely held. Gedaliah Ibn Jachia told at length about the soul of a Christian that had lodged in the body of a Jewish woman of Ferrara. He accompanied a group of distinguished men to observe this phenomenon and engaged the Christian soul in a lengthy conversation to learn from it what transpired in the hereafter, especially in Gehenna. "And I did not ask about the Garden of Eden", Gedaliah added, "because I knew that he did not come from there". Gedaliah assured his readers that he knew of other, even more amazing, events of this kind, such as what had transpired in Ancona where the spirits of people who were killed and hanged entered into human bodies. "Through incantations and blowing sulphur fumes and the like into the body's nostrils, the spirits would reveal their names and speak of themselves, what had befallen them, the place of their residence, and their sins..."

We have seen that scholars of the stature of Abraham Farissol and Jehiel Nisim da Pisa believed in the existence of demons. Other sages even exceeded them in the belief in demons and made them a subject of serious research. Rabbi Abraham Menachem da Porto was proud of having written "a treatise to prove the existence of demons" in which he disputed at length the opinion of philosophers, especially Giovanni Pico della Mirandola, who denied their existence. Johanan Alemanno went even further in a book that was recently discovered. This work contains lengthy discourses on practical Kabbala, angels, and demons. The author was thoroughly versed in the literature of magic and witchcraft.[2]

[1] See: *Sepher Chaje Jehuda*, pp. 12, 30, 34, and *Kirjath Sepher*, *Ibid.*, p. 274.
[2] See: *Shalshelet hakabbalah*, p. 128 ff.; *Minḥah belulah* by Rabbi Abraham Menahem Porto, Verona 1594, p. 201b; *Kirjath Sepher*, *Ibid.*

CHAPTER THREE

ASPIRATIONS AND MANNERS

From the depths of his spiritual complexity and life's entanglements into which his daring and extremism had led him, Renaissance man strove mightily to attain perfection in life and immortality afterwards. He destroyed the boundaries of the religious and social collective within which medieval man found his fulfilment, and became an individualist who established his own behavior pattern. The pursuit of perfection and happiness and the performance of acts that would set him apart from the mass and emphasize his individuality became his essential purpose. Many of the bizarre and discreditable acts by both Jews and Christians resulted from this desire to stand out from the gray mass.

These aspirations were common to most of the Jews of the Renaissance. Leon da Modena described his brother-in-law Moses as someone "who knew how to play an instrument, sing, and dance, and who possessed business acumen, wisdom, and the knowledge of books". In sum, he regarded him as a perfect personality. Special guides were written to instruct the Jew how to achieve perfection and ultimate bliss, and even Biblical exegesis was used for this purpose. Rabbi Isaac Arundi wrote his commentary on Job "because this is the most effective book that can serve man in the attainment of true perfection", and "shows what true human success is". The author of a guide for writing coded letters recommended his book as being useful "in managing the home, in political matters, and in matters of the soul". That is, everything must serve as a means of perfecting man's personality, successfully administering the household, and attaining a proper social position. Geḍaliah Ibn Jachia who sincerely believed in the immortality of the soul, dreamed of the attainment of "the soul's ultimate bliss in the world to come". He therefore wrote his book *Darke Noam* with the intention of "teaching man how to maintain the proper path throughout his lifetime, that he may merit ultimate bliss."[1] Significantly, those who

[1] See: *Sepher Chaje Jehuda*, p. 31; Introduction to *Sefer Zaphenath-*

dreamed of attaining ultimate happiness in temporal life, as well as those who only saw a possibility of its attainment in the world to come, used typical Renaissance concepts such as, "ultimate bliss", "benefit", and "true human success". For the Renaissance aspirations for perfection and success were very broadly conceived, and in their realm the inner desires of people of diverse character found a comfortable place.

The goal of personal perfection can be attained, taught the scholars of the Renaissance, through self-training. Immanuel of Rome greatly admired Job for his courage in facing his frightful ordeal. He maintained that this is why Job was referred to as *ish* rather than *adam* because "he had attained human perfection in its highest form..." The names of Job's parents were not mentioned "because he (Job) possessed nobility of character which is above noble ancestry". Gedaliah Ibn Jachia held a similar view. Addressing himself to his son he assured him that true nobility depends neither on wealth nor on "the length of the family's geneaology", but on the individual's own wisdom and knowledge. He therefore advised him "to conduct himself like the truly great men...."[1]

In describing the perfect man and the means of reaching perfection Jewish authors used as examples the lives of certain great personalities. Johanan Alemanno, like many of his contemporaries, regarded Lorenzo the Magnificent as the most perfect man who contributed to Renaissance culture very significantly. He was very enthusiastic about Lorenzo and the citizens of Florence, since "seven precious qualities are common to the people of this land". Paralleling the Christian Lorenzo the Magnificent was, in Johanan's view, King Solomon, the perfect Jew. In a long excursus he described the

paneah by Rabbi Menahem Cohen Porto, Ferrara 1557; *Shalshelet hakabbalah*, pp. 98, 175; *Ambrosiana Catalogue*, p. 20; Rabbi Isaac Arundi, it seems, lived in Italy. His book was printed in Italy by an Italian printer for Italian readers.

[1] See a fragment of Immanuel's *Commentary on Job* published by Pereau in his book *Intorno al comento inedito ... del Imanuel sopra Giobbe*, Corfu 1884, p. 7; the Hebrew noun *ish* (man) originates from a root with the connotation of strength. The other noun for "man", *adam*, refers to man's creation from dust. *Shalshelet hakabbalah*, p. 5.

political qualities that the perfect person might possess and
tried to prove that Solomon had them all. Johanan also
discussed human perfection in more theoretical and general
terms. He first traced the physical and spiritual development
of man from his youth to maturity. He then offered extensive
counsel in how a person should conduct himself at each stage
of his life in preparation of the attainment of perfection.[1]

A strong tendency toward pomp and solemnity accompanied
the desire for perfection and success. It by far surpassed the
desire for the beautification of everyday life (see above
section IV, chapter 3). Significantly, the North Italian Ashkenazim had a greater affinity for pomp than did the Italiani and
the Sephardim. The Italiani used to designate a great man or
a Talmudic sage in the manner of the Renaissance as *divino*.
But among the Ashkenazim this description was even applied
to an editor in a publishing house who did a competent and
faithful job. The Ashkenazim came to Italy from a country
where Jews did not have contacts with the gentile population
and its culture. They lived in ghettos devoid of external
beauty. When they arrived in Italy they therefore eagerly
turned to the rich life forms, and the craving for external
beauty was more articulate among them than among the
Italiani and the Sephardim. Thus it was the Ashkenazi
Joseph Castelfranco who ordered a copy of the Talmud on
extremely expensive parchment, and the Ashkenazi Hertz
Wertheim who undertook the construction of a synagogue
with gold covered walls.[2]

The predilection for pomp was further responsible for the
pursuit of all sorts of titles and degrees available in both
communities, the general and the Jewish. Wealthy Jews also
eagerly provided themselves with elaborate coats of arms.
The descendants of the few Jews who had the title of *cavaliere*
were very proud of it and mentioned it often. Many Jews
sought the degrees of Rabbi or *Ḥaber*, for they gave the

---

[1] See the excerpts from the Introductions to *Ḥe olamim* and *Ḥeshek
Shelomo* published in *REJ*, vol. 12; *Shaar haḥeshek*, Livorno 1790.

[2] See: *Leo Modenas Briefe*, p. 5; *Meor enayim*, Section *Imre binah*,
p. 130; A. M. Habermann, *Hamadpisim bene Soncino*, Vienna 1933,
p. 63; *REJ*, vol. 79, passim.

bearers the possibility of claiming a higher social status. This is well illustrated by an incident involving two impostors. One claimed that he was David Reubeni and had escaped from imprisonment by the Spaniards, while the other pretended to be an emissary from the Holy Land. Both also claimed to have the degree of *Ḥaber*, and when their connivery was exposed, the rabbis' first step was to divest them of this degree. The many attempts to annul the rabbinic degrees of rabbis of questionable conduct indicate that ordination carried important social prestige. This pursuit of titles evoked the scorn of Don Isaac Abravanel and he criticized the Italian Jews, and especially the Ashkenazim, "for ordaining one another". They did so, according to Don Isaac, because "they envied the practice of the gentiles to grant doctorates".[1]

A great deal of effort was lavished on the arrangement of funerals and the decoration of cemeteries. The Venetian cemetery, for example, was noted for its many elaborate tombstones. In his will Abraham Portaleone requested that his burial place be shaped like a room in which the casket should be placed, and forbade his family to cover it with earth. He was aware that his request would appear strange even in Renaissance society and pleaded with his sons to adhere to his wish. He concluded with the argument: "Let no one be astonished, because there is place for different attitudes". In his will Leon da Modena too asked of his sons to set up for him "a strong tombstone that would last the longest possible time". He composed an inscription for his tombstone when he was fifteen years old. In poverty ridden Sicily funerals assumed such a pompous character that an amazed visitor, Rabbi Obadiah da Bertinoro, considered them worth of a detailed description. The most lavish funeral, however, was that arranged by Rabbi Abraham Minz for his father Judah, the rabbi of Padua. Scores of rabbis and scholars surrounded the casket holding lighted torches, the walls of the room were covered with black drapery, shops were closed, and the

---

[1] See: *Sepher Chaje Jehuda*, p. 11; *Neppi-Ghirondi*, p. 42; *REJ* 30:304 ff. and *MGWJ* 75:130; *Kirjath Sepher* 15:128 ff. Isaac Abravanel, *Naḥalat abot*, Chapter 6, mishna 1.

entire community was kept in a state of mourning two full days. The pompous funeral provoked the anger of many to the point that Abraham was compelled to publicly defend his action.[1]

Renaissance people also desired to perpetuate their likeness on portraits or medallions. Samuel Archivolti praised a Christian artist in a Hebrew poem because the portrait that he painted "perpetuated a man's face for eternity". Leon da Modena was concerned about this too. After he lost the *ritratto* that the artist Tinelli had made for him, he again had "his portrait made in the form of a small square picture".[2] Leon's small picture has survived, and so have a number of other portraits of Renaissance Jews. But there is no doubt that these portraits represent only a fraction of the pictures of Renaissance Jews painted during the Period.

And yet, Renaissance Jewish intellectuals were well aware that their works would best serve to perpetuate their memory. Abraham Portaleone's *Shilte hagibborim* helped to preserve his memory far more effectively than the large tomb that he asked his sons to prepare for him. Immanuel of Rome sensed this keenly when he wrote:

"If I should die, my books will not!"

Even Leon da Modena knew this quite well. He wrote his autobiography because he recognized that thereby "I shall not die, but live". He also made unceasing efforts to publish his books. Many of his books were indeed published during his lifetime and even those that were not published were perpetuated in a bibliographical list that he incorporated in the autobiography. He introduced this list with a revealing statement: "Here I list some of my writings,... for it is a great consolation to me that my name will not be obliterated from Israel and from the world until eternity in spite of death..."[3]

[1] See: *Schiavi*, p. 497 ff. and p. 499; *REJ*, *Ibid.*, pp. 40, 43; *Iggerot Erez Yisrael*, p. 106. *Divan Modena*, p. 53.

[2] See: *JQR* 4:337 ff.; *Sepher Chaje Jehuda*, pp. 54, 70. Archivolti's poem was published by S. Bernstein, *Tarbiz* 8:62.

[3] See: *Maḥberot Immanuel*, p. 41; *Sepher Chaje Jehuda*, pp. 9, 42. Both Immanuel and Leon, no doubt, knew Horace's ode "The Poet's

CHAPTER FOUR

ELEGANCE OF EXPRESSION AND ORATORY

a.

Jews, like other Renaissance men, regarded the ability to use a refined linguistic style as one of the important characteristics of the perfect man. This attitude was a strong factor in stimulating the Italian Jews to acquire the knowledge of the Hebrew language, and to practice its use in a degree unknown in other contemporary Jewish communities. Letter writing, and even invective oratory, rose to a high level of artistry.

The Italian Jewish scholars were well aware of their linguistic superiority over their coreligionists in northern Europe. Leon da Modena believed that the Italian Jews' Hebrew pronunciation was grammatically more correct than that of the Ashkenazic Jews. A mid-sixteenth century letter expressed this view more emphatically: "...Verily, the Italiani are by far superior to the Ashkenazim in (the knowledge of) the grammar of the language of the Bible and in the proper ways of pronunciation, with all their rules". To be sure, there were exceptions as well. The chronicle *Shalshelet hakabbalah* was certainly not written in a Hebrew style elegant enough to satisfy the refined taste of the Jewish humanists. But this book and some others were exceptions. Most of the literature, including books in Rabbinics, was written in a beautiful style which was far above that common in the contemporary Hebrew literature in northern Europe. The concern of the humanist for a pure style is demonstrated by a chapter included by Samuel Archivolti in his work *Arugat habosem*, in which he gave "special instructions how to speak in an elegant style". He advised his readers to avoid the use of words from other languages and to employ clear and simple style, so "that your words be sweet to the listening ear". He further cautioned them to avoid expressions that were difficult to

Immortal Fame" and fashioned after it their thoughts about their own literary immortality. Comp. Horace, *The Odes and Epodes* with an English Translation by C. E. Bennett (The Loeb Classical Library), London 1960, pp. 278-279.

assimilate such as words with three similar letters, and not to substitute masculine for feminine or singular for plural.[1]

A product of the perpetual preoccupation with language and style was a new skill in describing nature, geographical phenomena, and the human form. Samuel Usque's lovely descriptions of nature and Azariah dei Rossi's excellent report of the Ferrara earthquake in 1571 are unique in Jewish literature. Azariah supplemented his dramatic description with keen observations of human reaction at the moment of terror and the serious economic consequences that ensued. Jewish writers also made efforts to describe the human figure. Leon da Modena's description of some members of his family is a good example. Far more extensive are Abraham Farissol's descriptions of the physical proportions of people in various distant lands in his work on geography.[2]

b.

The use of an elegant style, coupled with beautiful script, became all-important also to the letter writer. A substantial portion of time and effort in the educational process was devoted to these subjects. In sixteenth century Italy the well known saying "By three things may a person's character be determined, by his cup, his purse, and by his anger" (comp. Erubin 65b) was augmented with "and his quill". A letter from a teacher to his pupil contains a sharp warning on this matter: "...they will say that you are seventeen years old and show no capacity at all in writing, which is today a beautiful crown to all who know it". The teacher suggested that his pupil devote an hour or two every day to writing exercises. The subject of calligraphy was also included in the curriculum of the college founded by Rabbi David Provenzal. The noted writer Judah da Sommi, who apparently served as an elementary teacher in his youth, prepared for his students "pictures of the alphabet". He added a collection of epigrams

[1] See: *Historia de gli riti hebraici*, Part 2, Chapter 1, par. 2; *REJ* 105:56, *Arugat habosem*, Chapter 28.
[2] See: *Sepher Chaje Jehuda*, pp. 24, 36; *Iggeret orehot olam*, passim.

based upon the alphabet which reiterated the fact that "great is the power of script and the letter which is properly executed". He further advised his pupils to write only in standing position and to move their pens lightly. Throughout the lengthy poem he admonished his pupils to diligently improve their writing skill and, especially, "to train the hand and the eye (to write) in a correct and proportioned skript".[1]

The art of letter writing acquired in the school did not fully satisfy the desire of many to correspond in a superbly elegant style. The situation was remedied by letter collections prepared by gifted humanists. Two types of models are found in the collections: letters written by prominent individuals, including tourists to the Holy Land, and forms of letters that dealt with matters of everyday life. Epistles of prominent men were usually copied with deletion of names and dates that they might be utilized for exercise in the art of letter writing. Such letters often fitted various life situations and could be used directly with minor changes. This category also contained Hebrew translations of letters by Cicero and by the notorious humanist Pietro Aretino. Significantly, letters of non-Jewish origin were unhesitatingly used as long as they served the purpose of producing elegant correspondence.

The many manuscript collections of letter forms still extant attest to their popularity among the Jews of the Renaissance. One of the collections contains no less than one thousand forms. The frequent use of letter forms is further demonstrated by cases of plagiarism. One of the better letter collections *Megillat sefer* (also known as *Megillat haketabim*), was published four times during the Period. Among the forms were short letters dealing with everyday life and a number of marriage contracts. Joseph Hacohen composed forms of addresses, each fitting a letter recipient of different social position. Helpful to the public were also manuals of instructions for letter writing. *Maayan ganim* by Samuel Archivolti was outstanding in this

---

[1] See: *Louis Ginzberg Jubilee Volume*, Hebrew Section, p. 276, Note 33; S. Asaf, *Meḳorot letoledot haḥinuk beyisrael*, vol. 4, pp. 24, 26; paragraph 7 of Rabbi David Provenzali's school program, *Halebanon* 5:434; *Ẓaḥut bediḥuta deḳiddushin*, p. 141 ff.

category. Curiously, Leon da Modena accused Archivolti, his teacher, of plagiarising his idea of such a manual.[1]

The use of an elegant style was common also in the official documents and correspondence of the Jewish communities. At the beginning of the sixteenth century David Ibn Jachia tells that "every community employs a permanent scribe to write its letters and contracts, who is paid according to his stylistic proficiency". Like the rulers of Italian states who engaged scribes from among the greatest humanists, Jewish communities employed as scribes men as famous as Immanuel of Rome and Leon da Modena. Humanists attempted to attain stylistic perfection by writing their letters in rhymed prose and by quoting the writings of famous poets.[2] We have seen (section VIII, chapter 3) also that authors of rabbinic responsa made a great effort to compose their writings in elegant style. A sixteenth century rabbi went as far as to arrange a halakic responsum in the form of the Ten Commandments.[3]

c.

The aptitude in writing and expression was not always used as a constructive means of satisfying the quest for beauty. Literary talent was often used by quarrelsome humanists to defeat and ridicule their adversaries. There were quite a number of Jewish humanists who greatly enjoyed a fight and used their sharp tongues to smite their competitors. A good example is Joseph Arli, one of the most brilliant among them, who was perpetually embroiled in disputes. According to him, the primary advantage in learning the art of writing was its efficacy in a dispute: "(The writing craft) strengthens man's stand in his feuds, his business, and all his other endeavors". In a pungent letter addressed to an antagonist

---

[1] See: Sonne, *Zion*, N. S. 17:148; *Tarbiẓ* 8:172; *Catalogue Kaufmann* p. 165 (No. 494); *Louis Ginzberg Jubilee Volume*, Hebrew Section, p. 294; *Leo Modenas Briefe*, p. 148; *Oẓar Ha-sepharim*, p. 294, No. 464; *REJ* 16:31. I used Joseph Hacohen's manuscript which is kept in the Columbia University Library.

[2] *Maḥberot Immanuel*, p. 658 ff., p. 689 ff.; *Leo Modenas Briefe*, passim; *HUCA* 1:620.

[3] See: *Responsa of Rabbi Isaac de Lattes*, Vienna 1860, p. 14 ff.

he employed a battery of sarcasm and insults that makes depressing reading. He sensed that his words would evoke dissatisfaction among those who did not approve of this aspect of the pen's power and apologized: "for I am a human being and not God, and I also am formed out of the clay" (comp. Job 33:6). Joseph Arli's power of speech was as potent as that of his pen, which is illustrated by his encounter with two apostates: "...They slandered and berated him but... became frightened when he said: Do not speak, for you do not even know how to read the Pentateuch. He quarreled with them sharply and they were greatly abashed and embarrassed". Other humanists acted in a similar fashion. During a controversy in a divorce case Rabbi Moses Provenzal was derided and insulted by other rabbis much in the way the *melamed* Hillel was attacked by Elijah Baḥur (see above, Section III, Chapter 4). Joseph Hacohen went as far as to include in his work *Emeḳ habaka* a letter filled with invective that he addressed to Rabbi Joseph Ottolenghi. He thus made sure that his adversary's shame "will be remembered for ever". To be sure, Joseph Hacohen comforted his victim by insisting that he did the same to kings and their councelors.

An accepted tactic in such a war of words was to ridicule the antagonist by twisting his name and using all sorts of puns. Thus, Rabbi Judah Saltaro's antagonist described him as "jumping and treading upon the heads of a holy people", alluding clearly to his name (*saltare*, to jump). Moses Basola, a brilliant and quarrelsome humanist, opposed the decisions of the Ferrara congress of 1554, whereupon he wrote: "These are the troubles (*taḳalot*, instead of *taḳanot*, ordinances) created at the accursed (*ḳelali*, spelled with *ḳof*, instead of *kelali*, spelled with *kaf*, general) assembly". He accompanied it with many other sarcastic remarks. Significantly, a Jew was among the Roman humanists who used to attach to the statue called *Pasquino* biting satires in which they attacked and derided people whom they disliked. The text of one of his satires is still extant.[1] Some feuding rabbis and humanists

---

[1] See: *Louis Ginzberg Jubilee Volume*, Hebrew Section, p. 276; *Moses Schorr Memorial Volume*, p. 200 ff.; *Alim* 2:51; *Haẓaah al*

used in their correspondence such vile language, that the contemporaries considered the letters non-publishable. Rabbi Abraham Minz of Padua, for example, was notorious as a man of strife who used vile language. One of the rabbis remarked about him: "Are you one of the despicable (men) that you want to oppress (people) in spite of the law...And your threats and insults are not compatible with the behavior of scholars, but are the practice of knife wielders..." Elijah Baḥur who was a great novelist and grammarian wrote a poem in Yiddish filled with filthy allusions to his opponent's sex life. Joseph Hacohen, Rabbi Jacob da Fano, and others used equally objectionable language in their feuds.[1]

d.

Jewish society also produced an impressive number of brilliant orators and preachers. The homiletical literature of the Period, with all its beauty, reflects only in part the excellence of the Jewish sermon and oration. Virtually all sermons still extant served merely as speaker's notes or were jotted down for future reference after much of the orations' original charm had faded. Some circles, in their enthusiasm for the elegant oration, gave it preference over literary achievement. Curiously, among them was as brilliant and versatile a writer as Leon da Modena. His father, be it noted, desired "more than anything else" that the son should excel in oratory. The preference for homiletics was attested to by Rabbi Samuel Judah Katzenellenbogen when he stated that "almost everywhere people shun lectures in *halakah* but are eager to listen to discourses in *aggadah* and Midrash". A popular speaker like Leon da Modena had virtually unlimited opportunities to preach. During his stay in Ferrara he preached every Sabbath for three years on the community's invitation and in Venice he used to preach in three or four synagogues every

odot haget, Venice 1566, p. 32b; *Emek habaka*, p. 138 ff.; *Mikweh Yisrael*, Venice 1613, p. 9a; *Takanot ḥakamim*, edited by S. Z. H. Halberstamm, Brody 1879; *Natali*, p. 71.

[1] See: A. Marx, *Studies in Jewish History and Booklore*, p. 121, Notes 56, 57 and p. 141; *Palge mayim*, Venice 1614, p. 11b; *Sefer shaashuim*, p. 83.

Sabbath. Over the years he accumulated a collection of four hundred sermons that he had preached. When Rabbi Obadiah da Bertinoro came to Palermo, en route to the Holy Land, he succeeded in curing many social ills through his sermons. Some admirers of the art of speech went as far as to listen to Christian sermons. When Bernardino da Siena preached in 1438 before king Renato at Aquila in Southern Italy, numerous Jews were in his audience.[1]

In addition to the sermon that the people wanted to hear on the Sabbath, it was also customary to speak on various occasions such as circumcisions and weddings. The desire to add glamour to events of everyday life made an address mandatory for any kind of celebration. In a collection of liturgical poems, a remark following a marriage ceremony prayer says: "and it is customary to say something in Italian in praise of the couple". When Abraham Portaleone served as a circumcisor he used to enter in his record book not only the data on the child, but "the topic of the sermon" as well. The Renaissance Jews also had in their *yeshibot* a kind of graduation ceremony. A book of sermons by Rabbi Samuel Judah Katzenellenbogen contains a number of sermons which he preached on the occasion of awarding the degree of *ḥaber* to various students.[2]

The Renaissance sermon was characterized by its harmonious structure. The adherence to classical culture led Renaissance orators to mold their orations in the fashion of the great speakers of the Antiquity, primarily Cicero and Quintillian. Messer Leon offered a systematic guide for speakers and outlined the rules of eloquence in his work *Noṣel ẓuṣim*. He quoted Aristotle, Cicero and Quintillian at length and cited many biblical examples to illustrate his principles of speech.

---

[1] See: Leon da Modena, *Midbar Yehudah*, Venice 1703, p. 6a; *Sepher Chaje Jehuda*, pp. 17, 26, 30; Samuel Judah Katzenellenbogen, *Shnem asar derushim*, Warsaw 1876, p. 20; G. Pansa, *Gli ebrei in Aquila*, Auila 1904, p. 203. Bernardino spoke before King Renato, who was friendly to the Jews. Thus, it should not be regarded as a forced attendance.

[2] See: *Kebod ḥakamim* by David, the son of Messer Leon, Berlin 1899, p. 64; *Dabar beito mah tob*, Ferrara 1557.

The outstanding preacher Judah Moscato treated aspects of rhetoric in one of his sermons and also quoted the two principle orators of the ancient world. The relatively few extant Renaissance sermons, especially those of Rabbi Judah Moscato, Leon da Modena, and Rabbi Azariah Pigo, all are well organized and clearly structured after the pattern of the ancient oration.[1] They represent a new type of sermon hitherto unknown in Jewish homiletical literature.

Although virtually all the sermons that have remained in manuscript or print were written in Hebrew and only a few have been preserved in Italian, it is certain that practically all of them were preached in Italian. Leon da Modena attested to this in his work *Historia de gli Riti Hebraici*, and it is also evident from the fact that catholic priests used to visit Venice synagogues to listen to his sermons. Rabbi David Ibn Jachia also related that Christian scholars used to attend his sermons when he served as the chief rabbi for the Jews of the Kingdom of Naples.[2]

Although the evidence regarding the secular address is scarce, it may be assumed that Jewish speakers presented such orations quite frequently. For example, some of the marriage addresses surely had a secular character. Even more significant is the fact that Jewish humanists were as capable as their most illustrious Christian colleagues of delivering orations in the Latin language. The physician David dei Pomis relates that when the clergy tried to prevent him from practicing medicine, "I went to Rome to seek mercy and justice from Pope Pius IV and I made a lengthy plea in Latin before him and high officials and many cardinals and a large crowd of people, and I made a favorable impression and achieved everything that I had requested". Similarly, Abtalyon da Modena, Leon's uncle, spoke in Latin at the papal court in an attempt to obtain permission for re-printing the

[1] *Nofet zufim* appeared in Vienna in 1854; detailed studies on Rabbi Judah Moscato and Rabbi Azariah Pigo as preachers were written by Israel Bettan in *HUCA*, vols. 6 and 7. For Leon da Modena's sermons see Ellis Rivkin, *Ibid.*, vol. 23, Part 2.

[2] See: Leon da Modena, *Historia de gli Riti Hebraici*, Part 2, Chapter 1, paragraph 5; cf. *HUCA* 1:617.

Talmud. "And in 1581 he went...to Pope Gregory XIII and
spoke to him several times, and once especially before him
and several cardinals he spoke for more than two hours in
Latin as an interceder in behalf of the Gemara and returned
in glory, for he attained all that he had requested".[1]

CHAPTER FIVE

FULL PARTICIPATION IN LIFE

a.

In the framework of the admiration that Renaissance Man
had for talent and proficiency in the fields of cultural, social,
and political creativity, an individual's origin and religion
were often overlooked. While Italian Renaissance society
was not able to completely overcome its anti-Jewish prejudices,
it was, nevertheless, prepared more than any other pre-
Emancipation society to grant the individual Jew an opportunity for active participation in general life. This partial readiness
of Christians to remove the social barrier between themselves
and the Jews was met with a powerful desire of most Jews to
share the effervescent and interesting life of the Renaissance
society.

The tendency to bring about a rapprochement between
Jew and non-Jew was, however, energetically opposed by
powerful ecclesiastical circles. They feared the spread of
Jewish religious influence within Christian society, whose
religious foundations were shaken by the revolutionary
changes that the Renaissance had introduced into the entire
range of life. A certain opposition was also noticeable among
Jewish leaders who feared that Jewish society might absorb
too much of gentile culture. As a result, the rapprochement
between Jews and gentiles was limited and cautious. The
initiative was generally taken by individuals. However, they
were so numerous and their position in Jewish society,
especially in the cultural circles, was so important that the

[1] See: Introduction to *Zemah David*, Available in *Neppi-Ghirondi*,
p. 84 ff.; *Sepher Chaje Jehuda*, p. 12.

Jewish-Christian rapprochement became one of the characteristic phenomena of Jewish life in Renaissance Italy.

Jewish-Christian understanding is found first and foremost
among the humanists. Several leading Jewish writers admittedly were encouraged by Christian humanists to write their
works. Abraham Farissol related that he wrote his polemical
work *Magen Abraham* at the behest of Christian friends.
Johanan Alemanno similarly wrote his great work *Ḥeshek
Shelomoh* at the request of Pico della Mirandola. Elijah Baḥur
and Leon da Modena wrote many of their works specifically
for Christian readers. Leon and other scholars often printed
approbations for books that were written by Christian
colleagues and composed poems in their honor. Samuel
Archivolti wrote poems in praise of a Christian artist. The
number of panegyrics which Leon da Modena wrote in honor
of kings, princes, and Catholic priests was very large.[1] Quite
revealing is the fact that often sincere personal friendships
developed between rabbis and priests. Here too Abraham
Farissol, Leon da Modena, and Azariah dei Rossi are among
the outstanding examples.[2] Of even greater significance is the
fact that a considerable number of Jewish writers (Immanuel
of Rome, Judah da Sommi, and others) wrote Italian works on
general, non-Jewish subjects. Obviously, they expected their
writings to be accepted by the ordinary Italian reader.

The Jewish efforts to penetrate the broader society were
met, as mentioned above, with Christian opposition. Judah da
Sommi, who wrote far more extensively for the general public
than for his coreligionists, experienced it personally. When he
was proposed for membership in one of the Mantuan "aca-

---

[1] See: *Haẓofeh leḥokmat Yisrael* 12-286; Introduction to *Ḥeshek
Shelomoh* by Johanan Alemanno; *Divan Modena*, p. 93 ff., ten poems
in honor of gentiles, including princes and priests. Among these is a
poem composed by Leon at the request of the heads of the San Antonio theological seminary for recitation in honor of the doge's visit
to the school. Another poem was composed as an approbation of a
book describing the advantages of . . . the Catholic Confessional.
The author sensed that this would seem strange to his fellow Jews
and added that he could not "restrain himself from responding to
the request of a brother (i. e. a monk), who was a friend of the Jews".

[2] See: *Meor enayim*, Section *Imre binah*, p. 130.

demies", a rather powerful opposition arose, and even the energetic intervention of a duke was of no avail. The matter was compromised in a manner apparently characteristic of Jewish-Christian relations of the Period: Judah was not elected to membership in the academy, but became its "writer", that is, a sort of corresponding member. The war of the priests against Jewish-Christian rapprochement was far more serious. Where the Church was strong, as in Rome during the Counter-Reformation, Jews were banned from teaching Christians the Hebrew language, music, dancing and other arts. Christians were also forbidden to gamble with Jews. In places where the Church did not dominate, its preachers propagandized against non-Jews socializing with Jews. Bishop Diomede Caraffa in 1522 advised the Christians to abstain "from intimate conversation with Jews during meals or at dances". Another famous preacher Bernardino da Feltre in 1475 delivered a series of anti-Jewish sermons in Trent, with special emphasis on the need to break off social relationships with Jews. The bitter outcome of these sermons was the blood libel which resulted in the burning alive of a number of people and the obliteration of an entire Jewish community. Under these circumstances we understand the despair of a prominent Jewish preacher when he heard the sermons of an anti-Semitic monk. Moses ben Joab cried out bitterly against "...those who oppress us daily, these evil men whose love and hate are only devices to rob Jews of money..." [1]

b.

A drastic manifestation of the struggle over Jewish-Christian fraternization was the continuous effort to enforce the ecclesiastical law about the "Jewish badge". Its most characteristic aspect was its universality. Not only was it mandatory in the Papal States during the Counter-Reformation period, but even in those states that were most liberal toward Jews, such as Venice and Mantua, the governments

---

[1] See: D'Ancona, vol. 2, p. 406; Bertolotti, *Ibid.*, p. 262; *Ferorelli*, p. 226; H. Hildesheimer, *Simon von Trient*, Berlin 1903, p. 3; Cassuto, *Florence*, p. 371.

stubbornly insisted upon the wearing of the badge. Exemption from this obligation was very rare, limited mainly to physicians and individuals who were favored by kings or princes. Whenever a Jew earned the gratitude of a ruler, the first thing that he requested was exemption from the requirement to wear the badge, which indicates both the importance and the difficulty of obtaining it.

These exemptions obviously solved the problem only for a very few. However, the Renaissance spirit of freedom and the conviction of the Jews that they constituted an important element in the population, induced them to many varied efforts to get rid of the badge. The struggle was conducted by the Jewish communal authorities as well as by individuals. Even where a community was unsuccessful in its efforts, individuals would transgress the restriction and dress like the rest of the population. Violation of the law was widespread and flagrant, despite the harsh punishment meted out to transgressors. When the law of the badge was reintroduced in Florence in July 1571, it became necessary to prosecute Jews for its transgression as early as September of the same year. There were so many transgressors in Sicily that a special official was appointed to supervise its observance.[1]

The most effective weapon that Jews had was the *condotta*. Since many cities and states solicited Jewish pawnbrokers (see above, section III, chapter 1), they were compelled to permit them to settle in their midst under circumstances that enabled Jews to live unmolested as Jews. Thus, very frequently the *condottae* included paragraphs exempting the loanbankers from wearing the badge. The municipal council of Fano in 1464 placed all of its Jews under the obligation of wearing the badge but specifically exempted the loanbankers from the degrading requirement. Consequently, some Jews pretended to be pawnbank partners to evade wearing the badge. Whenever a city was in urgent need of a Jewish pawnbroker it was compelled to accede to his demands regarding

---

[1] Ample information regarding the struggle against the law of the badge and its widespread transgression is found in practically all monographs on Jewish communities.

the badge. However, when a new situation arose where the
city was no longer overly concerned with an extension of the
condotta, while the Jewish banker was anxious to continue it,
the clause offering exemption was removed from the contract.
Florence offers a striking example. The first *condotta* that was
signed in 1437 stated that Jews were not bound to wear the
badge. This clause was reiterated in the *condotta* of 1448.
However, in 1463 when the *condotta* was to be renegotiated,
and the Jews were afraid of steep losses if it were not renewed,
they were compelled to assent to the wearing of the badge.
In 1481 there were, apparently, far better prospects for the
Jews which enabled them to force the government to release
them from the wearing of the badge, although no clause to
that effect was inserted into the *condotta*. In a curious way,
aiming at satisfying both the law and the Jews, the matter
of the badge was handled in Pirano, in the Istria region where
the *condotta* of 1484 exempted Jewish women from wearing the
badge, but did obligate the men. However, the *condotta* adds,
if the badge should be covered by parts of the clothing, it will
not be regarded as a violation since the law of wearing the
badge has been obeyed.[1] Thus, the *condotta* did succeed in
freeing numerous Jews from the degrading obligation of
wearing the symbol, especially in the fifteenth century prior
to the attack of the monks upon the Jewish lending business
(see above, section III, chapter 1).

c.

The rejection of the badge was accompanied among the
Jews of the Renaissance by an aspiration for status symbols
common in gentile society, such as titles, family coats of arms,
and the right to bear arms. Leon da Modena related proudly
that his grandfather Mordecai was made a knight by the
emperor Charles V during his famous visit to Bologna. There

---

[1] See: Cassuto, *Ibid.*, pp. 40, 41, 48, 55, 115, 123, 141, 142; *Vogel-stein-Rieger*, p. 334 ff.; *RMI* 2:379 and 9:233; M. Stern, *Stellung der Paepste*, Part I, p. 15; Luzzatto, *Urbino*, p. 66 ff.; *Giovanni de Giovanni*, p. 37 ff. and p. 302; *REJ* 2:191; Colorni, *Magistrature maggiori*, p. 16.

were also knights in the Portaleone family in Mantua, designated in official documents by the titles *miles* (in Latin) and *cavaliere* (in Italian). Messer Leon was also called knight in an official document and there is reason to assume that as a result of the privilege granted to him by the government to call himself "Messer" he claimed a certain official authority within the Jewish community.

Family coats-of-arms were more common than titles. The latter were granted solely by governments, and were not too often given to Jews. Jewish families, however, could use coats of arms without difficulty. Numerous Jewish families had such emblems and their pictures have been left mainly in books and on tombstones. Leon da Modena related that he saw his old family home in Modena, "and in parts of it was our seal...a picture of a panther standing on two legs with a palm branch in its paw". There was a family tradition that this symbol was theirs for more than five hundred years. One of its members allegedly had patents from every ruler of Modena confirming the family's right to this coat of arms. Gedaliah Ibn Jachia in *Shalshelet hakabbalah* related that his family coat of arms consisted of the partially covered head of a negro. However, he had information that formerly the family had another coat of arms: A lion with a palm branch in its paw and an eagle underneath. He also tried to interpret its meaning: The lion symbolized the family's origin from the tribe of Judah. "And the eagle signified that all (members of) the family were swift in the study of Torah and in performing worthy acts". The Rapa family of Porto had a coat of arms depicting a raven and the hands of a priest (ready for the priestly blessing), while the seal of the tycoon Herz Wertheim of Padua consisted of a deer. Curiously, coats of arms that included figures of animals and birds were often depicted in written and printed books and painted on walls without concern over a possible violation of the Second Commandment. Some opposition was noticeable, however. We have seen (see above, section VII, chapter 1) how Herz Wertheim's attempt to put on the holy ark a curtain with his coat of arms embroidered in relief resulted in a violent conflict in the community of Padua. Gedaliah Ibn Jachia asserted that the Negro head in his family seal was half covered to avoid transgressing the prohibition of forming images. Gedaliah, be it noted, treated the subject of coats of arms at length in his book and tried to prove, in true Renaissance fashion, that the first family seals were instituted by the Jews and the nations learned from them to make "*bandiere* for the use of armies in wars, as well as for family emblems".[1]

A further symbol of social equality was the right to bear arms. While the efforts for the attainment of this privilege were not as forceful as the pursuit of titles and family coats of arms, they were nevertheless intense. On a number of occasions Jews who were close to the government were accorded these two privileges simultaneously, exemption from the obligation of wearing the Jewish badge and permission to bear arms. Obviously, these privileges were necessary for demonstrating one's social equality.[2]

Although the number of Jews who bore arms was rather small, Jewish interest in matters of the military and warfare was surprisingly high. Warfare was part of everyday life in Italy during the Renaissance. The peninsula was split into a multitude of artificially created small states with ambitious political aspirations. To attain a status of importance these states had to develop large military forces. This situation formed the background for the development of armies of mercenaries under the command of *condottieri*. In these armies a number of Jews served as suppliers or physicians. They also provided credit for the *condottieri* who were in constant need of it. When the armies of the famous *condottiere* Bartolomeo Colleoni were left penniless after his death (1475), they obtained a loan from Jewish moneylenders in Brescia and left

[1] See: Isaac Abravanel, *Naḥalat abot*, Chapter 6, mishnah 1; *Sepher Chaje Jehuda*, pp. 10, 11; Moses A. Shulvass, *In the Grip of Centuries*, p. 56 ff. and p. 62, Note 25; *Shilte hagibborim*, p. 188b; Colorni, *Annuario di studi ebraici* 1:173, 178; *Shalshelet hakabbalah*, pp. 11, 55; *Minḥah belulah* by Rabbi Abraham Menahem Porto, p. 17b.
[2] M. Stern, *Stellung der Paepste*, Part 1, p. 18 ff.; *Giovanni de Giovanni*, p. 302.

their arms in pledge. Few, if any, Jews served as mercenaries. They generally had better economic opportunities. However, in times of stress such as the War of the League of Cambrai, they took up arms alongside their gentile compatriots.[1]

There were a number of Jews who were experts in military technology. A Jew in Reggio advised the local ruler "during wartime". According to a contemporary, the Pope promised David Reubeni "weapons and Jewish and Christian experts". Evidently, there were expert artillerymen among Italian Jews. A sort of military genius was Abraham Colorni, who while still a child learned the art of fencing. Throughout his life he was busy designing weapons and advising the Italian rulers in matters of warfare. He was regarded as an expert on security matters. He was the author of a plan for maintaining internal peace within the state, which included detailed instructions on how to prevent planting of mines and damage by gunpowder. He was also an expert in fortification. His contemporaries admired him and believed that his inventions far surpassed those of other experts.[2]

In the Hebrew literature of the Period we find a curious treatise on the art of warfare. In the form of a speech by an anointed priest (who accompanied the Israelitic army on its march) Abraham Portaleone offered in his work *Shilte hagibborim* a comprehensive plan on how to conduct a war. Characteristically, the plan is very much reminiscent of strategic principles, as well as of weaponry, popular during the sixteenth century. The author manifests a remarkably thorough knowledge of military matters and gives instructions on the "making of gunpowder". In the course of his speech "the anointed priest" tells how the Romans waged war and describes weapons used by the Hungarians, Poles and Russians. He instructs us in how to carry out surprise attacks during the night and recommends that the soldiers wear white shirts over their armor, that they be recognized in the dark. At the

---

[1] See: *Kirjath sepher* 15:126 ff.; F. Glissenti, *Gli ebrei nel Bresciano*, Brescia 1891, pp. 14, 50; *REJ* 79:50.

[2] *Balletti*, p. 163 (2nd edition); *Iggeret orehot olam*, Chapter 14; G. Jarè, *Abramo Colorni*, Ferrara 1891, pp. 9, 50; *RMI* 9:147.

conclusion of the lengthy treatise the author apologized for having written it: "And it would not surprise me that many scholars who yearn to study Torah and are not ready to devote their attention to other spheres of wisdom, even though they may be related to the body politic...will, therefore, accuse me of having spoken too much on the subject of ramparts, bows, javelins, swords, spears, lances, and other weapons as well as on other matters of interest to warriors...Why cannot we too speak authoritatively of military issues, so that every Jew may know that we too are experts and need not have recourse to their (i.e. gentile) books...".[1] Obviously, Abraham Portaleone was of the opinion that if the Jews aspired to full participation in the country's life, they had to acquire understanding in all areas of endeavor, including those that were remote from their immediate spiritual and practical environment.

The feeling of equality with the rest of society gave the Renaissance Jews courage to protect themselves with arms against attacks of hostile gentiles. Such incidents occurred throughout the Period, especially during the second half of the sixteenth century. Jews defended themselves against rioters in Mantua, and in Rome too, when an army that had assembled for an expedition against the Turks tried to attack the ghetto: "And each one of them (the Jews) took his weapons and ran to the gate and fought with the soldiers, and protected the community and God saved them".

Another form of defense were the Jewish efforts to appeal to Christian public opinion when the peril arose of losing the social gains acquired during the Renaissance period. The most significant aspect of this struggle was the Jew's belief in the validity of such recourse to public opinion and expectation that their position would be understood. We have seen (section VIII, chapter 8) how David dei Pomis defended the Jewish physician when the Church attempted to introduce a ban on Jewish medical practice. Another writer, David d'Ascoli, in a volume entitled *Apologia Hebreorum*, attacked

---

[1] *Shilte hagibborim*, p. 35b-42b.

the entire array of Paul IV's anti-Jewish legislation. True, he was condemned to prison for this act. But the very fact that the Jewish writer only received a prison sentence indicates that there were grounds for Renaissance Jewish publicists to hope that their pleas would be heard. The struggle of Anselmo del Banco against the segregation of the Venetian Jews within an enclosed ghetto was typical of such Jewish pleas. He appealed for justice, but hinted at the same time that the Jews might leave the city in protest. Even when it became clear that the decree would not be annulled, he did not relax his efforts and virtually to his last day he persisted in petitioning the authorities to permit him to reside outside the ghetto.[1]

d.

The aspirations for full participation in life were accompanied by sincere patriotic feelings and by a desire to be active in the political affairs of the peninsula. The Venetian Jews had much admiration for the Republic, even though it was the first to enclose them within a ghetto. The stable regime gave them a feeling of security, unmatched in any other state. Elijah Capsali, a visitor from Crete, who watched the large scale immigration of German Jews to the Venetian territories, observed that they began coming "when they learned of the full power of the Venetian regime, its statutes, the fairness of its laws, and its other virtues". The exciting life of the city, then at the peak of political and economic success, also attracted the Jews most of whom came from an urban environment. Leon da Modena, captivated by the city's manifold opportunities, loved it sincerely with all its virtues and faults. He was miserable whenever compelled to reside in another city and he always returned to his beloved Venice where he spent most of his tempestuous days. Devotion to Venice was expressed in deeds. When the Republic was faced with the most serious crisis in its history during the War of the

---

[1] See: *Emek habaka*, pp. 145, 152; Moses A. Shulvass, *In the Grip of Centuries*, pp. 103 ff. *Vogelstein-Rieger*, vol. 2, p. 153; *Schiavi*, p. 325; Sonne, *Zion*, N. S. 3:126 ff. *Apologia Hebreorum* was published in Strassbourg in 1559.

League of Cambrai, many Jews volunteered to help in liber-
ating Padua, the cultural capital of the Republic. The Verona
ḳehillah flourishing under the Republic's protection, ruled that
one half of all the fines paid by members who transgressed its
ordinances, should be given for the *arsenale* of Venice, the
core of the Republic's military strength. There were also many
expressions of admiration by Jewish thinkers for the regime
of aristocratic democracy in Venice, regarded by them as the
ideal form of government. David dei Pomis wrote a special
tract to prove the divine origin of the Venetian republican
regime. He went so far as to ascertain that the Scriptures
contained an allusion to the Venetian victory over the Turks
in the sea battle of Lepanto (1571).[1]

Jewish inhabitants of Rome also lavished great affection
upon the city up to the time when the Counter-Reformation
popes initiated a policy of harsh oppression of the Jewish
population. They used to add the designation *ish Romi*,
Roman, to their names, much in the way Christians would
characterize themselves as Romans from Rome. When Cola
di Rienzi tried to renew Rome's grandeur in the middle of
the fourteenth century, the Jews supported him, for his
movement represented genuine patriotism that arose from
a deep love for the Eternal City. A remarkable expression of
a Jew's love of Rome is found in the will of Menachem ben
Nathan, a resident of Rimini. He left a substantial amount of
money as a legacy "for the repair of the walls of Rome, the
city where I was born", although he had left the city many
years prior to his death.[2]

Florence, too, evoked a great deal of Jewish affection.
Johanan Alemanno considered it to be the ideal state. During
the siege of 1529-1530 the poet Moses ben Joab composed "a

[1] See: *Sepher Chaje Jehuda*, passim; *REJ* 79:33, 50; Roth, *Venice*,
p. 187. Cf. Sonne, *Kobez al jad*, N. S. 3:151, for the half of the fine
that was paid to the arsenal. We also find a similar procedure in
Rome. In both instances it is difficult to ascertain whether these
were patriotic acts on the part of the Jews or whether government
demands prompted them. It is especially doubtful regarding Rome.

[2] See: *Kobez al jad*, 1903, p. 27 ff.; *Vogelstein-Rieger*, vol. 1, p. 310ff.;
Ibid., vol. 2, p. 130; Berliner, *Geschichte der Juden in Rom*, vol. 2,
part 1, p. 88.

dirge over the populous city of Florence, upon which God's wrath had fallen and the enemy's hand was raised". To be sure, periodically he had harsh words for Florence for oppressing the Jews. But whenever the homeland was in distress, the patriot's love awakened within him. During Siena's wars of independence Jews participated in the defense of the city and the expulsion of the Spanish army. Similar feelings of patriotic devotion were manifested by Jews in Rimini, Mantua, and other places.[1]

Jewish direct involvement in political affairs was quite common. The wealthy bankers regularly used to obtain from their agents reports on political events in the various Italian states. Roman Jews, as we have seen, took part in the revolt of Cola di Rienzi. The alarm that rallied the citizenry to the aid of the hero was sounded by a Jew, and after Cola's death the Jews were ordered to burn his body, probably because they were regarded as his most loyal supporters. A Jew was also involved in the bitter struggle between the various parties in Siena at the end of the fourteenth century. Jews were also involved in political disturbances in Florence in 1434 and in Naples in 1495. Jews also joined the mob in profaning the memory and statue of Pope Paul IV right after his death. Significantly, there was even some sort of Jewish involvement in the election of a pope. In 1590 Jews helped, presumably with money, in the election of Pope Gregory XIV. Prior to his election Gregory negotiated with the Jews and they received the impression that if elected he would grant permission for the printing of the Talmud.[2]

Jews served the various Italian states in the diplomatic field as well. There was nothing unusual in the appointment of Don Isaac Abravanel by the Venetian Republic to negotiate on its behalf a trade agreement with Portugal. Don Isaac was an eminent statesman and experienced diplomat. But we also

[1] See: *Haẓofeh leḥokmat Yisrael* 8:43; *MGWJ* 77:373; *JQR* 4:337 ff. *Kobez al jad, Ibid.*; J. Shatzky, *Alfred Landau Jubilee Volume*, p. 191 (Yiddish).
[2] See: Sonne, *Zion*, N. S. 17:151, 156; *Natali*, p. 149; *Vogelstein-Rieger*, vol. 1, p. 312; *Settimana Israelitica*, 1910, fascicles 43, 44; Cassuto, *Florence* p. 22; *Ferorelli*, p. 74; *Tarbiz* 2:488 ff.

find in the diplomatic service of the Italian states otherwise unknown Jews. In the fourteenth century a Jew served as an emissary of the city of Orvieto, and another Jew, a citizen of Trapani, negotiated a peace treaty between Sicily and Tunis. A Jewish diplomat is also known to have been in the service of the rulers of Mantua.[1]

Jewish interest in political affairs found further expression in the emergence of a political literature. The immigrant Don Isaac Abravanel, who in his works favored the republican form of government, was greatly impressed by the new type of state created by the Renaissance. Venice thus in his view was "a great power among the nations and a princess among the provinces" (comp. Lamentations 1:1), Florence "the beauty of all the lands" (comp. Ezekiel 20:6), and Genoa "awe-inspiring and powerful". Johanan Alemanno was greatly impressed by the Florentine republic and its citizenry. He enthusiastically enumerated the qualities of Lorenzo the Magnificent as a head of state and the "seven precious virtues common to all the people of this land". Out of these, according to him, grew Florence's perfect political order.

Messer Leon, Samuel Archivolti and Abraham Portaleone discussed political matters in a more general way. In his work *Nofet zufim* Messer Leon devoted a chapter to the question "what is a state". He discussed the necessary qualities of statesmen, problems of political order, and economic issues as related to the import and export trade. Samuel Archivolti included in his letter collection, *Maayan ganim*, models for correspondence between high government officials and kings. Although these sample letters were composed for the use of contemporaries, their "writers" were an Israelite kind and his ministers. By employing this method the author made his samples "Jewish", much in the way Abraham Portaleone had his instruction for warfare presented by an "anointed priest" of biblical times.

[1] See: J. Bloch, *Hebrew Printing in Naples*, New York 1942, p. 6; Cassuto, *Florence*, p. 30, Note 6 quoting G. Rezasco, *Del segno degli ebrei*; *Giovanni de Giovanni*, p. 302; *Menorah Journal*, Spring 1946, p. 90; *Balletti*, p. 164 (2nd edition).

Here again Abraham Portaleone surpassed all his contemporaries. In his discussion of the structure of the state he presented a detailed plan for establishing a society based on a multitude of different classes. The plan is reminiscent of the ideas of the great Greek philosophers in their search for the perfect state. He believed that ancient Jewish society was composed of two types of citizens: "Men who were suitable for (citizenship in) a good and desirable political collective, and the sages who guided people along the righteous path of Torah and *mizwot*". Among "the people suitable for the good and desirable state" he included one hundred classes, from the laborers and artisans to the merchants, manufacturers, the government officials, the army, the navy, and the king. He also listed twenty-nine groups of religious functionaries, and thirteen ranks of priests from the physically deformed priest (unfit for Temple service) to the high priest. He wanted to demonstrate by this comprehensive plan "that our sacred Torah is a panacea, and as it is not deficient in laws and statutes that lead to eternal happiness for the soul so that it may delight in the radiance of the Divine Presence in the world to come, similarly, it does not lack what is necessary to guide man toward collective political perfection in every age". And he proudly added: "And while some non-Jewish thinkers spent their entire lives searching for ways to act in times of peace and war, the Torah has effortlessly enlightened us and in an instant taught us the path to follow in human affairs and the actions that we should perform...".[1] The Jewish political literature suggests that a clear socio-political consciousness existed among Jewish thinkers, even during the dark times when Renaissance culture was threatened by the Counter-Reformation. A great deal of this socio-political thought was transmitted to seventeenth century Italian Jewry. Against this background Simone Luzzatto composed his work *Discorso circa il stato degli Ebrei* which was the most important pre-Emancipation Jewish contribution in the field of political thought.

[1] See: *Sefer haadam wehamedinah*, edited by M. H. Ben Shammai, vol. 2, Tel-Aviv 1948, p. 581; *REJ* 12:253 ff.; *Nofet zufim*, p. 99 ff.; *Maayan ganim*, the fourth group of letter forms; *Shilte hagibborim*, pp. 34a-35b.

INDEX

Aboab (family), 204n.
Abravanel, Bienvenida, 166
Abravanel, Don Isaac, 141, 174, 179, 276, 290, 307, 336, 336n, 357, 358
Abravanel (family), 14, 21, 59, 111, 127, 150
Abravanel, Isaac (of Ferrara), 141
Abravanel, Jacob, 260
Abravanel, Joseph, 260
Abravanel, Judah, 260
Abravanel, Leone, 290, 311, 313, 313n., 314, 315
Abravanel, Samuel, 158, 164, 166, 260
Abruzzi, 25
Abudarhin (family), 281
Abulrabi, Aaron, 208n.
Acqui, 19
Adelkind Cornelio, 231n.
Agrigento, 26
Alatini, Angelo, 249
Alatini, Azriel, 208
Alatini, Moses, 291n.
Alatino, Jehiel Rehaviah, 319n.
Alemanno, Johanan, 150, 150n., 151, 191, 202, 313, 313n., 314, 330, 332, 334, 335, 347n., 356, 358
Alessandria, 18, 54
Alexander VI (Pope), 59, 165, 245
Alghero, 103
Alharizi, Judah, 217
Alphonso II (Duke of Ferrara), 21
Anaw, Zedekiah, 287
Ancona, 13, 23, 24, 45n., 47, 55n., 57, 61, 61n., 86, 86n., 87, 98, 128, 141, 194, 205, 205n., 256, 272n., 332
Aquila, 207, 344
Archivolti Samuel, 37, 110, 131, 153, 154, 154n., 161, 170, 197, 200, 219, 235, 235n., 236, 239, 239n., 243, 244, 253, 287, 288n.,
294, 298, 329, 337, 337n., 338, 340, 341, 347, 358
Aretino, Pietro, 331, 340
Arienti, 220
Ariosto, 225, 232, 247, 331, 331n.
Arli, Joseph, 101, 102, 150, 177, 183, 193, 196, 269n., 274, 275n., 294n., 341, 342
Arundi, Isaac, 333, 334n.
Ascarelli, Debora, 167n., 229
Ascoli, 13, 24, 75, 183, 23, 238
Ascoli, David d', 354
Ascoli, Enoch of, 151, 258n., 295
Asher ben Jehiel, 269, 284
Asher Laemlein, 9, 210
Ashkenazi, Eliezer, 253n.
Asolo, 10n., 16, 46n., 136n., 146, 195n.
Asti, 11, 19
Avicenna, 221, 317

Bahur, Elijah, 35n., 41n., 42, 42n., 149, 151, 151n., 153, 154, 218, 224, 224n., 225, 226, 227n., 233, 237, 264, 264n., 282, 283, 287, 288, 288n., 289n., 306, 342, 343, 347
Balearic Isles, 25
Balmes, Abraham de, 151n., 152, 288, 289
Basevi, Abraham, 42
Basilea, Simon, 247
Basola, Moses, 99, 279n., 342
Beer, Elijah, 236n.
Behaim, John, 307, 308
Belgrado, Kalonymos, 272
Bembo, 296
Benedict III (Pope), 75n.
Benevento, Immanuel da, 177, 178, 196, 214, 218, 230, 231n., 286, 288n., 297
Benjamin bar Judah, 321
Benjamin Nehemiah of Civitanova, 9, 23, 299, 299n.

Pius V (Pope), 157n., 320, 331
Plato, 221, 294, 295, 311, 313
Plautus, 294
Portaleone, Abraham, 140, 140n.,
171n., 188, 209, 214, 232, 243,
254, 255n., 262, 266, 267, 280,
281, 287, 290, 291n., 292n., 293,
295, 300, 318, 319, 322, 323,
329, 330, 336, 337, 344, 353,
354, 358, 359
Portaleone (family), 316n., 351
Portaleone, Judah, 145
Porto, 351
Porto, Abraham Menahem, 73n.,
194, 237n., 289n., 307, 332,
332n., 334n.
Porto, Allegro (Simhah), 245
Provence, 20, 24, 30n., 149
Provenzal, Abraham, 255, 255n.
Provenzal, David, 172n., 196, 255,
284, 317, 339, 340n.
Provenzal, Jacob, 253n.
Provenzal, Moses, 280n., 342
Ptolemy, 294, 308
Pyrrus, Didacus, 292
Pythagoras, 243, 243n., 294

Quintilian, 294, 344

Raba, Menahem, 198, 199
Rapa (family), 351
Ravenna, 89, 98
Recanati, 327
Recanati, Menahem, 268
Reggio, 20, 21, 27, 28, 28n., 45n.,
53, 71, 82n., 90n., 113, 325, 353
Renato (King of Naples), 344,
344n.
Reubeni, David, 158, 173, 174,
201, 232n., 241, 281, 327, 336,
353
Reuchlin, Johann, 151, 265n.
Rienzi, Cola di, 356, 357
Rieti (family), 150
Rieti, Ishmael da, 173, 272, 275
Rieti, Moses, 95n., 190, 216, 217,
220, 221, 221n., 222, 229, 310,
311, 321
Rimini, 100, 104, 105, 128, 128n.,
208n., 356, 357

Riva, Solomon, 283
Riva di Trento, 152, 312
Rivoli, 95n.
Roberto the Wise (King of
Naples), 161
Rojas, Fernando de, 249
Romagna, 6, 11, 13, 19, 21, 22, 23,
24, 112, 113, 284
Romano, Judah, 252n., 291n.
Rome, 3, 5, 9, 10n., 11, 13, 16, 19,
21, 22, 23, 24, 26, 36, 39n., 40,
45n., 46, 51, 52, 52n., 61, 62,
64, 72, 72n., 73, 74, 75, 78n.,
80, 80n., 81, 82, 83, 89n., 90,
102, 107, 115, 122, 128, 136,
136n., 137, 143, 146, 147, 151,
152, 156, 163, 183, 184, 187,
192n., 206, 211, 216, 224, 230,
245, 247n., 256, 268, 284, 288,
290, 304n., 316, 327, 331, 345,
354, 356, 356n.
Rossena, Daniel ben Samuel da, 231
Rossi, Anselmo (Asher) dei, 244, 245
Rossi, Azariah dei, 33n., 57
110, 174, 191, 208, 209n., 219,
219n., 228, 253, 256, 259, 260,
263, 271, 291n., 292n., 293, 295,
295n., 297, 300, 302, 304, 304n.,
330, 339, 347
Rossi, Europa, dei, 244
Rossi, dei (family), 244n.
Rossi, Solomon dei, 150, 244, 245,
245n.
Rovere, 24
Ruschi, Francesco, 240

Sabionetta, 299n.
Saltara, Judah, 272, 342
Salonica, 315
San Marino, 128
Sardinia, 100
Sarug, Israel, 212
Savonarola, Girolamo, 119
Savoy, 5, 13, 17, 18, 107
Scala, Cangrande della, 230
Scandiano, 183
Seneca, 294
Sesso, Salomone da, 240
Sforno, Obadiah, 151, 191, 191n.,
295, 295n., 310